"THEM"

STALIN'S POLISH
PUPPETS

"THEM"

STALIN'S POLISH PUPPETS

Teresa Toranska

Translated from the Polish by
Agnieszka Kolakowska

With an Introduction by
Harry Willetts

Harper & Row, Publishers, New York
Cambridge, Philadelphia, San Francisco, Washington
London, Mexico City, São Paulo, Singapore, Sydney

This work is published in England under the title *Oni*. A hardcover edition of "*Them*" is published in the United States by Harper & Row, Publishers, Inc.

 For information address Harper & Row, Publishers, Inc., 10 East 53rd Street, New York, N.Y. 10022. Published simultaneously in Canada by Fitzhenry & Whiteside Limited, Toronto.

First PERENNIAL LIBRARY edition published 1988.

Library of Congress Cataloging-in-Publication Data

Torańska, Teresa.
"Them" : Stalin's Polish puppets.

"Perennial Library."
1. Poland—Politics and government—1945-1980. I. Title.
DK4438.T67 1988 943.8′05 86-45364
ISBN 0-06-091493-9 (pbk.)

88 89 90 91 92 FG 10 9 8 7 6 5 4 3 2 1

CONTENTS

TRANSLATOR'S NOTE

The people interviewed in this book, all of them in their seventies and eighties, speak in a peculiar dialect of their own. It is an idiom naturally determined by their age, their work, and their ideology: a way of speaking which combines the language of communist propaganda with stilted, archaic expressions and old-fashioned slang. The fact that most of them lack any kind of formal education heightens the general effect. Their sentences are clumsy, their grasp of grammar tenuous; they misuse words, and see language not as a way of conveying their meaning but as an instrument for distorting and concealing the truth. Years of mendacity and propaganda have made them adept at begging questions, skirting issues, and speaking in hints and allusions; when they feel cornered, they automatically lapse into textbook communist jargon, constructing phrases on such a level of abstraction that they become unintelligible: their words simply fail to refer, and the result is gibberish. This happens when the speaker has no meaning at all to convey but wishes to pretend that he does; when he is unwilling to answer a question and, equally unwilling to say so, tries to appear to be providing information while providing none. Sometimes, inured by years of speaking in this way, he genuinely thinks he can see meaning where no meaning exists, and really believes that he is saying something – indeed, that he is saying something true.

The language which these people have learnt to speak encloses them in a world of communist dogma which they cannot relinquish. Inevitably, a lifetime of this has permanently warped their ability to think for themselves. They repeat lessons learnt by rote, and can go on speaking for hours without saying anything, indeed without making any sense. This is why they must be stopped occasionally and reminded, in concrete terms, of what they are supposed to be addressing themselves to – a technique which the interviewer puts to frequent use. To wit, after a particularly stunning example of pure nonsense from Mr Berman, she says resignedly, "Yes, well, perhaps we'd better stick to the facts."

When language is mangled and pulled about in this way, any attempt at translation will inevitably be a compromise between intelligibility and faithfulness to the original. I have tried, wherever possible, to retain mistakes and misuses, and to provide similar-sounding English equivalents; in particular I have not tried to make sense, in English, out of nonsense in Polish. But propaganda and a communist-controlled press have lent a flavour of familiarity to certain kinds of nonsense, and in English it is not always possible to get this flavour across. As a result there are places in the text where the English sounds odder than it should – odder, that is, than the original. This is depressing, for it shows the ease with which nonsense ceases to be jarring once one is used to it. In Poland everyone is used to it; many have come to accept it; some have begun to use it. Over forty years of communist rule have produced a generation of young people who have difficulty constructing a simple declarative sentence without grammatical errors. This is perhaps communism's greatest triumph.

A.K.

INTRODUCTION

by Harry Willetts

Poles curious about the postwar history of their country and the mentality of its recent leaders get very little help from memoirs. Fallen communist politicians do not publish apologias, and those in power give no publicity to vanquished rivals. There is no Polish equivalent even of the official Soviet history of the CPSU: the Polish ruling party's prehistory is full of episodes embarrassing to the Soviet Union, and since 1945 one crisis after another has brought to power leaders eager to forget their predecessors. The gap in the public's knowledge of those at the very top has been partly filled by gossip: rival factions spread discreditable stories about each other, which often reach a larger audience by way of émigré journals or samizdat fiction. We shall, however, find there nothing nearly as substantial or as firmly based as Teresa Toranska's book.

An enterprising journalist closely connected with the Solidarity movement, she took advantage of the loosening of controls from 1980 to 1982 to carry out a systematic interrogation of persons prominent in the postwar Polish regime. Of her subjects, all born between 1900 and 1910, some ceased to hold posts of any importance as a result of "de-Stalinization", others during the subsequent ascendancy of Gomulka. The reason for their submission to Toranska's provocative and often abrasive questioning was obviously a need to justify themselves. This is as true of Staszewski, the only one of them to have renounced Marxism (becoming in his old age a "nonbelieving Catholic"), as of Berman (once one of the ruling triumvirs, here cautiously self-critical, but immovably loyal to the party which expelled him), or of the ferociously self-righteous Julia Minc. Faced with an inquisitor too young to have shared their experience, they repeatedly complain that she "understands nothing" (she understands only too well, of course, the lasting effects of their activity on her country) and seem to be appealing beyond her to the judgement of history. Without her they would have had no opportunity to do so. They seek understanding for the establishment, in the wake of the Soviet army, of a dictatorship wholly subservient to the Soviet Union, reliant on terror and the ever-present threat of

Soviet military intervention for its survival, and determined to reconstruct Polish society in accordance with a model which few in Poland found congenial.

"*Racja stanu*" (*raison d'état*), a concept much too frequently invoked in Poland's history, especially in the context of the country's relations with Russia, is their ultimate excuse for all the chicaneries and brutalities of the regime in which they held responsible positions. What, they repeatedly ask, would have become of Poland had it resisted Soviet domination and the imposition of socialism *à la russe*? It might have been annexed, to become the seventeenth Soviet republic. It might, squeezed between the USSR and a revanchist Germany backed by "American imperialism", have been reduced to the miserable dimensions of the Napoleonic Duchy of Warsaw, perhaps to become yet again a battlefield for East and West. Only the Polish communists, Toranska and we are asked to believe, saved Poland from such a fate, won for it not indeed "independence" (a suspect word to Toranska's subjects, belonging to the vocabulary of deluded and self-destructive Polish nationalism) but a measure of autonomy, and laid the foundations of a socialist state with an adequate territorial base for prosperity.

Prosperity is not yet in sight. Toranska pressed hard, and effectively, to gauge the limits of communist Poland's autonomy. Many things were done on the insistence of Soviet advisers, and not necessarily with the prior knowledge of the whole Polish leadership. There were Polish "men on strings", but none of those interviewed by Toranska would accept that description. They were, however, all "men with a noose round their necks". It is Berman's claim that although he had an oversight of internal security he did not know the extent of the repressions. Staszewski, who had a reputation for ruthlessness as a provincial party secretary, takes pride in remembering that he did not *himself* imprison people – he left it to the security services. (Having spent eight years in the Gulag he must have known better than most what arrest on a political charge was likely to imply, in Poland as in the USSR, under Stalin.) Bierut, first among the Polish leaders from 1944 to 1956, even contrived to be obstinately blind to the truth about the fate of most of the prewar Polish leaders. Staszewski's account of Bierut's efforts to extract from Stalin disproof of what he surely knew to be the facts, and of Beria's crude warning to him, is perhaps the grimmest anecdote of all in the book.

"We could do no other", "I did not know", "this was outside the sphere of my responsibility" . . . Besides these, another important self-exculpatory theme recurs in the interviews: that by cooperating in most things with their Soviet comrades the Polish leaders could and did moderate Soviet pressures on Poland and spare their country many hardships. Berman recalls that he kept the number of death sentences in political cases lower than it might have been, and that Poland, unlike Bulgaria, Hungary and Czechoslovakia, did not execute a single communist leader who had incurred Stalin's disfavour. Whether he would have been able to make this boast if Stalin had lived a little longer is doubtful. (Toranska reminds him that the persecution of *noncommunist* "enemies" of the regime continued after Stalin's death.) These survivors from the Polish leadership in the Stalinist period are proud too of their resistance to Stalin's call for rapid collectivization (accompanied, of course, by the dispossession of kulaks, estimated with the use of a Muscovite coefficient at 10 per cent of the peasantry). Resistance, of course, meant no more than making haste slowly – a policy adopted again in a less dangerous situation when Khrushchev decided that maize, maize and more maize was the cure for Polish as well as Soviet agricultural problems – Staszewski's feats of patriotic foot-dragging were performed in the cultural sector, where he deliberately "did not show excessive zeal" for the enforcement of socialist realism as the official aesthetic.

Toranska's book has much to tell us not only about the early years of the Polish People's Republic, but about the difficult period of readjustment which followed Stalin's death – and the death three years later of Bierut, precipitated, it seems, by the shock of Khrushchev's "revelations" (of things generally known) at the Twentieth Congress, or perhaps rather by dread of their impact in Poland. The relationship between the Soviet Union and Poland is, of course, not quite what it was when Berman was Bierut's right hand. The Soviet Union no longer concerns itself in detail with Polish internal policies, so long as they have no undesirable implications for the strategic situations of the Soviet Union and the stability of the Soviet bloc. In the early 1980s the Soviet Union, without openly threatening military intervention, could rely on the rulers of Poland to quell an upsurge of popular resentment much more powerful than any yet seen. Yet the underlying reality of the relationship has not changed since the days of those gruesome Kremlin stag parties at which Berman (as he tells Toranska) danced with Molotov (Molotov leading) while Stalin wound the gramophone. No one who wishes to understand the country's dilemma and its origins can afford to ignore what may reasonably be considered the most vivid and informative book in the literature on postwar Poland.

H.W.

JULIA MINC

JULIA MINC

Julia Minc, née Heflich, wife of Hilary Minc (third in command in Poland, after Berman and Bierut, until 1956), was born in Warsaw in 1901. Her father was a tradesman and a member of the SDKPiL, her mother a housewife. Her family spent the years from 1913 to 1918 in Moscow, thereafter settling in Poland. After finishing school, Julia and her sister, Ewelina Sawicka, were active first in the Union of Communist Youth and later in the KPP. In 1922 Julia was sentenced to two years' imprisonment as a result of the trial of Leon Toeplitz, a member of the KPP's military section. She met Hilary Minc after her release in 1924, and the following year followed him to France, where he had gone to study. They were married in 1925 and two years later, after being expelled by the French authorities because of their communist activities, moved to the Soviet Union for a further two years. They returned to Poland in 1930 and left again in 1939, this time for Lvov, by then occupied by the Red Army, and from there, after the outbreak of the war between Germany and the Soviet Union, to Samarkand, where Hilary Minc became professor of economics at the university. It was from here that they were summoned to Moscow in 1943. Julia was appointed to work at "Kosciuszko" Radio while her husband was recruited into Berling's newly formed army. They both returned to Poland in 1944. Julia became editor-in-chief of the Polish Press Agency [PAP], initially known as "Polpress", where she remained until 1954, a year of substantial personnel changes for propaganda reasons. She was awarded a "Banner of Labour" second class and appointed deputy head of the State Commission for Employment. In 1956, when the Commission was dissolved, both she and her husband went into retirement.

* * *

Mrs Minc, Mr Berman told me that –

How can you talk like that?

Did I say something offensive?

Yes: referring to a comrade as "Mr" is offensive.

But surely, Mr Berman is no longer a party member.

He may not be a party member, but he is a comrade. Before the war, even if someone only paid his Red Aid dues without belonging to the party, he was still a different person, and you addressed him as "Comrade". And if at any time you changed over and began addressing him as "Mr", that meant he'd done something wrong. One woman comrade talking to another ought to respect our old habits.

But Mrs Minc, I'm not –

There you go again with your "Mrs"!

Because we're in Poland. So, anyhow, Berman (is that all right?) told me that after he left he was surrounded by a void.

There's a Soviet novel where the main character describes how, after her husband had been put in prison, the house suddenly became very quiet. The phone stopped ringing and their friends stopped coming round.

Was your house suddenly quiet too?

I made noise.

And your friends? Didn't they call?

No political friendships last forever. I didn't blame them.

What about your private friends?

We didn't have any. There wasn't time for that. Minc was at the Planning Commission every day until midnight or one in the morning, and I was usually at the Polish Press Agency until ten o'clock at night, putting together the day's bulletin. Sometimes I was there until two in the morning, if someone was giving an important speech that had to be translated. One time, at one in the morning, I drove up to the house and there was Berman with Minc, walking up and down the street. They'd just come back from a meeting and they were still discussing things.

I'd go to bed at three in the morning, get up at eleven and drive to the Press Agency. That was what my day looked like. We all worked hard; people don't appreciate that nowadays.

And on Sundays?

I slept the whole day. So did Minc, unless he had a meeting. Everyone was exhausted.

Didn't you have any time to enjoy yourself?

Work was our enjoyment. It's a marvellous feeling to be building a new country from the very beginning and it's satisfying to see the results.

You're pleased with them, aren't you?

Of course. We're going through a difficult stage now, and there are some complications: the Solidarity revolt, American restrictions, and maybe the Gierek government made some mistakes as well, but the party said quite clearly at the Ninth Congress that it would put them right, and that's just what it's doing. And anyway, no one has ever claimed that socialism could be built in a few years. This is a struggle for socialism, and it will always go on, because that is what our communist song says: "All our life is a struggle".

Did you ever go to the theatre?

Of course not! There wasn't time.

What about the cinema?

The cinema came to us. We'd ring them up and they'd screen films for us at home. There was another cinema at the club.

What club was that?

The club in Konstancin. That was where we generally lived.

Not in Warsaw, in the villa on Klonowa Street?

We lived there as well, but only for a few months in the year. Most of the time we were in Konstancin; once we even spent the whole year there. There was a big garden, forest all around, and the air was better.

Where exactly did you live?

The road leading to our town was paved with red brick. Bierut had a house next to us, and a bit further off Radkiewicz, Jozwiak and people from the Soviet embassy.

What about Berman?

He did have a house there as well, but he lived in Warsaw most of the time. Our estate had a club, a canteen and a cook who was crazy about dogs. I had three in the kennels there – I love dogs, I've always had them; I've even taken them in from the street – and every day at two o'clock, when people were starting dinner, they'd be sitting outside the kitchen window, waiting. The cook would be cutting up meat round about then, and from time to time he threw them each a piece.

Did you eat in the canteen?

No, my dinner was cooked at home and they'd bring it up to PAP for me. We had a very good cook: she'd been a liaison officer for the Secretariat of the KPP's Central Committee before the war. Later she went to cook for Rokossowski. We also had Granny Garbaczykowa, as we called her; she was with us before the war. But I must say the house wasn't as well kept at it should have been.

So who ate in the canteen?

I don't know; someone must have.

Well, who went to the club?

Witek did.

Who is Witek?

My ward. The son of a good comrade who died at the battle of Lenino. His mother died after the war, when he was twelve. At first Zabludowski – he was head of censorship – took him in because he had a son his age. But the boys became friends and they began to run wild and get themselves into scrapes, and Zabludowski was afraid he wouldn't be able to handle them, so he asked me to take Witek. I said I would, and that was how he came to me. He was a smart little boy. He knew all our "nannies" [security men] as well as the ones from the Soviet embassy: every morning he'd stand out on the road, and he always found a car to take him to school. It's twenty kilometres from Konstancin to Warsaw, after all.

Couldn't you or your husband give him a lift?

He had to be in school by eight, and with us it varied. Anyway, he didn't want us to give him lifts. I once came to pick him up from school on my way back from PAP, and he said, "Mrs Minc, please don't come to pick me up any more, because I don't want my friends to see."

He called you Mrs Minc?

What was he supposed to call me? I wasn't his mother.

Well, Auntie, then.

But I wasn't his aunt.

Is he a party member?

No, he's an engineer and he never joined the party.

And your nephew, the son of the famous activist Ewelina Sawicka?

No, he's not in the party, and what of it? Others belong and that's enough. It's not important.

But it is curious that almost none of the children of old communists belong to the party, and most of them have emigrated to the West.

So what? Socialist ideology doesn't forbid people to go to the West.

Of course not. So, to get back to Witek.

Once when Bierut came to visit us, Witek said, "What do you do? Because we were told at school to write an essay about what the president does." So Bierut took him into a room, sat him down, spent a long time explaining it to him, and the following day Witek got an F. Another time he was even better. We were going to dinner at Bierut's and we took him with us. They seated him somewhere near the end of the table. The waiters came in and started to serve the food. Everyone was silent, of course, because you don't talk in front of waiters, and then suddenly, in this complete silence, there was a groan from the other end of the table: there won't be enough potatoes to go round. It was Witek, who loved potatoes. Bierut smiled and said, "Don't worry, sonny, when we run out they'll bring some more."

Bierut was nice, wasn't he?

Oh, very. Polite, well-dressed, well-mannered and a perfect gentleman with women. I once turned up at a party in just a plain summer dress, as I'd come straight from PAP.

Was the dress plain?

No, it was quite pretty, actually, but not an evening dress. I had my own seamstress. Minc had his own tailor as well, allotted to him by security, but he wasn't terribly good. Minc came up to me, outraged, and whispered. "Do you know what you look like?" Bierut heard him, took my arm and walked across the whole room with me, telling me that my dress was the prettiest of all.

What about your other neighbour from Constantin, Radkiewicz: was he just as nice?

He was an honest, calm, down-to-earth, principled comrade. We weren't very close. I was closer to his wife, who worked in films, but I didn't know Radkiewicz very well, because they lived too far away. We lived closest to Bierut, just across the street, so that was where we went most.

Did Ochab go there?

I don't remember. Ochab is a great traditionalist, a romantic of the revolution. When we went somewhere together he always liked to sing old revolutionary songs.

And Berman?

Berman didn't sing. I didn't either. Before the war, at demonstrations, comrades used to tell me, "Don't start to sing until the police ride up: it will frighten the horses and make them run away" [laughter].

You were under constant security surveillance. Did it ever bother you?

It's true they always had a couple of their adjutants around, but after a while you get used to being protected and you stop noticing it.

But someone like Bierut, for instance, wouldn't have been able to slip out to pick up some girls, would he?

Why should he slip out? They would have been brought to him if he'd wanted, or they would have come themselves. But Bierut certainly had neither the time nor the inclination for that sort of thing. He was very hard working, like all of us. I don't want to make too much of my own work, but do you imagine that building up a huge press agency like PAP could have been easy? We started off in Lublin with just a handful of people; at that time we were still directly responsible to the Minister of Information. A year later we moved to Warsaw and were allotted first one floor of a building, then another, and finally the whole building. The agency started to grow and people flowed in.

What kind of people did you take?

Anyone who was any good: knew how to write, had the appropriate level of intelligence and knew what was what: socialism, trade unions, a political party.

Would I have done?

Certainly not. You haven't grasped basic things and you ask too many questions. But you wouldn't have asked questions then. In those times we had order and discipline and people worked instead of gabbling on to no purpose.

What about people who'd been in the Home Army? Would they have done?

If they wrote what was necessary and according to the party line, I left them alone. Anyway, I asked them all at the start: do you agree with us, do you want a socialist Poland? If they said yes, they could stay.

They didn't lie?

No. You can always tell what someone's attitude is. I once had an editor who kept asking what this plan was that we were always overfulfilling. In the end I got tired of it and threw him out: how can you employ someone who doesn't understand the idea of competition at work? Someone else who worked for me was Swiatlo's sister: when Swiatlo defected, her whole family was transferred to Cracow. There was also Wieczorek, who later became head of the Council of Ministers' Office; they said he'd been involved in bribery. When he worked for me he was in charge of the economy section, and one thing I'll say for him, he was scrupulously honest. For instance, he once brought me a desk set. Then one of the editors needed it and asked me for it, so I gave it to him. I didn't see why I shouldn't. When Wieczorek found out about it he announced that desk sets were only for the use of vice-presidents, took it away from the man and brought it back to me. He was so honest in the fifties; I don't know what happened to him later. In general, the team of people we put together at PAP was really very good in every respect. They only arrested one of my people.

Did you intervene on his behalf?

Why on earth should I? After all, it's not as if he was family or anything. And I only knew him from work, so I couldn't have done anything anyway. But I did take him back after they let him out.

Our team was a good one because we used the right method of selection, especially in picking out young people. We would collect all the candidates and then see what they could do. There were the stupid ones who scurried around collecting bits of totally useless information, and the intelligent ones who knew what to look for and where to go to find it.

What did they find at political trials?

They were usually covered by the social section. We'd send out a reporter and he wrote down what went on. After all, they weren't secret trials.

What about prison trials? Weren't they secret either?

There weren't any trials in prisons. You've been picking up some peculiar information.

What kind of people were tried, then?

Traitors and enemies. I happen to know something about that, because I had a man working for me who'd been parachuted in from London. He used to come to me after every major Home Army trial and tell me awful things about the people who'd been sentenced. But he wouldn't do it before the trial: I suppose he didn't want to add to the defendants' charges.

But later all these traitors were rehabilitated, weren't they?

You'd have to make a list of them and check.

What were party comrades tried for?

Well, if one of them stole something, or tried to abuse his position, he had to be locked up – that's normal.

And what did Comrade General Kuropieska steal?

But he's alive. Efforts were made to protect him.

And Comrade General Spychalski?

Spychalski died a natural death a few years ago.

What about Comrade Gecow? You must have known him.

I did know him, indirectly. He is indeed dead: a sentencing error.

And Gomulka? Was that a sentencing error as well?

Don't be ridiculous, Gomulka was never in prison! He was only under house arrest, and he stayed at his villa in Miedzeszyn, near Warsaw.

What about Slansky?

A very decent sort. We worked together at Moscow Radio.

But he was a spy!

Rubbish!

Really? He was sentenced to death for espionage.

So what?

Nothing, except that PAP, where you were chief editor, said he was a spy, and now you say he was a decent sort.

Well, he was.

Did you tell your husband what you thought?

There was no point: he couldn't have done anything about it either. You're such a child: what do you think Bierut or Minc could have said to Stalin? What arguments could they have used? They had to come up with something, and Stalin could always say, quite truthfully, that Czechoslovakia was an independent country, that Slansky's trial was the Czechs' own affair, and that he, Stalin, wasn't officially involved.

That's what Stalin would have said. But what about you? What do you think?

Look, in banking you have assets and you have losses. We waged a victorious war against fascism, and there were some bad things. But the victorious war compensated for all the bad. And anyhow, if you have to choose between the party and an individual, you choose the party, because the party has a general aim, the good of many people, but one person is just one person.

Can he be killed?

The questions you ask! The party isn't a Christian sect that takes pity on every individual, with a vision of a heavenly tsardom; the party struggles for a better life for all mankind.

Can you rebel against the party?

You can rebel against particular people, but not against the party, because that would mean you were rebelling against socialism, which aims to better the living standards of the working class.

What exactly is this working class?

The working class is a class which owns the means of production and has its own party, which acts, and its actions represent the workers' participation in government.

Isn't it the whole working class that governs?

How could it possibly govern! We're not anarchists. It's the workers' avant-garde that governs, the most militant, select core: workers who are party members, representatives of trade unions and workers' councils. They are the ones who set the party's tone and represent the interests of the working class.

So the worker Walesa doesn't?

A worker isn't an iron-clad figure with a sign that reads, "Creed: Communism". Walesa is a worker who didn't follow the path that Poland is taking.

And what path is Poland taking?

The road to socialism. But Walesa was against this, and he was punished for it. Rakowski clearly said at the meeting in the Gdansk shipyards that he'd got his Ph.D. through hard work, whereas Walesa had done it by agitating against the good of Poland.

What is the good of Poland?

Work, building socialism and defence against imperialist war.

Who is going to declare this war?

You want me to explain that to you? It's quite clear who. And it won't be the Soviet Union, because if the Soviet Union declared war, it wouldn't be a socialist state.

But surely the Soviet Union has declared war more than once in the past. In 1939, for instance, against Poland.

Nonsense! In 1939 the Soviet Union took a stand in defence of the Byelorussian and Ukrainian people, and if it took possession of a bit too much, that was given back later.

What about the war against Afghanistan?

The Soviet Union is helping Afghanistan towards a revolutionary victory, and it isn't helping on its own initiative, but on the wish of the legal Afghan government, which is trying to build socialism.

What is socialism?

A higher standard of living for everyone, free education and social security.

Like in the West?

I know all about what it's like in the West.

Have you been there?

Not after the war, but I know. I see it on TV. It's very bad there. The shops are full, but people haven't got the money to buy anything: they go hungry and sleep under bridges.

And here?

Here we have no poverty, and we have social care, which anyone can take advantage of if they've suffered an accident of fate. We have child benefits, benefits for nonworking mothers, what more do you want?

In the West mothers don't have to work at all.

It's degrading for women not to work. Before the war they used to sit at home and rot, and gossip about clothes. It's only in People's Poland that they've been able to flourish in their own work, to be appreciated. They go to meetings, develop, widen their horizons and raise their consciousness. They know the meaning of war, the United States, and the general interest.

In the textile factory in Lodz that I went to see, none of the mothers I met go to the cinema, watch television or read books. They get up at three or four in the morning to be at work by six; when they finish their day's work they spend several hours scouring the shops for a pair of socks, a piece of elastic, a shirt or a pair of children's shoes, as well, of course, as queuing for meat; then they make dinner, clean the house and do the laundry; and very often, too often, after that they do a night shift at the factory, because eight hours' work spent on their feet amid the stink and din earns them half as much as your retirement pension, and in the end, counting the privileges which you have but which aren't available to them, they get one-third of that. That's exploitation.

That's not exploitation, those are difficult work conditions. Think about it: who could be exploiting them?

The state.

That's ridiculous: the state doesn't exploit, the state provides. It provides pensions, it provides benefits, it pays for education and, most important, it has got rid of unemployment.

Officially, yes – because it's hidden.

Rubbish. We don't have any hidden unemployment; all we have is a perfectly visible reluctance to work. If everyone pulled their socks up and got down to it, things would be better. But they don't want to. There's nothing I can do about that. They've got guaranteed employment, everyone in Poland has: that's a lot. Do you have any idea how humiliating it is not to be able to find work? I remember what it was like before the war: Poland in 1933 was full of unemployed lining up for their free rations of soup. The soup was full of added soda to make it expand in the stomach and calm people down. Or again, another example: we had a woman who came in to do the washing. She got fifteen zlotys a month – next to nothing.

Couldn't you have given her more?

What do you mean, "given"? That's what people were paid for that kind of work, and she thought herself lucky to have it at all. There was unemployment, after all. One evening, in 1934, around Christmas time, I was walking down the street when a man suddenly came up to me and said, "Either I take away your purse or you give me some money yourself." He didn't look like a robber, so I asked him why he was doing it. He said he was out of work and his wife and two children hadn't eaten for two days. I told him I didn't have any money, but I had credit at a Jewish shop, and would take him there. So we went, and I got some food for him. The man was very embarrassed by my attitude and whenever I saw him later (we lived on the same street) he would run away. You wouldn't see that kind of thing nowadays.

Really?

Nowadays if someone grabs your purse it's to get money for vodka, not food.

All right, so there was unemployment in capitalist Poland. And what about the Soviet Unon at that time?

They were building socialism.

And concentration camps?

There weren't any.

And did seven million peasants starve to death during collectivization, or didn't they?

I don't know where you get that kind of information. No one starved to death, and if they sent kulaks to Siberia, well, so much the better for them, because they got what they wanted: more land to cultivate.

And what is a kulak?

A kulak was a village exploiter who would lend grain to poor peasants before the harvest and then made them work to pay it off, and if they wouldn't, which was what happened in Russia, he would shoot at them.

I mean the definition of a kulak.

A kulak is a village exploiter who uses hired labour, and the labourers he hires are not a part of his family. For instance: if he has four nephews working for him and he pays them for their work, he is not a kulak, but if he pays strangers to work for him, then he is.

What if he hires his second cousin's nephew's brother?

That's an imaginary case. In PAP it was the head of the agriculture section who dealt with the collectivization of the countryside, and he propagated it very well.

Why, then, didn't the collectives work?

Because the peasants didn't want them, and it's quite clear why: they like to look after their own interests. But it's because the countryside wasn't collectivized that we now have a food crisis.

There was no collectivization in the United States, and they don't have a food crisis.

I've already told you what it's like in the States: people go hungry and sleep under bridges. Anyway, when they were decollectivizing in Poland I was no longer in PAP; I'd left two years before that, in 1954.

As a result of the struggle with cosmopolitanism? Along with Starewicz, Kasman and Staszewski?

I don't know what you're talking about. I left shortly after they'd gone. Bierut told me I had to leave, because that was the way it had to be, and I didn't ask him why.

You didn't ask your husband either?

I didn't ask anyone. I became Vice-President of the State Commission for Employment.

Was that a post created especially for you?

No, the Commission already existed. We studied the structure of employment in state administration units. We'd take a ministry, for instance, or a school, and we'd check to see how many secretaries the minister or vice-minister needed, and if there were too many, we asked what each of them did. The SCE was a very useful institution. After 1956 it was closed down and incorporated into the Ministry of Finance as a separate department; that was a great pity, and the work it did wasn't nearly as good after that.

After the SCE was closed down, you retired?

I felt fine, so I tried to find other work. Ochab suggested that I work on a military paper, but I didn't want to. Zambrowski said, "Fine, fine, we'll find something," but he never did.

You didn't try at the employment office?

Me? At the employment office? They don't find jobs for chief editors and no one like me would ever go there.

But workers have to.

The difference between a worker and a chief editor is that if a chief editor makes a mess of things, it takes years to correct his mistakes –

And when a worker damages an expensive piece of machinery, it doesn't?

If a worker damages a piece of machinery then he's a saboteur and he'll be locked up.

I gave up trying to find work and started doing translations from Russian.

And what did your husband do?

Nothing. He retired.

He retired on a pension fourteen years before the normal age; you retired five years before you were due to, and Berman ten.

It was all according to the law. There are legal provisions for such privileges for activists. After all, socialism is built on the principle of equality before the law, not total equality for everyone. And the law clearly states that those who have rendered services to the Polish People's Republic have certain privileges. They used to be certified by special ID cards; those have gone out of use now, but the custom has been retained. A very appropriate rule.

Rendered services? But surely they left because they'd made mistakes?

They made mistakes, yes, but they also did a lot of good; that should be taken into account, and it is. Individuals whose lives prove that they have worked for the good of People's Poland ought to be treated differently, just as a person who works more ought to have better living and resting conditions. Beirut had villas in Konstancin and Warsaw –

And in Lansk, and Sopot, as well as others at his disposal in Natolin, Jurat, Miedzywodzie, Krynica, and Karpacz. I didn't do the counting: Swiatlo did.

Well, was he supposed to stifle in three rooms? Everyone has to have appropriate living conditions guaranteed according to his rank and burden of responsibility. The time of total equality may come, but not until communism; under socialism you can't have a minister earning and living like a shopkeeper, mainly because then no one would want to be a minister. In socialism everyone should be given not an equal share, but a share according to his deserts.

I see. So that's why the woman doctor I met out in the hall rents a cubicle behind the kitchen in your three-room flat.

She's not being treated unfairly. She had a flat in Torun, but she gave it to her son and moved to Warsaw. She's trying to get a flat of her own and she will, eventually.

But when?

Dziunka [addressing the dog], bark at the lady, she's pretending to be a Solidarity fan.

December 1983

EDWARD OCHAB

EDWARD OCHAB

Edward Ochab was born in 1906 in Cracow, where his parents had moved from the village of Szowsko on the River San. He was one of six children. His father was a municipal clerk, his mother had been a farm labourer before her marriage. She died of tuberculosis, as did two of Ochab's five siblings, when he was twelve. Before the First World War he graduated from the Cracow Trade Academy (the equivalent of an economics school in modern Poland), completed studies on cooperatives in the agriculture department of the Jagiellonian University, and enrolled part-time in the Advanced School of Trade. He joined the communist party in 1929 and was subsequently imprisoned five times, for a total of seventy-eight months, for his party activities.

The outbreak of the Second World War found him in prison in Rawicz, with Marceli Nowotko, Marian Buczek, Pawel Finder and Alfred Lampe. He spent the war in the Soviet Union. In 1941, at the outbreak of the war between Germany and the Soviet Union, he volunteered as a soldier in the Red Army; he was not accepted for active duty, and instead was sent to work in the "Stroybat", an auxiliary army construction unit whose task it was, among other things, to dig trenches. This work took him to Kiev and Saratov, while his wife and children were in a kolkhoz in Uzbekistan. He joined the First Kosciuszko Division, a Polish army unit under Soviet command, when it was created in 1943, and there reached the rank of lieutenant-colonel.

His life from the summer of 1944 onwards was spent successively in a number of high positions. In July and August 1944 he was representative of the War Council of the First Army of the Polish Forces; in 1945, Minister of Public Administration in the PKWN; from 1945 to 1946, together with Wladyslaw Bienkowski and Zenon Kliszko, member of the secretariat of the Central Committee of the PPR; from 1946 to May 1948, first secretary of the PPR for Katowice, a post he took over from Aleksander Zawadzki; from May to November 1948, head of the Central Union of Cooperatives, where he was later succeeded by Oskar Lange; in 1949, head of the Central Council of Trade Unions, a post in which he was followed by

Aleksander Zawadzki, and a year later by Wiktor Klosiewicz; from 1949 to 1950, first deputy defence minister and chief political commissar of the Polish forces, a post in which he succeeded Marian Spychalski after the latter's dismissal and subsequent arrest, and in which he was promoted to the rank of general. From 1950 to 1956 he served as secretary, and from March to October 1956 as first secretary, of the Central Committee of the PUWP; from 1957 to 1959 as minister of agriculture; from 1959 to 1964 again as secretary of the Central Committee of the PUWP; from 1961 to 1964 as deputy head of the Council of State, from 1964 until 1968 as head of that Council, and from 1965 until 1968 as head of the National Committee of the Front of National Unity. He had, in addition to these posts, been a member of the Sejm and of the communist party's Central Committee since 1944. He resigned from all these posts in 1968 (remaining an MP until 1969) in protest against the anti-Semitic campaign launched in Poland by Wladyslaw Gomulka and Mieczyslaw Moczar. He retired at the age of sixty-two.

His four daughters are all university graduates. The eldest, the only party member among them, is a chemist and computer scientist; of the remaining three, one is an electrical engineer, another has a degree in Romance studies, and the last is a lawyer. His wife is a communist and a party member, but she has held no government positions in the Polish People's Republic.

* * *

What do you understand by the Stalinist period, Miss Toranska?

The years 1948–1955.

I think such a division is unfounded, indeed illogical. I reject the division into two stages, the Stalinist and the pre-Stalinist, because that would imply that previously, when the rule of the people was just beginning to blossom, the influence of Stalinist methods, of the Stalinist apparatus, or of Stalin himself, was smaller.

Wasn't it?

It was greater.

Greater?

Of course it was greater. Who was it, for instance, who deported thousands of people from Poland [into the USSR]?

What do you mean, thousands? I only know of the commander of the Home Army, the head of the National Council, the deputy premier of the Polish government and thirteen leaders of the main political parties.

That wasn't much compared to the thousands (from what I know) who were deported, suspected, often rashly, of connections with the London underground, nonchalantly organizing the sabotage of the communication lines of the millions-strong Soviet armies.

Couldn't you have protested?

The people to protest about were above all the troublemakers from London who urged our youth into battle with the Polish people's government and the Red Army, which was liberating the territories of Poland, Czechoslovakia, Hungary, Romania, Bulgaria and Yugoslavia. A fight to the death was taking place, for the defeat of fascism and for a new Europe. Millions of Russians, Ukrainians, Byelorussians, Georgians, Jews, Tatars and sons of other Soviet nations perished in that fight.

But couldn't you have protested against the deportations?

How? By declaring war? There already was a war. They had their communication lines here, their armies of millions; a battle was being waged over what Europe was to be; they didn't know whether the West might not try to attack the Soviet Union. So they had to be sure of everything here.

That I understand, but you, what was your reaction?

I'd been a member of the PPR Central Committee since August 1944; several comrades, seventeen or eighteen of them, had been Central Committee members then. Five comrades from the Central Committee membership at the time are still alive. There were even fewer of us to make the decisions: five or six. The decisions were difficult, because many issues had been born without us. Like all Central Committee and PKWN members I worked at trying to find solutions to the most urgent political, military, economic and social problems imposed upon us by the national and international situation. Above all, we had to concern ourselves with strengthening our people's armed forces in order to increase Poland's contribution to the victory over the Third Reich and secure our moral right to return to the Oder and western Pomerania. We couldn't have solved that problem without the all-encompassing aid of the Soviet Union.

Secondly, we had to make a concerted effort to ensure that the army and the city population were provided with at least some meagre food rations and to prevent unplanned and often unlawful levies being exacted from the peasants.

Thirdly, we had to build a new people's state administration from scratch, boldly promoting leading farmers, peasants and officers of the First Army's political apparatus to positions of responsibility.

Fourthly, we began a radical reform of agriculture and the transfer of factories to the control of the workers.

Fifthly, we were unstinting in our efforts to broaden the political base of the PKWN, drawing in, on conditions of partnership, yesterday's WRNists, populists, democrats and nonparty people.

Despite not very positive experiences in the regions of Wolyn, Vilnius and Eastern Galicia, where in any case we had no influence over the activities of the organs of Soviet security, we persevered in our attempts to win over the most far-sighted cadres of the Home Army to the idea of a new People's Poland, based on an alliance with the Soviet Union while returning to the ancient lands of the Piasts, all of which contained new and huge possibilities for the development of the Polish state. The London government was pushing the Home Army into what was practically an impasse. The fate of thousands of Home Army soldiers, who had spent years bravely fighting the Nazi invaders only to allow themselves, on the brink of total victory for Poland and the anti-Nazi coalition, to be pushed into antipopular and anti-Soviet positions, was often tragic.

We were also not always able effectively to oppose mistakes committed by our great allies. The troublemakers in London were urging their numerous supporters to commit anti-Soviet acts, but even so I think the Soviet organs of security were too rash in imposing on us their so-called advisers, even in district security offices. The PKWN couldn't answer for everything, and we certainly aren't responsible for the arrests made by the Soviet security services or for the deportation of Poles.

What else aren't you responsible for?

For the destruction of hundreds of factories, carried out by the "Spoils of War Divisions" [Russian: *Trofeinye Komandy*] as part of the so-called dismantling. Perfectly good factory equipment was taken apart, turned into scrap metal and transported out [into the USSR]. There was a factory called "Buna" in Auschwitz; it had been built by the Germans during the occupation. It was torn down. If there had been at least some real gain for the Soviet Union in this dismantling, it mightn't have been so bad, but there wasn't. I think

90 per cent of it was useless to them. But the dismantling did enormous damage, and our government was unable to stop it.

Did it so much as try?

I thought about what could be done, but there really wasn't much we could do. The dismantling was imposed upon us in the same way that the coal agreements in which we did not have equal rights were imposed.

How, specifically?

The matter wasn't discussed by the Central Committee, but I was informed by certain members of the Politburo that the Soviet Union was taking over the enormous wealth left by the Germans, and that in order to compensate for the great cost of liberating the Polish territories an equivalent sum was needed to help rebuild the Soviet Union. They would let us have the mines, without dismantling anything in them, while we were supposed to give them something of equivalent value. But in spite of everything I still think that this period, 1944–55, was a period of the most important, historically significant, revolutionary stage of development, a breakthrough, and no one can erase it from the pages of our history. I am convinced that it will remain throughout the centuries the foundation of a new era, a people's era, in the march towards a classless society. Those diseases, those rashes, may be painful for individual people; perhaps even for the nation; but it's not they who will decide our future, and besides, do you imagine that our dependence today is any lesser?

My child, we are basically a "garrison" state; a state which has many things imposed on it. But you have to start off by asking yourself: what would Poland have become if we hadn't been allied with the Soviet Union? Whose missiles are pointed at us? Who will defend our western territories if it ever comes to a conflict? We have Soviet garrisons in Poland. In my view they're quite unnecessary, and neither the Soviet Union nor the socialist bloc would be any the worse off if they weren't there, because, regardless of military reasons or intentions, they probably do more harm than good to the nation's state of mind. Their presence in the GDR would be enough. But I'm obviously not going to give these friends of ours notice.

Have you tried?

We have to go along with the Soviet Union the way it is. There's no other way for the Polish nation. We didn't only find fault with them. We agreed and we continue to agree on basic issues because we have common ideological principles and a common goal with the Soviet Union, and we will attain that goal, although the road ahead is a long one.

But do you have to do it at such cost?

At what cost?

So many, many people were killed in Poland after the war!

I don't know how you came by such a very peculiar claim. People's Poland serves workers and peasants above all, in spite of its deformations, which a young people's government can't avoid. It's true that there were great class conflicts in People's Poland, but mainly with the reactionary underground, which murdered about 30,000 people, including about 15,000 PPR members as well. The names and graves of the murdered are known. With that as a starting point, the security apparatus was unavoidably full of hatred for those who kill and shoot at defenders of the people's government. How many policemen did they kill; how many soldiers of the people's army; how many employees of the party apparatus? We, at least in my view, can claim to have exercised extreme leniency and indulgence in our treatment of the pro-London reactionaries, because we knew that alongside the people who transmitted orders from London – recommendations from reactionary groups – there were others whose motives were different, not reactionary. Various grudges, feelings of resentment, piled up: the ravages of Beria, the deportations of Poles, the memory, too, of previous stages in the history of Polish–Russian relations. But apart from considerations of a very general kind, in conditions of extremely acute class conflict, the fundamental problem was that of power. Power that couldn't be transferred. Who could it have been transferred to? To the reactionary fascist soldiery? Or perhaps we should have looked passively on at the exploits of the leaders of the armed reactionary underground? Were we supposed to stick to sermons and holy water in fighting the organizers of massacres, snotty reactionary hooligans and posthumous supporters of the Bereza regime? Or maybe we should have told our Soviet comrades: have faith in the democratic slogans of the people of the *ancien régime*, those who speak beautiful words about democracy, about equality, about freedom, about a "just" Poland, along with the great landlords and the great capitalists? We knew those reactionaries, we knew about their past; we knew about the twenty interwar years, about the prisons, about normalization, about the September defeat.

So instead of Bereza, where people did time, you treated us to the security services' prison, where people died.

There you go again, casually making comparisons which only show how many things you don't understand, and you are rash in making judgements about them. The reactionaries tortured thousands of helpless people, and prisoners who did not have a Catholic birth certificate [that is, who were Jewish] were treated with particular bestiality.

I don't know what you mean by your reference to murders at the security services' prison. You probably mean executions. During the years of struggle against the armed reactionary underground, mainly from 1945 to 1948, the military courts of the PRL passed numerous death sentences, of which several hundred were probably carried out. It was a difficult period in the life of our nation, but, viewed as a whole, it was the greatest turning point in our country's history. The national economy and the strength of our army both enjoyed an enormous boost, which was not without significance for the whole socialist camp. At that time the Americans had a monopoly on nuclear weapons. It is with great admiration that I look upon the Soviet Union as a country where important decisions were made to restrict the growth of consumption in order to obtain the means to break the American monopoly on nuclear arms.

Our coal. Let's get back to our coal.

In 1947 we were pressured to give the Soviets additional millions of tons of coal as part of the so-called three-year plan. We didn't have enough coal for our own needs as it was, and the miners worked day in, day out. I was secretary of the PPR in Katowice when a whole commission arrived in Upper Silesia, headed by the deputy premier –

Gomulka, that is: general secretary of the PPR

– in order to exend the miners' working day. They'd made their decision in the Politburo, of which I wasn't a member, and without bothering to contact anyone on the Provincial Committee they simply arrived in Katowice with their minds made up. They didn't want to include time spent in the lift as part of the shift, which consequently made it an hour longer than before. Thus a miner was supposed to work 8½ instead of 7½ hours.

Which meant that his working week would be lengthened by half a shift.

Even more. There was a row and I came out against the government's proposal. I didn't think the proposed changes would bring in any more coal; instead they would only further the disintegration of mining and lead the free labour force, which wasn't big enough as it was, to flee the profession; and there would be a strike, which instead of producing more coal would cause enormous damage.

I realized they would dismiss me and of course they did, but even so the implementation of the longer working week was delayed by a few months, so some good did come of it.

Didn't the Politburo follow your reasoning?

Oh, they followed it, but they probably thought they couldn't oppose the scheme, whereas I thought that in this case they could, and should.

Mr Ochab, in June 1948 a Central Committee plenum, a very important one, took place. As a result of it the fight against Gomulka's right-wing nationalistic deviations was launched. Do you remember?

Of course I remember, but it would be better if you consulted the documents.

The proceedings of that plenum were never published anywhere.

Bierut's later speech was, and so was Zawadzki's. I think that their arguments, and those of Minc as well, concerning the internal situation, the ideological significance of day-to-day problems, and the march forward towards a united future, are correct. I supported them then, and today I still believe them to be on the right lines.

But what did Gomulka say?

Gomulka basically attacked the Leninist traditions of the KPP; he told us to learn patriotism from the PPS. He did admit that KPPists were dedicated revolutionaries, but he said they didn't understand national concerns, because independence was a primary issue to which all other issues should be subordinated. Basically he also favoured, though not completely, the general ideas of Pilsudski.

Is that what he said?

No, what do you expect? I said "basically". His arguments were incorrect, anti-Leninist and anti-Marxist; they would have turned against the party. That's why Bierut, Zawadzki, Minc and other party comrades were right in taking a stand against him.

You look surprised. But it's true: the party has to adjust itself not only to the situation in Cracow or Warsaw, but also to that of the whole international revolutionary movement. Because if we were to decide that national concerns are predominant for the Poles and that all other concerns should be subordinated to them, then we would have to say that national concerns are also predominant for the Germans, and then the following question arises: can national considerations justify such international decisions as the return of the Recovered Territories to Poland, even though it was known that the majority of the population of those territories, indeed the overwhelming majority, was German? No. It's only on the assumption that international considerations, those regarding the proletarian revolution, are predominant in their role and importance that you can justify even those decisions which exceed the limits of a nation's right to self-determination. And not only in the case of Germany.

But Mr Ochab, do you need to justify them at all?

You have to. If we say that the issue of independence is predominant, then surely we also have to come out in favour of Basque independence and support their revolt.

Why not?

Nationalists try to justify themselves from a position of so-called national egoism; communists feel themselves to be the brothers of working people regardless of their nationality, and they seek justification for their actions in the predominant interests of the international communist and national liberation movement. We communists recognize the right to self-determination, even to breaking away, but that doesn't mean we're in favour of breaking away or displacement in every situation.

You're only in favour of those displacements which serve communism and communists, is that right?

Communism is the ideology and political stand of the international working class, which cannot liberate itself without at the same time liberating all working people from exploitation and from man's oppression of his fellow man. In this sense everything that serves communism, Leninist communism, serves all of progressive mankind and clears the way for a classless society. We recognize the revolutionary right to defend the revolutionary position and the overriding considerations of the revolution, and we don't support every case of displacement. Displacement is essentially counter-revolutionary. Such was the displacement of Poles by the Germans.

And by the Russians?

I doubt that the deportations of Poles by the NKVD during the period 1939–41 were in accordance with Leninist principles or with the interests of communism. I was against them when I was liable to be killed for it.

You're referring to the deportations to Siberia?

Yes.

Well, I'm talking about the displacements from Poland's eastern territories of 1945 and 1946.

Those weren't instances of displacement; that was the return and exchange of a population.

Return? What return? My grandmother, my great-grandmother, and my great-great-grandmother had always lived in Wolkowysk, so where were they supposed to be returning from?

They could have stayed.

Where?!

In Wolkowysk.

But they didn't want me to be Russian.

Ah, there's the fundamental difference. You want to or you don't want to, but you don't have to. About two million people were in a similar position. They didn't have to return. And incidentally, Wolkowysk is in Byelorussia, not in Russia.

Mr Ochab, I'm not denying international resolutions, nor do I want to make a case for our right to those territories. And I'll say more. I've reached the point where I don't care where the borders of this Poland of ours are just as long as it exists. But I will insist on the principle of calling the same facts by the same names. My parents might perhaps have had the possibility of participating more fully in the proletarian revolution if they had stayed, and they might have gone about building this communism of yours more happily, but they didn't stay, because they couldn't. And they couldn't because they wanted to live in Poland, regardless of what kind of Poland, just as long as it was Poland, and they didn't leave voluntarily. They were coerced, not in the same way as the Germans, because the coercion was psychological, but it was coercion all the same.

Not quite: they'd previously been living in Byelorussian territory. Only Polish nationalists thought that it was a bad thing if someone took over our territory and held on to it by force, but that it was all right for us Poles to appropriate someone else's land and pacify Byelorussian or Ukrainian territories. I'm not a nationalist and I never will be. It's a good thing we've put an end to this shameful outrage. I'm in favour of my nation's freedom, but also of the freedom of Ukraine and Byelorussia.

So am I, it's just a question of . . . calling things by their right names.

I support the rights of the Polish nation, and I'll defend the rights of the Polish nation, but as a communist I will also respect the rights of all other nations. With regard to this wretched Byelorussia or western Ukraine during the interwar years, I didn't propagate the idea of breaking off those territories; as a communist I was in favour of the broadest autonomy and the fullest democratic rights for Ukrainians, Byelorussians and Lithuanians. Let them decide what they want themselves. Let the majority of the population of those territories decide how it wants to manage its internal affairs. But the fascist Polish government used truncheons, prisons and pacification to deal with them; that government was the shame of our nation.

I understand. So let's get back to Gomulka. Don't you think now that he was right?

Right in what?

If only in his attitude to the PPS and to the issue of Poland's independence.

No, I don't think he was. I've always based myself on Leninist principles, and it's hard for me to engage in a discussion with someone who is probably not very familiar with Lenin's teachings. When you were a student you doubtless had to take the official exams: that spoonful of mush they feed you which neither explains anything nor wins your heart, and doesn't even inspire you to study. But to me Lenin was a genius. In difficult moments especially, I reach for his works. I'm repelled by people who sit beneath Lenin's portrait while in fact trying to revise the foundations of Lenin's teaching or to pass them over, yet spare no breath in making "patriotic" declarations which support his views.

Was there anyone who stood up for Gomulka then?

To some extent Bienkowski did – I think he even tried to defend him. He's got a head full of contradictions; basically he's always been distant from Marxism, and now he's clearly fighting against it. It's a pity; he once fought very bravely in the ranks of the underground PPR.

Kliszko also gave Gomulka partial support. And after that Gomulka was really on his own.

And you? What did you say?

I defended the KPP, which took the Leninist stand that we should fight for all democratic rights, and especially for a nation's right to self-determination, but that we also recognized, along with Marx and Lenin, that no democratic rights can ever override the right of the proletariat to its class rule.

Gomulka also condemned the collectivization of agriculture.

Perhaps he didn't actually condemn it, but he did reproach Spychalski by saying that he had had no right to accept such a principle in Poland as well, which he had done during a session of the Cominform devoted, among other things, to the issue of collectivization. Here Gomulka was also wrong. It was only in the matter of Yugoslavia that he managed to retain his far-sightedness.

This plenary discussion took place within a very restricted circle, since the Central Committee plenum did not, then as now, exceed a hundred people; why is it that it did not take place within the party?

You appear to be ill-informed: there was a discussion of this in the party, a very far-ranging one.

If you want to call a total condemnation of Gomulka a discussion, then yes, indeed, there was a discussion.

Look, the most important thing for us at the time (and I discussed it with Berman and Bierut) was to bring together both parties on the basis of Marxist ideology, to bring the three-year plan to a successful completion and to prepare the six-year one.

And did you really have to destroy the PPS in order to do that?

I don't know if I'd call it destruction.

There was a purge.

There was one in the PPR as well.

And so, duly purged, they were united.

I continue to see the uniting of those two parties as a great historical achievement.

Weren't you shocked by the speed with which they were united?

You have to remember that there was a civil war in Greece at the time and the Cold War with the West was escalating. There was also a civil war in China. The Kuomintang, with the support of the United States, brought out armies of millions against the "reds" in order to prevent a communist government coming to power in China. We had to balance the front. The imperialists also still had plans to attack us if the international situation was favourable to them.

What do you mean, "us"?

Admittedly, from the point of view of someone by the Vistula, this possibility might appear in a slightly different light. But you have to look at the international situation as a whole and consider the politics of the Soviet Union as those of a country that resists the ideas and schemings of billionaires and monopolists; a country of enormous deformities, yet one which represents a different road for the development of mankind, a road that in its broad outline is in accordance with the interests of the whole international proletariat. This is the road the world will take, and we in Poland as well, even though we still have to contend with reactionary forces which are foreign to internationalism and to the revolutionary movement.

What kind of forces do you mean?

I mean forces which are trying to overthrow the people's government and hand over power to the capitalists.

Do you see them? Because I keep looking and somehow I don't see anything.

Do you imagine they'll knock on your door tomorrow and say: we want capitalists?

I think I'm beginning to understand why it is that I sometimes lose track of what you're saying and can't keep up with your train of thought. Personally, I'd like it if Polish communists concerned themselves with the affairs of their own nation rather than with the world's.

Then they wouldn't be communists. We are working people, and we should unite ourselves throughout the world. We look after our own country, but we also reach out to other workers, regardless of their nationality. The revolution has to win on a world scale.

It's just this "has to" that I don't understand.

I don't doubt it in the slightest, my sweet. But since you're still young, I continue to hope that you will think over some things and one day come to understand them.

Yes, but my case is worse than you suppose, because you're talking about classes, whereas I don't even see those classes; but I'll do my best. Let's get back to the international situation in 1950. A difficult one.

There was the Cold War, the conflict in Indochina, and the situation in Korea was becoming acute. Some representatives of people's democracies, including myself, Rakosi, Slansky and Rokossowski, went to Moscow to discuss the problems of strengthening defence in socialist countries. Stalin, and in particular his military advisers, Marshals Vasilevsky and Sokolovksy, were of the opinion that, given the difficult international situation, the people's democracies, and Poland especially, ought to contribute more, in the name of common defence interests.

Meaning that they wanted to squeeze more out of us.

It wasn't so crudely put. It was said that we could afford it, that we were strong. It was with a heavy heart that we accepted these "suggestions" and their consequences.

Couldn't you have engaged in a discussion of it?

I did discuss it in a certain sense, keeping within the instructions of the Politburo. I told them what we could afford and what we thought doubtful. In addition I suggested that there were many details which Marshal Rokossowski, who was familiar with our social and economic situation, would be able to elucidate in his talks with the military staff. As for Stalin, he of course refrained from going into details; he talked about the international situation, which he was clearly better able to assess than we.

But couldn't you have formed a coalition with, say, Czechoslovakia or Hungary, and opposed, it together?

Why oppose it?

So that you would have had less to hand over.

Yes, my sweet, of course.

You mock me.

My sweet, to make agreements like that is to prepare your own trial. You know they wouldn't have hesitated for a moment.

No scruples at all?

None. The only thing we could do was to argue that our economic situation was difficult and that lowering the living standard of the population would be likely to result in strikes. Proposals were outlined at the military talks and subsequently considered by the governments of the socialist countries. Our government considerably increased its defence effort, which led to deformities and a lack of proportion in the Polish six-year plan. Clearly, it also meant that there would be less chance of an increase in Polish living standards, with all the serious complications that would then ensue. In other socialist countries the results were similar; difficulties increased, along with discontent among the masses. Certain countries began to look around for "scapegoats": I might mention the shameful trials of Slansky and Rajk. Slansky was accused of organizing a centre of Zionist provocation in Prague; Rajk and Kostov of being imperialist agents; and all this was part of a huge international act of provocation aimed against Yugoslavia.

That same Yugoslavia, one might add, which was bold enough to have its own road to socialism.

I wasn't at those trials, but I had detailed reports of them. Broken people, testifying in the glare of strong lights, being forced to confess that they had been part of the Tito conspiracy – it was shameful. And almost all of them said that they had conspired with Gomulka.

And that's how Gomulka became an agent. Did you believe it?

On the contrary. I had great doubts as to the existence of this "conspiracy", and for this reason I tried wherever I could to influence the people who were in fact responsible for the decisions made on the basis of the sentences that were forwarded to us from the whole series of trials. I tried especially to influence Bierut and Aleksander Zawadzki, with whom I was on good terms and whom I considered honest. I suggested that we ought to look in detail into the accusations against Gomulka which the allied countries were passing on to us, and to do so without haste.

But on the other hand you didn't deny them, either.

I couldn't say: he's not guilty, because they would have asked what proof I had of his innocence.

And what about proof of his guilt?

It was clear to me that we were being pushed into provocation, onto a criminal path. I was once told – in fact Bierut told me – of a decision to protect Gomulka from possible provocation. Apparently Soviet Intelligence, and maybe Polish Intelligence as well, had received signals that they were going to get Gomulka out of the country, kidnap him or organize his escape: we couldn't expose him to that and had to ensure his protection. What's it going to be, then, I said to Bierut, isolation? Well, yes, he said, you could call it that. I also asked him: have you talked to Stalin? Of course, of course, he said. At that point it became clear to me that we couldn't do anything in Gomulka's case, because on the one hand there was this international conspiracy against the Soviet Union, along with the testimony of all the accused, and on the other Stalin's agreement, which was in effect an order, to Gomulka's imprisonment. So I only said to Bierut: I hope nothing will happen to him that might offend against principles . . .

Still, Gomulka had no trial; who is to be thanked for that?

It's to a great extent thanks to Jakub Berman that things didn't take that turn.

Was that because he was next in line for destruction?

That's not the point. There was some sort of file on everyone; on me as well. Later, when they wanted to show it to me, I said, no, I don't want to look at it. Similarly, the Central Committee kept files on Bierut and Berman – on everyone. In Gomulka's case I think both Bierut and Berman were convinced that the acts of provocation were organized by Beria. They couldn't just go up to Stalin and say so outright, so they played for time and drew the thing out. I myself was witness to the pressure brought to bear on Bierut and Berman to bring Gomulka to trial.

But even such bitter things as this have to be viewed from a broader perspective. You have to see the long-term consequences of the stand taken by the USSR, by Cominform, indeed by all the communist parties with the exception of Yugoslavia. First of all: we had no possibility of resisting, just as we'd had no possibility of resisting in 1939, 1944 and 1948, even if the Soviet Union had been wrong, because in this specific historical situation we have to go along with the Soviet Union as it is, or was – and it's the same today. The fundamental interests of our state, our working class and, in fact, our nation, require that this alliance, and the common march forward, be maintained. I think Gomulka often failed to appreciate this. His autocratic tendencies hindered him from seeing national problems within a broader historical perspective. I don't, of course, wish to deny either his great talents or his great contribution, especially during his leadership of the underground PPR, when he was under furious attack from the reactionaries in London. I still think he's a fuzzy brain with nationalistic tendencies. The entire course of events shows it, for no one did more damage to this country than Gomulka.

You could find a few more.

A country, my sweet, is something you have to be responsible for; it's not enough if some little wench like you waves her arms about and utters a few lofty thoughts. You have to be responsible for a country not only now, but also in a historical perspective.

Mr Ochab, didn't you ever try to protest against the activities of the Soviet advisers in Poland?

Yes, there were times when I undertook such attempts; perhaps not in the form of a protest, but rather from a political stand. The Soviet advisers were more often than not the ones who had the final say in a number of ministries, and especially in organs of the Ministry of Public Security. They often didn't know any Polish and were ignorant of our difficult Polish history. I wasn't concerned with affairs of security, but I did get to hear how the security apparatus was being built up. In 1953 a commission was established, on which, along with me, sat three Central Committee members (two of them Politburo members); we were instructed to look into the charges against a certain group of officers who had been accused of conspiratorial activity.

You mean General Komar?

Among others, yes. Without going into detail I must say that as I was studying the documents of the "investigation" it became clear to me that the apparatus which was preparing the prisoners' testimonies and assessing the results of this investigation was making use of impermissible methods; shameful methods.

On whose instructions was this commission formed?

The documents are in the Central Committee.

Are you sure?

No, but there's surely something there.

They're impossible to get at.

Historians will get at them one day.

But people want to know now.

They don't have to learn everything from me.

Not everything, but a little at least.

The instructions were signed by Bierut and Rokossowski. Rokossowski because the matter concerned the army, and Bierut because it was of the highest importance. Some of the officers from the Second Unit were charged with anticommunist conspiracy and sentenced to death. It had been mounted by the Military Intelligence of the time, which was headed by Colonel Voznesensky, who was working closely with the central military prosecutor's office, headed by Colonel Skulbaszewski. In my opinion they were Beria's people.

In othe words, NKVD men. Who was the person to whom Voznesensky was responsible, directly responsible, in Poland?

Rokossowski. Military Intelligence as a whole was subordinate to the Minister of Defence.

A question, then: why did Rokossowski agree to such a commission?

He probably had to. Stalin was dead and Beria, even if still alive, had no power by then.

General Komar's son suspects that a different mechanism was at work. However, let's start with the arrest, as it's an interesting little detail. On 7 November 1952, General Komar and a group of officers from the Second Unit were present at the annual reception given by the Soviet embassy to commemorate the October Revolution. The reception must have been a fascinating one, since it was attended by those who were about to be arrested and who, ignorant of their fates, were having a very good time in the company of those who had already made the decision to sentence them. The arrest took place on 11 November. After almost a year of interrogation, naturally accompanied by torture, General Komar confessed to all the charges against him and stated that he was indeed an American agent, but the chiefs of the spy network were Boleslaw Bierut and Jakub Berman. The Politburo apparently took terrible offence at this, which fact was to be of some significance later, after the General's release, but at the time they formed this commission. Thus the point of the commission was not only to look into the charges against General Komar, but also to clear Bierut and Berman of the fabricated ones against them. This was in the summer of 1953.

It wasn't Bierut and Berman: Komar did indeed mention two names, but they were the names of two other members of the Politburo. Komar did sometimes go off the rails. For instance, he was also capable of saying that there was no need for Soviet garrisons in Poland.

Well, was there?

No, I don't think there was, but you don't go around saying things like that, because they're heresy to the believers.

Most of the accused weren't Catholic by birth [that is, they were Jewish].

The Marshal was.

Yes, he was . . . in the case of General Komar and Colonel Flato they used dreadful coercion, in various forms. When I began to look into the details I came to the conclusion that we wouldn't be able to get at the truth with Voznesensky and Skulbaszewski there; it was impossible to unravel the whole affair, especially the accusations against Komar, Flato or Leder, with these people from Beria's apparatus constantly controlling and deforming the investigation. So I proposed that Voznesensky and Skulbaszewski be dismissed. There was a great row about this with Bierut and Rokossowski, because it was a question not only of dismissing these officers from the Soviet Union, but also of dismissing a large number of interrogation officers from the security apparatus who in one way or another had been involved in the use of unlawful methods. Some of the interrogation officers started begging and pleading.

Who? Fejgin, Rozanski?

No, they weren't concerned in such affairs. The people involved were Poles with a good record of activity before the war and under the occupation, but they were demoralized and full of hatred, because most of them had lost their nearest and dearest in the struggle with fascism and the reactionary underground. They were Poles, and their main targets were "badly born" [that is, Jewish] officers.

I thought that some of the demoralized interrogation officers should be taken to court. The commission drew up a report, in which we wrote that there was no proof of conspiracy in the Polish army, that the arrested officers should be acquitted of the charges against them and released, and that the investigation under way should not serve as a reason to discriminate against them. These suggestions were accepted.

Who accepted them?

The Politburo – after a discussion which hadn't been easy. And I was supported particularly by Berman, Zawadzki and Minc. In Komar's case a kind of compromise was made: we expel him from the party, we reduce his rank and we let him go. Then Voznesensky and

Skulbaszewski were recalled from Poland, and the cases of some of the security officers were presented to the party control commission and the courts. I also pointed out the intolerable methods that were being employed and that they involved military men from foreign parties in intelligence work, which threatened the interests of those parties. I have the greatest respect for intelligence officers, but I think the combination of intelligence and party work is inadmissible.

Where did it come from?

It was simply that the Soviet Union was treated as the fatherland of the proletariat. Which was good, but the forms it took weren't.

And notice that so many years have passed, and yet to this day Voznesensky and Skulbaszewski haven't been mentioned: that's no accident.

Did you talk to the accused?

Of course. I talked to them in prison. That was when I got a better insight into the methods used to lead them astray. One of them appeals to this or that and – well, there's no point in going into details.

Please.

I don't really feel like it. But I can give you an example. One of the accused officers wants to summon another as a witness: he claims that this person will be able to say something in his defence. A few days later the person is arrested and confesses everything. It became clear to me that someone was behind all this, manipulating it. Besides, the different bits of testimony didn't hang together, and all those knots could only be untangled after getting rid of the "plants", who were a tiny part of a whole enormous group that had been active here for years and continues, in my opinion, to be active today. I have my views on various matters and various people.

But why did Beria mount this conspiracy?

There could have been various reasons. Among other things he wanted to implement a specific personnel policy in the Polish army.

Meaning what?

I should think it was meant as a solution to the problem of leadership of the great military units. Earlier, up to 1948, these units had been headed by many Polish officers. They may not have had sufficient qualifications for the job, but in that case we should have been bolder in promoting our young officers, as I suggested, and looked for people among the old officer cadres as well. General Kuropieska, for instance. He wasn't a general from Pilsudski's regime: he'd been a captain before the war, but an honest one, very knowledgeable, intelligent – and there were more such people. But Kuropieska and many other officers were manoeuvred out, or even arrested and accused, while Soviet citizens were brought in in their place.

Not long after the arrests of communist officers, nineteen officers of the Home Army were also eliminated.

I had no idea such a dreadful thing was being planned. I found out about their execution from an internal Central Committee bulletin.

I think the two operations were linked. But what was the point of it all? To destroy all Polish officers?

And why did they destroy the KPP cadres? Such is our painful history.

They finally released those wretched officers from the Second Unit – Komar, Flato and Leder – and Gomulka was released soon afterwards; but they held on to Spychalski.

On what charge?

His case was also part of a huge operation planned by Beria's apparatus to place their own people in the army, the party and security, either like puppets on a string or at least dependent on them.

Spychalski was accused of placing control of the army in the hands of old officers of the Pilsudski regime with anti-Soviet policies; and since he also had a brother who had been commander of the Home Army for the Cracow region, a professional prewar officer, Spychalski was suspected of passing military information to his brother, who in turn passed this information on to London. The person directly in charge of Spychalski's case was Bierut. I told him that nothing hung together in this case and that, on the contrary, all the evidence gathered by the security apparatus gave rise to doubts. I said: you can reproach Spychalski for his choice of officers in the army and for the danger of placing large army units under the command of officers connected to the old regime, but surely there is also danger in placing the command in the hands either of Soviet citizens or of people who, like Rokossowski, although they may take on Polish citizenship, in a difficult situation would certainly not hesitate for a moment in deciding whose orders to follow. I understand that we can't permit a conflict with the Soviet Union now any more than we could before, but nor do we wish to be a mere protectorate restricted to carrying out instructions, because that is something this nation will not accept. We can't force it to applaud, not with sermons and not with holy water. It will applaud if it has to, but its hatred and contempt will be all the greater. I was in favour of releasing Spychalski and perhaps of considering his case along party lines.

It's said they wanted to deport Spychalski to Moscow.

No, no, that didn't enter into it.

And then to kill him there.

If they'd wanted to kill him, they would have killed him. There was nothing to stop them. But both Rokossowski and Jozwiak were in favour of trying him, and some comrades abstained from taking a stand. So then, when Bierut realized what the Politburo's stand in the matter might be, he went off to Moscow to complain about me.

About you?

Well, not only me – the whole Politburo: Spychalski's case didn't come before the Politburo, it's true, but it was discussed outside the Buro's session and Bierut knew that most of the comrades were against putting Spychalski on trial. My conversation with him ended in an argument, so Bierut decided to punish me by not taking me to the Twentieth Congress of the CPSU. In Moscow, Khrushchev refrained from taking a stand. He apparently said: it's your affair, and you should take care of it at home. That was a profound shock for Bierut. He was even more shocked by Khrushchev's speech.

In March 1956, as first secretary, I brought Spychalski's case before the Politburo. I suggested that instead of declaring Spychalski innocent, which I didn't want to do in order to avoid putting myself at daggers drawn with Rokossowski, we close the case for the moment. I was convinced this would be the first step towards settling it. Some comrades avoided taking a definite stand. Mazur claimed he had to go to Moscow for treatment; it was true that his legs were bleeding as a result of the tortures he had suffered in the camps during the Great Purge. As for Jozwiak, he demanded a trial, and so did Rokossowski. But in spite of this the Politburo decided to release Spychalski. We instructed the office of the prosecutor general to return the act of indictment to us; but instead of doing so they informed Jozwiak, who, in defiance of the Politburo's decision, instructed the staff of the prosecutor general's office to hold on to the act of indictment and told them he was on his way over there. I took a car and went as well. In a sense I did it deliberately, so that the staff at the prosecutor's office and the officer lawyers would also know what they were dealing with. Jozwiak said to me that he had read the indictment through once more and that everything in it was correct. I said: comrade, the Politburo has made a decision. You can disagree with it, you can resign if you want, but we will carry out the Politburo's decision. They returned the indictment and Spychalski was released despite the gesticulations of Comrade Jozwiak – a corporal if I ever saw one, volunteered for the legions when he was a young worker, and as an older man also sometimes behaved with the soldierly unconcern of a volunteer. He gazed with awe at the USSR as if it were an oracle.

It was also then that you found out about Stalin's crimes.

It was like being hit over the head with a hammer. We'd already been aware of various deformities or crimes, but not on such a scale, and not such outrageous ones. Khrushchev's speech was a sudden blow for everyone, and required a decision: do we support the general trend of the resolutions of the Twentieth Congress of the CPSU, or do we opt for passing over in deathly silence the crimes of Beria and Stalin? The cost of revealing them was obviously great in the Soviet Union, and in Poland it could have been even greater. The question was whether our leadership had the right to pass them over in silence, rather than shooting those rapids as quickly as possible, telling the bitter truth the way we saw it and not losing hope of emerging into clear waters.

You chose the second solution.

I thought we had no right to conceal those crimes and no right to conceal what had happened at the Twentieth Congress, in spite of the complications that would inevitably ensue and the shock for the Polish party, indeed not only the party, but the whole of society.

Were there people who thought differently?

Even in the Soviet Union this whole affair wasn't clear-cut. Khrushchev didn't have full support at the Twentieth Congress, and shortly afterwards an "antiparty" group was formed – a somewhat unfortunate term, but one which was later used in the Soviet press. This group clearly wasn't formed at a meeting of the Politburo; it ripened gradually. It's possible that this group might have had sympathizers in Poland, and perhaps not only sympathizers, but people more closely connected with it; after all, Khrushchev's speech was also received with mixed feelings by people here. Reactions to the resolutions made at the Twentieth Congress resulted in the gradual formation of certain groups here as well; these groups would break up and reform themselves rather suddenly, but without the clear connections or discipline of factions.

There was the Natolin and the Pulawy group. You were considered as belonging to the latter.

I reject all suggestions that I was connected to the Pulawy group. I belonged to no group. My task, and not mine alone, was to bring people in the party closer together. I discussed this with, among others, Aleksander Zawadzki and Adam Rapacki. I said to them: we must prevent splits from forming. There's no need to break up the party; rather, we must strive for unity on basic issues, particularly on the question of planning a solution to our grave economic difficulties, which require a joint effort on the part of the whole party and the working class. These economic difficulties existed before, but now they've crashed down upon us twice as forcefully; their handling requires particular ability on the part of the party, a party which over the years has become unaccustomed to political action on a broad scale and has placed too much hope in administrative methods.

You publicized Khrushchev's speech in a way that no one else did.

It's true that in the spring of 1956 we were the only ones to do so, and I should add that our Soviet comrades reproached me for that a great deal when I went to Moscow in June to attend a Comecon meeting. They hadn't made the thing public at home, indeed they didn't do it until the Twenty-Second CPSU Congress.

In Poland copies of Khrushchev's speech were even being sold in the marketplace.

I wouldn't know about that, but the speech was sent to all party organizations, where it was read out and discussed. I also know that it was thanks to us that communists from the Soviet Union and other socialist countries had the chance to acquaint themselves with it.

Almost immediately after the Twentieth CPSU Congress, Bierut died in Moscow, and you were elected first secretary. Who were the other candidates for the post?

I don't know. I proposed Aleksander Zawadzki.

You didn't want to take it yourself?

No, for various reasons I didn't. There had been some points of tension between me and our Soviet comrades, and I didn't think that would be good for the cause. They remembered how I'd opposed the increase in the miners' working week in 1947, as well as my decision concerning the recall of Voznesensky and Skulbaszewski. They also remembered that I'd always considered the KPP, which had been so shamefully put to death, as embodying the best traditions of the Polish revolutionary workers' movement. And [after my election] I immediately had another run-in with them: again over coal. In June 1956 I went to Moscow to attend a meeting of the Comecon. Gerö made a fiery speech in which he attacked the Polish leadership for lacking the spirit of international solidarity. He was presumably instructed to say this. A few days before, *Pravda* had run an article about how a Soviet journalist had been making the rounds of Polish mines and all the miners were surprised at their low output, because they could be mining more. After Gerö came Ulbricht, and then Novotny as well, launching an attack on the Polish delegation to the effect that the Poles didn't want to provide coal and were forgetting internationalism. I spoke sharply in response, and the sharpness of my tone was not something the members of this distinguished forum were accustomed to. I pointed out to our comrades, not only the German and Hungarian ones, of course, that we were better able than they and their most distinguished correspondents to say what Poland could provide and what it couldn't. "Do not delude yourselves," I said. "Poland won't hand over any more coal because it hasn't got any more coal. It would be a good thing as it is if we were able to give you what we've agreed so far. The miners are working day in, day out; if you stretch that string any more, it will break; it's already overstretched. The miners are overworked. A strike in the coal industry could spread, but even if it were restricted to the coal industry it wouldn't produce any more coal, whereas the political damage done would be incalculable. We take responsibility for our country. We don't live by delusions."

Frankly, Mr Ochab, I find all this so peculiar. I mean the way it happened. They take someone, let's call him an envoy of theirs, and set him on you. He agrees to attack you in return for some concrete benefits, or perhaps just for favourable standing. Then you pretend not to know who's behind him and attack him in turn. I don't know, but . . . You laugh.

My sweet, that was the first time in the history of the Comecon, at least in the history known to me, that someone dared to come out with a fundamental objection.

That much I understand, but couldn't you have bargained with them a little, at least got some money for investment out of them?

You're being very childish. Of course I did so; Hoxha mentions it. His writings are very mixed up, they don't correspond to reality, and he held it against me in particular that I sometimes said what I thought about the kind of regime he had made, but in this case he wrote the truth: Ochab came out with a fundamental objection: you want Polish coal, give us money for investment.

Did they?

They did not. They were probably counting on my not being first secretary for very long and thought that I would eventually try to gain their support. But I never considered doing so, at any rate not at that price. Khrushchev was also annoyed that one of our planes had escaped to Denmark, and that we had distributed material from the Twentieth Congress very widely and that not all numbered copies had made their way back to the Central Committee. It's true that three were missing. The comrades in question tried to explain themselves by saying they'd burnt their copies, but surely they could have made further copies and sent back the numbered ones.

I knew, of course, that the Comecon conflict made my position among the leaders of the fraternal countries doubtful. I didn't want a further conflict, obviously. I later told my Polish comrades: we must look for a solution that will avoid clashes and short circuits of any kind, but we must also be firm in insisting that decisions on Polish affairs will be taken by us alone.

Did you expect any clashes in Poland?

Not armed ones. We expected a serious strike of some kind, but not bloodshed. I was concerned principally about the Coal Basin and tried to prevent a serious conflict there, because I was afraid that if that happened the mines would grind to a halt and there would be a coal shortage; but all in all things didn't go too badly there. I also expected some strikes in Lodz: the women there were very excitable, because their lives were hard. And on top of all that our propaganda, instead of explaining the solutions we proposed to this difficult situation, often added fat to the fire, even though we toned it down. In such conditions, when we were restricted in what we could say, no one could have managed.

How did the shooting in Poznan come about?

At the Politburo we couldn't deal in detail with each and every conflict, because there were many conflicts in many different workplaces. We tried to defuse them primarily by political and economic means, tried to find some way of pulling ourselves out of this wretched predicament. We made a number of decisions about limiting investment, releasing most political prisoners and introducing wage increases in many fields. We believed these increases had to be introduced even at the cost of our small reserves, which normally shouldn't be touched because the state has to have something put aside in case of crisis. But that time of crisis was now drawing near. The increases didn't alter things, however, because the standard of living was still low. In addition the international situation was difficult: the war in Korea was nearing its end, another war was escalating in Vietnam, the Cold War with the West was continuing and we had no guarantees that they wouldn't leap at our throats at any moment.

Who?

The imperialists, my sweet, the ones who organized the 1953 putsch in the GDR, for example. That's why, for all our poverty, we still had to spend considerable amounts on national defence. We tried to explain to our allies that our situation at home was dangerous, but we didn't always, or fully, succeed in cutting military spending. That was why even wage increases weren't always sufficient.

What happened in Poznan?

I'd like to stress that the short circuit there wasn't the result of any decisions taken by the Central Committee but of a wider set of circumstances that had accumulated over the years, and the fact that we weren't able to defuse it with holy water or by small material means, which in any case we didn't have, was only to be expected; it would have been impossible even if we'd been, so to speak, free to act as we wished in Poland. At the Politburo we decided as follows: the Politburo decides general policy in matters like limiting investment, increasing the wage fund, limiting the Defence Ministry budget, main Comecon problems and so on, while the comrade ministers and vice-ministers should take care of conflicts within the sphere of work of the ministries and the government.

So you're putting the blame on Cyrankiewicz.

Not necessarily. The Politburo sent the prime minister out to talk to the strikers in Poznan because Cyrankiewicz was more familiar with the Poznan conflicts. I was also relying on his political experience and his ability to make essential political decisions quickly and on the spot. But Cyrankiewicz was a man who'd lived through Auschwitz; a broken man. I've seen him in various situations, and he often, unfortunately, lacked character.

The news that there might be a general strike in Poznan reached me the day before the strike itself. I was rung up late at night by the first secretary of the Poznan Provincial Committee, who told me that the situation was difficult, that he had just returned from a railwaymen's meeting at the Railway Repair Yard, had listened to what various people were saying there and come to the conclusion that organized groups in Poznan were engaging in activities aimed against the people's government. Now I knew this man, and for the most part he was not easily scared off, but that night there was a new tone in his voice: he was very anxious indeed.

He claims that he'd also rung you several days earlier.

As a rule I talked to each Provincial Committee secretary every few days. But I don't think that previous, so to speak routine, conversation had had any particularly disquieting overtones. Day-to-day problems were dealt with by Central Committee departments or by the appropriate government ministries. When he rang I asked him why he hadn't rung me about it before and ended the conversation.

I immediately rang Pszczolkowski, the head of security, who said that he and Alster were just getting ready to go to Moscow to discuss things. Was it coincidence that it should have been just then? I don't know.

I said to Pszczolkowski: you can't both go. I want you so see what you can find out about those organized groups in Poznan. And I had Pszczolkowski go to Moscow while Alster stayed behind to look into things and see whether the danger was local and confined to Poznan or greater in scale.

You didn't suspect provocation?

It's possible. There were several possibilities, and I thought them all through many times, but I have no proof. Edmund later told me how, in Moscow, our Soviet friends had kept him informed about what was going on in Poznan: they communicated by radiotelegrams and were better informed than our security services.

In the morning I found out there was a strike. Some troublemakers in Poznan had spread the provocative rumour that a delegation of workers from the "Cegielski" plant that had gone to Warsaw the previous day had been arrested. This was a complete invention: the delegation had reached Warsaw, had talked with the minister and had returned with a promise that their problems would be quickly considered and solved.

Wasn't it possible to deny the rumour?

When? A general strike was already under way and things were developing uncontrolled by workers' organizations, in a state of near anarchy. The demonstration made its way to the prison; the warden didn't try to defend himself; the guards handed over their rifles and grenades; and a crowd in a state of anarchy released the criminals.

Surely not only criminals.

For the most part they were criminals, because I don't think there was anyone else there, or almost no one. Maybe there were some people on disciplinary charges, but I know there weren't any political prisoners.

The workers wanted to find their delegates.

They weren't there.

But they didn't know that.

Exactly. In any case, criminals formed the majority of the released prisoners. They took the grenades and machine guns and went off to attack the Security Office building. At that stage the discussion moves to a different plane: you don't appeal to rational argument any more. They wanted to kill. On their way they savagely killed a soldier from the Internal Security Corps and someone else as well, I think, and then began to shoot at the Security Office building. At that stage we couldn't allow them to occupy the building and murder the people from the security apparatus.

They'd been the first to murder people.

I don't want to go into whether or not the grievances against them were justified – although you have to remember that they, the little people from security, weren't the ones responsible for the situation. The people who worked in security in Poznan didn't really have any effective means of defence against an organized attack, because it was impossible to provide them with quick reinforcements, even with so much as a single Security Corps unit. That was when Rokossowski contacted me: at first by telephone, then in person.

Did he come alone?

Yes, we had a tête-à-tête. He suggested using army units against the armed hooligans who were attacking state offices. He also asked to be given a free hand and said he would take care of everything. I agreed, because we had to act quickly. My decision was accepted by the Politburo. But in the end Rokossowski didn't do a very good job of taking care of things: he got together several army divisions and set off to attack Poznan, and he brought in too many troops, far too many. It should have been done more calmly and more quickly.

But Mr Ochab, how are decisions to shoot made? After all, people were shot at on a number of occasions.

If they're coming at you with grenades and machine guns and killing people from the state apparatus, you don't respond to that with a speech: you respond with force. But you have to limit it to its essential minimum. If they're only striking the way they struck in Gdansk, then there's no justification for the use of force. Even setting fire to buildings doesn't justify it, because that was a response to unjustified repression against workers. In Poznan, however, an attempt was made at an armed attack against the people's government in Poland without any provocation on the part of the authorities. That's the essential difference between Poznan and Gdansk. I must say that I didn't expect the leadership in 1970 to show such stupidity in their handling of a conflict which to a large degree they had provoked themselves; I didn't expect them to be so overbearing with the workers or to reach for machine guns as their main argument. The comrades from the leadership that December made arrogant and autocratic decisions which roused the working class to anger. The responsibility for them lies not only with Gomulka and the prime minister, but with the Central Committee as well. For the Central Committee met when blood had already been spilt in Gdansk and not one member, not one, spoke up wanting to stem its flow, while many of those who today lecture us about reform and democracy voted in favour of the leadership's rashly provocative decisions and screamed about hooligans. Those weren't hooligans!

That upsets you; but those weren't hooligans in Poznan, either.

They were troublemakers and provocateurs exploiting the discontent and the workers' strike; they deceived the workers by lying to them about the alleged arrest of the workers' delegation, took over the prison with no resistance from the prison guards, released criminals from their cells, armed themselves with grenades and machine guns and proceeded, with the aid of the criminals, to attack the security building. And even then we were saying: this isn't just hooliganism, the roots of this problem go deeper.

You said it was the imperialists.

I rejected suggestions to that effect, as did most of the Politburo. There was even an acrimonious discussion with our Soviet comrades, who before the July plenum had suggested to us that the bloody Poznan clashes had been provoked by the imperialists. I told them there was no proof, and that I couldn't make a claim of that kind at the Central Committee Plenum.

How many people were killed?

As many as we said then. They wouldn't have concealed the true number of casualties from me.

How many from security and the army?

A couple, I don't remember exactly. Unfortunately most of them were chance victims; that's what always happens when you bring in too many soldiers. I later pointed this out to Rokossowski, saying: you asked for a free hand, fine, but why did you take in several divisions? A single company would have done. You had to defend the building, prevent the security people from being murdered and disarm the groups of troublemakers – that was all. They fired from the rooftops. How do I know whom they were shooting at? Or whom they shot? As usual, when that happens most of the victims are random – spectators.

Isn't there anything in this Poznan affair that surprises you, makes you think?

I looked over the documents afterwards. What had the whole thing been about – a dozen or so millions of zlotys. We should have taken them from those meagre reserves of ours; the economy would have survived.

Why wasn't that done?

I don't know and I don't want to talk about it. I'd just like to say that the clashes in Poznan probably wouldn't have assumed the proportions they did if the prison guards had not handed over their arms. I don't know exactly who had a hand in that or why, but I do know that the subsequent developments would not have been so dramatic. Unfortunately, in the event, we were unable to protect the country from an upheaval, and for that, of course, the leadership at the time is responsible. Naturally I never had, nor do I now have, any intention of denying my responsibility as first secretary.

That was said by the human being in you, but what does the politician say?

You don't philosophize; you grit your teeth and you hold your tongue. Politics is choosing the lesser evil, holding your tongue and sometimes playing with marked cards.

Choosing the lesser evil, not the greater advantage: that sentence sums up the whole tragedy of our Polish situation.

You have to see it as part of the whole international situation.

You mean it's even worse. Let's talk about Gomulka.

In 1953 I was already proposing his release from prison, and a year later I spoke in favour of his return to the party.

Klosiewicz says he was the first to put that proposal.

I don't know what he said, but I do know him, from back before the war. He was a good communist; a bricklayer. I spoke to a restricted gathering of comrades; after all, that's not the kind of thing you can just come out with all of a sudden, with no preparation. But of course there were many people at the time, Jozwiak and other external allies, who wanted to see to it that Gomulka would not be accepted back into the party.

And he wasn't, not by the normal procedure.

That was a very bad thing, because by 1956 the Gomulka affair had become pressing and some comrades were beginning to exploit it in their own party infighting.

The myth of Gomulka was also being propagated: the myth of that good man who was still being persecuted by the Stalinists.

That was some of the press giving free rein to their imaginations. I believed Gomulka's case had to be dealt with cautiously and slowly, applying some brakes, because otherwise it would be too much of an upheaval for the party. I said at the Politburo: we must recognize and admit with bitterness that we committed a great mistake in accusing Gomulka of anticommunist conspiracy, and we must now make it up to him politically. After the Twentieth CPSU Congress it was quite clear to me who had been organizing this "international conspiracy". I upheld my opinion concerning the ideological errors of so-called right-wing deviationism, but I also said: to a large extent this affair has been overtaken by life, and we have other problems to see to; we shouldn't discriminate against Gomulka or hinder his return to the party.

He was apparently offered the post of first secretary in Wroclaw.

I know of no such offers.

Two comrades came to see him with the proposal.

Many people came to see him.

You saw him too. On whose initiative?

Mine, I should think. I'd heard earlier about various meetings that comrades from the leadership were organizing for him, mainly in Poznan, unofficially and behind my back. Zambrowski started it; he laboured under the illusion that Gomulka had changed, and for this Gomulka later rewarded him generously. Zambrowski zealously strove to gain the support of the majority in the Politburo for his claim that "Wieslaw" had changed, had stopped shouting and insulting his comrades. Cyrankiewicz also trotted about after him – he had his reasons and I won't comment on them. They fell for those phrases of Gomulka's about patriotism and independence – empty phrases, basically, all of them. They seemed to think that by adopting Gomulka's phraseology we would win the hearts and confidence of the masses.

Well, didn't you?

Yes, but that doesn't give you communism; the differences are only beginning. There's not much use in patriotic phrases for the country or for communism.

Go on about Gomulka.

I said at the Politburo that we had to re-establish Gomulka in his previous post and accept him back into the party.

Did you invite him to come and see you?

Yes, we met at the Central Committee. I told him: the suspicion that you took part in a conspiracy has done you a grave and unjustified injury, and great damage to the party, and I sincerely regret that I might also in some degree have contributed to it, although I wasn't the one who organized that conspiracy, I wasn't even present when it was being organized. So we should not let that divide us today.

Did you address each other by your Christian names?

No, we addressed each other as comrade; I'd been on first-name terms with Gomulka before. Later I added: you displayed admirable far-sightedness in your assessment of the situation in Yugoslavia; we at the Politburo didn't see the danger of what was happening, as you did, but even if we had seen it, there was little we could have done. Now our country has new problems, difficult ones, and we have to look for new ways of steering it out into calm waters. We want to use you in active party work; we want to settle the question of your membership in the party, and we will take it up at the Politburo, but first you must say whether you want to be a party member. Gomulka just said yes, he did. I asked him further whether he accepted the party line. He said that basically he did, although he had some reservations. Reservations are all right, I said. I didn't offer him anything else. In the course of our conversation I mentioned neither his membership in the Central Committee or the Politburo nor the possibility of his being deputy premier.

Gomulka apparently claims that you did, though.

He's mistaken. Of course on the leadership level we talked about what we might offer him. At that time I was still considering making him a member of the Central Committee; I may have said something to that effect to my comrades, but not for the record, just unofficially, during the backstage talk at some Buro meeting. I later discussed the subject with Aleksander Zawadzki and Adam Rapacki: let him enter the Politburo, maybe as deputy premier, let him carry the burden for a while, and then, perhaps after some time, sooner or later, we could decide. I told them: you know how proud he is, how hungry for power, how limited; we shouldn't hurry this.

How did Khrushchev react to this?

He asked me about Gomulka's health. Khrushchev had attacked me at the June Comecon meeting, but up to the October tensions he'd behaved quite decently towards me. Sometime in July he asked me about Gomulka's health, saying that he had good specialists who would take care of him. I said I saw no need to bring the matter up with Gomulka or to try to persuade him of the merits of Soviet doctors, and that if they wanted to invite him over, they should ask him themselves. You know his address, I said, because as far as I know people from your embassy go to see him. In any case the Polish leadership would have no objection. Let him go if he wants.

He didn't go.

There were rumours that in October 1956, during the period of tension between Poland and the Soviet Union, Chou En-lai rang

Moscow and warned the Soviet comrades that he was opposed to an intervention in Poland.

I was well aware that in the event of a serious conflict in Poland the Soviet Union would not hesitate to deal with it, however grave the complications. That's why I tried to prevent a crisis situation and at the same time the isolation of the PUWP in our socialist camp. We thought it particularly important for the Chinese party to be well informed (so that they would not be surprised if anything happened) about our firm insistence on maintaining the socialist course in our national and international policies. With this aim in view I went to the Chinese Communist Party Congress at the end of September.

And, ironic though it may sound, it was precisely that Congress which passed a programme to build socialism based on friendship and cooperation with the USSR and the socialist countries.

I was accompanied by Franciszek Jozwiak, Oskar Lange, and of course our ambassador. I knew that Franciszek would immediately trot off to report to his people, but I counted on his either not noticing or misreading the sense of the parables I was using. I don't think I was wrong. In my conversations with Mao, Liu Shao-ch'i, Chou En-lai and Chou Te I tried to get across to our Chinese comrades some idea of our difficulties and our plans for socialist victory over the crisis. Oskar supported me with apt comments. Franciszek gazed with admiration at the Chinese and was for the most part silent.

Luckily?

Yes, luckily, although he wouldn't have changed much by then. Jozwiak, actually a friend of mine from prison, was an honest man in his way, but his gaze was concentrated on one single point in the world. So it was better that he did not mention the confidential information that we were intending to include Gomulka in the Polish party leadership.

What about Oskar Lange; weren't you afraid of him?

No. Oskar Lange grasped my metaphors and parables perfectly; he knew what the point was.

Did he know your purpose as well?

Yes, but that was something that had to be said. I talked to all four: Mao, Chou En-lai, Chou Te and Liu Shao-ch'i. The upshot of what I said was that we in Poland wanted to manage our own affairs ourselves. I also mentioned, among other things, that we wanted to include Gomulka in the leadership and to some extent make good the injury that had been done to him, which in this specific situation should strengthen and consolidate the party. The Chinese comrades were very well disposed towards our problems and I felt that they also had confidence in me personally.

Did you talk about the danger of intervention?

No, of course not: on the contrary. I stressed our alliance with the Soviet Union, which should be an alliance of equals and of the free with the free, if you can speak of equality between us and a world power. I also made reference to our poets: "Go forward with the living, go forward and be obdurate." I also said that our relations should be fraternal and also quoted: "For he who is not a brother in his heart will not come to know the soul."

I see; that was one of your parables. Do you remember any others, perhaps?

I remember the atmosphere quite clearly: the Soviet ambassador to Peking wouldn't leave our side for a moment and stuck close to me whenever he could. And there I was, trying to get something across to the Chinese comrades, wedged in by Jozwiak on one side of me and the allied ambassador on the other. I had the feeling that the Chinese comrades were beginning to get the gist of my efforts, but apparently not sufficiently, because just as we arrived at the airport and were about to leave, it turned out there was a defect in our plane. Presumably the Chinese comrades had helped arrange this, and as a result we still managed to talk to Chou Te for several hours while waiting for the plane to be repaired.

Wasn't the ambassador there?

Ours was, yes; but the other one hadn't anticipated such a situation. I had Oskar and Jozwiak with me. I explained to Chou Te that while it was true there were signs of an anti-Soviet mood in Poland, visible also in Poznan, this did not mean that we wanted to disturb or break off the alliance. The only thing we wanted was for the Poles to manage their own affairs at home within the general socialist framework, just as you, I added, want to manage yours. I also explained about Gomulka, saying that the charges against him of taking part in an international conspiracy were unfounded, that he had been wronged and that we were dismissing those charges, particularly since as we now, after Khrushchev's speech, knew and understood the roots of this "conspiracy". I also said I was in favour of Gomulka's membership in the Politburo, even though he wouldn't maintain his previous self-criticism, for surely there were more important things for the nation than arguing with one or another form of deviation: the nation found that kind of party language incomprehensible (I think I used the word "abracadabra" when speaking to the Chinese). I also said that on the basic issues Gomulka's views coincided with ours.

At one point the Chinese comrades complained that we were not releasing enough information on how Chinese workers and peasants lived. You must write, they said, about how difficult their lives are; hell, you have so much bread and so many apartments that you don't understand the Chinese situation.

Why do you laugh?

Because that was naive on their part. How were we supposed to get this information across? Our workers were quite well aware of how French, German and American workers lived, because there are millions of Poles abroad and they always compare their lives to those of the better off, not the worse off. So without adopting the suggestion that we publicize the misery of the Chinese, I nevertheless counted on their support in our difficult situation. Because in spite of everything I did take into account the possibility of intervention: never before or since has anyone played the kinds of tricks on our Soviet friends that they put up with from us [laughter]! Still, they didn't understand that at the time, but the Soviet Union also had something to gain from what I did, because it would have been catastrophic for them to intervene in Poland. Not because they would have lost – they had more than enough force to win – but because the consequences of such an intervention would have been tragic for them as well.

Did they suspect the game you were playing?

It would have been difficult not to. Indeed, worse, they thought that we might actually want to change sides, damn it, after all the blood they had spilt in Poland, the 600,000 soldiers they'd lost – all for nothing! A change of front in Poland would also have meant a change of front in Europe and the rest of the world.

So did you wish the Soviet Union ill?

No, but I trusted, and at one point feared, that the orthodox dogmatists and scholars of party texts would think of dealing with us other than with the aid of theological arguments. Mickiewicz had already suggested this kind of reasoning in his conversation between a tsarist governor and a priest: "And know you theology? Listen then, theologian, have you heard of the Russian whip?" So I had to upset those plans of theirs.

But where did you get the idea of talking to the Chinese?

Who else was I supposed to talk to? Novotny? Ulbricht? They didn't understand much. I must say that Ulbricht was a good communist, though, it's just that his brains were a bit defective. But China is something of an independent factor. And I'm convinced that for all our arguments about not yielding and being firm to the end, which did have an effect, if China hadn't sent its warning in time there would have been an intervention in Poland, and then you could have put flowers on my grave. But I'm sure that wouldn't have occurred to you.

No, certainly not, I was just a child.

I don't doubt it in the least, my sweet.

In what way did the Chinese help us?

I don't know. All I know is what Chou En-lai told us when he came to Poland in 1957. He said they had opposed the Soviet proposal to intervene in Poland and asserted that the Poles, even if they go astray, should find their own solutions to their own problems.

But how did they make this assertion? Did they phone? Did they send a message?

I don't know. It was enough to put it as delicately as possible. In affairs of great moment, when the gun is already on the table, you have to proceed with great delicacy, lest the gun start shooting by itself.

How did the other parties react, in the so-called fraternal countries?

My sweet, what do you expect? Obviously, the other parties agreed to an intervention, because they decided, following their mother, that counter-revolutionary forces were gaining the upper hand in Poland.

Tito as well?

No, not Tito.

What about Hungary?

Yes, of course.

But Nagy was in the Hungarian government.

But the party was headed by Gerö. Rakosi had already left. The Hungarians weren't going to intervene militarily; that would be done by our Soviet friends, perhaps with the Czechoslovaks, Germans and Romanians brought in to help. Anyway, Soviet generals and advisers were operating in each of those countries and I had no illusions about how they would behave. Later I even said to the Romanian prime minister: well, you agreed. He didn't answer.

You laugh.

Because it was very amusing. He was drinking tea; then he stopped, started to stir it again, and when someone came into the room he used the opportunity to change the subject.

Was a plan of the intervention already worked out?

They didn't report to me.

Yes, I know, but . . .

. . . but the fact that there were already tank movements is surely known to you. The whole of Poland knew, the whole world knew. And if it hadn't been for the Chinese . . .

But what were the Chinese counting on?

It's hard to say. They probably overestimated us. In January 1957 Chou En-lai came to Poland, and later Chou Te, and in 1960, when they were preparing to break with the Soviet Union at a meeting of communist parties in Moscow, Chou En-lai actually announced to the Polish delegation that they had helped us in 1956, and now the Poles ought to help them. It was unrealistic. We were neither able nor willing to act against the Soviet Union. People's Poland has developed its strength and is continuing to develop in alliance with the Soviet Union; we must stick to that alliance. However, our alliance should not take the form of a father and son marching together, the one holding the other by the hand. Our proud nation would never agree to such a situation. The Poles are very sensitive, sometimes oversensitive, in matters concerning national honour and respect for our country's dignity. Some of our Soviet friends failed to appreciate these profundities and were prepared to dismiss them as being of no consequence. This was a mistake. They may have seemed of no consequence to them, but not to us.

Did the other members of the Politburo appreciate them?

It varied. Some of them thought we had to repeat what our mother said.

Did you also talk with any other states in the way you talked with the Chinese?

No, there was no need. In September 1956 the Chinese were enough.

Still, I do know that in August a delegation from the Sejm went to Yugoslavia; surely they didn't go there just to establish bonds of love and friendship?

You could call it that. They went to establish normal relations, which had been suspended in previous years, and to get to know each other better. But all anti-Soviet overtones were avoided.

And you didn't meet with Tito?

Not then. I only saw him in 1957 and in the years following. I know Rapacki talked with the Yugoslavian ambassador in Poland, and of course they also discussed our situation at the time, but we weren't counting on the Yugoslavs then.

You said there were tank movements. Did you suspect that someone was planning a coup d'état, as the Europeans would call it?

I had no concrete proof that a "coup", as you put it, was being planned or that proscription lists were being drawn up; nonetheless it was possible to note various worrying symptoms. Comrade Rokossowski was insistent that energetic measures be taken against the press, which he said had "run amok"; at one point he even began to bang his fist on the table. I had to point out to him that this was a meeting of the Politburo, not a military briefing, and that there was no one here who was easily scared off or frightened, so he could keep his fists for another occasion.

Later he came to apologize. He said he'd been wounded many times and he lost his temper because his nerves sometimes failed him. I told him: Comrade Marshal, we have a high regard for your historic contribution to the liberation of Polish territories and the defeat of Nazism, but we must leave crucial decisions to the Politburo, and you should speak as a member of that Buro on equal footing with the other members of the leadership.

The Marshal was an outstanding army man and he was able to make a realistic assessment of the real disposition of forces, of what we could and could not do. But the situation that was developing in Poland was a difficult and dramatic one for him.

What could you do? You apparently discussed the subject with General Komar.

After consulting the then head of the Council of State, I talked with General Komar, commander of Internal Forces. I approved his plan to place units of the Internal Security Corps in readiness for possible action, in order to prevent the kind of thing that had happened in Poznan, where we hadn't even been able to send a single ISC company to the aid of the security functionaries who were under armed attack, and had had to take the matter to the Ministry of National Defence. I also instructed Comrade Alster to prepare, along with General Komar, an order from the Ministry of Internal Affairs concerning placing the ISC in a state of readiness. Various myths were later spread about that order; I won't comment on them. We were worried by information we had received concerning the mood of some officers in our armed forces. We recommended an intensification of political work, especially for the young officers, who often have a tendency to succumb to nationalistic moods.

Might there have been a clash?

I thought it would be catastrophic for us if it happened, a great tragedy, but I couldn't renounce that advantage – of being able, at any time, to say to our Soviet comrades: is that what you want, is that what you'd like to happen? We're only managing our own internal affairs; we may be doing it well or badly, but we're doing it. And it wouldn't occur to us to do what you're doing, to impose anything on you or to ask you what you're going to do. That was a very risky and very difficult game to play, of course. Khrushchev suspected it, that's why when he came to Warsaw during the seventh plenum he screamed at the airport: we know who's the enemy of the Soviet Union here! All in all it happened more or less the way I'd anticipated, but they did get a considerable shock.

Did Rokossowski suspect?

No. Rokossowski was an excellent military man but far weaker as a politician. He came to see me at the beginning of October and admitted that his authority in the army was weakening, and that discipline was visibly going in some units. He also wasn't sure whether the orders of every commander of a large unit would be followed in a crisis. Tension in Poland was rising and there was a danger of an uncontrolled explosion.

There were rumours that in October Stefan Staszewski, first secretary of the Warsaw Committee, distributed arms to workers. You laugh?

Well, where do you imagine he would have got arms from?

I don't know.

Gossip. Of course we couldn't rule out the possibility of isolated acts of provocation, for instance with bottles filled with petrol. I also couldn't rule out the possibility of the Central Committee or government buildings being attacked. Rokossowski came to see me and together we agreed that we had to be fully protected, and that certain special units would be posted in places which could turn out to be "excitable".

Some of them were placed near Warsaw.

That's where they stopped. Actually they stopped on an order from the Soviets. After all, those units were commanded by Soviet citizens. They were honest people and good communists, but if they had to choose we probably wouldn't be the ones they would listen to.

Soviet forces also moved out of their barracks. Why? To frighten us?

Yes.

How else did they try to frighten us? Did they write letters?

No, my sweet, when they write letters things aren't bad. I used to have visits from the Soviet ambassador, more or less . . . no, no, I don't want to.

You laugh.

I don't want to talk about that. In any case I loyally informed them which of their salutary bits of advice I would have to reject.

What were they?

Look. The people from the embassy had a lot of grievances against me, because they first had to send their reports to Moscow and then somehow adjust them to fit the Polish situation. So Ponomarenko was trying to protect himself when he reported, directly or by allusion, that the country was governed by opportunists or by people who were slipping down the path of opportunism. He made reference to various articles in the press, because the press at that time was letting its tongues fly and its comments, whether correct or incorrect, were always of the blustering kind, with no understanding of the country's situation; it was impossible to explain to them that it was better to be silent, that their articles would only irritate our friends and provide them with evidence that a counter-revolution had exploded in Poland or was about to explode at any moment. The people in the embassy, after all, studied the press carefully and picked out the appropriate quotes.

The other thing that worried me were the consequences of the amnesty for political prisoners. I knew it was necessary, but it also involved considerable risk, since I suspected that most of them would start making trouble again as soon as they were out. After all, these were people who had struggled with reality before, who'd been connected with the activities of the armed underground, and they didn't come to us bearing roses: they came at us with machine guns and they killed our people. It's true that the most active ones among them died fighting or were sentenced to death, but the majority of them were alive and considered themselves innocent, even heroes. However, the risk had to be taken; they had to be released in the interests of national unity. Of course they made trouble. Their unrestrained statements, along with those of parts of the press, must have worried our Soviet friends.

During the eighth plenum Khrushchev came to Warsaw uninvited. So we had to open the plenum and go out to the airport.

Surely you must have had some kind of message about his arrival before then.

The Soviet ambassador, Ponomarenko, had rung me late the previous night. That was the eve of the plenum, and he wanted us to put it off. I immediately summoned a meeting of the Politburo, which approved my decision to go ahead with the plenum. I informed the ambassador of the motions we intended to put at the plenum, without going into any details but mentioning that the Politburo had decided to propose Gomulka for the post of first secretary. They rang once again after that to tell me to put off the plenum and to warn me of their arrival. I repeated that we would not call off the plenum, so they came. I went out to the airport, accompanied by Cyrankiewicz, Gomulka, Zawadzki, Zambrowski, I think, and someone else. The first group to arrive consisted of Molotov and Mikoyan, and I think Kaganovich as well, all of them quite calm; we exchanged a few words and Khrushchev arrived about a quarter of an hour later. He'd barely come off the plane when he began demonstratively to shake his fist at us from a distance. He went up to the Soviet generals, a whole row of them, and greeted them first. It was only after that that he came up to us and started brandishing his fist under my nose again. The affront was of course meant not only for me but for the whole Polish party. There was a largish group of people standing around us: dozens of chauffeurs, security functionaries, Soviet military men, members of the Polish leadership. It was clear that the incident would become a public secret, and in these circumstances I had to remind our honoured guest of his manners. I said to him: we are at home in our own Polish capital; there's no need to make a scene at the airport. We're going to the Belvedere, which is where we normally receive our guests. Once at the Belvedere I told him: we won't call off the plenum. I've spent a good few years in prison and I'm not afraid of it; I'm not afraid of anything. We're responsible for our country and we do whatever we think fit, because these are our internal affairs. We're not doing anything to jeopardize the interests of our allies, particularly the interests of the Soviet Union. Mikoyan attempted to prevail upon me by friendly persuasion . . .

How, exactly?

He said they'd come as friends, not as enemies. . . . But I told him that we didn't use such methods towards *our* friends; we wouldn't back down, we wouldn't call off the plenum, and Polish affairs would be decided by *our* Central Committee.

What did Khrushchev threaten you with?

With intervention, obviously. Soviet army divisions were on the move. Khrushchev was still shouting: we'll see who's an enemy of the Soviet Union! Then Gomulka spoke: Ochab's an enemy, Gomulka's an enemy, it's the same thing all over again, just as before. Then Khrushchev said to him: we're happy to see you, we bring you greetings; we have nothing against you, but he – pointing at me – he didn't consult us. I asked Khrushchev, I think Mikoyan was standing beside me: and do you consult us about the make-up of your Politburo or your Central Committee? Khrushchev laughed: come now, don't be silly. But we didn't discuss it any more after that. Then we began our more detailed talks; they were bitter and difficult. They've been transcribed, and one day historians will pore over them. I won't comment on them. I'll just say that it was the Soviets saying one thing and us another.

You were at it all night.

Not quite; there was a break. Then we had part of the plenum, we adjourned it and went on talking. For the most part I was correct in my prediction of the actual course the talks would take.

Weren't you afraid? Many members of the Central Committee didn't come home for the night for fear of being arrested.

It's true, that did happen.

Later, on 9 November, Klosiewicz said in the Sejm that a list of

700 names had been drawn up, and accused the Pulawy group of having put it together.

I don't know whether it was the Pulawy or the Natolin group, but rumours were flying about. My name was on top of that list.

But was it only rumour?

I said rumours were flying about; I don't know whether any plans to deal with us in the event of intervention had been prepared. Of course there was uncertainty. Soviet divisions were moving towards Warsaw, so I imagine that some lackeys from the embassy, in security and in the army must also have received their instructions. So perhaps some lists did exist of who was to be arrested. I didn't want to concern myself with that. I told Gomulka after the seventh plenum to look into the matter. In my opinion the whole thing was instigated by Rokossowski and the people who had contact with the Soviet embassy.

Were there people who didn't?

It's one thing to have contacts and another to take orders. I knew that this whole matter of lists wasn't significant; it didn't mean anything. The real issues are decided elsewhere.

In Czechoslovakia in 1968 they deported the entire leadership.

I know what happened in Czechoslovakia, but in Poland the situation was different. This was most evident in what Rokossowski said, for as a politician he tended to say what was on his mind. Basically our Soviet friends wanted to make Gomulka first secretary.

Why?

As a rule first secretaries in garrison countries, particularly ones who resist –

– are dismissed.

No, they're used as back-up, so as to have alternatives. As a rule in that kind of situation the first secretary has to start defending himself and his position – his post, in quotation marks. But that wasn't the case with me. I drained that bitter cup because I thought someone had to, but I wasn't at all anxious to keep my position. Besides, I thought it might be better, in the end, if that function went to less sensitive comrades, or ones who'd had fewer conflicts with Soviet comrades in the past.

So Gomulka could have been that back-up.

Of course. At one point Khrushchev said to him: we bring you greetings. Presumably they thought Gomulka would put the country in order and was the one to stake their bets on.

And he did, too – it was a pleasure to watch.

In fact they'd counted on more. They thought I'd be portrayed as the two-faced enemy who was fighting against them and undermining them, that the nation would turn away from me, and that Gomulka would do what they told him. But Gomulka neither wanted to nor, indeed, could. In fact he displayed considerable toughness of character during those difficult talks.

But I still don't understand why you handed over power to Gomulka.

I didn't hand it over: I submitted to the will of the majority in the Politburo. I handed it over with a heavy heart, because I knew Gomulka and I knew also that given the circumstances in which he took power the trumpets would sound and proclaim him the saviour of Poland, and that would be a humiliation for the whole party. I had a choice: either put the matter of Gomulka's election to the post of first secretary at the Central Committee forum and come out against it, which would in fact be playing along with the slogans or suggestions of the interveners, or go along with the majority decision of the Politburo.

I don't understand: you had a majority in the Central Committee; you would have won the elections.

But there would have been a split in the party. And when there's a split you have quite a different situation.

What kind?

Intervention. We managed to avoid it, and by avoiding the worst we managed, despite a profound crisis, to keep the party from breaking up. The Hungarians didn't manage to do that then, nor the Czechs later. That's why I chose the second solution, which I knew was supported by millions of people, and handed over power to Gomulka in "peaceful" conditions, in accordance with the wishes of the Central Committee.

Gomulka didn't get off to a bad start. He managed to get compensation for the Polish coal that had been transported to the Soviet Union in previous years.

I'd already taken up the matter of compensation before that, in a conversation with Mikoyan in June or July. In the course of our conversation Mikoyan showed me a scrap of paper which he claimed was an account; according to it they had paid us more than we were owed. But Gomulka succeeded in getting compensation in completely different circumstances, and at the beginning he received favourable treatment. It's a pity he later failed to draw the most important conclusion, namely that we couldn't abandon the road to democratization. He was worried that democratization would open the door to hostile elements.

Weren't you?

I thought we had to take the risk, and that's why I proposed changes in the election procedure. They were minor changes, but they would have taken us at least that quarter of a step further.

In 1957 such an opportunity apparently existed.

It was accepted that we increase the number of candidates, introduce genuine secrecy in the ballot and stop being afraid of crossed-out names. But our new leading personality took fright: first he made one of his pathetic appeals in which he asked the people not to cross out the names of any candidates from the election ballots, because Poland's independence depended on it, and then he proceeded gradually to restrict the number of candidates, until we finally had a mute Sejm of nominees where the list of candidates in practice predetermined the results of the election. Even after my transfer to the Council of State, which was effected against my will, I said to Gomulka: we can't keep on with the kind of elections we had before; we have to look for a solution in the Front of National Unity, in voting for lists of candidates.

What was Gomulka's response to this?

That we couldn't afford to do so.

Because it was too great a luxury?

Because the enemy would start to muster his strength. But I was quite well aware, I said, of how the enemy would react, and that's why we had to secure our position; the best way to do so was through the Front of National Unity. I told him it was a risk we had to take.

Why was it a risk?

Because, my sweet, both for historical reasons and owing to mistakes committed, and in view of a number of responsibilities of an international nature, our party had no guarantees that it would win the support of the majority. The increase in its ranks also varied in different periods. But Gomulka believed that a few election ballots would clear the way for hostile elements. It's clear when you look at it now that he wanted to rule autocratically, and since this was an idea dear to the hearts of certain gentlemen outside Poland as well, it became yet another area of common interest between them. However, when they saw the national upheaval his behaviour had caused, and when the time came for them to choose, they scrapped Gomulka. And quite rightly, too, except that it would have been better for the party if it had got rid of those who wanted autocratic rule earlier and on its own.

Surely there were opportunities in 1968.

No. Gomulka, instead of concerning himself with the country's fundamental problems, had already a year before began to ferret out fascist "slogans" and to scream about how Poland was being threatened by Zionism, by a fifth column, and how he wouldn't stand for it.

Are you referring to the speech Gomulka made at the Trade Union Congress a few days after the Arab–Israeli war of June 1967?

Yes. Gomulka's claims also took the members of the Politburo by surprise. I told him afterwards that he'd had no right to say such things without the approval of the Politburo. Whereupon he started to explain how he'd been working alone, far into the night, without anyone's help. Stuff like that. By then it was obvious to me that the die had been cast and it was no longer a question of mere phraseology.

But you had a majority in the Politburo at the time; you could have protested.

No, I didn't; I didn't have a majority in the Central Committee. If I had I would have made a public statement at the Central Committee plenum and presented a fuller assessment of the situation. Of course I wouldn't have been alone: a dozen or so other comrades would have followed suit and we would have been shouted down and subjected to repression, and we would have lost. And then they would have gone outside with an appeal to this working class of ours, most of which was composed of yesterday's emigrants from the countryside, fledglings who hadn't yet grown claws, and they would have let themselves be duped into believing the arguments about why things were bad in Poland, why there were problems: because the Jews are in power or because the Soviets are grabbing everything for themselves. A decision had to be made. I already knew I wouldn't take part in this game, but I advised Adam, I mean Rapacki, to grit his teeth and continue pulling the wagon. But he said it was beyond his strength. I gave the same advice to other people too, but they wouldn't listen to me either.

I don't understand; after all this nation isn't that stupid, it might have understood your arguments.

It's a wise nation, my sweet, but it was gagged.

I still don't understand why you didn't make a public statement.

I told you. I could have made a statement at the Central Committee plenum; I would have had to dress it up and tone it down in the appropriate way beforehand; I wouldn't have got a majority, so I would have lost; and in the process I would have exposed a dozen, or several dozen, comrades to reprisals.

They were got rid of in any case.

That's another matter, and besides, not all of them. A lot of honest people remained. And after that, history took the course it took. To me it was clear by 1968 that the thing had to collapse. There were student riots. It's true that various trends were mixed up in that, but nonetheless it was an expression of discontent on the part of hundreds of thousands of people. Those students, after all, weren't fascists, counter-revolutionaries or any kind of bourgeoisie; that's why the situation demanded a serious consideration of our mistakes and serious talks. Of course you can break and defeat people with truncheons, but of the tens of thousands of students who protested most retained deep resentment and contempt for that kind of treatment for many years to come. Only the most demoralized student troublemakers, or the most susceptible to being demoralized, slid down into the morass. They, of course, were the ones who said: we won't make trouble: we'll make our careers with the people who hold the truncheons, and we'll keep up the wild anti-Semitic campaign that has been unleashed. Well, I was very decidedly opposed to that campaign, and thought that under no circumstances should the party tolerate it, much less sponsor it, because it would do the party great damage in the long run. I believed it had to be stemmed; that's why I wrote a letter, not to the Central Committee, but to the Politburo and the Central Committee secretariat. I said in it that I was resigning from all my party and state functions. I wrote:

"As a Pole and a communist it is with the greatest outrage that I protest against the anti-Semitic campaign being organized in Poland by various dark forces. In the situation which has been created in our party I am forced to express my protest by resigning my membership of the Politburo and the Central Committee of the PUWP. At the same time I offer a written resignation from my post as head of the Council of State and head of the Front of National Unity."

I was advised by comrades to talk to Gomulka and try to explain some things to him. I knew that such a conversation would be unproductive and useless; nevertheless I agreed. The matter was too important to be left without a response. I went to the Central Committee, where I found Gomulka unusually calm and collected. I think he realized, to some extent at least, that the anti-Semitic fuss was also aimed against him. He told me that we couldn't consider our situation without taking into account what was happening in Europe; that serious counter-revolutionary preparations were under way in Czechoslovakia, similar to the ones in Hungary in 1956. I told him I was not aware of anything of the kind. He then replied that he had material proof: Gierek's reports of his talks with Indra and Bilak. I said, well, all right, I suppose I can familiarize myself with this material, but the situation in the country is quite clear to me and I stand by what I wrote about an anti-Semitic affair being organized that is of no use to anyone and in which I will not take part. At that point Gomulka asked me to hold off with my resignations for the moment. I said I could agree to hold off for two weeks or so, and that my letter should therefore be treated as an announcement I would not go back on.

And is that why you wrote to the Sejm, "In view of my deteriorating state of health, which significantly limits the possibility of my continued work as head of the Council of State of the PUWP, I request that the Honourable Sejm allow me to step down from this post. Edward Ochab"?

I agreed because obviously I couldn't stoke up the student opposition and I still believed that the leadership would finally hold talks with them. But they didn't. The arrogant boors in the Politburo apparently came to the conclusion that police repression would suffice, along with expulsion from universities and that shameful cry in our press headlined "Workers of the World Unite!", which was supposed to patch up the autocrat's self-confidence and in practice clear the way for Moczar.

Did Moczar want the post of first secretary?

Perhaps not that, but he certainly wanted to be the first after the first secretary. He wanted Gomulka to be the official sponsor of everything while he, Moczar, effectively directed it all. That was the role that would have suited him, hence his involvement in the police operation, indeed his control over it.

He wasn't the only one in charge of it.

The country knew what those "superpatriots" were like. That whole Mafia is still there today! They control the security service. I said all this to Gomulka at the time. Kliszko and Cyrankiewicz were present at the conversation. I said that the operation was being directed by Moczar and security because they wanted to prepare positions into which to slot their agents and their intelligence.

Their *intelligence?*

That's not important: everyone knows we help Soviet intelligence, although it's involved in various things, good ones and bad ones. We mainly had to deal with the bad ones, the ones that made trouble. I don't know why we got ourselves into that situation.

Moczar and security came out against the badly born [that is, Jews], of whom there were twenty-five to thirty thousand in Poland at the time; now there are only about five thousand, the rest have been driven out. I told them: you're using our truncheons to drive out our youth, sometimes very talented youth; you're treating them like subhumans; that's something no self-respecting party should allow. You can't call them hooligans, even if there have been some acts of hooliganism, because tens of thousands of active young people are taking part in the protests – you have to hold political talks with them, not deal with them by police methods. But none of it helped. When the people from [the journal] *Znak*, albeit with different intentions, rightly and bravely spoke up in defence of our youth, they were spat at. I was sorry for them; they were literally hounded. And lo and behold, paradoxically the communists found themselves side by side with black reactionaries.

I remember Gomulka's speech of 19 March 1968. Who wrote it?

Gomulka did. The Politburo met an hour or an hour and a half before a conference of Warsaw activists. We wanted to read through Gomulka's speech but apparently it was not yet ready, so we got a few pages at a time handed to us at intervals; the final pages didn't reach us at all. The audience in the Palace of Culture had already been appropriately prepared: there were shouts of "Moczar" and "Gierek". Our honourable intelligentsia was silent, the saintly representatives of the Church also remained mute, so it was clear to me that there was no point in any talks, and that that game would go on without me. Adam Rapacki did try to send various memos to the leadership after the intervention in Czechoslovakia, where he expounded his thoughts, but that only encouraged their impudence. I thought it was pointless.

What use was Zionism to Gomulka? As part of a political strategy?

He simply had a nationalistic mania. But I'd never suspected he would go as far as an anti-Semitic campaign. Still, he shouldn't be seen in an entirely negative light; you can't judge him solely on the basis of his nationalistic mania, his autocratic aspirations, his lunacies – I think they were symptoms of a disease: megalomania and persecution mania. Such manias tend to flourish in the difficult circumstances in which our government is developing. Gomulka also did a lot of good for this country. I think one day history will judge him fairly; he can't be erased from our history.

Nor can you; hence my last question: is there any mistake that you have on your conscience?

In my political activity I've always tried to be guided by the principles of Marxist theory and not to forget the good and the bad experiences of the Polish workers' movement, so as to go forward without making fundamental errors of direction. And in my day-to-day work in the ranks of the communist movement, work that spanned over half a century, quite a number of day-to-day mistakes were made – must have been made. But I can die in peace, and I'll be able (in the metaphorical sense, since I am an atheist and I don't believe in an afterlife) to look calmly into the eyes of fallen comrade communists and all my brother soldiers who spilt their blood in the fight for a free People's Poland. We will meet in the pages of history, all those of us who conscientiously, boldly and fruitfully fought for the independence of the nation, for the rule of workers and peasants, for a new, socialist society in Poland and the world.

May–October 1981

ROMAN WERFEL

ROMAN WERFEL

Roman Werfel was born in 1906 in Lvov into a bourgeois family. His father was a lawyer, his mother a housewife, and his elder brother went to work in a bank. He joined the communist movement at the age of fifteen, while still in school, and by the age of sixteen was already a secretary of the municipal committee of the KZMP. Two years later, in 1923, he became a member of the KPP. Arrested in that same year and released on bail, he went to Vienna to study. In 1928 he was summoned back to Poland and sent to work in the communist party of western Ukraine. He was secretary of the KZMP for Stanislawow, and later worked in the party's operations department in Cracow. He then went to Berlin for a year, where he served as a courier, and after his return in 1931 became secretary of the Regional Party Committee in Stanislawow. Shortly afterwards he was again arrested, and remained in prison until 1935. The following year he was expelled from the KPP. In 1939, after the Red Army's occupation of Lvov, he became editor of the communist paper *The Red Flag*, collaborated with the paper *New Horizons*, one of Lvov's Polish-language newspapers, and became a member of the VCP(b). After the outbreak of the war between Germany and the Soviet Union he fled to Central Asia and was summoned to Moscow shortly afterwards. In May 1942 he was appointed editor of *New Horizons*, which had resumed publication under the editorship of Wanda Wasilewska. Among others who worked there were Alfred Lampe, Stefan Jedrychowski, Jerzy Putrament, Helena Usiejewicz (daughter of Feliks Kon) and Janina Broniewska.

Upon his return to Poland in July 1944 he went first to Lublin, and soon became the leading party ideologist. He held successive posts as editor-in-chief of the *People's Voice*; from 1948 onwards, after the merging of two party publishing houses, "Ksiazka" and "Wiedza", as director of the resulting "Ksiazka i Wiedza"; and from January 1952 to 1959, as editor-in-chief of *Nowe Drogi*, the leading organ of the Central Committee. He was, in addition, editor-in-chief of the daily *Trybuna Ludu* for two months from March 1956, supplanting Wladyslaw Matwin. He was succeeded by Jerzy Morawski for a month, by Walenty Titkow for three months, by Matwin again for several months, and finally, when "normalization" had taken place, by Leon Kasman, who had been the paper's editor-in-chief since its foundation and was to remain there until 1968.

In 1959 he was appointed propaganda secretary of the Wroclaw Provincial Committee, and in 1963 director of the Institute for the History of Polish–Soviet Relations at the Polish Academy of Sciences. In 1968 he was expelled from the party and retired. His wife and daughter have left Poland; the former, a KOR and Solidarity sympathizer, now lives in Vienna, the latter in England, where she is engaged in social work with juvenile delinquents, although by profession she is a biochemist.

In 1983, after fifteen years, Roman Werfel was accepted back into the ranks of the Polish United Workers' Party.

* * *

In Austria you have a wife, in England a daughter and in Warsaw one room strewn with books, a bathroom and a small anteroom with a kitchen niche. I doubt that's the kind of future your father, a solid lawyer from Lvov, intended for you.

No, but it's what I intended.

What did you want to be?

What I became: a professional revolutionary. I read Lenin's *What is to be done?* when I was still in high school – I don't remember whether I read the original or an abbreviated version – where Lenin maintains that the socialist revolution needs "professional revolutionary" cadres in order to succeed. Cadres who would be prepared, if need be, to spend months crawling along sewers and would be in charge, as he put it, of organizing the masses. That was when I said to myself: that's me. And I don't regret it.

What about your family?

My family belonged to two different traditions. One was the bourgeois tradition of going to work in the morning and chatting to doctors, lawyers and professors in cafés in the evening; the other was the tradition of rebellion. My father had a picture on the wall of his office of a handsome man in nobleman's robes; it was my mother's grandfather, who took part in the 1863 Rising. For this he was later locked up in the citadel, where he caught TB and died. But his sons, even though they went into business – indeed yes – kept his portrait.

Just in case?

Not only [laughter] and not primarily. Theirs was a post-Rising, positivist generation: you had your business affairs, certainly, but you retained a soft spot for romantic uprisings. My mother was very proud of her grandfather, much more than she was of the other, wealthy and business-oriented members of her family.

My father's father was another odd figure; it was from him that I got my middle name, Karol, for the Jewish "Chaim". Until the age of forty he'd been a wealthy rabbi, but then he decided that all this God and religion stuff was a swindle and a lie, so he became an atheist and went into banking. He didn't do very well at it, and lost a lot of money. He kept on losing and losing, but still he managed to salvage some of it, such as a huge German-language library of world classics, which unfortunately burnt down during World War II. I remember my father used to recount with indignation how my grandfather, when he was very ill with cancer, once sighed, "O Gott, Gott, Gott" (he spoke German at home). My father, surprised, asked him, "Have you begun believing in God again?" "So what am I supposed to say," my grandfather replied, " 'Oy vey mir' ['Woe is me' in Yiddish]? 'Gott, Gott, Gott' sounds so much nicer." My father always used to say that I was his punishment for my grandfather's sins. He had a typically legal mind; until his dying day he sighed for the emperor Franz Jozeph; we lived in a good district; and there I was, godless from the start. For although my family was polonized, in religious matters it was still loosely Jewish, which meant that you went to the temple four times a year, because it was done, because it was expected.

To the temple? What's that?

A "reformed" Jewish synagogue for the enlightened intelligentsia, where Polish was spoken instead of Yiddish, which you spoke at a proper synagogue.

The first time I kicked up a fuss I was in the fourth or fifth form at school. My father took me along to celebrate a Jewish holiday; it's customary for Jews to pick out young boys to sit and hold the Torah during the ceremony. They picked me. Well, by then I was already a militant atheist and I couldn't afford to look like a fool, you understand. So I said to my father, "Daddy, if you don't get this Torah away from me in five minutes, I'll throw it on the ground." My father was absolutely furious, and simply told the others that I wasn't very well. They gave me some scornful looks, picked another boy, and my father never took me to the temple again.

The second row also took place during a Jewish holiday. The tradition on that occasion meant bringing a matzo to school; instead I brought a sandwich made up of two pieces of matzo with ham in the middle. All the Jews in my class went for me. I came out of it one tooth worse off, but I gave them a pretty good beating as well.

At about the same time I began to take an interest in history, which I've retained to this day and which proved useful to me later. I was already buying *Workers' Culture*, a communist journal. The KZMP members from the upper forms at school noticed this and approached me. One in particular was a boy who later emigrated to France. I was hooked.

You have to understand: it was 1921. We'd lived through a terrible – as we thought then – First World War. Workers' families lived on *mamalyga* [hominy gruel], potatoes and bread spread with American "monkey" lard, as it was called; a section of the bourgeoisie – and not even the good one, but the worse one, the one we used to call "profiteering" – was feverishly trying to make it to the top; socialism was in the air. I became a communist, and only a year later I was one of the secretaries of the KZMP Town Committee. I was just over sixteen at the time.

That was quick.

It wasn't a huge organization in Lvov – 120 members – and the make-up wasn't very impressive: about 60 Jews, mainly small craftsmen, 10 high-school students, about 30 Ukrainians, most of them students, because there was an underground Ukrainian university in Lvov, and maybe 30 Polish railway workers.

Do you draw any conclusions from these statistics?

At least two. First of all, that oppressed nations lean towards rebellion, and when the leadership of that rebellion is taken over by communists who can lead it well and manipulate it wisely, then those nations lean towards communism. Hence the high percentage in the Polish Communist Party of Jews, Byelorussians and Ukrainians. A similar phenomenon occurred in tsarist Russia: the Poles were in a certain sense the Jews of tsarist Russia, and they played a tremendously important role in the whole Russian revolutionary movement, especially in the October Revolution. And they weren't just workers; some of them came from very good Polish families.

Like Feliks Dzerzhinsky, for instance?

For instance. And I can tell you an interesting detail, namely that

Feliks Dzerzhinsky and Jozef Pilsudski came from exactly the same social class, and that their parents' manor houses were almost next to each other. Dzerzhinsky himself (a detail remembered about him; I even wanted to publish it once, but they wouldn't let me), as a teenager, would lie on the church floor in a cross and pray for the rebirth of Poland.

To get back to the subject. The second reason for the relatively small numbers of Polish intelligentsia in the communist movement during the interwar years in Poland lay, in my view, in the fact that the Polish intelligentsia had many more barriers to surmount before it could accept communism.

More barriers, or more opportunities for diversity in political life?

Other people had those opportunities too: there were the Jewish and Ukrainian political parties. So I think the barriers were the deciding factor.

What kinds of barriers?

Well, Vilnius and Lvov, for instance, or the "Eastern Borders", as they were called then. The Polish Communist Workers' Party voted as early as 1923 for the self-determination of western Ukraine and western Byelorussia.

Yes, but that was on the explicit wish of the Comintern.

What's wrong with that? You're not thinking in historical terms; you're transposing today's situation onto the situation at the beginning of the twenties. Communist parties were still young then, just beginning to form (and I should add that the Polish party was one of the most mature), so it's no wonder they needed help, advice and even directives, especially as these were provided by a party which had already shown that it knew how to win – the Bolshevik party – and provided, moreover, in a situation where it seemed that a revolution in Central Europe would break out in a matter, not of years, but of months. It was to be an all-out revolutionary onslaught, not like the stationary wars of today. And for this a staff was needed which would engage particular units of the international army in combat or hold them back from attack. The Comintern was this staff, and we were one of its units.

The main question should be not whether the Comintern had the right to give us advice, but whether its advice was right. I think it was. After all, the Comintern directive reasserted, in Marxist terminology, the old slogan of Polish independence fighters: "for our freedom and yours"? By denying it you adopt the principle "for our freedom and your serfdom".

Please don't get upset; I'm really not the one who thought up the slogan that the Polish party is an agent of Moscow.

But you continue to repeat it. I once wrote in an article that it's not we who are agents of Moscow, but rather that Moscow is the first victorious agent of victorious communism, the first bastion conquered by communism. For the propertied classes every argument was good for discrediting the communists. The territories we conquered had originally been taken over against the will of the overwhelming majority of the local population; territories on which battles, sometimes bloody, had been fought throughout the whole of the twenty-year period between the wars. True, Vilnius and Lvov were Polish islands (there were other, smaller ones, as well), but in a Byelorussian and Ukrainian sea. This was a problem that had to be solved, and the communists were the only ones to propose a just solution to it.

What was that?

We thought the Ukraine belonged to the Ukrainians and Byelorussia to the Byelorussians, while we – I mean the interwar Republic – had the right to territories which were populated mostly by Poles, according to the nation's measure and its living scope.

Meaning the territories from the Bug to the Vistula, with Poznan to boot?

Land to the west of the Bug, all of Upper Silesia, Warmia and Mazuria.

That's too much. The KPRP said nothing about Mazuria or Warmia, but they did say quite a lot about Upper Silesia. Your slogan was "Upper Silesian coal for German workers!" when the Poles were fighting in the Silesian risings.

You don't understand what it was like then. The most important thing for communists at the time was not the issue of frontiers, but that of an all-European socialist revolution, whose outbreak was perfectly conceivable. There seems to be an implication, in what you've just been saying, that a great nation, a nation worthy of note, is one which appropriates the greatest possible number of territories populated by foreign nations. But this view is false. It may be correct from the point of view of the exploiting classes, which profit from such territories, but certainly not from the point of view of the people: they get some scraps from time to time, but later they pay for those conquests with sweat and blood. I get the feeling that you have the same nationalistic, chauvinistic tendency to which the Polish intelligentsia has always been prey. Provincial, parochial chauvinism, that's what it is!

And what about you?

In 1923 I got myself caught, along with the entire city committee of the KZMP; I got three years in the first instance, which wasn't much; my father got me out on bail until the appeal hearing, and I escaped through Czechoslovakia to Vienna. I studied and engaged in politics. All perfectly normal. I joined the Austrian Communist Party, where they advised me to join the Austrian Social Democratic Party: go, they said, and stir up opposition. So I did.

In order to break it up?

It was unbreakable [laughter]. It was a huge, mass party, and you could learn a lot from it, in particular how to work with the working class; it wasn't just a bunch of little Lvov –

– juveniles.

Why juveniles? I was one of the younger KZMP members, but we had a party organization over us which told us what to do, and one of its members was the father of [Adam] Michnik, a great figure in Lvov at that time. Those were the older comrades, and they taught us, as I discovered in Austria, quite well.

There's one thing that's sacred and essential for a revolutionary party: the party must display unity and solidarity in its actions, and its members cannot speak different languages. We were trained according to that principle and we stuck to it, perhaps even to excess, because after all if someone has been voted down it's difficult to ask him to take his place in the first ranks of those called on to carry out the resolution passed. For instance, I was organizing youth groups in the trade unions; I don't remember what the resolution concerned was, but at any rate I was outvoted. I lost my temper and said, right, one of you can go and defend that decision at the municipal trade union conference. Oh, no, they said, you're the one who has to defend it. So I went and defended it.

They taught you duplicity, then – or, to put it more delicately, flexibility.

Let's not exaggerate: they taught us discipline, not duplicity. Besides, that particular matter was a very minor one.

Minor matters are where it begins.

Look, when a resolution is passed, it's the duty of a communist to carry it out. So we were taught discipline and unity of action. That's not imporant when the party only has an election battle to deal with, but it's essential when it comes to organizing the masses for revolution. We were preparing the ground for that revolution, so we had to act as a unit.

And you stayed with that principle.

A lot was said about how the lack of democracy within the party was a result of its illegality. That's true and then again it isn't. Later, when I was the provincial secretary in 1931, I may have been able to dissolve every district committee and appoint others, and indeed I did sometimes after people had been caught, but I couldn't force party members to take instructions from such a committee.

But then, you see, they did.

They didn't have to, and they didn't necessarily. Even if they didn't manage to outvote it, they could stop coming to meetings, and thus vote with their feet. An illegal party is by its very nature democratic, because it cannot compel its members to do anything. I remember when the Polish party was going through a period of ultra-left fever after 1930. I was in favour of Warski's and Kostrzewa's policy. So I was dismissed from my post of KZMP secretary, and the party instead sent me to Cracow, and then to Berlin, where I was a "liaison man", meaning that I was a young man who ran errands. One of the features of the ultra-left fever was that people were constantly being called to demonstrations. But after three or four such calls our workers simply stopped coming. A few young petits bourgeois came, just for the hell of it and on a why-not-risk-it basis, but the old workers' cadres – they didn't come. They could get up and say their piece at a rally, they could elect their communist delegate to the Sejm and proceed to defend him afterwards, but as for going out on the street for no good reason, just for some commemoration or other, oh no, not they. They simply didn't go out on the street, and that was that.

And I'll tell you something else. A few years later the party adopted a "policy of division" in the trade unions, a line which was entirely false and basically opportunistic, since it reflected the mood of the crafts proletariat. It was comparatively simple to bring about a split in, say, a tailors' union: the workshops could divide into Polish and Jewish ones, or into red and PPS ones. There'd be a little communist union active in one and a little PPS union in another. The unions could conciliate one another and they were tolerated by the police, because it had informers planted in all of them, and everything was fine. But in a large factory such splits were harmful to the union, because they caused further splits on the shop floor. I presume Stalin imposed this policy of division on us for internal Soviet reasons. I was one of the secretaries of a district committee in western Ukraine and I had a party organization of about fifty people in the potassium salt mine in Kalusz. The trade union there was headed by a PPS man. In accordance with the Comintern line, I kept telling them they had to form a separate union, but they just kept on saying, "Well, all right, we'll see," all the time. They didn't say no, because the Comintern line is the Comintern line; they simply didn't create the split.

Gomulka has a habit of saying, "Yes, but . . . ." Couldn't one say, "No, but do it"?

And saying, "No, because . . ." to the Comintern would be too bold, would it?

Damn it, it hasn't got anything to do with boldness.

With what, then?

I've told you already: you have to maintain unity within an illegal party or an international army, because it's only through unity that action can be effective. Don't you understand that?

No.

Then I'll give you another example. In 1929 the entire KPP leadership – Warski, Kostrzewa – was dismissed.

Again, may I remind you, on orders from the Comintern.

Under pressure from the Comintern, not on its orders. A few supporters of Warski and Kostrzewa, including myself, began to discuss what was to be done. One of them said we should not recognize the directive.

Was he the one who was killed in the Soviet Union?

No, that wasn't him; he was killed in Poland during the Nazi occupation.

My view was that we just had to grit our teeth, allow ourselves to be dismissed if it came to that, and remain in the party. Especially since we didn't really know what was happening in this Russian party of theirs; we only knew, and the masses knew, that they were building socialism.

In 1938 as well, when they were dissolving your party?

Yes, in 1938 as well. But by then I was no longer in the party, anyway.

Indeed!

It's a whole long story. In 1931 I found myself in jail with a four-year sentence. They added another three years on top of that, the three I didn't do on account of my escape to Vienna. So I had seven in all. In 1935, however, I managed to get out temporarily for a health cure. I came to Lvov, and saw that things were not going all that well. That was when I still suspected that there was an *agent provocateur* in the CPWU. I left for Warsaw. I wanted to get a job in the central Warsaw editorial office, and made a few attempts through Minc and Pawel Hoffman, but it didn't work and I had to go back to western Ukraine. Before I left I bumped into a friend of mine and said to her, listen, if they find me with my brains blown out and say I was an *agent provocateur*, I want you to know it's not true.

A short while later an amnesty was announced for 1 January 1936. I immediately presented myself back at the prison to sit out the remaining three months so that I could be "legal" again when I came out. I did the three months, came out and discovered that I'd been expelled from the party as an agent of Ukrainian nationalists.

Why do you laugh?

Because it was so absurd. I found out about the party's resolution from my wife, who was then a courier for the Secretariat of the CPWU Central Committee. She at once asked them why, but they began telling her some rubbish about how I was such a terrible man because I'd raped my courier. Dziunka said, surprised: I was his courier and I can assure you that during our entire year and a half together he never raped me; he didn't have to. So then they started looking around for better reasons and they came up with two. I'd once written a united-front letter to the Ukrainian radicals' party – a right-wing party. A member of the CPWU Secretariat, a man from Warsaw who was totally ignorant about Ukrainian affairs, was supposed to approve the letter. He read it and at once insisted that it include a phrase about the need to defend "Soviet Ukraine". I said to him, Moisha (that was his pseudonym), you can't make a suggestion like that to radicals, you just can't! Whereupon he said, what, you mean they don't want to defend Soviet Ukraine? Of course not, I said, because they want a bourgeois Ukrainian state. "Moisha" was furious; he went to Warsaw and made some kind of report against me. Then there was the other matter: the Polish court had sentenced some Ukrainian nationalists to death, and I had put out two leaflets protesting against the sentences. They were in two languages, Polish and Ukrainian, and each one slightly different. In the Ukrainian one I criticized Ukrainian nationalism, while in the Polish one I tried to explain where it came from, what kept it alive, that it was the result of national oppression, and so forth. They didn't know any Ukrainian in Warsaw, and read only the Polish leaflet; so they accused me of defending Ukrainian nationalism and expelled me.

Didn't you appeal against the decision?

Appeal? To whom? The only thing that happened was that my hair turned grey. That was when I still had some hair [laughter]. As it was, I was lucky that all they did was expel me. I probably have Rylski to thank for that. He was a Comintern representative who worked with a friend of mine; she told him about the whole affair, and since he knew me and happened to be in Warsaw at the time, he began to ask all about it. He was a cautious man, so all he did was ask, and the people who did the expelling also turned out to be cautious, because that was all they did.

That, I believe, is what they call luck.

Why luck?

Because you're alive! And you didn't die as an agent of Ukrainian nationalists in 1936, or like that Comintern representative in 1937, as a "result of false charges".

I could still have been killed in Lvov in 1940. Some people were bent on sending me out to hunt polar bears [to Siberia]. They spread rumours about me. I was outraged, and like an idiot I went and complained to the NKVD that I was being harassed. I got a very cold reception from an NKVD man who said, we'll think about it, come back in a week. I came back in a week. The NKVD man greets me at the door graciously, almost warmly; he asks me to sit down, calls in another man, and they start asking me questions about hundreds of things: how the party functioned, who was in it, what did they do, and, finally, did I have a party card? A membership card of an illegal party, can you imagine! I looked at them as if they were out of their minds; they hadn't a clue what an illegal party was. Finally, they advised me to take the man to court for libel, because, unfortunately, they couldn't pin anything on him. Well, I wasn't so stupid as to go looking for justice from some kolkhoz member.

The president of the people's court, you mean.

Oh, don't be silly. So I left it at that. But the NKVD summoned me again to fire endless questions at me. What is the whereabouts of a certain CPWU activist who became a Trotskyist in 1937? I replied, truthfully of course, that I didn't know; how was I supposed to know? You're the ones who ought to know his address, I added.

Have you read Aleksander Wat's My Century*?*

He says in it that I was an agent for the NKVD: rubbish! If I'd been one of theirs, they wouldn't have asked Wat about me: they'd have known everything already.

All of you, Mr Werfel, have an excess either of completely unjustified faith in the Soviet authorities or of absurd suspiciousness towards your fellow comrades.

What do you mean, "all of you"? Everyone knows Wat wasn't one of ours!

Whose was he, then?

Who the hell knows? Probably no one's. Just one of the bourgeois literati.

A Trotskyist, perhaps?

No, there wasn't much Trotskyism in Poland, although there's no denying that Trotskyism was often an escape from illegal work. That's not to say, of course, that all Trotskyists are just a pain in the neck, but there were some bad ones. I had some boys who calmly sat around in the "commune" [prison; the communists in prison were very well organized], but when they came out they soon discovered they were Trotskyists, because that meant they could pose as martyrs who were being persecuted by the police and the communists. And later, when they stopped being persecuted, they took over their fiancées' hardware shops and lived the good life. They went on about how they could do great things if it weren't for Stalin. They never did anything.

But Stalin did, didn't he?

Yes, that's right. He defeated Hitler, and if it weren't for him we wouldn't be sitting here together sipping tea. That he did it in his own way is another matter. For that he's enormously to blame, but it was also the result of the situation at the time. All the difficulties the Soviet Union went through, all the mistakes and – let's be quite clear about this – all the crimes were above all the result of one fact: the isolation of the Soviet republics. To this day I'm still convinced that if the Red Army had made it through to Berlin in 1920, the fate of Europe, and perhaps of the world as well, would have been different. The Soviet republics would not have had to haul themselves up by their own bootstraps from that mud of backwardness which the tsars left behind and which Lenin described as "barbarity and pure savagery". There wouldn't have been the problem of an atrophied apparatus of proletarian rule, there would have been no Stalinist period in the thirties, no fascism in Germany, no Auschwitz, no Majdanek – words don't describe it!

Except that in Italy, France and Germany we would have had the dictatorship of the proletariat.

And it really would have been of the proletariat, because they had a proletariat there. It was possible; there were opportunities. The climate in the West was right for a revolution. The men came back from the front hungry and angry. Their armies had fallen apart; they had weapons, and the millions of women who had waited for them for four years were also angry, because their children were hungry. All that influenced the general mood. And the result? Hungarian and Bavarian Soviet republics were created; we had control of factories in Italy; we had a Red Army of the Ruhr Valley. So there were worker cadres in the West, a workers' proletariat, something which Russia already lacked because part of it had disintegrated during the civil war, while the remainder went into the state and party apparatus, and there was an influx of peasants and petit bourgeoisie into the factories. But it didn't happen, and it didn't happen, to put it precisely, because of two Jozefs, Jozef Stalin, who stopped the Red Army at Lvov and made it fight for four days instead of attacking Warsaw immediately, as Lenin had wanted; and Jozef Pilsudski, who took advantage of Stalin's own policy and stopped the Red Army outside Warsaw.

It was the nation, Mr Werfel, that stopped the Red Army. A nation that longed for its own state.

It wasn't the nation! The nation had nothing to do with it! The number of volunteers for the army was tiny, not more than a dozen or so thousand people; the army that fought the Red Army was an army of recruits. And as for independence, why shouldn't a socialist Poland have been independent? After all, it would have been part of a great socialist league of all European states. It's hard to imagine such a league being ruled by Russia, which Lenin said would be a backward, yes, backward socialist country after the victory of the socialist revolution in Europe. After the disastrous defeat at Warsaw, however, Russia had to build socialism on her own. But I remain convinced to this day that if the Red Army had managed to get through to Berlin, history would have taken a different turn, and we would have avoided the terrible experiences of the thirties. I mean we communists would.

There's an old Russian joke that goes: can you build socialism in one country? Of course you can, but what a pity for the poor country! So it was a pity for the country, but socialism had to be built.

Why?

What else was there to do? Return to capitalism? To the "Whites", who were responsible for all the backwardness? Remain a backward, exploited subsidiary of great Western-European capital? No, I tell you, socialism had to be built, and it really was a pity for the country. Things evolved in a way that had a harmful effect on Russia's development, and not on hers alone. Lenin had written earlier, in his *State and Revolution*, that in a dictatorship of the proletariat there would be no permanent army and no police; it would be a "non-state". The apparatus of force, along with all the attributes of power proper and essential to a state, would gradually fade away, and the state as such would also wither. When Lenin wrote those words, however, he had not anticipated a situation where only one socialist country would be created, surrounded by capitalist countries; he had imagined that the revolutionary movement would span the whole of Europe. When this failed to happen, new conditions had to be adjusted to. Thus in 1924 Stalin "corrected", or perhaps "supplemented" what Lenin had written, discovering that a state with a dictatorship of the proletariat must, when in capitalist surroundings, remain a state for a considerable length of time; we on our part accepted Stalin's formulation with relief, because he was right. What we failed to notice, however, was that Stalin had played a conjuring trick on us: the dictatorship of the proletariat which he proceeded to consolidate was not the dictatorship of the proletariat that Lenin had written about, for the state that Stalin began to build had its own apparatus of coercion over the masses, an apparatus which was not controlled by those masses and which needed to be strengthened and developed.

This, then, is where the problem arose. Every class system has, and must have, an apparatus of force – "units of armed men" – to protect the moneyed classes and the institutions created by them. But at the same time these classes create their own mechanisms whereby they, the moneyed classes, and not the people, are able to control that apparatus and prevent abuses of it. This can take a number of forms, from court cliques in an absolute monarchy to parliament in a bourgeois republic. But the intent is the same: control of the apparatus (at least, partial control, since the apparatus itself is not, after all, a passive instrument). In a dictatorship of the proletariat on the Leninist model, such control was not needed, for the proletarian masses *were* the state. On the Stalinist model, however, the apparatus gradually lost its dependence on the masses. Theoretically the soviets, the Councils of Workers' Delegates, should have been the instruments of control. But the Soviet proletariat was only in the first stages of its rebirth – indeed, for the most part it was simply being born a second time. Thus the apparatus of force was becoming independent of the class which had brought it to power, while, in addition, those in power had, as is usually the case in backward countries, two tasks facing them simultaneously: to ensure a greater degree of social justice (or, to put it more simply, a more egalitarian distribution of the goods of this world) and to develop productive forces so that there would be something to distribute. Now those two tasks are mutually contradictory: as the English say, you can't have your cake and eat it, too. You can't invest what you are consuming and you can't increase production without investing (sensibly, and not, as was often the case with us, unwisely). So you have to weigh up both sides; decide how much is to go on what. And weighing up means taking account of the real, hard facts, and not of the less real moods and demands of society. In this situation the danger of arbitrary, not fully thought through decisions on the part of those in "power" is particularly great, and the need for the ruling, that is working, class to have control over the functioning of this apparatus is particularly urgent. The trick performed by Stalin was pregnant with harmful effects, because the apparatus of the dictatorship of the proletariat under Stalin's leadership, and with his active participation, was taking a definite turn for the worse.

And now I'll tell you a story, a true one. In 1922 I was in prison along with a Ukrainian boy who, a year earlier, had crossed the border and presented himself for work at the NKVD. They were still pretty liberal in those days, so they took him on – of course as a simple errand-boy – and all at once he made a big name for himself.

And do you know how? They got an order to take down portraits of Trotsky and Bukharin, and no one in the NKVD offices, which were staffed exclusively with faithful Stalinists, wanted to take them down, because for them Trotsky was a civil war legend. They could disagree with him, they could vote against him, but take down his portrait! And my Ukrainian boy went and did it, because what did he care about some bearded Jew and another bearded Muscovite? I'm telling you this to show you that Stalin had to, simply had to get rid of the generation which had made the revolution and was bound to the Leninist conception of the party.

I discussed all this with Franciszek Mazur. Mazur was an intelligent man who loathed Stalin with a passion –

– but he did what Stalin told him.

What else could he have done? Become a supporter of capitalism? I asked Mazur whether Lenin (who claimed during the last weeks of his life that he would crush Stalin), if he'd lived longer, could have succeeded. Mazur thought for a long time before replying and finally said: well, you know, the mood of the activists was favourable to Stalin's ideas, but Lenin's authority was so great that he would have made mincemeat of Stalin.

What do you mean by the mood of the activists?

Stalin represented the cavalry charge line of thought: a generation that had grown up with the civil war and charged ahead with sheer force. Unlike the old Bolsheviks, it was not used to drudgery, to work that was long-term with no immediate, striking effects. So he decided to destroy his opponents, and no one was able to resist him. Maybe Kirov might have been able to, but he was killed.

Surely, that was why he was killed.

Perhaps. In any case Stalin was a mixture of primitivism, genius and ignorance of the world when it came to personal feuds and organizational abilities, while the old Bolsheviks were . . . noble-minded. Yes, noble-minded. Take Bukharin, for instance: a very nice man, and probably right in his basic idea that socialism couldn't be built without taking into account the peasant mentality. It would never have occurred to him that you could deal with something unethically and without scruples. Stalin had no scruples, and since the success of his idea required the destruction of an entire generation which remembered that things could be different, he simply did it.

Did he have to destroy them physically?

Probably not, but his Caucasian brutality and Asiatic savagery won the day.

Still, there are two ways of killing: by secret firing-squad and as a result of a public trial with foreign observers.

You have to remember that Stalin didn't take into account the whole world; he was concerned only with Russia. And in Russia, if he wanted to discredit Bukharin, he had to try him. Bukharin was, after all, the favourite of the party –

– as Lenin used to say.

Exactly. So Bukharin had to be forced to confess his guilt. And he confessed. Bukharin, Kamenev, Zinoviev – nearly all the Russians confessed. Torture and fear for their families had their effect. Only the Poles didn't confess, but they could be quietly shot anyway, because there would be no one to inquire after them.

But why do it at all? They surely posed no threat.

But they did, if only as witnesses to events. For instance page 161 of the *Short Course in the History of the VCP(b)* lists the people who became members of the Central Committee at the Prague Conference, and along with Lenin it also lists Stalin. Well, it's a lie. Stalin wasn't there. He wasn't there, and I ask you: could old Warski, who was at the conference, continue to trust Stalin? He couldn't.

But surely he would have kept silent.

He might have, or he might not. But this way one could be sure that he would.

How many were shot?

No one knows: some of them died in the camps. After the Twentieth CPSU Congress in 1956 our Politburo formed a rehabilitation committee to look into false charges against former KPP members. I was one of the people consulted by the members of this committee. We looked into about twenty cases; everyone could submit his case, myself included. We made positive decisions on all of them, although in some of them there was room for doubt. This was because in the thirties we had reservations, of a, so to speak, "police" nature about some of our comrades, and we sent them off to the Soviets for the matter to be cleared up. The result was that they were sentenced on quite different charges – simply trumped up. We rehabilitated them as well. Then, on 1 May, we published photographs of KPP Politburo members in *Trybuna Ludu*. It was a sensation, and the first thing the delegation of Soviet journalists did when they visited us was to ask for that issue.

Let's get back to Stalin.

He was a controversial figure. At one time it was popular among young Soviet historians to muse about who he really was. One of them asked me: what would you do with a comrade who had as many mysterious lacunae in his biography as Stalin? I said, "We'd give him the run around". Which means we'd tell him: we've got nothing against you, but there's something about you that's not right; maybe you bring bad luck. So you can pay your Red Aid dues, and you can vote for us in the trade unions, but keep away from illegal work.

One thing's certain: Stalin was a double-dealing hypocrite. I'll give you an example. There was an estate in the suburbs of Moscow where old Bolsheviks lived; each of them had his own little Finnish house. Stalin had one there as well, not a very grand one as yet, and Vera Kostrzewa lived next door to him. One day she was pruning roses in her garden. Stalin came up to her and said, "What beautiful roses". That same evening she was taken away and shot; Stalin knew about it. But in 1944, when our delegation came to see him, he suddenly asked, "You used to have such nice people. Vera Kostrzewa, for instance – do you know what's become of her?"

Does that surprise you?

Well, shouldn't it?

No.

There's one matter of psychology that you don't understand. Perhaps not everything in the Soviet Union was as it should have been, but for us at the time it was a country with a dictatorship of the proletariat; a socialist country, and thus an ally; a friend, even though it sometimes made mistakes. That is still what I think today. The Soviet Union has its problems, it has entangled itself in many matters, but it is the ally of progressive forces throughout the world. In the thirties there was one thing we were sure of: maybe it was true that there was something wrong with those trials, and there may have been some mistakes, but when Stalin defeats Hitler none of that will mean anything.

Stalin the victorious. So what if he appropriated the Ukraine, Byelorussia . . .

He took what he had a right to, what clung to him and what really did want to separate from Poland. I remember what Soviet Ukraine was like in the twenties. It was a genuinely Ukrainian workers' and peasants' state.

But they were displaced and killed off.

Only the cadres were killed; the same thing happened to Russian cadres in Russia. One of them blew his own brains out. I admit things were bad in the thirties; mistakes were made. Most of them, actually, tended to be the fault of the local bureaucracy. From what I read it seems they're now trying to put it right.

He took over Lithuania, Latvia, Estonia . . .

Latvia, Latvia! Latvia doesn't count.

I might be talking to a Byelorussian. The Ukraine, well, its a powerful country. And Poland's a big country, you have to take it into account. But as for these puny Estonians and Latvians, well . . .

There's no need to get upset. You just don't know any history. It was through a blockade of the Soviet Republics that those governments were maintained, and both Latvia and Estonia always remained vassals, first German and then English.

And now?

Now they are the Latvian or Estonian Soviet Republic, with their own culture and education. And I'll tell you something else. Books are published in Estonia that would never see the light of day in Moscow. Of course, one can speculate whether the USSR might not have done better to maintain the Baltic Peoples' Republics; that may have been a wiser thing to do. But Stalin did otherwise, and that's how it has remained.

I'm making a sober assessment, and I repeat for the tenth time that Stalin crushed Hitler, in the face of whom social democracy was helpless. The Soviet Union brought the Germans to their knees, and that's why we, their allies in that war, have to recognize that the strategy to protect the Soviet Union and the interests of international communism came through its trial by fire. That doesn't in any way mean that the Soviet Union is always and everywhere right. I merely think that historically, and for the moment, it is right, because it supports genuine people's revolutions throughout the world. The Soviets are committed to supporting progressive forces, just as the Americans are committed to supporting reactionary ones.

And just what did they support here that was so progressive?

How can you ask that? They supported the social revolution that took place after the Second World War; they prevented the rebuilding of capitalism in Poland.

By force.

No. We were fighting a civil war and the Soviet Army gave us no help in it.

No, it just stood there.

Well, so it stood there; what's wrong with that? Perhaps you think that the Red Army should have withdrawn beyond the Bug and allowed the United States to rebuild the old German Reich, so that this Reich could then proceed to submit (and realize) its claims on Szczecin, Wroclaw and Gdansk? Perhaps you'd like to install American atomic missiles on the banks of the Vistula? There have already been people who deluded themselves that Poland would supplant Germany as the American anti-Soviet battering ram. But they were fools. In defending our alliance with the USSR in that civil war we were defending the interests of Poland, the interests of the Polish nation.

Indeed?

There's one thing you refuse to grasp, which is that in a revolutionary situation, in the state of potential civil war in which Poland found itself after the Second World War, we were bound by revolutionary laws: either we destroy them or they destroy us. The law of the Wild West in postwar Poland. Whoever shoots first will be the one to survive. That may not sound very nice, it may even sound shocking, but that's the way it is. There were times when we exaggerated and went too far, because we had been trained, on historical precedents (the Paris Commune for one), on the principle that force is not only necessary, but also the best way. I now think it's necessary but bad. You think shooting people is good? Of course it's bad, but that doesn't mean it's not necessary in certain situations.

Besides, I've always thought that the ex-terrorist that goes home and becomes an accountant is better than the one that sits in prison and plots his revenge. Our revolution was quite mild, although it couldn't have been entirely mild, because the Polish moneyed classes didn't lightly forgo their ambitions for power.

You keep talking about a revolution, while what I'm talking about is a new occupation.

Come now, don't exaggerate. That terminology is false. I repeat: this is where our government, a government of Polish communists, was created, and whether you like it or not it was a Polish government from the start. In accordance, I might add, with the Yalta agreement.

Well, no: what was agreed at Yalta was that there would be free elections in Poland.

Oh, come on, don't be silly. One thing was agreed at Yalta: that the frontier between the great powers lay along the Elbe. That was what was agreed; the rest was just decoration. And it was agreed that Poland's government was to be friendly towards the Soviet Union.

Friendly to it, not a satellite of it.

A satellite? According to your (false) terminology, the Italian government is also a satellite of the United States, because the United States embassy won't allow communist ministers to be included in it. Everyone is dependent on everyone else in one way or another. Sticking to Polish affairs, however, I might point out that the Soviet Union had no partners in Poland, because all the parties, apart from the communists, were rabidly anti-Soviet.

That's another one of your myths: Stalin didn't want partners, Mr Werfel, he wanted people who would execute his wishes: blind, obedient executors. And he found them.

Maybe he could have settled for partners, although it would have been difficult. Only a few survivors remained from the old communist party. We're all survivors, people Stalin didn't manage to kill off in time – the third set of KPP cadres. The international situation was also a decisive factor, and the international situation precluded a partnership. The United States, in particular Truman, was not favourably inclined towards an agreement with the Soviets; this is even evident in the memoirs of Bliss Lane, their ambassador to Poland at the time. When they open up their archives you'll see how much money the United States poured into stoking up the civil war in Poland.

And you, of course, are counting on the American archives being opened.

Of course. That's when you'll see how much money went into supporting all the reactionary forces in Poland.

That was the majority of the population.

Oh, no. We were the ones who had a large part of the peasants and working class behind us, and as for the population as a whole, nearly all of it supported us, albeit without confidence. *Ex post*, let's say. It approved our agricultural plans and it responded to our call to rebuild the country. I suppose most of them thought, well, you have to admit these communists are doing good work, we ought to give them some credit. Of course they had a lot of grievances, about the functioning of the security services, for instance, and about Rozanski, to mention a symbolic name.

Rozanski: director of the interrogation department at the Ministry of Public Security, member of your party and, I should add, brother of Jerzy Borejsza.

Perhaps he was a psychopath? I knew him quite well: devilishly clever, very two-faced, a Dr Jekyll and Mr Hyde. But I'd like to remind you that security services have their laws, and the apparatus of force has its laws: they promote people who are efficient. Swiatlo was efficient: before the war he'd had nothing to do with communism, whereas after the war he advanced very rapidly, because he didn't share the scruples that other people had. Rozanski also was efficient, very much so. I asked him whether they beat people.

Why did you ask?

Well, because . . . because people were talking! And Rozanski swore several times that they didn't. He even quoted to me, in Russian, a saying of his Soviet adviser's: if you beat people, then you'll find that the victim will even call his own mother a whore. But I still wasn't entirely convinced they didn't beat people, because I knew that they'd done it before the war, and I was really only asking because I didn't want people to be beaten. The point is that beating causes degeneration not only in the person who's being beaten, but in the person doing the beating as well. So it's better to shoot someone than to beat him. Although I admit there are situations where I don't know myself what I would do. I don't mean, of course, beating in order to force a false confession from someone – that's always the ultimate, disgusting trick – but you do get particular cases where beating is the only way out. If I met someone who knew the location of an arms cache that would be used against my men tomorrow, I'd pound him myself to get it out of him. I'll give you another example: during Tito's first visit here, the security services were alerted to a coup being planned against him. One of the would-be assassins was taken in a square, weapons in hand, and many people were arrested. I don't know exactly what happened, but there was no coup. I'm sure people were beaten. Besides, people are beaten all over the world. Even in England – the Irish. It's bad and we have to fight against it, but it will always be like that, especially in conditions of civil war. There's one principle you have to stick to in beating, however: Johnny has to be beaten by Johnny, and not by Moshe. I can see now that there were too many Jews in the security services, because we hadn't considered the security services in that light. We'd considered trade, since everyone had some memories of that that were not too pleasant. I had some from Uzbekistan. I was standing in a queue along with some Russians, Poles and Uzbeks, while three Jews from the cooperative carried out bread from the back. The whole queue was screaming that the Jews were robbing them, and I couldn't say a word. The Jews knew the ins and outs of trade all too well, and already in Uzbekistan we decided that we weren't about to let them into internal socialist trade in Poland. Let them go into foreign trade, into publishing houses, into the press, but stay away from internal trade. It was a pity we didn't consider security as well, because, as I said, it's Johnny that has to beat up Johnny.

What did you want to achieve?

Do you know the song: "With the thud of feet we rip through the night, today for a different Poland we fight, for a Polish Soviet Republic!"? I wanted socialism; a socialist Polish state.

Meaning what?

I'll tell you something, at the risk of your thinking me a terrible conservative, but I don't care. All these concepts – socialism, workers' rule – have retained their validity everywhere in the world; it's only here, in this provincial, parochial Poland, that they've become fuzzy. This was supposed to be a Polish socialist state: a socialist state, and thus a state where the means of production are nationalized. We wanted to create a new society, different from the one we had before 1939. A society without class conflicts, a modern, more enlightened society ruled by democratic laws – for those, of course, who believed in the principle of the system, in the principle of socialism.

So, to sum it up: first, not for the PSL; second, not for the PPS; and third, not for part of the PUWP, either.

No, no, our only enemies were the reactionaries: the moneyed classes whose interests the PSL looked after.

So, in accordance with the party line at the time, you proceeded to go about eliminating them.

Yes, I did take part in destroying them publicly. I wasn't involved in the operational or security side of the matter. I opened journalistic fire – rightly so, I still believe – on Mikolajczyk's supporters in the *People's Voice* and in various pamphlets.

Of course. You were merely justifying the activities of the security services when you wrote, for instance, that "the PSL voted en bloc *with Nazi agents in the referendum", or that "underground bandits, insinuated into PSL organizations, are supplementing speeches at rallies by shooting democrats in the back".*

Well, wasn't that the way it was? Mikolajczyk's supporters at the time really did collaborate with the armed underground. And as for shooting in the back, have you seen the book that lists our people who fell in those battles? It contains 18,000 names. And that doesn't account for all of them.

What about ours?

I'm not sure you'd feel all that comfortable among those "ours" of yours. But never mind. There was a civil war on, and they were a side taking part in it. When I myself went from Lodz to Warsaw I used to have to clear my way ahead with machine guns. Once we came to a roadblock made of stones. We were nearly killed, but luckily we had a good jeep, so the stones were pushed aside while we went at it with our machine guns and escaped.

And why do you think you were shot at?

Because we were communists and they were anticommunists – simple. They wanted to defend the capitalists, to protect their rule in Poland.

Perhaps it was independence they wanted to defend?

Independence! Rubbish! Independence for capitalists and landowners, yes; independence from land reform and from a nationalized industry. And at Truman's command, at that.

The PPS as well?

That depends which PPS. Its right wing – yes, I think so. But not the left wing. With them we negotiated.

By eliminating them.

By uniting with them. Ex-PPS men like Cyrankiewicz and Rapacki became PUWP Politburo members, after all. As for the merits of uniting, I still think it was the right thing to do. It's a very complicated problem, but I'd venture to say that Lenin was right when he took the line of uniting the workers' movement in 1921. For the more united the movement, the stronger it is. But there it was united under the banner of ultra-Stalinism, and that was certainly a mistake.

After dealing with the PPS, you began, in your journalism, to deal with Gomulka, who, as it turned out, had also ceased to believe in the principle of the system.

I regret that very much. The pamphlet entitled *Three Defeats for the Reactionaries* is the only thing in my life that I'm really ashamed of. Because as for the rest, I'm not. And if I were to start my life again, knowing everything that I know today, I wouldn't change its basic line: I would just formulate certain articles more cautiously, I'd go to bed with a few women whom I wanted and who wanted me, which I didn't do for sectarian reasons, and I wouldn't write that pamphlet on Gomulka.

So what would have happened to Gomulka?

I must tell you that his speech at the June 1948 plenum was a tactical mistake on his part, and if he had come out with his "injustice" to the KPP then, we'd all have followed him, and we would all have been crushed. Simply crushed. Luckily he didn't, but I still think that at the time it was impossible to oppose the Soviet party. I remember coming home from the plenum completely shattered, and my wife asking me what was the matter. It's a catastrophe, I said; a split. I realized that a split in the party meant blood.

One group's blood spilt by another?

They'd spill each other's, and Stalin would watch.

Oh, no: he was preparing a third.

You said it, not me. After that I went to Wroclaw to see Wladyslaw Matwin. We were sitting there, a bit sad, chatting, when a woman – she's a big figure in Solidarity now – bursts in and starts screaming at us about Gomulka: how could you have let that bastard stay in the Central Committee? There are some women who are rabid by nature. Wladyslaw and I looked at each other and I don't remember which one of us first said to her, well, you know, there's always time to expel him; and then, when she'd left, we said, she must be mad, she's out for blood.

For us, I mean for the party, it really was a difficult situation.

Bierut was playing for time and he won, while we were trying to smooth things over. You can check that in the transcripts of Rajk's trial. It says there that Gomulka was an agent closely allied to Tito, but in the Polish version that doesn't appear. As soon as I saw Gomulka's name, I rang Berman and said, Comrade Jakub, there's something wrong with these transcripts; we don't write about Gomulka like that. So he said: cross it out. And I did.

You falsified an official transcript.

So what? It was better to falsify it than to let it go as it was.

You falsified a historical document.

It wasn't a document: it was an abbreviated translation. Making cuts in such a translation isn't falsifying it. Historians can always refer to the Hungarian original. What was I supposed to do – show Polish readers charges against Gomulka that we didn't uphold? It would only have muddled people.

I'll admit there might have been times when I didn't like that kind of thing – for instance, when large chunks were deleted from Mehring's book on Marx that I was publishing – but I acknowledged the interests of the people's government, and I understood that you can't publish things which could activate a counter-revolution or harm the party. You, of course, can't understand that because you don't know how to think in terms of class; you're ignorant of the world and you're sick, like those little boys from Solidarity who run around the streets throwing "frogs" [small home-made explosive devices] and shouting "Poland, Poland", unaware that they're pawns on the chessboard of a great international game. The majority of this nation suffers from the disease of parochialism – hopeless Polish provincialism, that's your disease!

Yes, I'm sick, and that's why there is nothing, no circumstance and no form of coercion, that would make me "shorten" an official transcript, and nothing that would lead me to write a 160-page pamphlet entitled Three Defeats for the Polish Reactionaries: Remarks on the trial of the espionage group of Tatar, Kirchmayer and others. *Of course, all of them were rehabilitated after 1956.*

I've already told you my views about that pamphlet: it was contemptible. I've never been in a position of having to do something under the threat of arrest or of being shot, but that doesn't mean that everything I did was done on my own initiative. I was, and am, as I've already told you, a professional revolutionary, and that means that I could be ordered to carry out a particular task which accorded with a common goal. I signed my name to the *Three Defeats . . .*, although the text was later gone over by members of the Politburo. There was one phrase I wanted to smuggle through, and I succeeded: the Polish road to socialism. But actually, that only showed how naive I was, because it was a question of facts, not of words. The "Polish road to socialism" was a lost cause the moment the Cold War began.

The facts were that you accused completely innocent people of espionage, treason and other extremely serious crimes.

I want to stress that I was convinced that what I wrote in that pamphlet (which, after all, reflected the testimony given at the trial) was in accordance with the truth. The accused were for the most part members of the prewar "Number Two" [the second unit of the General Staff: an intelligence unit], and "Number Two" was known for its excellence in penetration and the manipulation of people.

Do you want me to start citing the insults that you flung at them? At them and at Tito, Spychalski, Kuropieska . . .

I was wrong, and it pains me. They were innocent people. They weren't enemies; indeed, perhaps they were allies. But in a political struggle, sharp, and sometimes even insulting, words are permissible. But only where they reflect the objective truth; only where they correspond to reality. An enemy can be treated in an insulting way, even though such treatment is generally both pointless and wrong, but innocent people should never be either accused or insulted.

Is that a self-criticism?

No, because I'm against self-criticism. It's a disgusting Stalinist custom which derives from the Orthodox Church. Lenin used to say, rightly, that self-criticism had to be carried out in deeds.

Those years, 1952–3, were really difficult times. The Cold War threatened at any moment to escalate into a hot one. After the Tito affair, Stalin saw treason everywhere. When I went to see Minc after some sudden changes – clearly for the worse – in the six-year plan, to ask him what was going on, he said: we have to be prepared for the worst; a world war can break out within a year, at the most in two years' time; we're reprogramming the economy for arms. And Berman sat poring over quite a few *Trybuna Ludu* editorials. Sometimes I would even laughingly say to him: Comrade Jakub, do you really think my readers will notice that you've switched that sentence over from one paragraph to another? Berman would smile sadly and say: your readers probably won't, but there are certain others who might.

Did you know him before the war?

No, I didn't. I'm rather atypical: I spent all my time working in western Ukraine and when I was in prison it was mostly there as well. So I didn't know either Bierut or Ochab. I did know Guta Berman, though, because she was the one who took care of your teeth when you came out of prison, and I also knew Minc and Mazur slightly.

People say that Mazur was an NKVD man.

One thing is certain: in the Soviet Union, where Mazur had worked since 1917, all party personnel with any responsibility were in one way or another connected with the security services. After the war I was also acquainted with many of our security people, and they were all free to consult me about this or that or to ask for my views on a particular subject. Of course, none of them would actually have dared to order me to do anything, but they could certainly ask questions. It was the same in the Soviet Union.

I met Franek Mazur in peculiar circumstances. He gave me the fright of my life. It was like this: sometime in 1929, I think, I received instructions from the party to take a very important person, someone, I guessed, from the CPWU Politburo, across the Soviet–Polish border. We left at night. You reached the border by a small path near some woods, and after walking for two or three hours you came to a place with a broken tree; that was where you were supposed to turn off. If you continued along the path, it would take you straight to a police post. We're walking along, I look at my watch – we've been walking for four hours and there's no sign of the tree. It's not so much going to prison that worries me, but, much worse, that I'll look like an *agent provocateur* in the eyes of my comrades, and that means moral death. I feel myself going weak. What had happened was that, in my nervousness, I'd failed to realize that this important comrade was an older man and walked more slowly than I did.

He wouldn't get through today.

I took him across, and got to know him after the war: Franciszek Mazur. We often met; he was a very good comrade. There was one thing about him: I could go to him for advice and he would advise me wisely and honestly, as best he knew how; but if the result turned out badly he wouldn't say a single word against it. He wouldn't say anything to support it, either; he'd simply remain silent. He'd had enough of the Lubyanka after the several years he'd spent there.

What about the others?

I knew Stach Radkiewicz well, back from our days in the Siedlce prison, where they took us out for exercise together. Radkiewicz was in a particularly difficult position during the fifties. He knew what the consequences would be of bringing the class conflict [that is, fighting the enemy] into the party. His brother, after all, an outstanding CPWB activist, was killed in the USSR in the thirties, while his sister was sent to a camp – he managed to get her out after the war. Radkiewicz was very obdurate in his opposition to anything he thought unacceptable. He handed in his resignation several times because he thought there were some things you shouldn't do.

But he did them.

Well, what choice did he have? Going over to the other side? Besides, he didn't do everything, far from it.

He could have left.

He couldn't, because he wanted to save the party. He watched over it like a guard dog. I'll tell you something. When I was editor-in-chief of a publishing house, I received some material containing things I didn't like, and I decided to talk certain parts of it over with Radkiewicz. I rang him to say I wanted to see him, and he said fine, come over.

When I got there the secretary said: the minister's occupied, he has General Romkowski with him. I have an appointment, I said: please announce me. After a moment she asked me to go in.

Radkiewicz had Romkowski and Fejgin in his office. He asked me: where were you during the twenty years between the wars?

I said: you know where I was; except for the periods in Vienna and Berlin, I was here all the time.

Radkiewicz said: I'm not interested in the details. You were here, and you were in constant touch with the party.

I said: of course.

Radkiewicz: did you see a Trotskyist faction in the party?

I said: well, there were a few small fry.

Radkiewicz: I don't mean them. Did you see a Trotskyist faction in the party leadership?

I said: no, absolutely not.

Well, would you have noticed it if there had been one?

Certainly, I said.

You see, Radkiewicz said to Romkowski, you see? The man was free, he spent all his time on the job and he didn't see it, and yet you say there was one.

Romkowski replied: well, my material says it existed. At this point Radkiewicz dismissed the subject and said: well, we'll discuss this at the Politburo. Romkowski and Fejgin left.

You understand, this conversation wasn't taking place in the Party History Institute; it was taking place in the Ministry of Security, and you could smell blood.

But these were your party comrades.

Oh, no. Fejgin wasn't a comrade of mine and none of the Lvov communists had any contacts with him. I didn't either. He played a dirty trick on one of our comrades in Lvov –

The one who was dismissed from his post in the sixties for economic corruption?

That was all fabricated. Mietek came from a Christian Democratic family: before the war he worked for the party in a factory. He was had up for it. A dozen or so communists, also Ukrainian, were in the dock, and the judge said to him: you come from such a decent family, and yet you're an enemy of Poland? To which he replied, no, that's not true, I'm for Poland's independence precisely as a communist; and then he continued to testify just as the party line dictated. But the journalist who was reporting the trial as usual got something mixed up.

When the Soviets came in, Mietek was released from prison and returned to work at the factory, where he was welcomed back with open arms. Fejgin came to work there as well, and decided to get rid of him. He found the trial report in the newspaper and took it to the Lvov regional party committee, where he started shouting that Mietek was a Polish nationalist. We all tried to persuade him: leave off, Tolek, there's nothing wrong with Mietek, there are witnesses. But Fejgin wouldn't listen to us and went off with the cutting to the regional committee. Now the regional committee was, of course, dim-witted: how could it not be when people posted to western Ukraine were only there because the Russians wanted to get rid of them? Mietek was in great danger. He was lucky that the "people's gatherings" [this is said in Russian: *narodnye zbory*] were taking place just then, with the aim of passing a resolution to incorporate western Ukraine into the Soviet Union. The boys who had sat in the dock with Mietek came to Lvov and paid him a visit. When they found out what was going on they took their red deputies' cards and rushed over to the regional committee crying: don't believe the slanderers! The committee took fright when it saw their deputies' cards and left Mietek alone, while Tolek Fejgin never again had any authority in Lvov.

But in Warsaw, on the other hand, he became head of a department of the Ministry of Public Security, which concerned itself with the purity of the party ranks.

I warned Berman, but he wouldn't listen to me.

You needed people like that.

No we didn't, and neither did he. Berman simply, and wrongly, trusted him, because he'd met him in the course of his work before the war, and in Poland at that time the same process was taking place as in the USSR under Stalin: the state and party apparatus, and in particular the apparatus of force, slipped out from under the control of the masses and ran amok.

You mean it placed itself above the party?

I'd be careful in making such a claim. It's true that the apparatus of force and the party leadership united themselves, which meant specifically that the head of security or of the military also took up his place in the party's Politburo, but Radkiewicz wasn't above the party; he took his orders from the Politburo. He was responsible to the first secretary, and he stood to attention before him.

And then arrested him, as in the case of Gomulka.

He arrested him on the orders of the new secretary chosen by the Central Committee.

Who, in his turn, acted on orders from Stalin?

I wasn't the one sitting by that telephone.

Didn't you have any ambitions for a more independent policy of your own?

We did, and we were even implementing it.

Perhaps you could provide an example, because the fact that you abstained from murdering Gomulka, well, you'll forgive me, but it's not very much to go on.

Remember we didn't even allow him to be tried. I once wrote an article entitled *The Gallicanism of the KPP*, in which, with the aid of a metaphor, I expounded the meaning of our policies. Gallicanism is a concept from the Catholic Church. The Church in France was loyal to Rome, and the French did quite a thorough job of massacring the Protestants. At the same time the Church was divided between, on the one hand, the Ultramontanes, who stuck by Rome, and, on the other, the Gallicans, who thought that the basic principles of the faith should be decided by the Pope in Rome, but that decisions specific to France were better left to the French themselves. I transposed their thinking onto Polish–Soviet relations. We in Poland knew better what was needed.

Could I have an example, please.

There are lots of examples, but I'll give you the first one that comes to mind. Collectivization in Poland failed because we weren't particularly assiduous in implementing it.

No, no, Mr Werfel, you did everything you could to make it work.

You remind me of a certain young man who as recently as a year ago was still trying to convince me that there was no force strong enough to crush Solidarity, while I kept telling him that there was, because every revolution begins by dismantling the army and the police, and in this case they were both untouched. Similarly, we had enough force in Poland then to implement collectivization. But I repeat: collectivization in Poland didn't work because we were in no hurry to go through with it. We were in no hurry because we knew what the Soviet collective farms were like, and we knew that the things going on in some of them were – to put it delicately – not all that nice. The reason was that in the USSR, collectivization – or, rather, the pricing system of collective farm products – was a form of primary accumulation, in order to speed up the industrialization of the country. Was it necessary? A lot of Western academics, even anti-Stalinist ones, think that it was. I don't think so. I think this form of collectivization, when you take into account the damage it caused to Soviet agriculture – "haste makes waste" – didn't compensate for the advantages of the revenues obtained thereby. In Hungary, on the other hand, in East Germany and in Czechoslovakia, collectivization produced good results because it was was based on the principle of equal exchange between the cities and the countryside. Here, in Poland, in the fifties, we didn't have the means for this, but there was also no need to exact that kind of tribute from the countryside. We thus had neither the need to implement a Stalinist form of collectivization nor the means to apply the Hungarian and Czechoslovakian variety, and for this reason we thought we should not implement it at all.

Gomulka said the same thing, but no one backed him up; not to mention, so as not to irritate you, the PSL activists.

It wasn't possible. At that time – when the parties were "centrally" governed – we thought of turning a blind eye. You couldn't say no when the whole of the international movement was saying yes, but you could draw the thing out. After all, all those philosophers who are so active now survived the Zhdanov period because they were given work translating classical philosophy. And now Poland has an excellent collection of all the important philosophical works in translation. That was also a case of turning a blind eye. Soviet philosophers weren't so lucky.

You were the leading ideologist of the Stalinist period, ready to justify every move of the authorities, ready with an answer to everything.

Leading ideologist is probably a bit much. Rather, I was the party's leading journalist, and it's the job of a party journalist to justify the party line, a line I believed was right. Now I'm non-party and retired, but I haven't stopped being a communist, even though that irritates you somewhat, and I reply to questions in accordance with what I think, in accordance with my convictions. Nor have I lost interest in politics. Besides, I'm still better at policy, as the English say, than at politics, that is, at knowing what goals to set rather than what tactics to use in order to attain them. I know that tactics are important, very much so, and I can appreciate the talent of the late Antek Alster, whose little machine of a brain was always ticking over, and also Zambrowski's cunning, although I think that in his case an excess of politics triumphed over policy; I was never able to do that. And that was why I did more work in ideology than on operative tasks. I'm not claiming that the way we evolved was ideal, but I do maintain that it's better than it would have been in a capitalist system.

Times have changed and your answers no longer suffice. Thirty years ago precisely you could write in a pamphlet with a run of 200,000 copies: "During these thirty-five years the working masses of the Soviet Union have transformed their country into the culturally and economically leading state of the world . . . ."

I wrote that? There's a lot of exaggeration in it, but who would deny that during those years of Soviet rule, and at the cost of considerable sacrifices, a backward Russia was transformed into a world power of huge, albeit still insufficient, economic force? Who would deny that she went from being a country of illiterates to being a country of people who passed out of high school? The Soviet Union is burdened with enormous defence expenditure and that slows down its process of development (and ours as well, when all factors are taken into account), but that can't be helped. That's how the world is; if the Soviet Union hadn't had the factories that were built during the difficult years of successive five-year plans, Hitler would probably have sauntered his way to the Pacific Ocean. And from that point of view Reagan isn't any better.

"Steel today means bread, meat, clothes and housing tomorrow"?

Well, doesn't it?

Have we got any of it?

We have more than we did before the war, and we'll have much more.

When? You promised us – this is from your pen: "In the Poland we are building the working classes and the working intelligentsia will find constantly growing employment, better and better working conditions, greater and greater means of access to culture and education. . . . In the Poland we are building the entire mass of citizens will live full, joyful, creative, cultural, wealthy and industrious lives."

We are, it seems, discussing me, and not the history of People's Poland, so in this context I can't give you a detailed analysis of the past forty years. But there's one thing I'd like to say at the outset: we slogged our way through quite a chunk of good work during that time, for Poland and for the Polish nation. Mistakes and distortions undoubtedly happened, and undoubtedly there were too many of them when I was active, but they were outweighed by good, solid work. Poland is no longer the same country it was in 1939, let alone in 1944. Do you know how many people there were to a room in Warsaw in 1931? 2.07. The figures for other cities were similar, varying between 1.7 and 2 people. And how many in all the cities of Poland in 1981? 1.03. Almost half as many. Let's compare that with a few countries in the developed capitalist world. In Great Britain, for instance, there were 0.85 people to a room in 1931, whereas now there are 0.6. That's a quarter less. In Germany we have 0.98 and 0.7, and in Italy 1.36 and 1.0. Yes, they are progressing, yet they're progressing much more slowly than we are. It's true that in 1981 they were still better off than we were, but we've been catching them up, and making good time. That's a success for the system.

No.

I know it's hard to talk about it at a time when a crisis is raging in Poland, in considerable degree caused by the false economic policy of Gierek's leadership of the PUWP. But I'm not afraid of irony or of outrage and I tell you categorically that, yes, we accomplished a lot (although without those mistakes much more could have been done). I know we've now lost the propaganda battle. But we lost because our propaganda was not backed up by facts. Something began to go wrong from about 1952, and the apparatus alienated itself from the masses. Take Gomulka, for instance: a totally honest man who once, over the radio, confessed his surprise at hearing there were no tights to be had, because his wife found no difficulty in buying them. What did that imply? Surely not that he was stupid, but rather that he didn't know Poland: he simply didn't know the things I knew. And when the director of a department store rang me up and said, comrade, do you want me to put aside a raincoat for you, they've just arrived, I would say, no, better not, I'll do without one. I didn't say that because I didn't need one but because I knew that he would put aside another ten under cover of the one for me and sell them on the side. Gomulka didn't know that, although he himself was beyond reproach, which you couldn't say about Gierek. But now, in 1980, the entire apparatus has been taught a lesson, and I think the party leadership has drawn some conclusions from that lesson. Sure, it's hard, it's hard for all of us, and it's difficult to persuade people by rational argument: many of them now think in, so to speak, irrational, gut terms. You as well. That's a normal reaction at a time of crisis, and we need time for it to begin to lose its hold. And perseverance. And good policies. I think the party is up to both those things. I'm convinced we'll find a way out of the crisis. The example of Hungary, where the situation was much more acute, shows that every predicament has a solution. And of course capitalism will help us. Such is its character [laughter]! [This is said in Russian.] Some of those who went to the West in search of paradise will begin to return, they'll tell us about the unemployment and the difficulties, and that, too, will go to show that ours was the better way after all.

You were saying the same thing thirty years ago.

Well, different things happened in different countries. Now the difficulties are growing on a world scale, I can't help that. But I do think that if I manage to live long enough, the time will come when you'll admit I'm right.

No.

June–November 1982

STEFAN STASZEWSKI

STEFAN STASZEWSKI

Stefan Staszewski was born in Warsaw in 1906. His parents both perished in Treblinka; an older brother, who was a communist, was killed in the USSR in 1937 during the Great Purge. Staszewski joined the communist movement at the age of fourteen; by 1921 he was a member of the KZMP. In 1926, after being arrested and then released under caution, he left for the Soviet Union to study at the Comintern's international advanced school, where he met Bierut. He returned to Poland as a party official, becoming first secretary of the KZMP Central Committee for western Ukraine, a post he held for a year, and later a member of the KZMP secretariat. Arrested and released under caution once again, he went back to the Soviet Union in 1934, where he lectured on the history of the workers' movement at the Comintern school.

In 1936, after a loyalty check on party members, his party card was withdrawn. He was arrested two years later and sentenced to eight years in the labour camps of Kolyma. He was released in 1945 and returned to Poland. He became secretary in charge of propaganda for the party in Katowice, then head of the press section of the Central Committee of the PPR until December 1948 and of the PUWP until January 1954. He was then appointed deputy minister of agriculture, a post which he held until September 1955, first secretary of the Warsaw Committee until 1957 and editor-in-chief of the Polish Press Agency until 1958.

From 1958 to 1968 he worked as an editor with the Polish Academic Press. He was expelled from the party in 1968 and retired.

Staszewski is sympathetic to KOR and to Solidarity.

* * *

What, in fact, are you?

I'm a politician. A *homo politicus*, who lives and thrives on politics as an art, a skill, a profession.

Were you at least a good one?

I not only was but still am, I think, and will always remain one. For politics is a way of thinking about reality; it is an ability, probably innate, to subject to analysis events which take place, trying to understand the course they are taking and the forces which cause them to follow one trend rather than another; it is also the capacity to construct solutions to particular situations and to predict the consequences they will bring. To be equal to this task one needs brains, knowledge and political imagination. In my view these characteristics are more important than experience and theoretical training.

Gomulka was a politician, although a limited one. Zambrowski was a very good politician, with political imagination; so was Minc. And there the list of postwar politicians from the communist pool would end.

Were they better than you?

Lampe certainly was. He was an exceptionally talented and intelligent man who knew a lot, had a lot of ability and great political instinct, but for many years was almost totally unknown to the more general public, since his widow, fearing that his manuscripts would be destroyed, hid them deeply away. Many people – Jerzy Borejsza, Antoni Wolski-Piwowarczyk – tried to steal or get hold of them by various methods, but luckily they did not succeed, which is how at least some of them could be published after 1956. Lampe was a model for me. One thing I certainly learnt from him: that you can't shape reality to your own conception of it; on the contrary, you have to appreciate it. It was thanks to this that I was less doctrinaire than many other people.

According to Henryk Vogler [the author of Self-Portrait from Memory*] you were "Tall, with an erect bearing and sparse, fair hair that was smoothed down, with a parting; a man of few words, with a permanent cynical smile which seemed stuck to his lips and evoked fear and anxiety in his subordinates. He was nicknamed 'the blond Bestie', since his cold determination concealed something of a Germanic leader's ruthlessness and brutality . . ."*

And according to Leszek Krzemien [author of A Drop in a Flood*] this is what you were like: "He talked and commandeered a lot . . . he knew how to wriggle out of dangerous work and climb the ladder of a party career. . . . His grand, lordly ways, his contempt for simple people and his imperious manner made him offensive. . . . I thought: this son of a great merchant was and has* *remained at heart a bourgeois who does business in the workers' movement."*

Rubbish! Compare me with other people – with someone like Minc, for instance. He was a man of high calibre with an outstanding thinking apparatus, but all his ideas were false, because they flowed from the wrong source, Leninist–Stalinist Marxism; and he lacked the imagination to see that he wasn't the only one who could change the world, that the world changes without his help. Minc's system of opinions, primarily on economic matters, since they were the main object of his interest and work, for years remained basically the same as it had been twenty or thirty years earlier, and did not change even though significant and ever newer events were taking place. It seemed that on Minc they had no effect whatsoever, and not because he wasn't flexible – it's got nothing to do with flexibility, because flexibility presupposes a certain amount of opportunism and Minc wasn't an opportunist – but rather, I'd say, because he became arrested in his development once he was fully formed.

A smart person, a person with imagination and a sense of reality, will, when practice or life in general fails to confirm his views, begin to ask himself what is wrong here and why it is wrong. Minc was not only least inclined but indeed unable to make such revisions. Zambrowski was more inclined to; he and I were friends for a very long time, then our paths separated and never met again, although the route he covered was as long as mine and the evolution he underwent almost as profound. But areas remained between us in which I was already moving about freely, whereas he wouldn't or couldn't enter them. We met sometimes, on the street, in the course of a walk, always by accident; and from the few words we exchanged I realized how very much he had understood, how his consciousness had changed, how different a person he had become. But he was constrained by limitations typical of communists, and he couldn't cross . . . the Rubicon and say to himself: I am not a communist; my programme, the programme I believed in, has not been realized and will not be realized.

I'm pleased to say that I wasn't afraid to cross that Rubicon, knowing all the consequences and implications of such a step. Perhaps that was partly a result of my character, or perhaps of the imagination I possess, but at any rate I did say to myself, at one point: I am not a communist.

At what point?

There was no single decisive moment, but there were critical turning points which together made up the whole process of leaving communism. My speech at the November meeting in 1954 was already a clear sign of that. I said in it that terrible things had happened, things that were unthinkable to a communist, because we had joined the party in the belief that we would create the fullest democracy and the best system, and really implement a great Magna Carta – and we were disillusioned. Surely these words reveal that a great crisis was taking place inside me, even though I naturally still thought of myself as a communist, but probably no longer was one in the eyes of the general public and those of the party itself.

Why? What is a communist?

A communist is someone who has absolute faith in the party, which means that his faith in it is uncritical at every stage, no matter what the party is saying. It is a person with the ability to adapt his mentality and his conscience in such a way that he can unreservedly accept the dogma that the party is never wrong, even though it is wrong all the time – something the party itself actually admits with every new stage it enters. A new stage really begins with a criticism of the previous one and with the promise that, although the party had made mistakes up to that point, it would now stop doing so. Whoever is able to reconcile that contradiction or, to put it in Marxist terms, that dialectical process – the party's infallibility and its fallibility – is a communist.

You also pulled off quite a nice stunt: in 1945 you began a new life erasing all you had learnt from the previous one.

My dear lady, people often ask me: why did you, on your return from Kolyma, from camps where I spent seven years, camps of very hard labour in gold mines, totally isolated from the world, camps where Bruno Jasienski died of typhoid before I left, camps where corpses were laid out between the barbed wire, like logs of wood, incredible amounts of frozen corpses, and where, out of each truckload of twenty-four people going from Magadan to the Taiga, two survived the winter –

– why did you go on doing the same thing, you mean?

As you say, doing the same thing. The fullest and shortest answer is this: I returned to Poland a communist. Which means that I was bound, by my ideals and by my whole life, to the programme and ideas propagated by communists, in other words by people with whom I had worked together for very many years. This kind of tie between combatants plays no trifling role in a person's life. A common or similar fate is an important factor in shaping not only our opinions but also how we act in practice. Besides, these people who joined the party with me before the war, a time hardly favourable to the making of a career, weren't looking for positions or a better life in it. At that time, by the very fact of joining the party they were manifestly jeopardizing their careers and their existence. These people were locked up in prisons, expelled from their studies, dismissed from their work, and very often they sacrificed their personal happiness in order to be able to realize their aims and ideals. You mustn't forget that the party's slogan was one of social justice, along with the slogan of making good social wrongs, and these were slogans to which any decent and honest person would subscribe – he didn't need to be steered by Moscow for them to occur to him.

I realize that after the experience of the past thirty-eight years you may find this difficult to understand, but try to imagine an opposition movement trying to combat social injustice in a capitalist or feudal system. That kind of injustice exists in every system, so it always has a genuine basis for development. And imagine, too, that a little group called a communist party is one branch of this opposition movement, in Salvador or in Honduras. A communist from Salvador isn't like one of our party members after years of communist rule. He loathes opportunism, and he strives with total dedication to realize his *idée fixe*. And he accepts help from anyone who offers it. For the most part this help flows from one source with a specific aim in view, but our hero does not concern himself with these extremely distant aims, putting them aside to be judged at the time of victory – a tardy time. I returned to Poland convinced that here we would not have the same thing as in the Soviet Union, because we were different, different in culture and customs and raised in a different tradition of private and public life. I returned convinced that we would create a new model. In principle, of course, a common and related one, but different nonetheless.

A better one, right?

Better and different. When I came back from Russia I was convinced that there were two worlds, and I was taking part in creating the world of the future. I was taking part in building a better socialism.

But surely you knew it well enough by then.

I know it even better now and I assure you that people have gone on at me about it before: you're not the first one to ask me these things.

So that means there's something difficult to understand there, as in Mazur's case.

They always tortured their own people. I, dear lady, was inside with an NKVD man, so I know. He suffered merciless torture.

Well then, there you are.

Well then nothing. Mazur remained Mazur and went on doing what he'd done before. You have to approach these things individually, and if you're interested in Mazur's case, I'll tell you: Franciszek Mazur came to Poland from Moscow before the war as an envoy of both departments, in other words as an agent delegated to the communist party of western Ukraine. Then, in 1939, he went back to the Soviet Union, where he was arrested and imprisoned. I saw him when I got back from Kolyma. He didn't say how, when or where he had been tortured, so I don't know the details. But I do know that he never broke the connection with his department. So you see his case is not, in my opinion, the most apt, and you should treat Mazur as a man from there, which is what he was and what he remained. And whether he was imprisoned or not is no proof of anything. I was also imprisoned, like many others. From autopsies I got to know the methods of extracting confessions, the Asiatic cruelty. But the fact also remains that, instead of running as far away from communism as I could, after my return to Poland I joined in the building of socialism.

And prisons.

In some sense, yes; indirectly, by supporting those politics. But there's no point in setting the limits of responsibility too wide, otherwise we might think our way to the conclusion that everyone who in any way contributed to creating this Poland became answerable for everything, including the prisons. And there were tens, hundreds of thousands of such people.

Let's stay with the tens.

Really? And what about members of the Polish intelligentsia who helped the government – do we leave them out? What about someone like Andrzejewski – an example off the top of my head, but a typical one – who wrote *The Party and the Writer's Profession*, do we leave him out too? Here was, to put it bluntly, this intellectual, this humanist, this Catholic, and you mean to tell me he didn't know what he was doing? He came to us of his own free will; no one forced him, no one pressured him; and he joined the party not because someone was urging him to but because he accepted that party's programme and principles. And not only did he join it: he wanted to play an active role in it. He wanted to justify the party's principles and persuade others that the party was right. I don't know how you interpret his *Ashes and Diamonds* after all these years, but it's a novel whose function, if you'll forgive me, was among other things to bring the nation round to this regime and show that there was shooting on both sides, and that Maciek was a victim of accident and misunderstanding. Whom does Andrzejewski justify, who does he think was right, historically right, in this novel? Maciek? No, Szczuka: a communist. No one asked Andrzejewski to do that; no one asked for the pamphlet, *The Party and the Writer's Profession*. My question, then, is whether a writer, a moralist and a Catholic, a person raised in the Polish tradition of independence, who for the whole of the occupation was connected – not fighting, but connected – with the London independence camp, and who went over to the other side, to the party, burning his bridges behind him – whether or not such a person becomes answerable for that party's mistakes. And let's not deceive ourselves by asking: did he know or didn't he? He knew. I could tell you, but I won't, that he knew more than I did, because he was in contact with persecuted circles whereas I wasn't. So he knew what was going on behind the security walls and I didn't. I never come out with the argument that I didn't know, but I really didn't know. I could only surmise, and subconsciously I was afraid of something. I asked everyone, from the gentlemen from security to Bierut, whether it was possible that people in Poland were being beaten, tortured and forced into confessing. They swore to me on their word of honour that it wasn't so, that it was out of the question. And later, as you know, all the members of the Politburo as one man insisted that they hadn't known.

Mr Staszewski . . .

So if you really want to talk to me about whether my involvement in this or that was right or wrong, whether what I said about this or that was mistaken or not, I'll tell you that it was mistaken, entirely wrong, false and misguided, and I turned back from that path. And I turned back not as a result of any calculations that I would be better off, but because I became convinced that I couldn't and I shouldn't go on doing what I was.

Mr Staszewski . . .

For years I was able to retain the conviction that we could make something of this party; for years I thought that within this party we could fight for a socialism that would accord with the interests of working people and of this nation, but that's all over. I no longer have that conviction. And not at all because I thought that everyone in the party was a criminal or was making mistakes –

Mr Staszewski . . .

Talking with you is like sitting on a stool with Jacek Rozanski in front of me.

I'm sor—

That's all right, I'm treating my conversation with you as a conversation with myself, so I'm not evading anything and I've got nothing against touchy questions, because sometimes you have to answer all the questions for yourself.

A squaring of conscience?

My dear, you were never in power; it's a pity. There's no one point at which a person sits down, puts his head in his hands, becomes absorbed in thought and proceeds to square his conscience; that's not how it works. You're constantly squaring the account of your conscience. Doing this took me very far, because I finally adopted a position which was not typical for a communist and which set me apart from the others: I dug down to the foundations of the reasoning by which I had until then been guided and I stopped being a communist.

The whole of Warsaw knows about that, so let's put it differently: what do you have on your conscience?

What I have on my conscience, Miss Toranska, is my activity in the PRL in more or less responsible posts, and my involvement in making right or wrong decisions. I have on my conscience the fact that I faithfully served the party, but a party that never proclaimed it would organize trials on the basis of false testimony or falsely accuse innocent people. A party that never proclaimed the predominance of security over politics, but rather publicly called for a people's democracy. And I wasn't the only one to fall for this people's democracy bit. Polish society, it must be said, also fell for it. It accepted this government – with suspicion and mistrust, after a period of struggle and the laying down of arms, but it accepted it, even with the knowledge, on the part of its more aware sections, that Poland would not have full sovereignty, that it was going from one kind of occupation to another; but it didn't think that the two occupations, the Nazi and the Soviet one, were equal. The difference was obvious, however you looked at it. A Polish government was installed; a Polish army, Polish schools, Polish institutions. After five years of the terrible Nazi occupation Polish books began to be published in millions of copies; Polish theatres and Polish universities were opened. So it wasn't difficult to win society over to the new politics, although of course it required a certain amount of effort and sufficiently deft and flexible tactics.

Deceit.

To a certain extent, yes. Claiming that what wasn't there was there and pretending that what wouldn't and couldn't be there would be there. But even those who saw through those politics had to admit that the new Polish government was better than the Nazi occupation and that it represented something Polish.

On the principle of choosing the lesser of two evils?

Rather of choosing another possibility, without realizing that it is doomed and cannot evolve in a positive direction. Besides, after the war we entered a period with very large scope for organic work: building, rebuilding and creating new values which would serve the nation. No one suspected at that time that it would all be wasted. That's something you have to understand, because then it won't seem strange to you that so many people decided to collaborate with the communists and conquer their mistrust or indeed their hostility. I, of course, didn't share those misgivings; I threw myself into the work with total enthusiasm, and despite the critical attitude I have towards myself today, I'm far from wanting to claim that everything I did was wrong and guided by base motives. That's not how it was. In Silesia, for instance, where I found myself in 1945 in the post of economic secretary of the PPR Provincial Committee – that's just the first example that occurs to me – I helped to organize and rebuild industry to get factories and mines working again. I was very pleased to be with people, working among people. I'd worked in Silesia before, actually, organizing the working class there – strikes, trade unions. I went back there with great enthusiasm and I can't say that my work there was contemptible or that it was a form of betrayal.

And you weren't bothered by the dismantling of post-German factories?

By the time I got to Silesia, Miss Toranska, the dismantling had ceased. And in fact in Upper Silesia it had never taken place at all. I inherited my post from Eugeniusz Szyr, who went to Warsaw to work for Minc, but I only took over from him in one aspect of the work, as economic secretary of the Katowice Provincial Committee; I didn't take over his function of representative at the military headquarters in Legnica, which dealt precisely with dismantling. That was something they simply didn't trust me with. Minc's view, in fact, was that "in their eyes you're unreliable, finished, because you came back from a camp; they'll always treat you with suspicion". I, too, had not the slightest inclination to have anything to do with them, so we decided that someone else would be delegated to Legnica.

That kind of lack of trust must surely have been terribly painful for a good communist.

No, because you see, in that party no one ever had complete confidence in anyone. Your first duty was revolutionary vigilance, and then party vigilance. And it was convenient for me: I preferred to keep away from them.

I had a lot of happiness and a lot of fun in Katowice. Every mine, every factory and workshop that we got going was a great event for us. There was hunger, so I was to a large extent responsible for seeing that people got enough to eat. Especially since, food being scarce, strikes kept breaking out, and although they were short-lived and ended with an accord being reached (brutal solutions were not resorted to then), they were still an aggravation.

I remember how we chased after nineteen trainloads of wheat that were supposed to be going to Upper Silesia; they'd escaped from Opolszczyzna and Lower Silesia towards the eastern border.

What do you mean, "escaped"?

Just escaped. Trains that were supposed to be for us went off in another direction: they were abducted! And we only had a three-day supply of flour. The things that went on then! The Internal Security Corps and organized groups of workers chased them through the whole of the Lublin and Rzeszow regions. Nineteen trains! We caught up with them and turned them back. The tremendous feeling of satisfaction we got at times like those absorbed us completely.

What did I do that was wrong? I was wrong to take part in stifling the opposition, the PSL and the PPS. To take part in kicking out of the PPS all those whom we, the communists, found unsuitable. The PPS actually hadn't been the strongest party in Silesia before the war

– the Christian Democrats had been the strongest – but the PPS did have its traditions rooted there; good traditions, and old ones. We manipulated the PPS: people who were deemed inconvenient were removed from it, and others, who declared their loyalty and obedience, were put in their place. Those were disastrous, wrong and contemptible actions on our part.

Is that all?

No, I'm sure it isn't all.

That's good, because at the third PUWP Central Committee plenum in 1949 you said, "I think there's a limit at which lack of vigilance ends and the class enemy begins. It seems to me that our right-wing nationalist deviationists, with Comrade Gomulka at their head, have found themselves somewhere in the vicinity of that limit."

There were others who thought so, but of course that's no argument. There were two reasons I said that. First of all I was convinced that Gomulka really was a right-wing nationalist deviationist, and secondly I was on the side of Gomulka's opponents, in other words those who didn't approve of Gomulka's ideas during that period. And since I am in the habit of formulating my views very clearly, concealing nothing, I stressed my position sharply. Of all the things I said I remember one that was probably the worst and the saddest; I said, namely, that Gomulka was opposing the Soviet Union. For I saw him as someone who was in some way hindering our relations as fraternal allies. I thought at the time that this was because of his position on the Yugoslav issue. Pretty it all wasn't, but then the behaviour of his friends, with whom he'd been closely bound for years, was no more pretty. Gomulka was hideously betrayed by his friends; they finally dissociated themselves from him. All of them except Kliszko. Of course, Gomulka forgave them for it later; he was incredibly understanding of human weakness. But he had to forgive them in any case, because it's one of the communist dogmas that if the party condemns me, and then people condemn me, then it's hard to hold it against them that they obey the party and not me and trust the party while ceasing to trust me. For the party is simply the party: it is a word which replaces all known concepts and expressions; it is an absolute, an abstraction. It is always right; it is our honour, our happiness, our life's goal. And if you ask any communist about its infallibility, and if you also prove to him that for the past thirty-eight years of its existence in Poland all it has done is commit mistakes, he will say to you: the party didn't commit mistakes; people committed mistakes. The leadership, abusing our trust, committed mistakes. In that context Gomulka really could forgive everyone. He didn't have to forgive me, because I'd never been either a friend or an ally of his, so I didn't have to support him or to reject him.

Only to finish him off.

That wasn't finishing off, Miss Toranska, that was a discussion.

And how did it end for Bukharin, Zinoviev, Kamenev and others, Mr Staszewski?

You don't have to remind me of that, because I know how it ended, only too well. I was in Moscow as a guest at the Fifteenth VCP(b) Congress in 1927 and I was able to observe in detail the mechanisms of factional struggle. I also saw Stalin then. A hard, unyielding communist and a bad speaker whose ideas were primitive but prepared with exceeding care. He would take a cardboard file, unfold it and announce: part one – the international situation . . .; then he would put it away and begin on another file. He didn't really read from the files, but that's how he laid out his speeches. Sometimes he would argue a point, but mostly he would just assert: it's plain that . . . Everything was plain to him.

At the Fifteenth Congress I saw him in action. There was Trotsky, a great virtuoso of the art of oratory, whose words mesmerized you and swept you away; there was the excellent Bukharin; and there was Stalin: small, pockmarked, wearing high boots and a green tunic. The discussion was fierce. Suddely Stalin accused Kamenev of having sent a wire to Mikhail Romanov, the brother of the tsar, from Irkutsk in 1917, during the February revolution, thanking him for renouncing his claim to the throne. The matter had been cleared up while Lenin was still alive, and Lenin had denied that such a thing had occurred, but Stalin had no scruples about dragging it out again. Kamenev shouted from the floor: "*vryosh*" – you're lying – whereupon Stalin shouted, in his horrible Georgian accent: "*malchi*" – silence – or you'll regret it, and his voice sent a chill of terror through the room.

After that I was in Moscow during the purges in 1937, when the NKVD was dragging people out of their homes. All my friends and acquaintances were taken away. So you don't need to remind me of anything. You see, things were never on a level in that party, and no one ever abided by any rules of the kind that we commonly call principles of fair play.

But I see that there's no point in this; I'm wasting my breath, because you don't understand anything. I've already told you what a communist's faith is and what the party means to him, haven't I? There's an old Latin saying that goes, "Plato is your friend, but truth is a greater one". To parody: a person can be your friend, but your greatest, your most important, your only genuine friend is the party, my sweet, the party! We can drink together and be friends and while away nights chatting, but in a situation where this friend of mine loses the party's trust and the party condemns him, who should I support? Well, who?

The truth.

The party, my sweet, the party, because the party is truth, it is the right and the good. Of course my aim in asking this question was purely theoretical – a communist doesn't ask such questions. He knows. Do you still find it strange that my position on the case of Gomulka, Kliszko and Spychalski was the communist one, which at the time I unfortunately thought was the only right one? Besides, that struggle concerned basic principles: that period was a turning point. Gomulka made a self-criticism which I remember to this day. I still remember self-criticisms that were made in Russia in the thirties, and I remember Gomulka's.

Was it sincere?

Show me one self-criticism that's sincere! I at least don't know of any. Communist acts of self-criticism are indications either of betrayal or of political destruction. I know of no case where a communist who wasn't threatened in any way suddenly, because of his experiences or of some inner need, or because he had thought things through, came to the party and confessed what he had done wrong or what he had thought wrong. There's only one way people would interpret something like that: the guy's showing clear symptoms of mental illness. It generally took place according to the well-known schema: someone attacked him, saying: we know you've got this or that on your conscience, and then, as a result of peer pressure or on orders from his superiors, or just out of ordinary, physical fear, the guy would come to the conclusion that he should make a self-criticism. As a matter of tactics.

And what happened to revolutionary courage?

Sure, it's there, or rather it was there; it just manifested itself on another level – an external one: in conflicts with enemies, to put it succinctly. But faced with his own party, every party member is an absolute coward. He's scared of the party, really scared of it. If that weren't so we wouldn't see such blatant displays of opportunism, conformism, or just plain, disgusting cowardice in the party. And there's another factor that comes into it: the ordinary desire to live a comfortable life. I don't mean just material comforts, which everyone who comes into contact with the ruling classes has, but above all the moral advantages whereby any opinions or events which might come into conflict with my conscience and bring about an internal split in it get relegated to an entirely different plane, an external one. I have no internal conflicts, you see; I simply don't have any, because I have faith in the party and I carry out its instructions, be they good or bad, right or wrong; and if it turns out that they were fundamentally wrong I can calmly sit back and wait for the party to act, make a decision and resolve those conflicts in some way. This faith which party members have is not a result of the traditions in which they were raised, nor of any profound thoughts they may have had, but simply of their decision that it will be better for them and for others if responsibility for everything that happens to them or to others is transferred to someone else, to the party, in other words to an abstraction.

Did you do that as well?

I can regret it now, but I can't deny it.

So you don't deny that you were one of those who introduced Stalinist terror in Poland?

That I contest, because Stalinist terror had been introduced in Poland earlier: at the precise point when the feet of Soviet soldiers touched this country's soil and when the borders of the Soviet empire were marked out.

In 1944, you mean?

Yes, exactly; in 1944. That was when the whole security apparatus was formed and its structure established, except for Department X, which was created later to combat enemies within the party. And that was also when most of the people who in the following years became directors and deputy directors in the Bureau of Public Security were hired.

What was the planned scenario?

What do you mean, what was it? That's clear, surely: the sights were set on the view from the East. Nationalize all economic life, destroy cooperatives and private trade and bring everything under the state monopoly. And if you have the administration, the money, and all the material means under your control, it's not difficult to nationalize society as well, by creating fictitious organizations, fictitious structures and a fictitious ideology.

Still, appearances were maintained: Mikolajczyk, the PSL, and the PPS.

When they murdered Home Army people in security service cellars they weren't maintaining any appearances. And they kept up no appearances when they arrested thousands of people, because even Wachowicz, a prewar PPS member from Lodz who became deputy minister of the MBP in the coalition government, had no power. They would arrest a guy; Wachowicz might decide he'd been wrongly arrested, so he gave the order to have him released; the guy was released, and the next day he was arrested anew. This game of hide-and-seek went on until Wachowicz got kicked out, but it was a game, not an attempt to resolve a complicated political situation.

I will strongly contest the claim that the period after 1950 was some kind of extraordinary growth, because it isn't true. Tendencies to destroy the Home Army were already apparent in 1944. When did Wlodzimierz Zakrzewski paint the poster that said, "The Home Army, filthy reactionary dwarf", in 1944 or 1945?

In 1945.

It doesn't matter. But what did that mean? It meant that the Soviet Union had no intention of sticking to the international commitments it had made. So if, for a period of time, certain appearances and a certain façade were kept up or certain concessions were made, it was only because Stalin hadn't yet made up his mind to strike. But, good Lord, there was nothing to compare with the period of violence, cruelty and lawlessness that Poland experienced in the years 1944–7. Not thousands but tens of thousands of people were killed then, and the official trials that were organized after 1949 were merely an epilogue to the liquidation of the Home Army, of activists of independent parties and of independent thought in general. That's how it was, and I think claiming that the Stalinist period begins when communists start getting locked up is a terribly misguided view. It is from that untruth that Gomulka and his allies derive comfort and justification, for they divide Polish postwar history into two parts, the period up to 1949 and the period that followed, and they present the first one as follows: well, it may not have been idyllic, but it was some kind of decent situation and the political struggle was waged with relative decency; and the struggle with the underground was taking place because the underground provoked it: there were armed bands in the forests and there was a civil war situation, and when that happens shots get fired and people get killed. According to them, Stalinism came after that decent situation, in the years from 1949 to 1955: numbing Stalinist terror; but we weren't responsible for that. Of course Gomulka isn't responsible for locking up communists, but for the destruction of the Home Army and the destruction of the PPS he certainly is.

While you were responsible for propaganda?

What do you mean, "responsible"? I was head of the press section in the Central Committee.

Isn't that enough?

Of course not. I was made head in 1948, when the idea was born to divide the enormous propaganda section into five smaller ones. The person who was to coordinate all this was Jerzy Albrecht, and Jerzy Borejsza was his deputy. My candidacy for the post of director of the press and publishing section was put forward, I think, by Zambrowski, and he informed me that I had been nominated. So I left the *Workers' Tribune*, which I'd been editing in Katowice during the previous year, and went to Warsaw to organize the section.

So you were the one who hired Rakowski, the current deputy minister?

I don't remember, but I think he was already there when I arrived. A smooth man, and very energetic when it came to carrying out orders. I neither liked nor disliked him, which was my attitude towards everyone, in fact. He was just there and that was that. The person I liked least was probably Haber, my deputy that they'd assigned to me: a rather ridiculous and completely useless figure. I even asked Ochab, when he took over control of the press, to get rid of him, but Haber was a wartime friend of Ochab's from Russia and Ochab asked me to leave him in his post. Haber didn't actually get in my way, and he turned out to be a relatively decent type, as opposed to Janiurek, Wysznacki or Rakowski.

And what did you do?

At first I didn't do anything. I wasn't the one who thought up the socialist-realist model. I don't want to shield myself by pleading lack of authority, but the fact is that the question of whether or not socialist realism would be launched in Poland was not one that I decided, or that anyone else in Poland decided, for that matter. Socialist realism was an element in the politics of the entire bloc, and that was something you couldn't question. That whole struggle with formalism and decadence, and later with hostile influences in art and literature – all that was general party policy. And if you want to accuse me of having implemented it, I assure you I implemented it with all the restrictions I was able to apply, and in fact some people held that against me.

Who?

Sokorski, for instance, and Pawel Hoffman. Imagine the following scene. The national artists' congress was on, and vigorous attempts were made at it to persuade our artists of the value of socialist realism. Sokorski and Hoffman foamed at the mouth and shouted with fire in their eyes. They received calm retorts from Professors Eibisch, Kobzej and Pankov, while I just sat in a back row and said nothing. When the session ended and we were leaving, Sokorski and Hoffman grabbed me and said, it's all your fault, you're the one who's egging them on, you're the one. . . . I was surprised, and said, come on, don't be silly, you know there's nothing I can do. Whereupon Hoffman gave the amusing reply: we know that, but they don't.

And what should you have done?

I should have joined in the shouting. If you keep quiet and don't shout, that means you're not a supporter and you're taking the side of the opposition. Which, granted, I wasn't doing, but then nor was I displaying excessive initiative in implementing the Soviet model of culture in Poland. True, I did hold the view that the bathetic style of grand-scale building propagated in Russia should be grafted onto Poland and that Polish society should be infected with it, but the forms that this grafting process was taking didn't seem effective to me. And I assure you that that's why we were able to reject and get rid of socialist realism with such relative ease: because first of all it was not rooted in our cultural tradition, and secondly we weren't excessively enthusiastic in implementing it. Wherever it was possible to wriggle out of some act of servility, we wriggled out of it. Above all we managed to wriggle out of a large part of the junk of Soviet socialist-realist literature; we published relatively little of it and we didn't propagate it much. On the other hand, we did publish quite a lot of Russian classics, which was in part an act of servility, but I think it was good for Polish culture as well. So if they published the whole of Dostoevsky or Tolstoy –

– not the whole of it –

Well then, almost all of it – that wasn't a bad thing to do, on the contrary; but the odd thing is that this literature didn't prove popular with our public. In Poland if something's translated from the Russian that's enough to put people off reading it.

We also published all the Polish classics: Mickiewicz, Slowacki, Sienkiewicz –

– well, no. You didn't publish the messianic writings of Mickiewicz or Slowacki and you didn't publish Sienkiewicz's By Fire and Sword *or* Master Wolodyjowsky.

Yes, all right, but we did publish almost all of Zeromski, with the exception of two or three stories: "At the Presbytery in Wyszkow", "Progress and Snobbery", and "Whiter than Snow will I Become". There were discussions about publishing those as well, but the issue came up against the Politburo and the Politburo decided against it.

The Politburo decided about the publication of two or three stories?

Of course. Zeromski was ready for printing, the censors questioned two stories and the matter went to the Politburo.

Of course, apart from the classics we also published heaps of junk, but that was often a decision made by publishing houses, which claimed it was necessary, and one could hardly forbid them. And sometimes writers themselves displayed a quite irrational stubbornness. I remember my conflict with Konwicki when he wrote his book *Power*. I was against publishing it because I thought the book was bad and written in large degree under the influence of Borejsza, so Grzegorz Lasota went off to complain about me to Berman, on his own behalf and Konwicki's. Berman had *Power* published and to this day Konwicki is still ashamed of having written the book.

But however we assess that period we do have to admit also that many good things were done. An impressive printing network was established. Several printing houses were built, among them the "Dom Slowa Polskiego" ["House of the Polish Word"], the October Revolution printing house in Warsaw, and others in Torun and Poznan. We brought Poland to the stage where 120 million books were being printed annually, which made 5.5 books per capita, more than now and about three times more than before the war.

On the other hand you dissolved hundreds or even thousands of journals – no one had taken a precise count of them before the war – and created a model of the press that was so permanent it has stuck to this day.

It's a familiar model, based on the old, unchanging Leninist principle of the press as an organ of the party, the party's tool and mouthpiece. Thus papers can be attractive or not in varying degrees, they can be more or less strident and aggressive, depending on the needs and temperament of their editors, but they must always, in varying forms, express and propagate the party line.

Stefan Kozicki wrote that they should also rebuild reality. He would go off to the country, write about a production cooperative that didn't exist, and after his piece was published the cooperative would be created.

Well, if it did happen it could only have been after his articles, because there was no danger of it after Kusmierek's.

I set up provincial party journals, which didn't really exist outside Warsaw, Lodz, Wroclaw and Katowice.

Why did you do that?

Obviously, if you assume that all newspapers are amalgamated and subject to the same directives, then it should follow that they're not needed: one is enough. And it should also follow that there's no need for provincial committees because one is enough. But that isn't so. The committees were and remain the effective provincial authority and not everything that goes on there is ordered and directed by the Central Committee. The basic line is, yes, but not the details of its implementation. And so those details, which depend on the particularities of the province and the temperament of the activists working there, had to find their expression and transmission channel in the press. So party newspapers were necessary and had quite a large amount of freedom, be it in the use they made of agency material from the Polish Press Agency or the Workers' Press Agency or in their selection of articles, especially those dealing with local matters. Indeed party newspapers weren't the only kind of paper being established at that time; a whole network of so-called "Czytelnik" newspapers sprang up.

Why?

You expect me to provide you with clearly formulated answers; very well, then: the "Czytelnik" newspapers arose in order to give the appearance that Poland had not only a party press but a nonparty one as well, basing itself on the positive principles of the party's programme. In fact that's why the publishing house and newspaper concern "Czytelnik" was created. Set up in 1944 by Jerzy Borejsza, it was in fact controlled by the party, but formally it was independent, in order to attract as many well-known nonparty people as possible – people who'd been famous before the war – and with their help to draw the mass of nonparty readers into the party's sphere of influence.

First to draw them in, and then to take control of their consciousness.

In order to be able to administer their consciousness, yes. Which in any case, as you can see, did not succeed.

What were your contacts with the Soviet embassy?

They only made polite, formal visits, with no attempt to impose anything on me. I maintained more frequent contact, by reason of my position, with *Pravda*, *Izvestya*, and Tass correspondents, but those contacts were of an entirely different nature. For correspondents I was the chief, so even if they'd wanted to make critical comments of any kind I wouldn't have had to take them seriously.

We once had a visit from a member of the CPSU Central Committee who was editor-in-chief of a Cominform organ with the long title, *For Lasting Peace and People's Democracy.*

That title was thought up by Stalin himself.

Yes, I think so. The editor came here from Prague, because the journal was published in Prague, and expressed the desire to talk to me. The talk was in part funny and in part threatening, because at one point he asked me: what will you do with your kulaks during collectivization?

I'm not sure I understand the question, I said; what collectivization?

Whereupon he said: surely you know you'll have to go through with collectivization sooner or later and the problem of kulaks will arise, so what will you do with them?

You know, comrade, I said, I don't think anyone's thought about it here.

He was outraged: what do you mean, no one's thought about it? He began to explain it to me: Poland, he said, is a country of limited geographical space; how many peasants' farms does it have?

Up to four million, I said.

Well then, it's simple, he said; you have 400,000 kulak farms.

I don't quite understand, I said; what kind of calculation is that?

He told me: we assumed that kulak farms make up 10 per cent of peasant farms, and it must be roughly the same here, so you have a total of 400,000 kulak farms, which means at least half a million people to resettle or arrest. Where will you resettle them?

I said: we don't have that problem. First of all, we have never thought about how many kulak farms there are, secondly our concept of a kulak is entirely different and we have no kulaks of the kind that you define as capitalist, and thirdly no one here has any intention of resettling or arresting half a million or a million people, because that would be lunatic or catastrophic.

The editor was very disapproving when he left my office and went off to complain to someone in the Politburo that the head of the press doesn't know what a class enemy or a kulak is, and after all a kulak is an animal, as Lenin said. Zambrowski later told me that this editor expressed concern about whether I was the right person for a position of such responsibility.

Surely that wasn't the reason you stopped being head of the press section in January 1954.

No, of course not. There was just one reason: they dismissed me. But I must confess I'd also had enough of it myself; I was sincerely bored in that post and I had an increasing sense of the fruitlessness of what I was doing, because more and more acts of servility were required from me.

And what was the real reason?

All right. I left because the Soviet embassy demanded it. More specifically, the Soviet ambassador, Popov, in an official *démarche*, demanded the dismissal of Staszewski, Starewicz, Kasman and about two other comrades. They had got back on their old anti-Semitic course, and we were Jews. Bierut said to me outright: it pains me, but it's not our decision.

Did it pain him?

Yes, I think it did. After all, I'd known Bierut quite well since before the war and met him during various periods of his life. First in 1926, when he came to the Comintern school in Moscow together with

"Jasia", Marek and Aleksander Fornalski. He was a "majorist" then, and when he'd finished his course at the school a discussion arose in the Polish section of the Comintern about whether he should be allowed to go back to a country where the "minority" had taken power. The view that he should not be allowed to go won the day and Bierut was posted to the Ländersekretariat, as it was called then, in other words to the Comintern section which dealt with the Balkan countries. He returned to Poland in 1931 and became first secretary of Red Aid. I was in touch with him from time to time during that period in my capacity as representative of the KPP secretariat in matters of aid to political prisoners. After the war we met again, and at first our relations were cordial. I told him, without concealing anything, about my own fate and that of his friends, most of whom had been killed in Russia. He was very interested in Warski, Krajewski and Stefanski in particular. He was very shaken by what I told him, because Stalin and Beria were constantly telling him that these people had been swallowed up somewhere in that huge country and couldn't be found. I told him exactly what had happened to them, so that he wouldn't have any illusions.

Did it change his attitude towards Stalin?

No, of course not! He made a brief remark about how tragic it was and said that perhaps individual people were still alive somewhere, so he would go on looking for them, asking about them and trying to obtain their release. He frequently talked to Stalin about them. Whenever he was in Moscow he would go to see Stalin; Beria was always present at those meetings. Bierut would say, what's happening about these Polish communists who aren't here, and then Stalin would turn to Beria and say, Lavrentii Pavlovich, where are they? I told you to look for them, why haven't you found them? He would play out this comedy every time.

Once, I think it was the beginning of 1950, or maybe near the end of 1949, Bierut returned so shaken from one of his trips to Moscow and so shocked by what had happened that he came back here and described it. He'd gone to see Stalin, asked his question, Stalin repeated his little circus with Lavrentii Pavlovich, and Bierut and Beria left Stalin's office together, whereupon Beria said to him (please excuse the coarse and straightforward party language): why are you fucking around with Iosif Vissarianovich? You fuck off and leave him alone. That's my advice to you, or you'll regret it.

Bierut took the hint, which was no longer a hint but a final warning, and never again brought up the subject of his friends with Stalin.

You mean he was scared off?

I don't know; Bierut was cautious, I suppose, but he wasn't a coward. Besides, at that time he still had nothing to fear. Above all he was shocked, because no one had spoken to him like that before or threatened him in that way, and here, all of a sudden, was a comrade, a friend, a brother, a representative of an organ which he respected and to which he was attached, speaking to him in that way. I suspect that two or three years later he did begin to be afraid. I don't know whether it was fear for himself from the start, but I think he gradually began to fear for himself as well. The Russians got the idea that prisons had to be built in Poland and one of them had to contain a special section for members of the party leadership. A project was even drawn up; Mietkowski was in charge of it. You understand: the Russians thought of it, but the Poles were the ones who were supposed to build it, build it for themselves, and each of them could very well anticipate that he was building himself a one-family cell.

I've no doubt that Bierut must have been aware of the grimness of the situation. And I'll tell you this: Bierut, who never drank, and under Hempel's influence had been active in the Temperance Society before the war, now, near the end of his life, began to drink. I don't know if he drank a lot or a little, alone or in company, but the fact is that I saw him several times when he was clearly over the top. Drinking was probably an escape for him, perhaps from fear, perhaps from bad premonitions. I saw him once at a party – I think it was an important one because the Soviet ambassador was present – in 1954, I think, or 1955 at the latest, certainly after Stalin's death. Possibly it was to celebrate the 22nd of July. As usual there was one huge table placed across the room for the most important guests, while the rest of the tables were placed lengthways down the room. Everyone was eating, drinking, talking. Bierut got up from his table along with the Soviet ambassador and began introducing him to people. He came up to where I was standing with a group of others and said: Comrade Staszewski, introduce yourself to our ambassador. We've already been introduced today, I replied. And then I heard a frightful thing from Bierut's lips: never mind, you can do it again, he said, you can greet our ambassador again.

Bierut was pissed, and I saw it as a symptom of the man's decline, a kind of fall and a loss of dignity. I'd never seen him like that before. I thought for a moment that this self-humiliation of Bierut's was in a sense an indication of the death of his spirit, although it seemed to me that there were no grounds for it, since the Soviets' attitude towards him was surely very positive, and had always been positive.

That was already after Swiatlo's defection as well. Did panic break out then?

Not immediately. I remember that a few days after Swiatlo's escape – so it must have been December 1953 – someone told me that Swiatlo had gone to Berlin with Fejgin. They were walking along the street when Swiatlo said to Fejgin, wait for me a minute, whereupon he went into a shop and evaporated. Our security men suspected he'd been abducted. I didn't believe that. Listen, I said to someone, he wasn't kidnapped, that's not the way you kidnap people; he flew the coop. But they hadn't expected that from Swiatlo; he'd served the PRL government from the first and he had begun his career as deputy chief of security in Cracow (Swiatlo's own deputy for political matters was in turn a journalist with thc *Evening Express* – Kozlowski). That was when I first met him. He was crafty and smart, a wise guy, certainly intelligent and certainly primitive.

Swiatlo had disappeared into the blue and some people began to suspect that perhaps a girl was involved. There were plenty of girls in West Berlin, each more beautiful than the next, and one might suppose that he'd got himself entangled in some kind of affair. I don't know whether it happened before or after the Prawin scandal. I think it was after.

What scandal?

Jakub Prawin was a general, the head of the military mission in Berlin. The mission was located not far from a nice bar, the "Bodega" it was called, a bit Spanish-like. Prawin started going there, took a fancy to some girl or other, and it looked like quite a serious affair was in the offing when suddenly the girl turned out to be an agent for American intelligence.

I see that one can't hide anything from you.

Ten days passed, maybe even two weeks, and Swiatlo still hadn't come back. Some kind of official announcement had to be made and they were wondering what to say in it when suddenly the bombshell came: Swiatlo had requested asylum and then Radio Free Europe announced a series of broadcasts with him. Many people panicked and got frightened.

You too?

No, because I had no reason to, but I listened with great interest, becaue I was learning a great deal myself. It was mainly the security people who were scared.

Which of them did you know?

Not many, because I never gave them an opportunity to get close to me or to ask me for anything. I didn't allow any friendliness or familiarity from them. That's why I didn't know any of them socially except Luna Brystigier, who definitely shone above them by her intelligence.

She was the only woman in security; was she at least pretty?

She had quite a nice face but she was terribly ungainly, square and short with very fat legs. She was aggressive and headstrong, one of those women who announce who is to take her home today.

And did they take her home?

Of course.

You as well?

I was excluded. I went around with girls I found attractive.

Oh, but surely if she'd ordered you to . . .

Order me? Not likely! She could order Piasecki about, but not me. I didn't have to and Piasecki did. Soviet intelligence probably passed Piasecki on to her along with his whole bunch and she dealt with them to the end.

By drawing them into collaboration?

Mostly into bed. Luna was a typical political subversive: she was in charge of the Church and the intelligentsia. She didn't take part in the struggle with the armed underground and she wasn't involved in extracting forced confessions or rigging trials; she was assigned typically subversive tasks which required a lot of intelligence. Cultured, eloquent, not at all shrill, she was the type for social encounters. In fact it was she who decided the fate of Pawel Jasienica, who was in prison. She had interesting discussions with him which made her understand that he would be more useful at liberty than in prison.

And Pawel Jasienica was brought out of prison and taken to these interesting discussions while awaiting the execution of his death sentence, right?

Of course. Later Luna brought about his release and rang me up. She said: listen, there's this rather interesting guy that's just been released, you may have heard of him – Pawel Jasienica. He's a historian with a lot of literary talent and it would be good if he weren't completely bottled up so that he could write and publish things.

Jasienica came to see me, actually on the advice of Jozef Sieradzki, a historian at the Jagiellonian University. He said he wanted to write a series of articles about Biskupin. I thought this was a very good idea and I had them published in *Zycie Literackie*.

Did you also get him a job?

No, Jasienica didn't have a full-time position anywhere.

In January 1954 Starewicz was transferred from his post as director of the section dealing with publishing houses to the Central Council of Trade Unions; Kasman was transferred from being editor-in-chief of the paper Trybuna Ludu *to deputy minister of light industry; and you were transferred to agriculture.*

The position they offered me was highly unattractive: I became deputy minister of agriculture without knowing anything about farming, your typical city cat, and my wife had to teach me to distinguish rye from barley.

But you gained notoriety – in the worst possible sense.

Yes, and this is where a well-known period of my life begins, but many different things are jumbled up in it. Organizing requisitioning was unconnected with the post of deputy minister of agriculture.

Maybe not with the post, but certainly with you, according to Putrament.

A moron, and a liar into the bargain.

So how many people did you finally lock up?

What?

How many people did you lock up in the Wielkopolska region in the autumn of 1954? According to Putrament it was several tens of thousands.

My love, not one; not one single person did I lock up.

Because of course locking people up was a job for security.

Not only because of that, but because I'd gone out to the Poznan region as a representative of the Central Committee. There was a shortage of wheat, and people said that the peasants wanted to starve the cities and wouldn't provide any wheat voluntarily, so they had to be forced to sell to the state.

Not "people said"; you *said.*

The party said, Miss Toranska; all I did was repeat what it said. The decision was made and a whole huge apparatus was activated. It was headed by representatives of the Central Committee who were delegated to each of the provinces. To each of them. I was one of many, delegated to the Poznan province. I do emphasize that this procedure was put into effect absolutely everywhere. The Central Committee representatives were in charge of organizing the apparatus on the next levels down – the district or community level. They recruited people from among party members in the city or the general region of their province. In addition, each province was assigned a team of representatives from the Ministry of Procurement [of Agricultural Produce], a team of representatives from the Prosecutor's Office, and a team of representatives from the Ministry of Public Security. Each apparatus worked parallel with the other three. Of course, the province also had its own Provincial Committee along with its whole regional apparatus, its own security offices which functioned there, and administrators from the national councils. The apparatus of party representatives from the Central Committee had as its primary task to mobilize the party in the wheat department; the apparatus from the Ministry of Procurement was assigned to the local purchase apparatus and the community cooperatives, which were to exert additional pressure by way of provisioning; and the apparatus of the Prosecutor's office and the Ministry of Public Security was active in the area of repression. So any peasant failing to fulfil the plan of requisitioning established by the apparatus from the Ministry of Procurement, by the apparatus of purchase and provisioning in the province, its districts and communities, and by the administrative and party apparatus – for they established the quotas – any such peasant came under the powers of the Prosecutor's and security apparatus representatives, and there a whole mechanism of how to proceed had been provided for. First the peasant was summoned for a talk, then for another, and finally he was arrested. He was normally held for anything between a couple of days to two weeks and his goods were confiscated.

How many did you arrest?

I don't remember exactly, but more or less the same amount as in Pomerania, up to eight thousand.

Of course, as a plenipotentiary supervising the activities of all these services you knew about it.

Yes, I knew about it.

And?

And nothing. Quite frankly, I thought it was right, because it accorded with the principles of our politics.

Mr Morawski, who was propaganda secretary in Poznan then, remembers how you used to rant on at meetings – because of course the province you were in charge of had to be the best – and he was horrified at the scope of repression, many different kinds of it. Provincial Committee employees who were working in the countryside would come and describe how in some villages it was hard to find even a single house that wasn't painted over with the word "kulak", which was supposed to be a signal to the security services. The painting over was of course done by our valiant youth from the KZMP.

That's all true, and I must say no one ever made a point of holding my activities in Poznan against me until I went over to the opposition.

That's one thing I can believe.

This system of requisitioning wheat from peasants wasn't any kind of discovery. It was copied – you can guess from whom – and repeated in all the people's democracies. Here, too, it was generally applied until 1949, and its scope was greatest in those provinces where production was highest: the Poznan, Bydgoszcz, Opole and Wroclaw provinces. In fact no plenum ever concerned itself with the methods applied to requisition from the peasants, since they were thought suitable.

They got concerned over Gryfice.

That's because blatant acts of violence were committed against people there: there were beatings and tortures. People were made into public laughing stocks and forced to sit on barrels.

What do you mean, sit on barrels?

Precisely that: on barrels. They'd set up a barrel in the middle of the village and make the guy sit astride it; then they'd round up all the peasants and make them watch their neighbour sit there for several hours. And finally there was a scandal. Bierut thundered about it, the

Politburo stepped in, a resolution was passed, but the system of requisitioning remained the same and the methods remained the same, only less drastic.

Because all that happened in Gryfice was that they went too far, right?

Exactly; they went too far.

I sat there learning about agriculture and gathering material for over a year, and I finally came to the conclusion that our agricultural policies were fundamentally wrong. Minister Pszczolkowski thought they were right and I thought they were wrong. Pszczolkowski thought we should aim for cooperativization of the countryside, while I maintained that it would take a civil war to cooperativize the countryside and that even if we won it, it would lead the state to bankruptcy, because as it was we were spending horrific sums of money subsidizing existing cooperatives, and if any more were created we would finally run out of funds.

Gomulka was already saying that in 1948.

In 1948 everyone was saying that and swearing by all the saints that there would be no cooperativization.

Well, then, before that.

Before that the authorities distributed the land and said: farm your land and don't worry, there won't be any cooperatives. But at some point Stalin decided that that was all very well and we should have said it earlier, but now the time had come to speak and act differently.

Let's forget Stalin for a moment; after all, he wasn't the one who cooperativized the Polish countryside.

Everyone was responsible.

Everyone meaning no one.

Just a moment, I haven't finished. I want to tell you about the rest of my activities in the Ministry of Agriculture. When I'd collected all the data I wrote a memo to the Politburo in which I set out my views on our agrarian policies. I wrote about the amount of money these cooperatives were costing the state and the sums we were pouring into them; about how we were bribing these supposed cooperative members to remain in the cooperatives, at least formally; and about how extending the cooperatives would cause a greater deficit. My conclusions were to the effect that until we opted for equivalent exchange with the countryside, Polish agriculture would continue to deteriorate and would finally become incapable of feeding the population.

Before sending off the memo I showed it to Zambrowski, who at one time had also dealt with agriculture. He read it and said: of course, there'll be a terrible row and "Tomasz" will be furious, but send it anyway; you're not risking anything, since you've no particular desire to stay on in this ministry.

There was no row. Bierut decided that the arguments I'd put forward weren't convincing and that the agrarian policy practised up to that point would continue. At most we would have to cut down or cancel the deficits of production cooperatives and that would be that. My reward was that I was withdrawn from the post of deputy minister of agriculture without a bad word being said against me.

So it was a question of successful tactics.

Not at all. It's true I didn't feel comfortable in the ministry and I wanted to leave, but I could also have done the opposite: I could have written that our agrarian policies were absolutely right and should be consistently applied, at best improved; I could have suggested some changes which would have made the system more efficient and tried to get a post in another ministry. I was in that pool, after all, so I had a chance. I could have tried for the post of deputy foreign minister or ambassador, but I didn't want to. I didn't want to and I didn't think about it. At least not then – I'd be lying if I said I never wanted to be an ambassador. Later I'd have liked to; it's nice to travel abroad.

So why in fact did you write that memorandum – which I haven't read, actually, because I couldn't find it anywhere?

Because that's what I thought.

I don't understand. First you valiantly organize the purchase of wheat in the Poznan province, packing thousands of people off to prison, and then literally a few months later you change your mind.

Well, perhaps my eyes were beginning to open? Haven't you thought of that?

I find it difficult.

Writing that memorandum, which totally negates the value of the policies applied until then, took courage, because there was a danger that I would be pushed off the ladder. Especially since my position wasn't all that secure, particularly given my unsuitable origin.

You want to make a fetish out of it.

Well, it's important, especially for the Soviet comrades.

And yet they left you alone.

Apparently there was no reason not to. The comrades decided that I was wrong; that Comrade Staszewski was put off by difficulties, so apparently he must have been incompetent and not very resilient, not seeing the right way or the correct solutions, but not because he is some kind of secret enemy. No, not at all; they didn't see me as a secret enemy that had to be eliminated. Rather they simply came to the conclusion that Staszewski is a person who has questioned our policies (which in itself is not yet a crime) because he doesn't understand them, because he yielded in the face of the difficulties with which he had to cope in his work; but we, by facing those difficulties and overcoming them, will prove that we were right. That's the kind of attitude I encountered. I was told: if you don't want to, then too bad, you'll have to resign. We'd like you to stay on, because you're a good organizer, energetic, decisive, and strong-willed, with excellent insight.

And so they gave you another post, a better one.

Well, yes, shortly afterwards. But before that I met Khrushchev and I must tell you about him. Khrushchev came to Warsaw to persuade us to switch to corn. He had a kind of corn-mania then. So first a meeting of the Politburo was called at which he made a speech proposing that our economic plans be revised and demanding that two million hectares of land be allotted to corn in the following year's plan. Utter despair descended.

Impossible.

I'm telling you, utter despair descended. Even Minc was completely crushed. He said: this is a disaster; we'll be short of those two million hectares for wheat and there will be hunger. Bargaining and negotiations of some kind began and the Central Committee was summoned to an agricultural conference. About two hundred people must have been invited: secretaries of provincial committees for agriculture, employees of departments of agriculture, directors of State Farms' associations, presidents of production cooperatives and representatives of about ten scientific institutes and agricultural academies. Bierut asked me, as a fluent Russian speaker, to sit next to Khrushchev and translate for him what was being said.

Khrushchev came out with his corn programme and strongly encouraged us to go over to cultivating corn throughout the country, indeed by the following year. First two million hectares, he said, and then more, and you'll see for yourselves what a boon it is. A discussion broke out after his speech and that was when disaster struck. Everyone, directors and professors alike, began to oppose the proposal and assert that it was absolutely impossible, because the soil was wrong and the climate was wrong and that corn is known and even cultivated in some regions in Poland on a small scale, for grain, and in some places a variant of it, the so-called horse's tooth, for fodder, but only in small quantities because it is not a worthwhile crop on a large scale – a waste of grain and a waste of land. I remember the remarks of Professor Lekczynska, a Central Committee member from the Institute of Plant Cultivation and Acclimatization; she said she was very surprised that something like this was being proposed in Poland, as if Polish scholars and agronomists were illiterates, which she assured us was not the case. Khrushchev was sitting beside me and I was translating for him; he got terribly upset by this and at one point, no longer able to contain himself, he burst out at me, completely forgetting where he was and whom he was speaking to: so, you hear that? You hear what they're saying? That's Poles for you: they always think they know everything better than we do! It's incredible! They mean to tell me I don't know anything about it and they do; that's so Polish.

Then he realized he'd said something he shouldn't have, cooled off and fell silent.

Khrushchev had brought us five sacks of seed, the best seed, as a present, and promised he would send more. Then he went off to some production cooperative, where his corn plan wasn't received with delight, either, and then he got into some kind of conflict with a zootechnician who tried to convince him he didn't really know what he was talking about. Khrushchev was very displeased with it all and thus the corn issue in Poland came to an end. A few hundred thousand hectares of it were included in the plan.

But why did you include any at all?

What do you mean, "you"? It was Minc!

All right, so it was a colleague, but why?

It will console you to know that nothing ever came of this corn business, anyway.

You mean everyone cheated?

That's right, everyone cheated. For the sake of peace and quiet they allotted not 2,000,000 but 500,000 hectares in the plan, but only 100,000 were cultivated.

But why cultivate any at all? I don't understand the reasoning behind it.

It's very simple. Khrushchev was being insistent, so there was no point in battling with him: we include a bit in the plan and it won't be done anyway, but at least appearances will be kept up, and next year we'll see.

Did Bierut also think you should plant it?

Bierut thought that above all we should do as we're told. He wasn't convinced of the value of corn, but he was convinced that one couldn't oppose the comrades from the CPSU, and especially not Khrushchev. And he also thought there was no point in provoking a clash and getting into a conflict over a trifling matter.

It would have escalated into a conflict?

For Khrushchev everything was potentially the beginning of a conflict – not in the sense of intervention, but a conflict. Especially since he was utterly convinced that corn was a cure for all ills; he really was convinced of it. It was in this way that he also plainly aggravated the crisis in Soviet agriculture.

A system of total deceit, with everyone deceiving everyone else to more important or less important ends. My God, how depraving.

You're quite right, because in the end people begin to believe in the rightness of things they'd only a moment ago considered wrong and indeed disastrous. That was what happened with the Polish "Ursus" tractor and the Polish "Warszawa" car, and it happened with many other things. At the beginning we'd been convinced that these undertakings were useless; later, people gradually began saying that perhaps they weren't so bad after all; later still they were claiming it was a very good idea; and finally they were claiming that people who were opposed to the project had a sneaking distrust of Soviet technology and scientific thought, and drew very far-reaching personal and political conclusions from this. The whole plan for the industrialization of Poland was based on extremely backward Soviet technology and was thereby doomed to failure from the start.

Billions had already gone down the drain. But you couldn't oppose it because it was difficult; and you also couldn't oppose it because if you tried you immediately took on terrible political hues. The argument went like this: you have no faith in the leading role of Soviet science and technology and Soviet industry, and if that's so, then what's your position, whose side are you on?

That's the way it was, and I suspect still is today, to a large degree. I'll give you another example, at the same time another anecdote about Khrushchev. I'm not sure exactly when, but I think it was at the sixth plenum in 1956 that Khrushchev was describing how times had changed when he came to power and how different he was from Stalin. You know, he said, when Stalin was alive I was the secretary for Moscow, for Moscow oblast, and I had a chief agronomist. One day we got into an argument and he told me at one point that I knew nothing about agriculture. Can you believe it? *I* didn't understand anything about agricultural economy! He actually claimed I didn't understand it! He actually said that. Well, of course I could have done anything I wanted with him, I could have destroyed him, I could have arranged it so that, you know, he would disappear from the face of the earth. But I didn't. Instead I said to him: get out, out of Moscow, and don't ever let me see your face around here again. That was all, and he went off to Siberia.

Do you understand? He, Khrushchev, considered that throwing someone out of Moscow and sending him to Siberia was a display of kindness and humanity, because he could have locked him up, murdered him, destroyed him, but he didn't, that's what a good person he was.

And you went around applauding him, happy that there was no danger of another Siberia for you.

Well yes, we did applaud him, but what was important was that he met with opposition here.

On the issue of corn.

Yes, he met with opposition on the issue of corn, and the important thing was that it wasn't only the peasants who had no intention of following his orders but even party members as well.

A victory indeed.

Of course it was a victory. It wasn't for no reason that Khrushchev said: that's Poles for you. None of them have any love for Poles, and above all they have no love for the Polish readiness to pick a fight and the possible resistance they're liable to encounter here; after all, there's never been a period when everyone here obeyed them and treated them like an oracle. After the November conference in 1954 and the third plenum in January 1955 this resistance became plainly visible.

In September 1955 the Politburo resolved that I would become first secretary of the Warsaw Committee, replacing Stanislaw Pawlak, later a member of the Natolin faction and an extremely primitive, dogmatic and doctrinaire type who was unable to cope with the Warsaw organization, the Warsaw activists and in particular with the intelligentsia. For we had entered a period when comrades were beginning to take a critical look at their own and their party's past and to wonder whether the party had acted rightly. When you have a feudal party which demands uncritical faith and obedience such a period is called a crisis in the party. History teaches us that rarely do such discussions arise from within the party's own bosom; rather they mature under pressure from non-party circles. For the fact is that a party member sees and understands practically nothing of the circles within which he normally lives. I say practically, because it would be hard for him not to see anything at all, hard not to see his children, his family, his colleagues from work; but these surroundings do not trouble him. A party member knows what is being said when the party is criticized, but he can always say: it wasn't me, it was the party. But when the mistakes and absurdities pile up and grow to a stage where they reach the limit of society's tolerance, then the party member's circle of family and friends will no longer ask him the reasons for this or that, but will instead start jabbing at him and pointing out specific cases of nonsense and idiocy, so that he can no longer defend himself in a rational or effective way. The profundity of the party's crisis is measured by the level of acuteness of the jabs that are made at him.

And what about communists? What does a communist think at a time like that? Assuming he's an ideological one, of course, and that he joined the party in order to realize the slogans of social justice.

The paths of those people are undoubtedly more complicated. Many of them took the path designated by the party in the belief that it was the only way to realize the ideals of their youth. Of course it turned out to be rather different from the way they'd imagined it in the past, harder and dirtier, so to speak, when it came to real life, but it was the path that was supposed to lead to the goal of their dreams. It wasn't easy to abandon this belief, for what would it mean to do so? It would mean breaking with the past, crossing out your whole life, and admitting that the dictatorship of the proletariat is not the way to socialism and democracy. The histories of false ideologies, which lead to terrible self-destruction and to the total destruction of everything near them, are actually quite well documented; so communism isn't something entirely new.

But what is it in practice, not in theory?

It's the rule of the minority over the majority. The restructuring of society against the wishes of the population. Forcing people to maintain the official doctrine as the only correct one, binding for all. Absolute intolerance towards other social and political conceptions. Finally, communism means deprivation of liberty: depriving people of their fundamental civil liberties and of the freedom to decide their own fate and that of the society in which they live. Lenin was the one who began to introduce these principles, while Stalin proceeded to develop this sytem, to strengthen it and perhaps even to modify it –

– to improve it.

Oh yes! So I'm not claiming that Stalinism is an exact replica of Leninism or even its continuation. Stalinism really is something new in Leninism [laughter], and perhaps that's why it has proved so lasting. The conceptual system, the system of proceeding and the system of rule formulated by Stalin in the *Problems of Leninism*, or in his excellent work, *The Foundations of Leninism*, and later introduced and developed in practice, has been retained almost in its entirety to this day. Of course, it's been somewhat amended, but then, after all, when Stalin was in power there were also various stages of intensified terror, somewhat lesser terror, terror that destroyed the whole of society and terror that only destroyed a part of it.

The screw was simply tightened, loosened, unscrewed and screwed in, but it always remained in place.

That's right.

And in 1955 it started to be just a little bit loosened?

That year was the beginning of a thaw, or in party language a period of crisis, when discussions broke out, and in these discussions the Warsaw party organization took the lead. I was summoned either by Bierut or by Alster, the head of the organizational department, I forget which one of them it was, and was told that the Politburo had decided to transfer Pawlak to the Warsaw provincial authorities and to recommend me for the post of first secretary of Warsaw, which was tantamount to nominating me. Then someone from the Central Committee took me to a meeting of the Warsaw Committee, where this resolution was approved.

In other words, an election was held.

That's right, of course – an election. For clarity's sake: elections in a mafia aren't democratic and elections in a gang aren't democratic, because it, the mafia, isn't democratic, and a gang is the negation of democracy.

So you were nominated first gangster of Warsaw.

Please, just don't ask me again whether I knew. I knew, and I didn't resist it. I could have represented other political conceptions, I could have supported democratic elections, but I knew full well that genuinely democratic elections could never take place in an abnormal party.

In a normal party you might not have been so lucky.

Sweetie, I'm perfectly well aware of that. I don't want to imply that God inspired someone or made them see the light or performed a miracle; I'm just saying that's what happened and it was a stroke of luck for me. Presumably I had characteristics that influenced the choice. People probably said about me that I was one of the intelligentsia, a good organizer and knew how to talk to people.

And a good communist, tried and tested in battle.

Certainly; no one had the slightest doubt as to that. And the situation in Warsaw was complicated; it required someone who would be acceptable to very different and varied circles, someone more open that Pawlak. Hence the conclusion that Comrade Staszewski ought to be able to manage in Warsaw.

What was your programme?

Well, the programme crystallized gradually; it wasn't drawn up at a desk but developed in a more spontaneous and sometimes dynamic way.

But what did you want to achieve?

I wanted to develop closer and stronger, firmer relations with the great factories and the big schools, mainly the universities.

In order to control them?

No, not so much to control them as to breathe some life into the organizations themselves, so that they might set the tone for the Warsaw organization.

Those are pretty words, but let's get down to the crux of the matter: you went "into Warsaw" to impose order and method, and order and method has always meant the same thing.

Not for me, and the facts bear that out. I was the one who began to introduce new people into the Warsaw Committee: I also brought in many people from the factories. This led to an inevitable conflict with the permanent staff of the Warsaw Committee apparatus and the apparatus of district committees; it was faint and not much in evidence at first, but later it began to take the form of a political conflict. The apparatus, formed and shaped in the Bierut period, was conservative and dogmatic, and unwilling to renounce the position it had attained in party life. Unwilling and in fact unable to.

But you were also a product of the apparatus.

That's true, but even though I'd been part of the party apparatus I opposed its monopolistic and hegemonistic role in the life of the party. That was what my dissent, my apostasy, consisted of: that although I was the product of that apparatus I also in some sense opposed it. Indeed, I was opposed above all to the way in which the party apparatus saw its role and to the fact that it prevented those things which came from below – from big factories, enterprises and schools – and which in my view brought life, vigour and creativity to the party, from breaking through to the surface of political life.

In your view, or in fact?

At that time in fact. People said what they wanted and what they considered important. Party members, instead of blindly obeying, were beginning increasingly to use their own powers of reasoning.

That year, 1956, was the beginning of your great period, some people think your only good period. It began in March, did it not, at the sixth plenum?

No, before that. Do you know that a great conference was held during the sixth plenum, lasting three days, I think, in the course of which Bierut died?

Perhaps we could begin at the beginning. First there was the Twentieth Congress of the CPSU.

A Polish delegation attended the Congress. I don't know whether it was actually while it was in progress or directly afterwards that Bierut began to feel ill, and it turned out that he had a temperature. The delegation came back with the news that Bierut had flu with complications and had therefore remained behind. Then the flu developed into pneumonia. We didn't have the patience to wait for Bierut to come back before hearing the report from the Twentieth Congress, and demanded that a conference be called. Rumours had already begun leaking through to Central Committee members and party activists that something important had happened there. So Central Committee members began demanding a report from the delegation, and indeed within a few days a conference of the central party activists was called – not a plenum, because we were waiting for Bierut for that – in which about 70 to 100 people took part. It was thought that a general report on the Congress and Khrushchev's speech would be enough to satisfy their curiosity for the moment. It was not to be, however. From the one day intended for it the conference grew into an affair of several days, in the course of which everything took a ferocious bashing. The leadership gave a rough account of what Khrushchev had said about Stalin, and we naturally took advantage of the opportunity to have a chat about Stalinism in Poland. Some people spoke several times; I myself took the floor about three times. Passions became inflamed and a great attack was launched against Bierut and the whole leadership.

Did Berman preside over the conference?

Certainly on the first day, but I don't remember whether he also did on the following days. At any rate he was there throughout. As I later found out, transcripts of this conference were sent off to Moscow, to Bierut, every day. Khrushchev told me about them when he came to Warsaw for Bierut's funeral. I said to Khrushchev then: we consider that Bierut is also responsible for what happened here and that the leadership should thoroughly elucidate these matters and the extent of its own responsibility for them. Whereupon Khrushchev replied, almost word for word: we had full confidence in Bierut. And then, half-jokingly: there was an absolute cult of Bierut. And I'll tell you something else about Bierut, he said, pointing his finger at me: it was you who killed Bierut.

What do you mean, I killed Bierut, I said, surprised. I never killed anyone.

And Khrushchev said: no, it was you who killed Bierut, because this is what happened – and here he told me the following story: we were ill; Bierut was ill and I was ill, we were both in bed and we constantly telephoned each other. (At this point Khrushchev proudly stressed: only I was tough and he was weak, so I got better and he died, and we've just buried him.) And this is what happened: every day Bierut would receive transcripts from the conference you'd organized here; he was horrified by what was happening and would ring me up to give me accounts of it. He also read your speech to me. Comrade Bierut was of the opinion that you hadn't understood the Twentieth Congress.

I asked Khrushchev: well, is that true? Did we really fail to understand it?

He replied: I won't go into how you understood it, but the fact is that Comrade Bierut got so upset about it while he was ill that at some point he suffered a heart attack. He had pneumonia and he wasn't going to pull out of it, but at some point he did suffer a heart attack and you're to blame.

Now I hear that there are no transcripts of that conference and never were. That's a lie. They're there somewhere, here or there, I don't know, but they do exist somewhere, hidden away. Everything's hidden away, because the party is ashamed of its history.

So finally we know who killed Bierut; there was so much speculation.

It's hard to live with the consciousness that by my speech I could have had a hand in someone's death. That's not how it was intended, but it's true it could have happened that way, with Bierut getting upset, and since he was weak after his flu and his pneumonia . . .

Because of course you spoke more sharply than anyone.

I spoke about Bierut's responsibility and about the responsibility of the leadership, and about how it was not just a question of Stalin but of the system as well. It sounded terrible at the time, absolutely monstrous.

And did Berman try to justify himself?

It was a very inadequate sort of justification. Berman had already been attacked by us earlier, and at this conference I attacked him again. So he knew I was against him and wasn't shocked by my speech, but a day or two after the conference he rang me up and asked if I could drop round to see him. He was still in the Politburo, as yet untouched. I went round. He asked why I had launched such a sharp and categorical attack against him. I said, well, I'm afraid that's how it is; you know everything you've done deserves condemnation. Especially since you knew that the accusations you made against many people were false accusations. Gomulka, for instance, and Spychalski, and that whole rigged-up affair of Tatar's trial: you knew that it had no basis in fact, that it didn't hang together, and yet you sent people to their death while knowing it wasn't true; you handed your friends and acquaintances over to the police. Well, you have to answer for that. I used words like "betrayed" and "sold".

Berman was weeping – I'd never seen him in such a state before – and he said, sobbing: I also went about with a noose around my neck; I knew that sooner or later I'd go to the gallows.

I'm not destined for the role of confessor who hands out absolution, and I felt very uncomfortable in it, so I said: yes, I believe that; everyone had a noose around his neck, especially since history has confirmed that we were on the verge of a new great purge on the scale of 1937, or perhaps ever greater. But even if you have a noose around your neck that's not sufficient reason to sentence innocent people to death; no one can be excused by the fact that he was at risk himself. And that was the end of my conversation with Berman.

Berman, too. First Bierut, then Berman – not bad.

Berman was totally discredited; he had to go. But still neither his departure nor that of Radkiewicz is any reason to draw general conclusions about an absolute change in politics or government. This system simply exchanges the used parts of the apparatus and replaces them either with new ones or with the old ones in new packaging. Often people who are thrown out don't know exactly why they got thrown out, but they understand that the party has to suffer some losses, and they're ready to sacrifice themselves for it. Naturally, they think removing them is a mistake, since after all they served the party faithfully and guarded its strength and unity, but they understand that in a difficult social situation the party sometimes has to yield to the pressure of society's demands and make it appear that it's embarking on a new course. And a new course requires new people and new faces. So they leave, considering it a sacrifice offered up on the altar of the party, and are ready to return when the party summons them. That's just how it was with Gomulka.

Gomulka wasn't a new figure, but society was looking for him (the party didn't begin looking for him until much later). Polish society knew it wouldn't be able to get rid of communist government, so it looked about for a communist with – as it thought – a more human face. For Gomulka's later fate wiped from people's minds the memory of what he had been until 1948 or 1949. People forgot that Gomulka had been a tougher and more consistent communist than either Bierut or Berman, and they forgot that he bore equal or even greater responsibility for what happened in Poland from 1944 onwards. On the other hand they remembered that he'd been dismissed by those Stalinists whom they despised, as a result of some not too clearly defined conflicts, and that these Stalinists had put him in prison. Polish society has always had a liking for martyrs, so it had to glorify Gomulka as well. An extraordinary situation arose: Gomulka didn't want to push his way into power – society wanted to push him into it. Initially he was happy to be released from prison at last and able to relax a bit. I doubt that he'd been thinking about returning to power, but when he saw that there was a crisis, a general social, economic and political crisis, he decided that his time had come and began preparing himself for the role.

The coffin containing Bierut arrived from Moscow by train, open and accompanied by Soviet generals. Bierut's portrait was carried ahead and behind it the open coffin, with the head lying on a pillow; it was a horrible sight.

Finally there was the funeral. A group of us met at the cemetery – myself, Matwin, Morawski, Kole, Starewicz and Zambrowski – and we decided to get in touch with Gomulka. We delegated Starewicz and Morawski to do this. We had initially wanted Albrecht and Morawski, but Albrecht thought his relations with Gomulka weren't good enough, so perhaps he shouldn't, while Starewicz is the kind of guy who's right for any kind of job, and when he'd sniffed out the advantages he'd get from it, he accepted readily.

Did the "Pulawy" group meet at the cemetery?

There was no such group. There was the "Natolin" group and then there was everyone else – the people who firmly dissociated themselves from it.

Still, it's thought that the "Pulawy" group existed.

It didn't. It never existed. The name came from the fact that Klosiewicz, in order to defend himself against the charge of creating a "Natolin" faction within the party, retorted that the "Natolin" was not the only such group, because there was also a "Pulawy" group, which met at 24–26 Pulawska Street, a building inhabited by Kasman, Werfel and Mazur, but also for a while by Kliszko – by very different people, in other words, and if anything linked them it was only this: that they were all firm opponents of the "Natolin" group. But even this opposition sprang from different motives and views and was maintained by them with varying consistency.

That's enough for a start.

But you can't build a programme on that basis. The exact situation was this: there was a strong "Natolin" group – conservative, opposed to any kind of change, in favour of maintaining the status quo, and often supported informally by various people from the state administration and the economic apparatus, who were by definition hostile to reforms or democratization of any kind; and then there was the rest – a bunch of little groups. That's how I would describe those divisions. I consider myself a member of my own group, the Warsaw Committee; the people I was close to were the people with whom I worked in the Warsaw Committee executive. I never visited Kasman, Werfel or Mazur in Pulawska Street. I once sat with Kasman at some kind of conference, either the November one in 1954 or the third plenum in January 1955; it was purely coincidental. Radkiewicz made a speech in which he talked about abuses in security, and I said to Kasman: well, how about it, do we take the floor? Let's go ahead. I'm putting my name down, and you sign up as well. So we each wrote a note to the presidium, and both of us made speeches that were very similar in tone, without in any way consulting with each other beforehand about what we were going to say. Our speeches caused a fantastic row. We warmed to our task and spoke once more – I think I even spoke twice more – and there was a big to-do, but Kasman and I hadn't agreed anything on any subject. Sure, we'd talk and exchange all sorts of stories when we met at various plenums, but it had nothing to do with the existence or creation of any kind of group.

The "Natolin" group, however, did exist, although for a long, long time we knew nothing of its existence. We heard about it when someone spotted Nowak, Zawadzki, Klosiewicz and several others having dinner together at the Council of Ministers building in Natolin, and he told us: listen, Zawadzki's organizing dinners with a select little group.

Cyrankiewicz had probably known about it much earlier because he went to Natolin every day – there was good food and fine wine, which he liked, and he treated the Natolin villa almost as if it were his own house – but he didn't tell us about it. Naturally, he didn't take part in Zawadzki's dinners, but still he didn't tell us – typical of him. It took someone else, who just happened to be there and see it. And that's when it was revealed that Zawadzki, who saw himself as a potential successor to Bierut, had decided to surround himself with a select group of people and establish political relations with them.

On the instigation of the Soviet Union?

I know for sure it was on Zawadzki's own initiative. I suspect it was at these little gatherings that they started talking about the yiddification of the party and state apparatus, because you could tell that from the speeches they made, and those took place in – please note – 1955 and thus after Swiatlo's defection and after the November conference, at which the security apparatus came under criticism. They probably also agreed on the tactics of cleaning up the apparatus in such a way as to escape responsibility themselves, and decided the best thing to do would be to shove the responsibility onto – well, who do you think? – the Jews, of course.

Didn't the Jews resist this?

No, because you see the Jews were one group which didn't feel threatened at all. People from security might have felt threatened, but I myself, for example, had nothing to do with them. I didn't see Mietkowski or Rozanski for years at a stretch, and nor did other people with whom I worked.

The "Natolin" group was the most aggressive, the most vigorous and the best organized – a sort of mixture of "Grunwald" and the "Katowice Forum".

In other words they were agents?

Certainly some of them were. I think Klosiewicz was connected with the Soviet embassy, Nowak definitely was, and so was Witaszewski, by the very nature of his work.

What about Zawadzki?

I have my own private opinion about Aleksander Zawadzki – I would reply positively, that he was. In my opinion he began when he became director of the so-called army group in the KPP, the section assigned to subversion in the Polish army, and by reason of this function alone he must have had some links with Soviet intelligence and counter-intelligence. It couldn't have been otherwise, for that section wasn't under the control of the KPP. Because of his activities in the army group Zawadzki was arrested and sentenced before the war; later, near the end of the war, he was chief of the Partisan Staff in Minsk. He had Soviet officers under his command, at least formally, and I've no doubt at all that the Staff, officially overseeing partisan activities within Poland, was in fact connected with Soviet intelligence and counter-intelligence and with clandestine agents placed in various posts. Stanislaw Wronski was also there.

Ochab proposed Zawadzki for the post of first secretary.

I think he only did that for two reasons: out of genuine modesty and because he really didn't want to be first secretary himself. And in his eyes Zawadzki had all the qualities for the job: he was an old communist, a man used to fieldwork, devoted to the party, and he'd spent eight years in a Polish prison.

That was true of Zambrowski as well.

Zambrowski's candidacy was never a possibility, for one thing because Zambrowski was a Jew. It's true that no statute forbids it, but it was just self-evident that that would be going too far. Thus Minc or Berman, for instance, could never have been first secretary. At least formally, the limits of the posts they could take up were determined from the outset.

The sixth plenum began on 20 March 1956, with Khrushchev's speech, which he summarized, adding a few very piquant details from Stalin's life – among other things how Stalin had murdered his brother-in-law and driven his wife to her death. I found out about the circumstances of Alliluyeva's death while I was still in Moscow; rumour had it then that she had shot herself after some kind of fight with Stalin, and this information was considered reliable. Voroshylov was very pained by this and is alleged to have said publicly that everyone found Stalin insufferable, he was so obnoxious. But I hadn't known about the murder of the brother-in-law, a murder executed in an underhand, terribly Eastern way, until Khrushchev talked about it.

A recess was called after Khrushchev's speech in the hope that he would avail himself of the opportunity to say goodbye and leave. As it was we were surprised that he stayed for the plenum at all; we'd assumed that the first secretary of a great party didn't have too much time on his hands and that he would leave directly after Bierut's funeral. Khrushchev, however, announced that he wasn't leaving and would stay for the second half of the plenum as well. The recess was to be a long one, lasting about two hours, because of the continuing deluded hope that Khrushchev would leave; we went out into the corridor and I went up to him and asked, on behalf of several comrades, whether we could have a talk. Khrushchev said, certainly, when? I replied, let's go now, and he said, fine.

Behind the Central Committee conference hall, where most meetings take place, there are separate rooms used as secretariats and lounges. We chose one of these and sat down. There were five of us; later Hilary Minc also joined us.

I asked him: will you have something to eat? No, said Khrushchev, I'll just have some tea. So we all asked for tea.

I asked Khrushchev whether it was true that Stalin's death had interrupted preparations for a great purge. I added that it was not my intention to question the fact that his death had been a natural one, but that we had heard something about the doctors' trial.

Khrushchev said yes, he didn't mind telling us about that. And he began:

"There was no doubt in our minds that we were all in danger, because Stalin was preparing another purge. The trial of the Kremlin doctors was provoked by Stalin, and Lydia Timashuk, who testified to their guilt, was a tool manipulated by his people. Of course, there were more tools like her. The death of Kirov was also a provocation, and we still don't have all the details of his death. Stalin didn't like Jews."

Whereupon I said, "That's true, he was an anti-Semite."

"What did you say?" Khrushchev asked.

"Well, you know, he was an anti-Semite," I said.

"Well yes, something like that," said Khrushchev, "but it's not that simple, my friends." And he began to explain it to us:

"Stalin was a great revolutionary and a distinguished Marxist. Everything he planned was done with the revolution in mind and in the light of whether or not it would be ideologically advantageous for world revolution. And now imagine the following situation. After the war we had displaced the Tatars from Crimea. I won't go into the whys and wherefores of it now, but the fact was that Crimea became deserted. At that point comrades from the Anti-Fascist Jewish Committee, a committee created during the war, came to see Stalin. The group consisted of Ilya Ehrenburg, the famous Jewish actor Michoels, comrade Frumkina, and Lozovksy, who was then secretary general of the trade unions' international. They suggested to Stalin that Crimea be used as a place in which to resettle Jews from Byelorussia and the Ukraine who had survived the Nazi occupation. Stalin understood all the dangers that threatened our world, so his reasoning on the matter was as follows: the spokesmen for the

Anti-Fascist Committee represent Jews, and we all know about Jews: they all have some connection with the capitalist world because they all have relatives living abroad. This one has a granny, that one has an auntie, that one a grandpa. And Stalin thought: the Cold War is beginning, the imperialists are plotting how to attack the Soviet Union, and these Jews want to settle in Crimea. You understand," Khrushchev explained, "here's Crimea and here's Baku and the oil basin. So Stalin's conclusion was that through their connections the Jews had created a network of agents to carry out America's plan of attack on the Soviet Union, and that Crimea would be the base for an American attack. So he squashed it all – well, you know the story. Michoels was the victim of a street accident, run over by a car; Lozovsky, Frumkina and others were shot; only Ehrenburg was left alive. Stalin was very fond of Ehrenburg."

"Quite," I said. "Stalin was an absolute, rabid anti-Semite."

"Well, no," said Khrushchev, "that's not quite true." When discussing any issue, Khrushchev would always begin by saying that Stalin was a great Marxist and revolutionary, and it was as if he was teasing me and quibbling on purpose: what did you say? An anti-Semite? Well, yes, it was something like that.

"At the end of 1952," he said, "Stalin called us together and told us to organize groups of armed men."

At this point Khrushchev broke off. I said, "What for?"

"Well, to kill," Khrushchev replied.

"To kill whom?" I asked.

"Well, Jews," he said.

I asked, "You mean he wanted a pogrom?"

"Well, yes, something like that," he said.

We all felt a chill run down our spines, and Khrushchev went on:

"But you know, it was a difficult business for me, because my father, an illiterate miner, took pride in the fact that he hadn't taken part in the Jewish pogroms organized by the tsar in 1905–7 in the Ukraine. And when Stalin started to talk about planning pogroms I thought to myself: how can I, his son, in my high position, go around organizing groups of armed men?"

A silence fell on the room, and then I committed a great indiscretion, for I asked him, "And what did you decide, Nikita Sergeyevich?"

Khrushchev looked perfectly pleased with this question and said: "Well, you know that Stalin fell ill and died shortly after that, and not long afterwards, at the first meeting of the Politburo after his death, we resolved to release the doctors and submit their case to revision. Not all of them, of course, because by then some had died."

There's just one thing Khrushchev didn't say, and that is that the motion to release the Kremlin doctors was put by Beria – an incredibly smart and cunning and quite unusual man, and also a great criminal, almost as great as his boss. Almost, because no one could outdo the boss. After Stalin's death, Beria realized that the era had come to an end and that somehow he would have to do an about-turn. Which he did, but Khrushchev passed over his name. He said, "We later rehabilitated those doctors."

"Not all of them," I said.

"You're right," said Khrushchev, "not all of them; after all we had a certain nationalities policy." And he started talking about it in a way which almost made us fall off our chairs. Minc came up to stand beside me and said in a terrified whisper, "Stop it, for God's sake stop talking to him, he doesn't understand anything! Stop!"

"What kind of policy?" I nevertheless asked Khrushchev, "because we heard there was a *numerus clausus*, a quota, at your universities."

"And what about you?" Khrushchev asked, "what quota do you have?"

"We haven't got one," I replied.

"Yes, well then, Comrade Staszewski, tell me," he said, "how many Jews do you have here?"

"I don't know."

"What do you mean, you don't know? Come on, how many have you got in the Warsaw organization?"

"I really don't know," I said, "it never interested me. I don't know who thinks of himself as a Jew and who doesn't. We never concerned ourselves with that."

"It never interested you?" Khrushchev said; "well, it should. In the Soviet Union we have 2 per cent, which means that ministries, universities – everything – is made up of 2 per cent Jews. You should know that."

"We thought calculations of that kind were contrary to revolutionary ideology," I said.

Khrushchev said, "No, that's not true. I'm not an anti-Semite," he hastened to add, "indeed we have this minister who's a Jew; he's a good minister, Dimschitz is his name, and we respect him, but you have to know the limits."

Well, how many Jews were *there in the Warsaw party organization?*

I really don't know. No one counted.

The recess came to an end, we returned to the conference hall, and the Politburo proposed Ochab for the post of first secretary. Everyone thought this candidacy was the only right one. I suspect Khrushchev had counted on Aleksander Zawadzki becoming first secretary, but he quickly reconciled himself to the new one and made no objections. And for all Ochab's protests at the meeting of the Politburo, at the plenum he accepted his election as a *fait accompli*, and recognized with a soldier's obedience to duty that he would have to shoulder new responsibilities. He's the kind of person who, when a decision has been made and a resolution passed, thinks that the only proper thing to do is to submit to it. The Central Committee proceeded to the election of members of the Central Committee secretariat, and this was when we encountered blatant anti-Semitism on the part of the "Natolin" group. To people who were active and involved, and especially to those who had taken part in the conversation with Khrushchev, this came as a shock. The issue of nationality emerged when Zambrowski was put forward as a candidate from the floor.

Why not you?

No, no, working in the apparatus was the last thing I wanted: I've never been hungry for leadership, please believe me.

I don't believe you.

A pity, but never mind. I was happy to find myself heading the Warsaw provincial organization. It meant contacts with all sorts of organizations and factories and being surrounded by lots of people. I like being surrounded by lots of people.

I can see that.

A few days after the plenum we got the full text of Khrushchev's speech at the Twentieth CPSU Congress from the Soviet Union. The Soviet party publishes transcripts from its congresses and plenary sessions in A4 format, printed in two columns on each side and bound in red cardboard. The cover bears the heading: *Sovyershenno Sekretno*; inside there is the title and below it the words, *rozsylaetsya yegerskoy pochtoy*. I was astonished by this term when I saw it for the first time, much earlier, for the form and terminology are ones that were introduced at the time of Tsar Nicholas I. The word *feldyegerskoy* referred to an old military formation which had been transferred to the gendarmerie and was used for the transmission of special mail and top secret documents, and also for escorting prisoners.

It was this kind of folder that Ochab received a few days after the sixth plenum: one copy, numbered. Ochab informed me of its arrival and I at once demanded that the text be made accessible not only to members of the secretariat or the Politburo but to a wider audience as well. Ochab agreed, and Khrushchev's speech was initially placed in one of the Central Committee rooms at the top of the building for people to read. However, it could only be read by members of the Central Committee and editors of the main papers who knew Russian. It was a direct transcript which indicated applause and included interjections from the floor. After a few days the issue of its translation came up, since a lot of Central Committee members knew no Russian. Ochab agreed and a few people translated it; then a few dozen numbered copies were made on the Gestetner and sent off to all the provincial first secretaries, Central Committee members and their deputies, but with the proviso that they should return the copies after reading them. One copy was also sent to the Warsaw Committee. After some hesitation it was agreed by me and a few members of the executive that the speech was an important document which everyone ought to read. We made an official announcement that we would print a run of three thousand numbered copies; unofficially we told the printers to run off fifteen thousand, repeating the numbers, the printers themselves ran off some additional copies on top of that, and thus the seal of silence on Khrushchev's speech was broken. I personally handed a copy, hot off the press, to Philippe Benn, the *Le Monde* correspondent, and to Gruson from the *Herald Tribune* and Flora Lewis from the *New York Times*, three foreign journalists whom I knew and who immediately telexed the text of the speech to the West. In this way I violated all the principles of party discipline; the bomb fell and there was an explosion. Khrushchev tried to deny it all and to claim that the speech was a forgery, and the Central Committee of the French communist party, headed by Thorez, supported him, but it was no good: Khrushchev's speech had become a public secret.

How disloyal.

As you know, they've been refusing me a passport for fourteen years now, and people say it isn't because security has determined to give me a hard time. They tell me: the Soviets have got you marked.

Did you betray them, or disappoint them, or what?

They don't like me. And it's not any kind of irrational dislike, I can assure you. In their eyes I really was doing something terrible. In their view I'd always represented a profoundly misguided revisionist line, and they knew me very well indeed. I remember an astonishing thing that once happened when Mazur and I and one other person went to the airport to welcome Bulganin, on 22 July 1956 – he'd just arrived. We were standing there on the tarmac and Bulganin came down the steps and stretched out his hand to me in greeting, saying: "*Zdrastvuytye*, tovarisch Staszewski, how are things in Warsaw?" He already knew – they must have told him on the plane – that the guy standing between those two others was that man Staszewski from the Warsaw Committee.

It could have been a gesture of friendship, not hostility.

Oh, no, impossible. They were observing me, and if you observe somebody it's always because you suspect him. Besides, the way the situation in Poland was developing was hardly to their liking, and they knew I supported the direction it was taking.

By May 1956 it was already plain to everyone that Ochab was neither able to make up his mind in favour of serious and far-reaching reforms nor capable of coping with the mounting tension in the country, and that things might reach the point where his position as first secretary would no longer be tenable, since the line he represented diverged too much from society's expectations. That was when some of us began to consider the possibility of putting Cyrankiewicz up for the post of first secretary. Apart from him and Rapacki everyone was discredited. And Cyrankiewicz had a beautiful past: Auschwitz, the resistance movement – and he also held very liberal and reformist views. In addition he had many valuable personal and intellectual qualities, and was indisputably an agile politician, intelligent and respected. His PPS past had ceased to be an impediment and could become an advantage in dealing with society, a bridge between society and the party. I talked to Rapacki and Zambrowski about him and they both agreed he was a possible candidate.

Did he have a chance?

Yes. Of course, Poznan ruined his chances, although I thought his speech was more the result of lack of character than of lack of imagination. Those were his instructions, and he carried them out.

Twice.

But the difference between his speech in 1956 and his speech in 1970 was that while in 1956 he probably hadn't yet become aware of what he was participating in, by 1970 he was fully aware of it. In 1956 it was decided not to negotiate, not to attempt to mediate, but to strike out and crush the revolt. Cyrankiewicz followed these directives and made a terrible speech at the cemetery in Poznan, threatening to cut off the hands of those who would raise them against socialism, and he lost face. At that point my plans became outdated.

But surely Cyrankiewicz said no more than what was repeated, perhaps in a less drastic form, at rallies that were called throughout the country – in Warsaw as well. Vandals, hooligans, American agents – the usual stuff.

Of course a lot of condemning was done at the rallies – that's the ritual – but the scope of it was relatively small. The point was rather to implement the party's current line by loudly condemning the Poznan riots, but in fact the tendency in the factories at the time was pro-Poznan. Indeed attempts were made by people from Poznan to make contact with Warsaw, and on the third day of the events delegations from Poznan turned up in some places in the capital. And then, in July, at the sixth plenum, it was resolved that the Poznan workers' protest had been right –

– but that hooligan elements hostile to the system of the PRL had joined it and exploited a justified workers' protest.

How did you know that?

There are simply a few basic phrases that I've committed to memory. Haven't you?

I know them [laughter].

It's autumn. Your good days were still continuing, and a rumour was going around Warsaw to the effect that you were distributing arms. Mr Ochab denied this. He said: he didn't distribute any because he didn't have any.

I didn't, that's true, but only in part. The Internal Security Corps distributed 800 rounds of ammunition and a few machine guns and hand grenades to the workers' militia which had been created in a car factory in a suburb of Warsaw. Various self-defence groups were springing up then in many industrial factories, but that was the only armed group. It was led by a man called Wasik, a veteran of the

Spanish Civil War. The workers in this group were supposed to organize the defence of Warsaw against the Polish troops marching on the capital from Pomerania on the orders of General Huszcza. Soviet troops, independently of this, were also making their way to Warsaw, but since they stationed themselves further away the direct danger came from the Polish troops commanded by General Huszcza. The workers' militia went out to meet them; it had been instructed to disarm the troops politically, and it did: the workers entered the ranks, began to agitate, and the troops did indeed stop. I made that decision without consulting anyone, because I was afraid that Ochab would oppose it.

What kind of scenario did the Russians have planned?

I don't know exactly. But I do know that they anticipated intervening. We found out the details the day before the eighth plenum. The commander of the military district of Warsaw, a Russian general called Andrievsky, had summoned the commanders of all the units situated within the Warsaw garrison and those in the vicinity, together with the army political staff, and held a conference with them in the Citadel. Two officers, a major and a colonel, left while it was in progress and came to see me at the Warsaw Committee. They said that a coup d'état and a plan of arrests were being worked out at the conference. I immediately rang up Ochab, Ochab got in touch with Gomulka, and we held a meeting at about noon, with Ochab, Gomulka, Rokossowski and myself. Ochab broached the matter by saying that Comrade Staszewski here has just brought information to the effect that a conference called by General Andrievsky is in progress at the Citadel, orders which are peculiar to say the least are being issued, and does Rokossowski know anything about this. At first Rokossowski lied and said he didn't. Ochab seemed surprised and said to me that perhaps I'd better check, because surely Comrade Rokossowski would know. I said there was no doubt whatsoever and Comrade Rokossowski had perhaps better consult his memory to make sure he was not mistaken. Whereupon Rokossowski blushed – in general he had a tendency to blush like a young girl and when he was upset he would turn pale and get flushed. And thus, cheeks aflame, Rokossowski said he really had no idea, but that was how it was these days and there was really nothing in the least strange about a commander, who is after all responsible for maintaining law and order in Warsaw, meeting with his officers. So the conference, in his view, could be of a preventive nature, to safeguard against riots and unrest. At that point Gomulka, who all the while had been silent, spoke up, presumably in order to make it clear that he understood what was going on, and said: having troops occupy public sites and buildings is something you do in a state of emergency, Comrade Marshal, as I'm sure you know.

Rokossowski repeated once more that that was how it was these days. Then Ochab remarked: well, then, everything seems to be clear, I don't think we need to explain anything to one another any more, I would just ask the Comrade Marshal to be so kind as to revoke these orders. And the meeting ended.

What was clear?

That Rokossowski wouldn't revoke the orders, because he wasn't the one who had issued them and they hadn't originated here.

That conversation took place at noon, and the following morning Khrushchev arrived with his suite. Units of the Soviet war fleet were sailing up the Polish coast and docking in Gdansk, and Soviet troops, both those within the country and those stationed along the borders, began to march forward. Events succeeded one another with lightning speed: talks with Khrushchev, the eighth plenum, and finally the rally in Procession Square. I wanted to call one immediately, thinking that we should take advantage of the mood of euphoria which had swept Warsaw, but Gomulka opposed this. He said: the masses are excited, they're fired up, we shouldn't be hasty. He didn't want a rally at all, he didn't like rallies.

How could he not like them, when they're an element of the ideology?

Not all of them, though; not all of them.

What kind of rallies are good?

The Gierek rallies were good, especially in Katowice. People would shout: Gie-rek, par-ty, par-ty, Gie-rek, na-tion, par-ty. That kind of rally is good. Spontaneous rallies, on the other hand, when you never know what's going to happen, are useless.

But surely they would have shouted Go-mul-ka on Procession Square just as before they had shouted Sta-lin and Bie-rut; wasn't that clear?

It was clear that they would shout Go-mul-ka, but it wasn't at all clear that they would also shout par-ty. Gomulka was scared. He was scared that the wave of unrest would burst and overflow into new forms and shapes which he could not predict, let alone control. And he was scared of anti-Soviet sentiment. He said clearly: we have to wait, the masses are restless. And in any case he didn't need that rally. He knew he already had power, that he had won the day; he didn't need people shouting as well. And it must be said, incidentally, that he wasn't vain. Of course he didn't dislike hearing people shouting in his honour, everyone likes that, but he wasn't particularly anxious for that kind of thing. Unlike Gierek.

But the Warsaw Committee insisted that Gomulka appear before the people and tell them what had happened, and after lengthy battles and urgings Gomulka finally agreed. The rally was to take place on Wednesday, ten days after the eighth plenum. During those ten days Gomulka never stopped ringing me up to ask whether we could guarantee that it would go well and was constantly asking: will we have a riot or won't we, will we – won't we.

Before the rally he asked me whether I intended to speak. I said yes, I'd open the rally with a short speech. He didn't like that; he wanted his speech to be the only one made at the rally. He jumped at me: what exactly do you intend to say, anyway? I lied and said I wasn't sure yet, as I wasn't about to start confessing to him. I'll give a brief opening speech, I added, and say a few words about what we've achieved and what we must protect. Gomulka, who'd always been suspicious as hell, opposed this and said, no, I'll do that. I said that in that case I didn't see why I should be there at all. "You," he dictated, "will open it."

What did you want to say?

Five, ten sentences. I hadn't written them yet but I'd thought them through: we have achieved something called the possibility of self-determination, which means that from now on we will determine what Poland is to be and what roads Polish socialism will take. This is our greatest achievement, and it is you – here I wanted to address the audience – who must safeguard it, who must protect it, all of you who are here.

That's pure demagoguery.

No, that was the only thing to say. I didn't want to talk about the Soviet Union or to make any promises, just to bring out that possibility of self-determination.

What did you finally end up saying?

People of Warsaw, I hereby open this rally and I ask Comrade Wieslaw to speak.

Is that all?

I'm afraid so. Masses of people, a sea of faces, three o'clock in the afternoon on Wednesday, 24 October. Between 300,000 and 500,000 people. We went through the underground passage from the Palace of Culture. Rokossowski began pushing his way through to the tribune: he was very anxious to be up there along with the members of the Politburo. I started to be afraid that something would happen when he got close to the barrier: the crowd might charge at the tribune or start throwing something at him. He was tall and thus very visible. I came up to him and said, Marshal, please go back, but he didn't understand me. And as a soldier he wasn't in the habit of turning back, so he asked: why? I said: please, Comrade Rokossowski, I really would ask you to turn back, this auditorium isn't for you. He returned to the back rows, pale and with clenched lips.

There were banners and red-and-white flags, and for the first time signs supporting and expressing solidarity with the struggle of the Hungarians; there were particularly such signs near the tribune. Gomulka was terribly, frightfully anxious. He declared: enough of rallying, let this be the first and the last. To work!

The crowd started chanting: Spy-chal-ski! Spychalski, after all, was the other persecuted one, and could be contrasted with the Moscow man who, because of his tallness, was still visible. A roar went up: Spy-chal-ski! I told Spychalski to say something. He was put out by this and resisted, but finally he spoke, and it was embarrassing. He'd never been a good speaker, but this time he was dreadful. He mumbled and stuttered and I felt sincerely sorry for him. He stopped after a few minutes and I breathed a sigh of relief.

It was beginning to get dark, and suddenly there was more chanting: Wy-szyn-ski! Wy-szyn-ski! Gomulka anxiously asked me what they were shouting. "They're shouting 'Wyszynski'," I said.

He said, "Dissolve the rally, then."

I dissolved it. People began to disperse but a whole crowd of them still remained, about 70,000. And this mass of people started shouting slogans in support of Wyszynski. "Wyszynski to the Buro," they chanted. Meaning the Politburo, of course, which to us sounded paradoxical, but it reflected the mood of the people. Gomulka, shaking and white as a sheet, ran off to the Palace of Culture and drove to the Central Committee. I was left on the square with Gozdzik, the first secretary of the committee at the car factory outside Warsaw. We tore our way through the crowds of demonstrators to a building where a small, improvised broadcasting station had been set up on the fifth floor. Gozdzik called for calm and asked people to disperse, which they began to do. I went back to the Warsaw Committee. Here, in front of the building, I met a handful of writers: they'd come to defend the committee. It must have been Putrament's idea, because they didn't know who they were supposed to be defending it from. At the committee I was told that the crowd had turned back and was making its way towards the Soviet embassy, and that a rally had been called at the Polytechnic. Gozdzik went off to the Polytechnic, and I asked the workers from the car factory for their help and made my way to where the crowd was.

Wasn't the Internal Security Corps on the alert?

They had a battalion or a company standing by, but this meant nothing in practice. First, the security service didn't mean anything at that time; secondly, we couldn't allow a clash between the demonstrators and the Security Corps; and thirdly, we couldn't allow people to get near the embassy. Besides, if we used the Security Corps the results would be tragic. So that left negotiations. The workers from the car factory arrived with fantastic speed, and we put them in front of the Security Corps unit, which was stationed at the corner of two streets on the way to the embassy. And thus began attempts at persuasion, explanation, cajoling.

Gomulka was shaking by his telephone and rang constantly to ask if I could guarantee that the demonstration wouldn't reach the embassy and produce riots in Warsaw. At one point he got the idea of calling in the army. Don't you dare, I told him, I don't want the army here. People will calm down; they realize they can't riot or demolish the Soviet embassy. He asked me again: can you guarantee it? I guarantee it, I said.

Could you?

Look, a crowd that isn't attacked or provoked will always disperse in the end, however long it takes.

On 4 November a conference took place in the conference hall in the Palace of Culture, and I was increasingly convinced that the October battle was lost and that Gomulka had begun to go back on what he'd said and had no intention of keeping his promises. It was not a successful conference. After that we had a meeting of the

Warsaw Committee which Gomulka attended and at which he subjected the committee to a barrage of shattering criticism. He accused the Warsaw Committee of activities that were – can you guess?

Counter-revolutionary?

No, not yet. First you accuse people of extremism, and only afterwards of being counter-revolutionary; that's the proper order. Gomulka knew the rules of the game, so he decided that the Warsaw Committee was extremism incarnate, saying that its aims and demands were inciting social unrest and unrest in the party, and that the Warsaw Committee was an obstacle to the party's unity and consolidation.

From Gomulka's point of view there was some basis for this, since in the late summer of 1956 we had created a commission whose task was to draw up proposals concerning the role of the party apparatus. The commission was headed by Romana Granas. It drew up a document which proposed, among other things, that the numerical size of the apparatus be reduced by at least two-thirds, that permanent staff be elected at a provincial conference, and that they should be responsible to delegates to that conference and to participants in plenary sessions. The commission's proposals were premissed on the fact that the role of the party apparatus was to serve the party and its members and that it should periodically give an account of its activities. These proposals were accepted by a Warsaw Committee plenum and approved by the executive, whereupon they were forwarded to the Central Committee. There they made a big impression, since this was the first time we had made so clear and blatant an assault on the monopolistic position of the apparatus. Some members of the Politburo approved of the proposals, although they expressed surprise at the report's audacity and doubt about whether it might not have gone too far; others saw them as an attempt to dismantle the party by demolishing something that the party had built up with enormous effort and that it considered its most precious asset – its apparatus. But the most furious resistance came from the apparatus itself. After some time Gomulka, despite his earlier promises and the activities in which he was engaging to give them a semblance of reality, came out on the side of the apparatus.

I knew what would happen then, because Gomulka was an excellent tactician, who never lost sight of his goal, and he was pretty good at planning his political games.

How did he play them out with you?

Very simply: he launched a campaign against the Warsaw Committee, with the participation of his most active supporters: Strzelecki, Moczar, Kliszko and a gang from the army and security, going hand in hand with the "Natolin" group. And you also have to remember that the campaign against the Warsaw Committee was nothing other than a campaign against all we had gained in October, since it was precisely this organization which had had the greatest part in drawing up and launching the October programme.

For the second time Gomulka came to a meeting of the Warsaw Committee. I said I wanted to talk to him and brought some demands with me. I said that it was, after all, the Warsaw organization which, together with Warsaw society, had prepared what had happened in October, and it had done so not only in order to have "Wieslaw" at the head of the party but also in the name of the demands which were not yet fulfilled. I put these demands to him; there were about ten of them. To each of them Gomulka replied: negative. I demanded the creation of freely elected workers' councils. Gomulka was outraged: it risked throwing the state into anarchy. I presented him with the proposal to create a State Tribunal and a Constitutional Tribunal.

"A State Tribunal?" he said, surprised. "That means we would all be putting ourselves in prison, right?"

Finally I brought up the proposal to sign an accord with the Church and dissolve the PAX organization. I said: if we are to negotiate with the Church in order to reach an agreement to be honoured by both sides, that agreement must be honoured above all by us, and to this end the dissolution of PAX is essential, since PAX is a subversive organization created to combat the Church. At this Gomulka said: I know, you'd like to leave me alone with Wyszynski, but I'm not going to do that: I'm not going to make the rope to hang myself with.

This conversation took place in private, just between the two of us, but it left me with no illusions as to what course future events would take and what would happen to me.

And you, hardly a newcomer to political games yourself, were unable to frustrate his plans?

No, I couldn't. And in any case I wouldn't have found anyone to support me: the fascination with Gomulka was so horrific that it's difficult to imagine if you haven't lived through it. Saying anything the slightest bit unfavourable about Gomulka was some kind of inconceivably monstrous crime. Gomulka was given credit, enormous credit without any security – if you read his speeches now, the ones he made at the eighth plenum or at Procession Square, he really promised very little. But still, people invested the enormous burden of their hopes and aspirations in him. Even someone as intelligent as Zawieyski was fascinated with Gomulka, and before the elections to the Sejm in January 1957 tried to persuade Wyszynski that he really should support the elections and join his voice to that of the Politburo in the call to vote without deleting any names on the ballot. There was something the primate didn't like about the election campaign: he suspected dissembling and deceit; but our dear, naive Zawieyski suspected nothing. I saw him a few months later at a July 22nd party at the Council of Ministers' building. He was head of the parliamentary delegates' group "Znak", while I was already editor-in-chief of the Polish Press Agency. We met in the gardens and Zawieyski said:

"Mr Staszewski, do you remember that you and Gomulka signed a promissory note for us in October?"

"But this is July, Mr Zawieyski," I reminded him.

He didn't understand what I was talking about, so I told him outright: I withdrew my signature from that note a long time ago, half a year ago, and I'd advise you to take it to court.

To what?

To court, Miss Toranska; that's where you go if a promissory note has not been honoured. The court appoints a debt collector, and the debt collector executes the court order.

And your signature can be withdrawn without informing the interested party?

Of course you inform them – at the bank [laughter].

Zawieyski stared at me incredulously: you're joking, surely, he said.

I wasn't joking. Since December 1956 I'd been fully aware that I would have to go, otherwise I would be given an exemplary political funeral, so when they asked me to put my name down on the list of candidates to the Sejm, I said I wasn't having any part in it.

But why did Gomulka still want you in the Sejm?

All first secretaries are put down as candidates in first or second place, that's been the known custom since the beginning of People's Poland and no one had any intention of changing it. In January 1957

I resigned, but Gomulka wouldn't accept my resignation. "The Politburo," he said "rejects your request."

I'd expected that, actually. Gomulka was anxious for me to hold up the elections and keep guaranteeing the promissory note. I held them up. After the elections the matter of the Warsaw Committee came up again. The Politburo met; I was there with my second secretary, Stanislaw Kuzinski. I gave a report of the committee's activities, and that was when Gomulka launched into his attack. He began shouting about subversion in the committee. I interrupted him: what kind of subversion? You're the one who's responsible for it.

Gomulka said: you can't even deal with the distribution of leaflets that's being organized against you.

I said: of course I can't, because those leaflets are printed up by the general staff, by security, by the provincial Warsaw Committee and by the Central Committee.

There were various kinds of leaflets, for "Wieslaw" and against "Wieslaw", anti-Soviet in part, and all printed with the aim of sustaining the nation's belief in the myth that Gomulka wasn't going back on the promises made in October and of calling upon the people to vote without crossing any names off the ballot. It was cunningly thought out. On the one hand there were the organized leaflets, and on the other a number of groups were set up, not only in Warsaw, to create a warm atmosphere around the candidates chosen by Gomulka who were threatened with a boycott – in defence of Cyrankiewicz, for instance. Neither I nor the Warsaw Committee had anything to do with these operations, which were directed by Kliszko and Cyrankiewicz.

But you had leaflets printed up as well.

The only leaflets that were really printed up with my approval were two little posters designed by Starowieyski. One portrayed a dove of peace with blood dripping from its beak, and the other a Soviet tank crushing the streets of Budapest.

Were they signed?

No, of course not. They were anonymous.

And what purpose, to use a favourite newspaper slogan, did they serve?

They simply reflected popular sentiment.

No. They inflamed it.

Dear lady, it couldn't have been any more inflamed than it was. And in any case the leaflets were printed in October or November, and Gomulka was talking about January.

No one spoke at the Politburo meeting; everyone stared at the table. After a lengthy duel of words with me Gomulka finally said: there's nothing we can do except agree to Comrade Staszewski's request to resign. Still there was silence, so Gomulka added: the request is granted; thank you; we'll take a cigarette break.

He broke his "Sport" in two and stuck half of it into his holder. Everyone began to get up and take out cigarettes, because there was no smoking during meetings, and then Ochab came up to me. He whispered to me in sympathy, in Russian: be brave, soldier. That pissed me off so much, if you'll forgive the expression, that I nearly punched him. The guy had kept quiet all the time, just like Rapacki and Zambrowski – not that I want to make a thing of it, but they were supposed to be all for me – and now here he is, all sympathy. "Edward," I said loudly, so that Gomulka would hear, "are you out of your mind? I'm not a soldier any more, remember that, and as a friend I can tell you one thing: he's going to shoot you all down like sitting ducks, one by one. Rapacki and Zambrowski and Jedrychowski and you, he'll shoot down all of you. He'll deal with you like sitting ducks. Remember that. Goodbye, see you."

I came home and announced to my wife: you've got a choice: divorce me or stay with me. If you choose the second, remember that you'll be going through some hard times, the hardest of your life; it'll be terrible, and you'll get a chance to prove yourself. So choose. Whereupon Danka said: that's just fine.

You do like to exaggerate, don't you? It's not so terrible. You have the most beautiful apartment of all the ones I've seen – five huge rooms, a bathroom and two toilets, the most beautiful furniture, mostly antiques, the most people at your parties –

– so does Bienkowski, Kisielewski –

All right, let's drop it. You joined the opposition?

No, I became editor-in-chief of the Polish Press Agency. Where I didn't last long, actually, because I made a great mistake at the very start. I went abroad to inspect Agency posts and I made the discovery, which in fact I'd anticipated, that our correspondents, instead of concerning themselves with Agency work, were burdened with tasks for an entirely different agency. Before returning to

Poland, I had a conversation with one of our correspondents in London which was very characteristic of the way those gentlemen think. I announced to him that he was going back to Poland; startled, he asked: why, when? I replied evasively that we needed a new man in London, someone qualified as a journalist; whereupon, still not catching on, he asked me: but comrade, have you cleared this?

I pretended not to know what he was talking about: cleared it with whom? He was thrown off balance: no, it's nothing, he said. But I persisted: please explain to me with whom I'm supposed to clear my decisions. He wouldn't reply, but he began to excuse himself, that perhaps he really was a bad journalist; his actual words were: I'm a lousy journalist, but I'm loyal.

And thus without knowing it he described, in simple words, the party's personnel policy: no one has to be competent in any post; he merely has to be loyal.

Naturally, my decisions caused a certain amount of confusion. A colonel from the department which apparently controlled PAP journalists got in touch with me and reproached me for recalling people who were important to him. I said it didn't interest me and that I resented any kind of interference.

Then Antek Alster called me – the deputy minister for internal affairs. I hear you've had some kind of conflict with Colonel Sienkiewicz, he said. I replied that no, there hadn't been any conflict, I only asked him kindly to stay out of my affairs; let him have power, by all means, but only over his security men. And I added: listen, Antek, you've got opportunities enough for placing your people where you want them, but I think that combining those two professions doesn't do anyone any good, and whether you like it or not, as long as I'm in PAP, whenever I see any osmosis between you and us I will eliminate it.

To which Antek replied, with some wit: I don't want to worry you, but I'm afraid you won't be there for long.

Apart from that he agreed with me, noting, however, that we would unfortunately be isolated in our views.

He anticipated correctly, because I didn't stay long in PAP after that. One day, in the summer of 1958, Zambrowski rang me up – he was a member of the Politburo then – and announced, when I had come to see him as bidden, that by a decision of the Politburo I was no longer editor-in-chief of PAP. The decision, of course, was not the Politburo's but Gomulka's, and it was a perfidious one. I'd been about to go to Yugoslavia to sign an agreement with Tanyug and to

West Germany on the invitation of *Spiegel* and their press agency, the DPA. Two days before I was supposed to leave, Gomulka came to the Politburo meeting and announced that he had heard that Tito was organizing a congress of the revisionist international in Belgrade and that I was going to Yugoslavia with the purpose of taking part in it. He proposed my immediate dismissal from my post. Of course, no one at the Politburo meeting demanded to be shown any evidence of this, or even to have this information checked; they all accepted the decision in silence.

As usual, and as you had done in previous years.

Zambrowski was assigned the task of imparting this information to me. He didn't attempt to explain anything, he merely said: you know the man, he's possessed; he told me to ask you what you want to do, what kind of post you want, only it's to be no higher than director of a department. I said: Roman, if you really want to do something for me as an old friend, there's one thing you can do, as a gesture of mercy: stop concerning yourself with me. I'll find some work myself, and I'll do something, or I won't do anything, but please for God's sake stop concerning yourself with me any more.

At that point Roman, not listening to me, offered me the post of director of the welfare department in the Ministry of Health. You know, he said, you can help poor people there.

Roman, I said emphatically, fuck off. I don't want to know you. Please, stop concerning yourself with me.

I thought I'd achieved my aim. But it only seemed that way, because they caught me; they had to catch me.

I left PAP, and Professor Gieysztor suggested that I come to the Polish Academy of Sciences and take up history, while my old friend Bromberg offered me the post of editor-in-chief of PWN [Polish Academic Press]. I refused to be editor-in-chief, so he suggested I become editor of the *General Encyclopedia*. I accepted.

You get your encyclopedists according to your revolution, as you used to say in Warsaw cafés.

Well, it's true, isn't it?

The post had to be approved.

Of course; like any post. But I warned Bromberg from the start that I wouldn't go anywhere and wouldn't ask for anything. You're the one who suggested this, I said; you arrange it. Bromberg rang up

Zambrowski to ask whether the Central Committee would approve it. Zambrowski declared that the post did not fall under the control of the Central Committee *nomenklatura* and that on his part he would contribute by not asking anyone for permission. Thus thanks to Zambrowski and Bromberg I had a few years of peace and quiet. Until, of course, Gomulka began preparing to spring again and the wave of Moczarism broke.

When exactly was Moczar's group formed? After the meetings of combatants in the Kielce region at the beginning of the sixties?

It's impossible to give a precise date; the meetings of combatants were gatherings which accompanied the formation of the group. They were one of Moczar's tricks, and were quite well conceived. He would organize camp fires with baked potatoes and sausages on sticks, and then he'd invite veterans from the Home Army and the People's Army in order to show them that we old combatants, we should stick together; we wandered around forests together and now here we are by the camp fire – let's join together. Fortunately not all the Home Army people fell for this, and some of them remained aloof, but there was quite a large group which, out of political stupidity, clearly did join.

One of those meetings of combatants was attended by Jan Jozef Lipski. A few months earlier there'd been a search at his apartment and a few of his books had been confiscated, including the manuscript of his book about PAX. Jan Jozef got the idea of going to a camp fire meeting in the hope that perhaps he might be able to get Moczar to give him back his books. At some point, when things were rolling along very nicely, everyone was tipsy and full brotherhood reigned, Jan Jozef asked Moczar for the return of his things. Moczar, of course, told him that he didn't know anything about it and had had nothing to do with it. And in this way Jan Jozef lost his virginity. It's true that not everyone attaches major significance to this, but Jan Jozef does. However, this is how the adventures of all virgins must inevitably end when they think they will be able to outsmart the rapist.

The formation of Moczar's group is connected, in my opinion, with a new stage in Gomulka's regime. At the end of the fifties or the start of the sixties, opposition tendencies, or rather opposition moods, resulting from a feeling of disillusionment with Gomulka's rule, began their process of formation. It was clear by then that Gomulka had no intention of keeping the promises he had made in

October and that the ideology of reform, democratization and society's participation in the process of government was not at all to his liking.

Because he couldn't or because he didn't want to?

He didn't want to, of course he didn't want to, because the word "democracy" has no place in communist ideology and Gomulka was a good, old communist. I don't want to demonize him, but I'm convinced it was Gomulka who instigated the actions which brought disaster upon Poland.

I've never liked Gomulka, so it's difficult for me to be entirely objective when judging him – although believe me, my assessment of him doesn't spring from my dislike. Nor does it spring from any personal animosity, although to me the man is obnoxious and repellent, but not cynical. Gomulka was a man with a passion for politics; he was very absorbed by his own activities and capable, I'm sure, of sacrificing much in order to realize his own conception of the world and of government. He wasn't the kind of man who finds it easy to sell his own convictions, but he had a low opinion of other people; he broke people, and his view of the world and of social and interpersonal relations was very narrow. In this sense he was very primitive, albeit stubborn. A good tactician, he was resolute and at the same time patient when playing political games, waiting for just the right moment to strike or to come out with his own point of view.

I'll give you an example, one that's very characteristic of him. In 1965 they did a survey of students' answers to the question: name a figure who fascinates you and who should be emulated. The results of the questionnaire were announced in the paper *Zycie Literackie*. The answers contained not a single name of any communist activist, past or present. There was a row. Gomulka summoned Professor Schaff and said to him: why the hell do you do these surveys in the first place, what do you want to find out from them? That the youth is against us? We already know that, and there's no point in asking them about it. That was what Gomulka was like. He was undoubtedly an honest man, but he only had one single political vision and knew only one road; and that road and that vision were absolutely communist and doctrinaire, and for the average Pole they were contrary to the interests of the Polish nation. Gomulka wouldn't allow the thought that it might be possible to create a system that was different from the one he knew and held up as a model – the Soviet system. The whole period of Gomulka's rule shows this. His evolution, from his coming to power to his fall, was an evolution from an opposition stance towards what we call the Stalinist period to a communist-fascist stance, in other words to the stance which most approximates that of our neighbours.

Was it also inspired by them?

That was difficult to gauge in any situation: you get feedback between elements of pressure from Moscow on the one hand and reactionary and backward-looking elements existing with Poland on the other. This process goes in both directions and only varies in intensity according to the situation. We have a similar phenomenon now. On the one hand there has been, and there still is, pressure from Moscow, and on the other an active and quite large group of people in Poland who are opposed to democracy and reform and who are hostile to the increase in tendencies towards freedom. The bureaucratic party, army and security apparatus have found sympathy and a readiness to cooperate among the most reactionary ideological elements of prewar Poland – imperialists and chauvinists. It's no accident that old National Democrats gravitate towards old communists at such times.

Something similar happened in Poland at the beginning of the sixties. Gomulka disappointed large numbers of the intelligentsia, especially some distinguished intellectuals who had supported him passionately during the first period and felt deeply bound to him. He also disappointed some of the young, who were aware of the increasing economic difficulties or concerned about the government's way of dealing with the so-called revisionists, most of whom were people with enormous authority, like Leszek Kolakowski, for instance. Thus a situation arose where Gomulka's arsenal of political and ideological means was nearly exhausted, and, especially in view of the increasing complications in the economic sphere, and hence the social sphere as well, an urgent need arose to bolster the thinning ideology with new elements that would lend a certain offensive character to Gomulka's policies. It was in these circumstances that the Moczarist trend was formed, a trend which on the one hand inaugurated a new period of Gomulka's rule, a period marked by repression, and on the other introduced into political life tendencies previously unexploited in the history of the PRL – nationalist tendencies, or, more specifically, fascist and anti-Semitic tendencies. A powerful government and a strong state which knows how to deal with society while disregarding its interests, and the army – the armed branch no longer merely of the party, but of the nation as well. Of course, as is usually the case with communists, this whole ideology was built up out of lies, distortions and by magnifying various facts out of proportion, and all in order to be able to say: we struggled for a Poland that is free, independent and just. Admittedly, we were not alone, because we had a partner that we decided to acknowledge – the Home Army, the underground representation of the government in exile, the government in exile itself, the underground state. There were differences between us, but let us forget them now and join together in one organization, one ideology – the ideology of combatants. All of us together, meaning me – Moczar – and Radoslaw Mazurkiewicz. The huge ZBOWiD [Union of Fighters for Freedom and Democracy] organization was formed, a whole propaganda machine was activated, and enormous amounts of money were provided in order to make good the injuries done to Home Army soldiers on the one hand and to flatter and bribe those same soldiers on the other.

Up to now you've made it seem more like "hire".

Oh, very good – you learn quickly. Yes, of course, hire. You don't bribe traitors, because you can never be entirely sure of them; you hire them.

In this way quite a large group of people was created. The ZBOWiD tendency was shaped at the very least under Gomulka's protectorate, if indeed it was not inspired by him in the first place. For Moczar had been one of his close collaborators after the war as well as during the occupation. True, he later betrayed Gomulka, but then he was not alone in this. Gomulka greatly contributed to the creation of the myth of Moczar – Moczar the partisan, Moczar the great guy.

Rakowski once discussed him with Gomulka. Well, you know what he's like – he didn't know whether to stick to Moczar or not. He always wanted to play the liberal, the man of broad European views, and this Moczar fellow, with all his obscurantist and anti-Semitic views, didn't really seem to fit in too well with that. And he was becoming more and more significant and important with every year. Rakowski decided to ask Gomulka what he should do. And Gomulka told him: they're trying to create differences between Moczar and me, to drive a wedge between us, but they won't succeed, because we are one. Whereupon he joined together two fingers of his hand and showed Rakowski how they were one. Rakowski later publicized this widely.

Wasn't Gomulka afraid of being dominated by Moczar?

If he did wake up to it at some point, although I doubt it, by then it was too late. Gomulka needed Moczar. Once he'd scattered the revisionists, if I may put it that way, he proceeded to broaden his field of attack. Remember the attack on the Church in connection with the Episcopate's letter to German bishops? Its importance is not appreciated, but it was one of the most important, pivotal moments in Gomulka's rule, for in those conditions an attack on the Church was tantamount to an attack on society, society in the broadest sense of the term. It was not successful, and evidence of its failure is visible today, but it caused a certain amount of disarray. Then came 1966, the year of the Millennium. The police came out on the streets. A lot of police. In fact that was when my road towards the Church began: I'm a nonbelieving but passionate supporter of the Church, and that was when the full awareness of the enormously positive role which the Church plays in our lives hit me.

My wife and I attended a variety of celebrations connected with the Millennium in Warsaw. There was an Ordination of Bishops at St Anne's: a hundred thousand people on their way to the Cathedral. We didn't make it to the Cathedral, getting bogged down on Castle Square. The square was surrounded by police and riot police, and the ORMO [police reserves] had been brought out as well. At some point I decided to leave my wife on the square and go for a stroll around the Old City. Swietojanska Street was lined with rows of ORMO, and behind them the police. One of the commandants turned to me and said: you won't get through, Comrade Staszewski. Why? I asked naively. Because I won't let you through, came the answer. Further along, Brzozowa Street was filled by about 500 armed policemen in helmets. The ceremony came to an end, and by some miracle my wife and I succeeded in pushing our way through to the street in front of the Cathedral. About a hundred party activists were stationed there, and as the bishops began to file out of the Cathedral, Bishop Modzelewski was visible among them, and was greeted by shouts of: "You oaf, you stupid oaf!" Then the Primate, Wyszynski, emerged, and some atrocious harridan, who by then had apparently lost all that remained of her wits, shrieked: "You . . . you . . . you Bolshevik lackey!" That's how the production had been organized. And what of the picture of Our Lady of Czestochowa, which had made the rounds of all the churches in Poland? It was being madly pursued by the militia, party activists had been mobilized to go after it, force was used, and at one point even the picture itself was arrested. Throughout Poland attempts were being made to obstruct the Millennium celebrations. Everywhere, that is, except in the Podhale region, because they were afraid to touch Podhale. The campaign against the Church then was as strong as the campaign against Solidarity today –

– and the campaign against the Home Army earlier.

Yes, well, that was much earlier.

The only difference being that you organized the first, participated as a spectator in the second, and are now being harassed by the third.

That's because the party always has to have an enemy in order to consolidate its ranks. If the external enemy is crushed it will find its own internal one, just as it found revisionists or right-wing nationalist-deviationists. But it must always have enemies.

In 1968 the enemy appeared in the form of the students. That was when I first heard your name mentioned, yours and Zambrowski's. On Friday 8 March there was a rally at the university – at that point I didn't yet know of your existence – and on Monday 11 March I read in Trybuna Luda *that I had shouted, "Staszewski and Zambrowski to power!" at the rally. None of my friends knew your name.*

[Laughter] The first thing they did was to launch a furious assault on the editors of the PWN *General Encyclopedia*, which was made up of a bunch of revisionists and Jews.

Formerly prominent figures.

You could say that. Tadeusz Zabludowski, formerly editor of *Glos* [*The Voice*] and chief censor, worked at PWN, as did Jerzy Baumritter, formerly deputy to the editor-in-chief of *Trybuna Ludu*, and Pawel Hoffman, editor-in-chief of *Nowa Kultura* and director of the culture department at the Central Committee who in 1956 printed Wazyk's "Poem for Adults". Thus the *Encyclopedia* was a good target to attack, and one pretext was found in the entry under "concentration camps" in volume 8, which said that under the occupation there were labour camps and extermination camps, which corresponded strictly to the truth, that such-and-such a number of Jews, Poles, Russians and Gypsies had perished in

Auschwitz, and that almost four million Jews had perished in the extermination camps. For Moczar's group, to give the number of Jews who had been killed was almost a challenge flung at the Polish nation; it was also a pretext to launch a furious anti-Semitic campaign. Additional piquancy was lent to the whole affair by the fact that this entry was signed and approved for publication by a member of the *Encyclopedia's* academic council, a historian by profession, one Henryk Jablonski, minister of education at the time. When this whole row broke out I went to see him.

"Henryk," I said, "you are the president of the ZBOWiD historical commission which unleashed this rabid campaign; would you like me to remind you of something?"

"I have no part in it," he said.

"Oh, but you do, you do, if only as the president of the historical commission. Should I remind you of something, Henryk?"

"What?" he said.

"Of the fact that it was you who approved that entry for publication."

Henryk Jablonski was put out. He went pale, his eyes began to swivel around, he had nothing to say, and the conversation came to an end.

Jablonski's turn will come. Everyone gets his turn.

They needed Staszewski then – a Jew and a revisionist, a man who was much disliked and who in addition had contacts with Michnik, Modzelewski and Kuron. And Zambrowski as well, for his son was connected to the opposition movement of the young intelligentsia. The conjunction of those two names was beautiful. Here were two party members who had played a role in the past and who had ceased to support Gomulka's policies and refused to obey him – in my case it was earlier, and in Zambrowski's not until 1964, when he criticized Gomulka's agrarian policy at the plenum. In fact I'd never made a secret of my attitude towards Moczar and his fascist-obscurantist views, and this was additional grist for the mill of that whole group's loathing for me.

Why? Were you a danger to anyone?

Me? Of course not; I'd already been dealt with. And Gomulka wasn't interested simply in a bunch of Jews who played no role in political life and never could. They'd been pushed out of the picture a long time ago. Nor was he interested in the few members of the leadership who resigned voluntarily as a result of the anti-Semitic campaign.

After all, he didn't need to get rid of Ochab or Rapacki that way. With Ochab it was enough to say: Comrade Ochab, I'm transferring you to another post, or: Comrade Ochab, you will resign; and Ochab, disciplined as always, would do what he was told. There were several things which concerned Gomulka. First, he wanted to strengthen the repressive regime to make it even more repressive so that it would instil fear and ward off any signs of discontent. Second, he wanted to win over all the National Democratic and National Radical elements, of which there were quite a few in ZBOWiD and which might in future contribute to spreading opposition tendencies. Gomulka decided to make them his allies. And he anticipated correctly: these elements put up no resistance to his offer, especially since it would give them additional privileges and authority. And third, he needed to find some sort of explanation for the deteriorating economic situation. People were seeing the Soviet Union as the cause, so what could be better than giving them Jews as the cause – indeed there was an abundant tradition of this: when something's wrong, blame the Jews. Anti-Semitism was always used as a screen for dirty business, diverting the attention of people who were not well informed and were ignorant of what was going on from the genuine and significant causes of the difficulties. It was here, in fact, that Moczar and Gomulka slipped up: they hounded all the Jews out of Poland and now there's no one to lay the blame on. How lovely it would sound: Solidarity taken over by Jews! But now all that's left is extremists, and that's just not the same. It really isn't the same.

Ochab claims that the point was to clear new posts for people in security.

Yes, but that was only by the way. The first thing was to dismiss all those who were known for their liberalism or who had contacts with opposition circles. So the faculty of the departments of philosophy, sociology and political economy at the university was shunted off, and their place was taken by the so-called "March" professors [supplanting those who had been expelled after the student riots in March 1968], but these "March" professors were needed only to fill the posts which were now empty. In fact it wasn't only Jews who were expelled from the university; they expelled Poles as well.

People said that some of the students were inspired by certain members of the Politburo.

There's not an ounce of truth in that; it's another of those fabrications, although I don't know whether this one comes from

Gomulka or directly from security. Not only was there no inspiration from the Politburo, but every member of the Politburo was totally opposed to what the students were doing. I don't know a single one who in any way collaborated or helped the students, or even sympathized with them. And that includes Ochab.

When Adam Michnik, Jacek Kuron and other members of the Workers' Defence Committee "KOR" were arrested in 1977 or 1978, I very much wanted to talk to Ochab. I thought that even if he didn't support them politically, he might still react to their arrest in some way, by saying that persecution was not the right way to go about things. I talked to him for a few hours. He not only refused to sign the petition or to encourage others to sign it, he actually said: I've got my own disagreements with the leadership and I criticize their policies, but I will not come out against the party in this kind of company. In 1968 his position had been similar. Of course he was against the anti-Semitic campaign, the base chauvinism and the security methods, but he never supported the students in any way. Nor did others, like Morawski or Albrecht, who were considered liberals. But the children of many former or current prominent figures got involved in the opposition movement, and this was no accident, in the sense that they got a lot of their knowledge about politics and the world from home and had easier access to it than others. Because of this they were undoubtedly more intellectually alive and aware, and perhaps also more intelligent. Today, looking at their further development, one can say that this was a group of intellectually outstanding students of which any university would be proud. Their participation in the opposition movement was of course magnified for tactical reasons; nonetheless, this does not alter my belief that it grew out of society's opposition stance, which became clear two years later.

Did you meet with them?

I saw them from time to time – I think that's a more appropriate description – in cafés, and told them that they should hold meetings and write memoranda, build up a strong movement among the students and develop a rapport with young workers. That much I said. I was not, however, in favour of their going out on the street. I kept telling them that such demonstrations would be exploited and used to destroy them.

And they didn't listen?

Nothing could convince them. I told them, Leszek Kolakowski told them, a few other people told them – but their perception of reality was different, their experiences were different, or perhaps it was their lack of experience, and they believed that if they went out on the streets society would support them, because they were right. They didn't realize that you can be right and lose; that being right doesn't guarantee victory.

Over a dozen people were given prison sentences, dozens were expelled from universities, hundreds drafted into the army and thousands forced to emigrate. What happened to you?

To me? Nothing. I was just vilified in the press.

You weren't even interrogated?

No. I could be arrested, but not interrogated. And they only tried to interrogate me once, a year later, after the arrest of Adam Bromberg, the director of PWN. They wanted to try him for various abuses. There was a fashion then for putting Jewish directors on trial on the pretext of abuses or bad management. Bromberg was accused of needlessly spending money on various publications. Rubbish. I was summoned to police headquarters to be interrogated as a witness. This did not prove useful to the interrogators. They asked me what I thought about Bromberg and I replied that I thought he was the best editor in Poland. Poland had never before had a publisher of such organizational talent and scope. And, I added, he's a man of unblemished honesty.

"Well, then," they said, "what happened with that encyclopedia about Poland that was supposed to appear in several foreign languages, and where you were supposed to edit the Russian edition?"

"Despite the advanced stage of the work," I said, "it was never published, because the Russians withdrew from the agreement, fearing that they would get something other than what they were expecting."

Then they asked me about the qualifications of the encyclopedia's editorial board and academic council.

"Surely," I said, "you've seen the names of the professors, deans, doctors and members of the Polish Academy of Sciences."

"We've got plenty of their kind downstairs in storage," they said.

Underneath the police headquarters, as I'm sure you know, there's a prison.

"And you," the chief of the investigative bureau, a colonel, asked me, "what qualifications do you have for editing the Russian edition?"

I explained that I had graduated from university in the USSR, had lived there for many years, and had been a lecturer there.

"A lecturer?" they said, pricking up their ears. "Where?"

"I was a lecturer at the international advanced sociopolitical school in Moscow, which was a communist school of the workers' international. Bierut and Gomulka, among others, studied there," I said.

A hush descended on the room. It lasted several minutes. Unable to restrain myself, I said: "I'll bet you I know what you're thinking now."

"Well, what?" asked the colonel.

"You're thinking about how to get rid of that transcript."

For there was a captain sitting at a table next to us, taking everything down.

The colonel looked at me and made up his mind: "Captain, may I have that, please."

The captain gave him the transcript, whereupon he tore up the last page, threw it into the wastebasket and left. When an hour had passed and he still hadn't returned I told the captain that I had to go to dinner, as it was 2.30 already.

The captain turned on his heel and left the room. He returned with the prosecutor, who wanted to interrogate me. I refused. We agreed that I would sign the transcript, but only with the last page included. I dictated this page to the captain and left. I wasn't summoned again.

Until 1982.

That's right. In the course of this past year I've had two very scrupulous searches of my apartment and several summons to headquarters in Rakowiecka Street.

There's much talk about them in Warsaw cafés, because after each one you describe the witty and apt replies you made, the way you led the interrogators up the garden path, the way you made fools of them –

[laughter]

– and after a year of meetings with you I'm still asking myself: who are you really?

1982

JAKUB BERMAN

JAKUB BERMAN

Jakub Berman was born in Warsaw in 1901, into a moderately wealthy bourgeois family. His father, who perished in Treblinka, was a trade representative; his mother, who died before the war, a housewife. There were five children in the family, all of whom went on to university. The eldest brother, a surgeon, also perished in Treblinka, along with his wife; one sister, a Ph.D. in Germanic languages, was killed during the war; another, a pedagogue, survived the war in the Soviet Union. The other brother, Adolf, was a psychologist. Before the war, Adolf had been an activist in a leftist Zionist party; in 1943 he crossed over to the Aryan side of Warsaw from the Jewish ghetto, was active on the praesidium of the Jewish National Committee and worked as secretary to the Home Army's Council of Aid to Jews. After the war he was a delegate to the KRN and an activist in the Central Committee of Jews in Poland. In 1950 he emigrated to Israel, where he became a member of the Mapam Party, later of the Communist Party of Israel, a member of the Knesset, and a member of the praesidium of the International Federation of Militants of the Resistance Movement. He died in 1978.

Jakub Berman graduated from the faculty of law at Warsaw University in 1925, and became a teaching assistant on the history of social systems. He wrote his Ph.D. thesis on the structure of Polish cities on the basis of lists from 1791, and wrote an article entitled "Household servants in Warsaw at the end of the eighteenth century", dealing with the foundation of the trade union of butlers. He could have pursued an academic career.

While at university he became involved with a left-wing student organization, and in 1924 with the KZMP. After graduating, from 1926 to 1928 he was a "Papagit" activist in the Central Committee. He was transferred to the KPP in 1928, at the age of twenty-seven, and appointed director of the department dealing with the intelligentsia at the KZMP's Central Professional Section. He was a member of this section and director of its editors. In 1939, after the outbreak of the war, he left Warsaw and made his way to the Soviet territories: first to Rowny and then to Bialystok. In the spring of

1941 he was sent to Minsk, in Byelorussia, to work on the paper *Standard of Freedom*; he edited the correspondence pages. The *Standard of Freedom* was an organ of the Byelorussian Communist Party. He came to Moscow shortly after the outbreak of war between Germany and the Soviet Union. He worked briefly at "Kosciuszko" Radio, and later became a lecturer and director of the Polish section of the Comintern school in Kushnarenkov, where he prepared the second group of PPR activists for their parachute drop into Poland. In December 1943 he was appointed secretary of the National Section of the Union of Polish Patriots, and in April 1944 he was coopted into that union's central council. In December 1943 he also took part in the foundation of the Polish National Committee as a member of the organizational committee. At the end of December he helped to found the Central Bureau of Polish Communists in the USSR, where he was responsible for Polish affairs and communications with Poland.

In July 1944 he took part in the foundation of the PKWN, but did not join it. In August 1944, while the leadership of the PPR was changing, he became a member of the party's Politburo. At that time he held no particularly prominent posts. He was successively undersecretary of state in the Ministry of Foreign Affairs (1945) and undersecretary of state in the praesidium of the Council of Ministers (1945–50); he also took part in the sessions of the Central Coordinating Council of Political Parties (1945–7). In 1947 he was an adviser for the communist party's meetings in Szklarska Poreba, when the Information Bureau "Cominform" was founded.

In June 1948 he was a PPR delegate to the Information Bureau's conference which condemned the communist party of Yugoslavia and decided to collectivize the countryside. He was active in the joint PPS and PPR commission, where he was one of the editors of the PUWP's ideological and programmatic declaration. In July 1948, at the PUWP's first congress, he became a member of the Politburo (until May 1956), of the secretariat of the Central Committee (until 1954) and of the Central Committee's Organizational Bureau; he was now officially responsible for ideology, education, culture and propaganda, as well as for foreign affairs and matters of security. Together with Bierut and Minc, he was a member of the party's highest leadership. He was also a member of the Government Presidium (1950–2), Deputy Premier (1954–6), and Member of Parliament (1945–56). After Bierut's death he left the Politburo and the government (in May 1956), was expelled from the Central

Committee in the autumn of 1956 and from the party the following year. (Stanislaw Radkiewicz, Minister of Public Security, was expelled with him.) He was judged responsible for the "period of errors and distortions". He spent the following years as an editor in the publishing house "Ksiazka i Wiedza", remaining there until 1969, when he retired.

He died in April 1984, in the course of authorizing this interview.

* * *

For ten years you were the second most important person in Poland after Bierut. You were the brain behind the party; you were its highest authority. Then they accused you of the gravest crimes, the worst acts of treason a man can commit. After that you were crossed off, finished. They even crossed you out of the General Encyclopedia.

Of course. When you're cast out, you cease to exist. When I was in power they even included me in the Soviet one, but later they deleted the entry. But then, they've always manipulated their history, and the Poles are succumbing to the same thing. Gomulka, who instigated that, didn't display any generosity towards me. It may have been partly under my influence that he'd submitted his self-criticism to the party in 1948, and I suppose that was something he could never forgive me for; presumably that was why he had some kind of aversion to me, at least there's no other explanation that I can see. His stand on a number of matters remains a mystery to me to this day, particularly as I'd considered him to be a more reasonable man who would be able to control his aversions. Even if he didn't like me (after all, not everyone has to love me), still he knew me well enough not to have to make my party card into an issue of debate for years to come – and yet that's what he did! The resolution concerning me included a clause to the effect that I could apply to be reinstated in the party within three years after my expulsion. I took advantage of the clause and did so, twice, and both times Gomulka replied that the time was not yet ripe.

Personally?

No, his secretariat sent the reply, which made reference to the resolution passed by the Politburo. Naturally, there was no one who could oppose him, even though they all knew me. After that I tired of it and stopped trying.

Werfel has been applying at every party congress for the past fifteen years.

There are such fanatics, but I'm not one of them. When Radkiewicz, who'd been expelled along with me, was ill in hospital, Gomulka sent him a party card: he forgave him, but he didn't forgive me. I hadn't anticipated such a decision, especially since I'd resigned from all my posts of my own accord; so when the motion was put to expel me from the party, I voted against, along with twenty or so other comrades. But there was a majority in favour. My expulsion from the party came as a shock, and I felt that a great injury had been done me.

And what did you feel in 1937 and 1938, when thousands of communists were being murdered in the USSR?

I assumed that the terror of the Great Purge was a side effect of the search for a solution to the Soviet Union's extremely difficult international situation, and possibly also a result of Stalin's own internal struggles and contradictions; they in turn may well have been connected with his extreme suspiciousness, which had become pathological. I didn't try to justify what was happening; rather I accepted that it was a tragic web of circumstance which drew an enormous number of victims into it. Naturally, I tried desperately to cling to the thought that you can't make omelettes without breaking eggs – a superficial little saying, actually, but at that time, in 1938, it was current among us, and I imagine there were some who found consolation in it in the situation that had arisen. A violent purge had begun in the Soviet Union; in some sense the trials that took place cast a cruel cloud over the history of the communist movement. A number of party members began to have various doubts. The KPP's last secretariat delegated me to attend various meetings, mainly with the intelligentsia.

Why you?

Although I didn't hold any position of responsibility in the KPP – I was head of the intelligentsia section at the Central Professional Department – the party nevertheless entrusted me with the task of explaining the situation. The arguments that the party hacks produced at these meetings were difficult to refute because of the clumsy and artificial way in which the Moscow trials were constructed. Old communists with a long record of service to the party were put in the dock and accused of spying for the Japanese, for the Turks and for the devil knows who else. It was something I simply couldn't accept. I thought that these people, if there were any doubts or reservations about them, ought to be dismissed from their posts or transferred to some other kind of work, not sentenced. It was also a mystery to me why Bukharin, for instance, or Kamenev, were submitting to such totally absurd self-criticism at their trials and confessing to crimes they hadn't committed. I assumed they'd been talked into it by being told, look, the only thing you can still do for the party now is to take these sins upon yourself, whether you committed them or not. At that point the accused may not yet have known that he was going to be killed, eliminated; it was probably just a matter of a trial and a public confession. So quite often he agreed to perform a service for the party if the party demanded or expected such a sacrifice of him, because for the old communists serving the party was not merely a goal but an inner need in life. I expect other methods were also used against them, depending on a given person's weakest and most sensitive points: thus hunger, for example, or fear for his family, may have played a role. But I suspect that these personal aspects served only as an additional argument, not as the main one. Many an old Bolshevik may have suffered torments, struggled, been afraid, even, but would not have gone through with a self-criticism unless he had found what he took to be overriding considerations to justify it – considerations which were to a large extent illusory, but which, at the given time, bound him to that course of action.

At the meetings I tried as best I could to explain what was happening; to clarify the background, the situations full of conflict and internal contradictions in which Stalin had probably found himself and which forced him to act as he did; and to exaggerate the mistakes of the opposition, which assumed grotesque proportions in the subsequent charges against them and were further blown up by Soviet propaganda.

You had to have a great deal of endurance and dedication to the cause then in order to accept what was happening despite all the distortions, injuries and torments. I don't want to go into the rights and wrongs of the ideological conflict which had arisen in the Soviet Union, since it was, after all, unavoidable. I don't even want to go into who was right, Stalin or the opposition. At the time I found Stalin's arguments more persuasive than Bukharin's, but that's not to say that I was able to accept the charge of espionage against Bukharin – not in the least. I could also see how there might have been individual, isolated acts of treason, but I couldn't believe the claim that everyone was a traitor, which was how the situation was portrayed at the time. I also found it hard to accept the guilt of the KPP leaders, whom I knew and who had now been sentenced to death. So I found consolation in the thought that some day, perhaps in many years' time, people would arrive at the truth, and the injuries that had been done would be made good.

How?

People would be rehabilitated.

What was your reaction to the Soviet invasion of Poland on 17 September 1939?

We were familiar with the official communiqué, which had come as a shock to us. It was impossible to believe at first. However, we understood that when the Soviet Union reached its compromise with Germany by signing the non-aggression pact in August 1939, it did so obviously not out of any love for Hitler – they'd seen through the rogue completely – but in order to extend the period of peace with Germany for as long as possible, since Stalin was perfectly well aware that he was unprepared to take on the powerful German machine. I found myself in Bialystok, where I became a humble work inspector. Wierblowski was the director of the inspectorate, and as he was an old chum he did me a favour and took me on. I made speeches, public appearances.

In what capacity?

Mainly during the election campaign.

You mean the one where they voted in favour of annexing Bialystok to the Soviet Union?

Deputies were being chosen for the National Assembly of Western Byelorussia, which was to pass a resolution to that effect.

How did the elections go?

I wouldn't say the enthusiasm was enormous, but they did cause quite a stir. Differences emerged. Some people went to vote with conviction, and some without.

Did they go because they were afraid?

Some people went because they were afraid. In any case they understood that they had to. And even if they didn't think they'd be subject to repression if they didn't go, they still thought it better to be on the safe side so that no one would be able to reproach them with anything.

And what did you think?

I thought that in that situation you had to vote without crossing out any names from the ballot. Anyway, anything else was impossible. Apparently there was greater freedom in Lvov, where you could retire to the little screened booth that was supposed to be there when the election ballots were cast, but there was no booth in Bialystok.

Were there Byelorussians there?

Perhaps not *en masse*, but yes, there were. I think they constituted the greatest group in the countryside.

In the countryside in the Lomza region as well?

I don't know the figures.

According to the prewar encyclopedia the Bialystok province (which also included the district of Lomza) was inhabited by 1,004,370 Poles (77 per cent), 162,912 Jews and 119,392 Byelorussians. Bialystok itself was inhabited by 39,602 Jews, 35,832 Poles and 1,358 people of other nationalities. However, these proportions changed every month to the disadvantage of the Poles, who were being imprisoned and transported to camps on a huge scale.

Indeed, that's true. In anticipation of a war with Germany the Soviets were trying to clear those territories of uncertain elements.

A war? But they were allies, surely. In December 1939 Stalin, while thanking Hitler for the telegram he had sent on the occasion of Stalin's sixtieth birthday, also gave his assurances as to the firmness of the German–Soviet alliance, which had been "cemented with blood we have spilt together" (doubtless in Poland); in June 1940, after the occupation of France, Molotov was congratulating the Germans on their "glorious victory"; while in April 1941 Stalin went so far as to go to the railway station, something he never did, in order to meet with the German ambassador, Schulenberg, on the pretext of escorting the foreign minister of Japan. He put his hand on Schulenberg's shoulder and said: "We must remain friends and we must do all we can for this cause", while to Colonel Krebs he said: "We shall remain friends whatever the circumstances".

It was a rather unwise game he was playing in an attempt to salvage peace, if only for a time, but he was playing for considerable stakes – for life. The Soviet Union wanted very much to avoid a war but realized at the same time that war was unavoidable. And the fact that it did realize this became clear to me just under a year after the elections, when Ponomarenko, first secretary of Byelorussia, gave a reception for Polish communists who had taken up residence in Bialystok and Baranowicze. It made history as the "tangerine" reception, because among other things tangerines were served; they were a wildly exotic rarity for us at the time. It was a turning point for me.

What was your position by then?

I was director of the teachers' institute and an activist in the teachers' trade union.

And a Soviet citizen as well, weren't you?

Yes, I assumed citizenship at the very beginning.

The meeting at Ponomarenko's reception took place after Molotov's trip to Germany, from which he had returned with definite and negative impressions. Molotov was clever enough to see right through Hitler's game, and the stakes were considerable. The Germans were preparing to invade France and bomb London, and a neutral Soviet Union would have been very helpful to them. So when Molotov went to Berlin he was promised the earth: India, the Far East, anything to keep Stalin from interfering in Hitler's conflict with the West. This was not, however, something Stalin could accept, even though France and England were a thorn in his side: they bothered him, and their role during the Munich period seemed to him to be more than doubtful. Still, he suspected that the war with the West was only one stage in Hitler's war, and by no means the last one. Stalin must have come to the conclusion that things would soon come to a head and that the present situation could not be drawn out for long.

Ponomarenko, who was the only speaker on the Soviet side, expounded to us, in rather general and non-committal terms, his assessment of the situation, naturally without reference to Molotov's talks with Hitler; but I was soon able to see what his real meaning was. He said: great tasks still await you. There might be a further stage to the war, when the question of Poland will become the order of the day, and then new perspectives will open up for Polish communists.

We had not been addressed in this way since the dissolution of the party; even our membership in the KPP was not acknowledged. Some people were therefore astonished as they listened to the speech.

I was not, because it confirmed my earlier expectations and premonitions, which I had formed after the defeat of France, when the Moscow press had published an article by Ilya Ehrenburg. The warmth and sympathy towards France which his article expressed was quite unmistakable, and to me this signified that something was changing in the unanimous chorus of criticism against the West; a new note, new undercurrents were appearing.

I took up Ponomarenko's tone, and was joined in this by a few other people. I got up and said that we had been awaiting this moment.

Why you? Why not Lampe, Finder, Nowotko or Fornalska, whose services to communism were surely greater, and who were also in Bialystok at the time?

If Lampe had been at the reception he would surely have made a statement, but he hadn't been invited, and nor had the others. Presumably there were still some old grudges against them which enjoined reticence in dealing with them. Lampe was an experienced party man, undoubtedly distinguished, and a member of the KPP Politburo, but until 1941 he remained on the sidelines. The people Ponomarenko invited to his reception were middle, not high level.

Whose man was he: Stalin's or Beria's?

He simply carried out instructions from his headquarters, which doesn't mean that he summoned us on Stalin's orders, although he must certainly have expected Stalin to approve. In my view he was carrying out a plan, different from the one Khrushchev was carrying out in Lvov, where he organized no such reception, and indeed allowed the arrest and imprisonment of, among others, Wladyslaw Broniewski and Aleksander Wat, both ardent supporters of communism. It may be true that the situation Ponomarenko had to deal with was much less tense and complicated, but still it's fair to say that at times he displayed more far-sightedness and directness than Khrushchev. For instance, he repealed the decree, or resolution, concerning education. At the outset, in their zeal, Soviet administrators closed down Polish schools and replaced them with Russian or Byelorussian ones. Ponomarenko ordered a return to the previous state of affairs, a move which was, so to put it, a government one [that is, such a decision would normally be made higher up, as part of government policy]. And although he clearly would not have done it if he had thought that it would not be well received in Moscow, the very fact that he made the decision on his own testified nonetheless to a certain amount of courage on his part. He also displayed courage in his treatment of us, despite the considerable risk he was taking in doing so – if only the risk that news of our meeting would be intercepted by German intelligence, for he had to recognize that if you invite a dozen or so people, who have families, friends and relations, sooner or later news of your meeting will leak through to the outside.

Whom did you tell?

Lampe. Lampe showed no surprise either at not having been invited to the reception or at the subsequent course of events. A few months earlier, he and Wanda Wasilewska had put the problems of KPP members before Stalin, and their letter had been favourably received, which signified that the Soviet comrades' fears concerning the KPP would finally be blown away. When Wanda got news of this she informed Lampe that Stalin had agreed to reinstate KPP members in the VCP(b), counting their time in the KPP as VCP(b) membership. I didn't take advantage of this opportunity because Stalin's instructions about crediting our time in the KPP hadn't penetrated everywhere, and after various hassles they agreed to accept me, but without counting my time in the KPP, so I abstained. A number of people, such as Romana Granas, Leon Kasman and Olek Kowalski, who were in Lvov, received party cards.

Did you see Lampe and Finder frequently?

Finder rarely, Lampe more often.

Whom did you deal with on an everyday basis?

With Wierblowski and with Regina Kaplan, who headed Red Aid in Bialystok. As you know, Kaplan was of Soviet origin, a member of the VCP(b) and the KPP; the party sent her to work in Poland, where she was sentenced to fifteen years.

On the charge of preparing an armed uprising with the aim of breaking off western Byelorussia from Poland and annexing it to Soviet Byelorussia.

She got out of prison thanks to the war and came to Bialystok with a Soviet party card that was still valid. Because of our work together before the war we now gathered around her, since she represented some kind of protection for us.

After the "tangerine" reception I was sure that the outbreak of the war would be delayed, but would take place nonetheless. Ponomarenko launched a daily paper in Minsk which would be under his personal control, and the *Standard of Freedom* was born. I wasn't included in the paper's initial founding group. Wierblowski and a few other people went to Minsk to work on it. But the four letters, namely the NKVD, were vigilant, and managed to dig up some charges to bring against two of the *Standard*'s editors. After their arrest, in the spring of 1941, I was summoned to join the editorial team and assigned to the section dealing with contacts with readers – a humble position, but even so it had probably been approved by the party committees in Minsk and Bialystok. One of my major feats was to publish, on the first of May, an article about the third of May, which as you know is a national holiday. I worked on it for quite a long time, sitting in the Lenin Library in Minsk, trying to recall the facts. I had to think about the articles of the Constitution in a new light and a new situation, and tie them in with the discussion that had been going on before the Seventh KPP Congress. For a long time our approach to it had been rather sectarian; we'd discounted it. During the interwar period the 3 May Constitution had been the domain of the National Democracy and all the other bourgeois groups. But now I wrote about it in a more favourable light, in the spirit of a return to our "people's front" line. My article made a considerable impression, so much so that even the Lvov paper, the *Red Flag*, reprinted parts of it. It was also very much seized upon by readers, even though it wasn't any kind of revelation, for people were waiting for that date to be remembered and commemorated, and they viewed my article in some sense as an act of courage.

In June the Nazi invasion began. Bialystok was already being bombed; the first trucks carrying activists began leaving the city. But in Minsk it was still calm. We were living in a residence for film makers, who had gone on holiday. One morning I went round to see Wierblowski, who lived down the corridor from me, because Lampe and Finder had just arrived from Bialystok; they'd got a truck from the committee, and in their flight into the depths of Russia they had made their way to Wierblowski.

I was sitting in their room, talking, when suddenly the bombing of Minsk began; one of the first bombs fell on my room. So I escaped by a miracle, only because I'd left my room. We decided to make our way to the editorial office. We were walking along the street, wondering what we should do, when I suddenly got the idea that somehow Poles should be seen to participate in the war, and that a Polish battalion should be formed to fight alongside the Red Army.

Did you know how to use a gun?

Not very well; I only learnt in Kushnarenkov. I shared this thought with Regina Kaplan. She took up the idea and immediately contacted the committee in Bialystok; the others also managed in time to get hold of the Central Committee of Byelorussia in Minsk. They told us to leave Minsk, but to keep in touch with them and they would consider whether or not to approve our plan.

Who did Kaplan talk to?

I don't know, but I'm sure Ponomarenko must have been informed, and in his turn must have consulted Moscow, since he wouldn't have made such a decision on his own.

That same day my wife and daughter arrived from Bialystok by the last train. They'd had hundreds of adventures on the way: the train had been bombed, everyone had fled for cover in ditches and she had acted as midwife to a woman who had given birth in the train. My daughter was wounded in the foot when they arrived at the station in Minsk.

In the late evening a whole group of us started eastwards. Broniewska, who lived in another part of Minsk, took off with Lampe in a truck, bound for some kolkhoz, while we, with no way of communicating with them, set off on foot. There was no transport. Bombs fell all around us, we spent most of our nights in cemeteries, and my daughter was limping, her wound suppurating. She was just a child, but she was very brave. We finally reached Mogilev, where Regina Kaplan made contact with Minsk. She was told: it's been approved, you can start organizing your battalion; we'll send you instructors, and you'll receive your next orders in Gomel, which will be your gathering point. Round up volunteers on your way.

How many did you get?

Eighteen or twenty people.

Communists?

Yes, but there were more people who wanted to sign on, so that, when it came to forming a unit, we thought we could probably count on getting several hundred people.

We duly stopped in Gomel, where I took leave of my wife and daughter and with the others set about preparing to organize our unit. We were now soldiers, part of a future battalion. We drew up a statute, wrote a proclamation and decided to get in touch personally with the Comintern in Moscow. We wanted to get an idea of what real chances we had for further action. So we sent a "leadership" delegation, consisting of Finder and his wife, Wierblowski and his wife, Regina Kaplan and Skonecki.

Did they have a "summons" from Moscow permitting them to travel within the Soviet Union?

No, they didn't, but Regina Kaplan was able to move about thanks to her party card, and she could vouch that the others had received a summons in Mogilev to present themselves in Moscow and make contact with the Comintern. They managed to get hold of a truck on their way, as luck had it, and got to Moscow. After some ten days or two weeks they sent a message saying that the thing was off: apparently in the meantime Maisky and Sikorski had signed an agreement to collaborate that was based on different principles, and our battalion was naturally too minor a thing in comparison with the idea that had been born there. Our "leaders" were summoning us to join them. Pressing on through blazing territory, with bombs falling around us, we finally made it through to Moscow. I found a place to stay with Daniszewski in his room at the Lux Hotel, which was inhabited by Comintern activists of various nationalities. The Poles who were there apart from us by then included almost the entire editorial staff of the Lvov *Red Flag*. The Soviet authorities were considering what to do with us. We were received by Jan Dzerzhinsky – Feliks Dzerzhinsky's son. He was in charge of cadres at the time, delegated by the Central Committee of the VCP(b).

Was he a Chekist as well?

No, no, he was a Comintern functionary. A very nice man, very human. I don't know the precise details of his life story, but apparently when he was young he ran away from home, rebelled, searched around for his own way, and then, as usually happens in this world, he settled down, got married. But he was at a loss for a long time. During the thirties he lived in the government residence [*Dom pravitelstva* in Russian: a residence for Comintern activists], where he survived the difficult years of the Great Purge. He was already established in his post when I met him: very responsible and disciplined, extremely meticulous in the fulfilment of his tasks, but also kind to the people entrusted to his charge. He also spoke Polish well, since the Dzerzhinskys had always spoken Polish at home. He sent Wierblowski, myself and a few other people to work as editors at the "Kosciuszko" radio station, where his mother, Zofia Dzerzhinska, was director.

In the summer of 1941 Poland and the Soviet Union resumed diplomatic relations. In the agreement signed with Sikorski, the Soviet Union renounced the territorial changes in Poland that had figured in its pact with Hitler in August 1939, committed itself to granting an amnesty to all Polish citizens who had been imprisoned and agreed to help in the creation of a Polish army on its territory. This army was to be a part of the independent Polish Armed Forces, equipped and provided with rations by the Soviet Union, which received American aid on the lend-lease system. Poland, on her part, renounced any war reparations of compensation for the occupation of half of its country, the imprisonment of 250,000 of it soldiers and the deportation of 1,500,000 of the Polish civil population to Russian camps or forced labour. That was Stalin's version which was played out in the international arena; what was the version in Moscow?

I'm not sure that's the right way to look at things. The Soviet Union was in mortal danger and Stalin was searching for various ways out of a critical situation.

First of all: the Comintern training school which prepared the leaders of the future communist party in Poland – when was it created?

In the spring of 1941, before the outbreak of the war between Germany and the Soviet Union. Certain activists were sent there to prepare themselves for the future course of events. The group included Marceli Nowotko and Pawel Finder, members of the First Initiative Group, who were delegated to form the PPR. The school was on the outskirts of Moscow, in Pushkino, and Nowotko and Molojec considered themselves heads of its Polish section.

Secondly: what about Berling?

A survey of prewar Polish officers was conducted, in which they were supposed to say whether they wanted to return to Poland, that is, to Nazi occupation, remain in the Soviet Union and continue to fight or go to a neutral country. A dozen or so opted to remain in the USSR, Berling among them. They later constituted the central core of the military group.

And thirdly: what about Wanda Wasilewska?

By then Wanda was already a member of the Supreme Soviet of the USSR and of the VCP(b), and the only Pole to have a *vyertushka* telephone, the most secret and exclusive telephone in the Soviet

Union: it was a direct line to Stalin, among others, and it testified to her high position. Wanda developed a sense of mission – a great thing – as a result of her prominence. It agreed with her, although she must sometimes have felt the burden of the responsibilities she had taken upon herself. She must have been bothered that she, a former member of the PPS, was in a sense taking the place of KPP members who by virtue of their age and office should have held high positions. We didn't hold it against her, in fact we were rather glad that she was clearing the way with Stalin for reactivating the Polish communist party, since this reactivation had, after all, been the most sacred aim of our efforts. Stalin held Wanda in very high esteem, and he also appreciated her literary work. You see, Stalin was impressed that the daughter of a well-known prewar Polish minister was a writer and a communist.

Did Stalin like her? Was there anyone at all that he liked?

[Smiling] Presumably he liked his daughter, but as to Wanda, it's hard to say. The familiarity that grew up between them required a lot of moral courage on Wanda's part, and she had that courage, perhaps to a greater extent than did KPP members, since she wasn't used to the extremely strict discipline that was deeply rooted in Polish communists, sometimes restricting their freedom of expression. But in my opinion Stalin's positive attitude towards Wanda flowed from his sense of realism: Stalin was very calculated in his actions, and he valued people who were useful and necessary to him.

With whom was she in contact?

With Khrushchev, who was first secretary of the Ukraine. At Khrushchev's she must have met General Serov, Beria's deputy, who was installed in Kiev, and General Georgi Sergeevich Zhukov from the NKVD (not to be confused with Georgi Zhukov, Marshal of the Soviet Union), who exerted an enormous influence over her for a long time.

And what about you?

I was in contact with Manuilski, who was a member of the Comintern executive. He would often ring me up when he wanted to get some information or have something explained. I was involved in a funny incident with him once. I was staying at the Lux Hotel with my family, in a little servants' room on the fifth floor, and the telephone was in the corridor. One day it rang. It rang on and on and no one answered it, and I certainly wasn't going to rush around answering every phone that rang in the corridor. Finally, after a long time, I lost patience and answered it. Manuilski was furious. But thanks to that I got a better room, with its own phone.

I didn't live there for long, because on 18 September Moscow was evacuated. The Comintern, its school in Pushkino and the radio station moved to Ufa. The school was installed in an old manor house in Kushnarenkov, eighty kilometres from Ufa, and I became a lecturer there. In fact I was put in charge of the Polish course, which prepared the second group of future PPR activists for their parachute drop into Poland. The first group was ready by then.

So you were promoted. Why?

Because there was a dearth of people, and I'd had a university education, and possibly greater experience and familiarity with the problems of Marxism–Leninism and the workers' movement. I also suspect that Nowotko had a hand in my nomination.

Why the trust in Nowotko? Was it only because he was a proven communist who hadn't been "contaminated" by membership in the KPP leadership?

I don't know. The old fears and complexes might presumably still have had some influence on the attitude towards old communists, although in fact by then they were fading away, and Lampe gradually began to inspire confidence and to be assigned party work. But at the time Nowotko was indisputably the most important person in the Initiative Group, marked out for first secretary of the PPR. The second most important person was Finder.

Why the PPR and not the KPP?

There was a long discussion about the name of the party, not only in the Comintern but also within the First Initiative Group that had been formed. Some people were in favour of keeping the old name, while Dimitrov tried to convince them that the name ought to be changed, and they resisted this. On the one hand they understood that the PPR would create greater possibilities for work, since it would broaden the base for political influence in Poland and facilitate access to the masses on a wide scale; on the other hand, they were attached to the old party, which had become something of a symbol for them after its dissolution and the loss of its leadership. On the one hand they understood that a return to the old name would in effect mean reactivating the KPP, while on the other they knew that it would be inconvenient for the Russians, because the KPP still trailed the fact of its dissolution around behind it. In the end Dimitrov's version won the day and they agreed that they ought to be guided by the overriding concern, which was indisputably the need to create a new and wider formation with the aim of establishing a national front – an aim which diverged from the ideas of the prewar KPP.

So the new party was to be founded by old KPP members?

We had to base ourselves on someone, and who other than communists from the former KPP and KZMP? A month later the first drop of the PPR Initiative Group ended in disaster. The entire group, I think with the sole exception of the radio operator, returned to Ufa after a brief stay in Moscow. Their plane had crashed just after take-off and Nowotko had broken a leg. The situation was depressing. There was much speculation. Considerable differences were becoming apparent within the Initiative Group, in particular within its leadership, which consisted of Nowotko, Molojec and Finder. I knew nothing about the cause of the conflict, but it was always possible to glean something by way of the grapevine. It appeared to centre around the question of which group would wield supremacy in Poland, the party or the army, and whether the party would be in charge of the army or the other way around. From the outset, Molojec was the person marked out to be in charge of the army; his task in Poland was to form the People's Guard, and then the People's Army. Nowotko, in contrast, was to be first secretary of the party. Molojec naturally had his supporters, not only within the Initiative Group but in Ufa as well.

Who were they?

I don't want to be flinging names about, because the army had its own internal differences as well.

General Shcherbakov, chief political administration of the Red Army?

I wouldn't swear to it, but I suspect so, yes.

And who was backing Nowotko?

The Comintern, that is Dimitrov and Manuilski, who were in charge of its foreign policy.

And higher up? Beria? Serov?

I have no basis whatsoever for making such conjectures. But I do know one thing: echoes of these conflicts prompted discussions in Kushnarenkov. In the group I was in charge of, Olek Kowalski was in some sense a Molojec sympathizer. He was rather abrasive, actually, in his attitude towards me, although this was evident only in his general demeanour, since Kowalski was, of course, appropriately subordinated.

The Initiative Group stayed in Ufa for about a month, during which time they held talks with Dimitrov, the general secretary of the Comintern, drew up party documents, and all the time awaited the next drop, which was set for mid December 1941. Nowotko came to Kushnarenkov to say goodbye to the "girls", as he called them, before he left; he was much liked by them, as he was by everyone. He was warm in his dealings with people and easily able to communicate with them. I'd known him from previous years, and in the course of this month our relations had become quite close. So I decided to have a talk with him, and this talk may be the key to solving the mystery of his death. I had two things to discuss. Naturally I began by asking him to take me with him to Poland.

But surely Nowotko wasn't the one to decide that.

No, of course not; it was probably Dimitrov. But I asked Nowotko. He replied: listen, I'd love to, but you know you're needed here; someone has to prepare our people, so your departure is out of the question.

Both Nowotko and I were aware, although he didn't say so to me, that taking me to Poland wasn't simple, because under the occupation a Jew would have caused countless problems.

Wouldn't Finder have caused such problems as well?

Yes, but they had to send someone with the right qualifications, after all.

I told him: I understand, so there's another matter I want to discuss with you. I've heard there's been some friction in your group, and I'm very worried about it. Couldn't you solve all your disagreements here, before you leave? Why lug all that around with you?

Nowotko didn't deny there was some conflict, thereby confirming its existence, but he tried to allay my fears: don't worry, Jakub, he said, I'll manage. I always manage.

Well, he didn't. He was killed.

In Kushnarenkov, for five months after the Initiative Group left we had no direct news from them. We were lost in speculation. Finally, in May, we discovered why: Nowotko had broken his leg again during the drop and Finder had had to begin organizing the party by himself. The transmitter was also lost during the drop, and it took a long time to find it again.

In the meantime I was preparing the second group for a drop into Poland. It consisted of Malgorzata Fornalska, Janek Krasicki and Aleksander Kowalski.

What did you teach them?

There was an obligatory course for everyone, a short course on the history of the VCP(b), which was taught by some Bulgarian; in addition to this, each national group organized its own lectures. I lectured on the history of the workers' movement in Poland and analysed the past ten years; I also lectured on Polish history, and analysed and passed on the material we were getting from Poland. In addition I gave talks on literature and drew up reports on the international situation. Actually, I did these press reports for the use of the whole school, since I was quite fluent in Russian and the director was only too happy to delegate the task to me.

Where had you learnt Russian?

In Warsaw. Before the First World War I'd attended a Russian high school. The reason I found myself there was quite original, because I was made to do the first year over again in the same form. And do you know why? Because of the *numerus clausus* – the Jewish quota. It wasn't imposed in private Polish schools, but in all state Russian schools it was obligatory.

Just as it is now?

Apparently Andropov is abolishing it. Under the tsar there could only be 5 per cent of Jews in each class.

I knew Russian well, and from time to time I gave lectures for the whole school on the international situation and about the battles on each front. Once a week at most I would go to the Comintern in Ufa, where I had access to the French, German and émigré press, and where I read the coded messages from Poland. These messages constituted our spiritual fodder, even though the information contained in them was not always encouraging. As it turned out, the conflict between Nowotko and Molojec had been escalating. It reached a tragic resolution in late November of 1942: Nowotko was killed, on Molojec's orders, by Zygmunt Molojec, Molojec's brother.

And on whose orders was Molojec himself acting?

That I don't know. His real motives remain a mystery to me to this day. I've thought about who could have given such an order and I can't see who it could have been. I don't believe that either Molojec or Nowotko were agents of the Gestapo. So I'm inclined to think the answer is to be found in the character of Molojec. He might have suffered from some kind of pathological jealousy or craving for power. Molojec was, after all, a distinguished activist, a veteran of the war in Spain; later he directed the Initiative Group of the party in France, where they even began to put out their own bulletin, so his role was considerable. Perhaps, when he was recalled to the Soviet Union, he was shocked that it was not he, but in fact Nowotko, who was designated leader of the Polish party. Perhaps his activities in France fired ambitions in him which he was later unable to renounce. And then there were also various sympathies and aversions, grudges or differences – it's hard to tell if you weren't involved closely in what was going on. Some light is shed on the escalation of the conflict between Molojec and Nowotko by Spychalski in his memoirs, where he writes that Molojec insisted on party members' swearing an oath of loyalty to the People's Guard, which meant that he intended to make the military command into the central decision-making authority in the country.

Nowotko was opposed to this, but Molojec wanted to force him into a situation where he would have no alternative. He accordingly went to France, where he had good contacts and many supporters. There he rounded up a few Spanish war veterans who were loyal to him, which was actually quite a useful move because they already had military training, but with the tensions that existed within the leadership it certainly can't have been received with enthusiasm by Nowotko or Finder.

Quite. But had you not considered the possibility that sending them to Poland together, in conflict, was either a compromise between the Soviet army and the NKVD, or motivated by the desire to transfer their conflict to Poland?

I don't know, because these things are impossible to find out. So why make speculations which, though they admittedly have some sensation value, have nothing much to back them up? Divisions or conflicts were never publicly played out, indeed they were concealed. The external façade that was always imposed was that of a unanimous Politburo, behind which stood Stalin, who was *ober* – arbiter and decider at the same time. Still, the fact remains that even then I found it surprising that Nowotko and Molojec should have been sent to Poland together. In my opinion the problem with the First Initiative Group was that the question of who would impose law and order in Poland, the party or the military, had not been solved: so we're back to the same thing. For a solution to that question would impose a different way of proceeding, or a different division of authority.

After the assassination of Nowotko, Boleslaw Molojec immediately declared himself *de facto* first secretary of the party – not *de jure* because there were no legal provisions for an election. At that point he was joined, for a short time, by Olek Kowalski, who was in Poland by then and highly approved of Molojec's conception of things, as he had done even back in the Soviet Union. Gomulka is alleged to have urged him very strongly not to bother, because there was no point in supporting Molojec. But he soon discovered this for himself. According to the accounts in our possession, Molojec's guilt was proven. Gomulka made quite a long and detailed report, in which he described the investigation and all the complications involved as it unfolded.

That, apart from the enigmatic declarations of Jozwiak, is the only document there is.

But it's a reliable one, something you can't say of Jozwiak's account, which is mysteriously opaque. Besides, I've always considered Gomulka an honest man, and he had no reason to lie. He wrote that Molojec's brother, Zygmunt, who was head of military intelligence, received an order from Molojec to shoot the man Molojec was going to meet. Zygmunt didn't know Nowotko – they checked that – and he carried out the order. Indeed, when they began to interrogate him he didn't make any attempt to deny having done it. He was sentenced to death and the sentence was carried out. Then they shot Molojec.

Janek Krasicki shot him.

That whole affair was the most terrible thing that ever happened to the Polish communist party. In previous years, fierce factional struggles, where people leapt at each other's throats, had never ended that way. This way of solving conflicts was something we simply couldn't conceive of, and hence the various suppositions that Molojec was purportedly hiding behind instructions or powers of some sort, the devil only knows whose.

At the third plenum of the PUWP Central Committee in 1949, Boleslaw Bierut said: "It is a fact that the first secretary of the

PPR, Comrade Nowotko, was murdered by a provocateur *sent to the party by the Second Unit [the Second (Intelligence) Division of the General Staff]." He didn't mention the name, and thus, in the natural order of things, Molojec was crossed out of the history of the party.*

That was a plenum at which I didn't speak at all. I didn't like the atmosphere there, nor did I like that claim.

In Ufa you used to see Dimitrov. What was he like? According to Djilas: "Each time I was struck by the appearance he had of a sick man. His breath was asthmatic, his complexion pale and unnaturally red, with dry patches around his ears, as if from eczema, and his hair so thinning that it revealed his parched, yellow skull. His thoughts, however, were quick and fresh, in total contrast to his slow, tired movements. This prematurely ageing, almost broken man still bubbled with enormous conscious energy and heartiness. His features, also, attested to this, especially the bright look in his bulging grey eyes and the aggressive thrust of his nose and jaw. And although he didn't reveal his every thought, he nonetheless spoke honestly and with confidence."

Djilas likes to exaggerate and overplay things. I had only a few direct conversations with Dimitrov, and I gathered from them that he took great interest in our problems: they preoccupied him a good deal, and he had a lot of trouble with the First Initiative Group. The question of which of the forces entering Poland would impose law and order, the politicians or the military, had not, after all, been definitively answered, and yet it was undoubtedly a significant one, for it was connected with deciding how to proceed and with determining the division of authority. Dimitrov was very involved in this conflict, and tried to find some sort of human, not brutal, solution to it. The most important matters, however, were not decided by him alone, but discussed collectively, so he had to take advice from other people.

From whom did he take advice directly?

From Manuilski, for example, who was a member of the Comintern executive and had quite a lot of experience and knowledge of Polish affairs. Though he was not always right.

Did he dissolve the KPP?

It wasn't for him to decide its dissolution.

But he provided the evidence.

I don't know if it was him specifically. The evidence was collected, or rather fabricated, by another department. Manuilski had been assigned to political work: he formulated generalities, engaged in debates.

What was Dzerzhinsky's wife like? She was directly in charge of the Polish group.

Basically she was quite an unhappy person. In general being the wife of a famous person isn't a cause for joy, and being Dzerzhinsky's wife in particular. He was an unusual man, extraordinarily complicated, with an extreme concentration of willpower and idealism. He must have been interesting.

What's so interesting about him?

The impression of him that has been preserved in Poland is an extremely simplistic one, but if you read his diaries, if you ever came across people who were close to him and particularly if you saw the lists of the women who had loved him, only then could you really come to know him as a living being, with all his faults and obsessions. He was an extraordinarily brave and self-sacrificing man – a mixture of nobleman and revolutionary. Dzerzhinska, his wife, continued to live under his spell. From a young age she'd been active in the SDKPiL; she was very attached to Warsaw, to Poland; indeed she still spoke beautiful Polish even after many years. At the same time she was never particularly warm towards people. Comintern activists who held various high posts had particular national groups entrusted to their charge. Whenever "*no pasaran*" Dolores Ibarruri, for instance, came to Kushnarenkov, there was great joy among the Spaniards because their mother was coming, bringing them what she could – sweets, shoes. Dzerzhinska visited us twice; I would say her behaviour was rather withdrawn. She wasn't unkind and she didn't have any unpleasant tendencies, but she treated us with aloofness, without particular warmth or emotional involvement. This coldness, or even standoffishness of hers, in a situation when people were far away from their country, was perceived by some as offensive. Especially since people often tend to idealize someone who's been in the party for as long as she had, and who in addition had lived for a long time with a distinguished man.

With two of them – there was also Warski, Secretary of the KPP.

Very briefly, and much later. So I wouldn't want to speak negatively of her; rather, I see her as a woman who didn't give much of herself and was very rigorous and unwavering in carrying out her instructions. She was more rigid in her opinions than Dimitrov, who was her superior.

And ideologically?

Dzerzhinska stuck to the canons. Whether or not behind them stood people who formulated them I don't know, although of course it's possible. But I think that what above all dictated Dzerzhinska's stand was that she had been trained to think in a certain way, which imposed on her the use of familiar solutions and well-trodden paths.

Did you ask her about the circumstances of Warski's murder?

No, it would have been particularly awkward to bring that up in a conversation with her.

What about Dimitrov, did you ask him? He allegedly remarked to Tito, on the subject of the Great Purge, that it had been necessary to bleed the healthy tissue in order to get rid of the diseased parts.

No, I never asked him. I wasn't on those kinds of terms with him. And he'd spoken quite warmly to me of Tito back in 1943: perhaps because the Yugoslav party was full of internal conflict at the time, and it was presumably in Tito that Dimitrov had found support for consolidating it.

I tried to discuss the purge with Manuilski, but he prevaricated. He wouldn't even say whether or not they were alive.

Did he know?

Definitely. He must have known. He was a very clever man, actually.

An NKVD man?

I don't think so. Rather, he tended to slither about, keeping his options open. He belonged to the Comintern *vyerkhushka*, its leading group, which had gone through all the experiences of that time, but which in fact was to a great extent the executor of Stalin's orders, though in minor matters it made its own decisions. Manuilski, however, was useful to us inasmuch as he had a good grasp of Polish affairs, spoke Polish quite well and had picked up a number of things during his years of supervising the KPP. Of course, the conclusions he drew from his knowledge were another matter. But he was easier to talk to than others.

So, Manuilski manoeuvred, but what about the rest? What was the structure of the interdependencies between people?

You're asking about top secret matters of which I couldn't have any knowledge; besides, any attempts to pigeonhole people like that would result in dangerous oversimplification. The only thing I could do would be to mention a few members of the Politburo, but that wouldn't take you very far if you don't know exactly what kind of work each one of them did – for that also was considered a secret. There was Malenkov, a very intelligent man, but I didn't really know him. The person I saw most frequently was Molotov, who dealt with Polish affairs until the end of the war. He was certainly close to Stalin, but also often very harshly treated and threatened by him.

February 1943 was the victory at Stalingrad; in March the creation of the Union of Polish Patriots was announced; in April the Katyn massacre came to light and the USSR severed diplomatic relations with Poland; in May the Comintern was dissolved and Berling's army was formed.

The victory at Stalingrad, which can't be overestimated, determined later decisions. The role of Shcherbakov, chief political administrator of the Red Army, increased.

Did you know him?

No. If I ever came across him, I don't remember it.

What about Zhukov? Djilas says that he was "slim and fair-haired, still young and knew his way about . . . not without a sense of humour and a refined cynicism, assets rarely found in a member of the secret service. . . . Zhukov was an excellent administrator and, on the basis of experience, placed greater faith in force as a means of realizing communism than in ideology."

I had almost no conversations with Zhukov and I didn't really know him.

According to Berling, Zhukov was "a very intelligent and energetic major in the NKVD, which in the Soviet hierarchy was equivalent to the rank of major general. He was blindly devoted to Stalin body and soul . . . he was his eyes and ears."

Zhukov was a liaison officer in Anders' army, and later fulfilled the same function in Berling's army. Berling never lost his attachment to him. I really only had one conversation with him. One day he asked to see me to hear my opinion on opening a ZPP centre in Teheran, where it had just been decided to establish one. It was to be our first diplomatic outpost, so I expressed my support for it. Zhukov suggested some candidates for the posting and asked me what I thought of them. I approved of the choice and said so. I don't remember any other conversations with him. I do know, however, second-hand, that he didn't do much to help in Polish affairs. One of his tasks was to assess our people to see which of them should to go Poland, and later to organize the drops. He delayed the departures, which would have taken place much more quickly if the system of decision-making had been different; this was strange, because it was not a question of making any choices about who would be sent, our people or his – he could send his as well, as many as he wanted, and by sending ours he gained another perspective on many Polish affairs. So presumably he was just a *strakhovshchik*, a coward who did all he could to put off making decisions and in addition didn't understand where the crux of the solution to Polish affairs in the future lay: in intelligence work or in the political work done by communists. As a good (to his own mind) administrator in his own department, he believed that it lay in intelligence and in people who were to a large extent dependent on intelligence, and for this reason he failed to grasp the political significance of sending communists to Poland, where they founded a party which became the beginning of a new government in Poland.

What conflicts appeared among the Polish communists as a result of the struggle for power and influence in the Soviet leadership?

No, no, there weren't any conflicts.

Well, then, let's take them one by one. There was a conflict in the army between Berling and Sokorski on the one hand, Minc and Zambrowski on the other.

It's hard to call that a conflict. It was in Lublin, in 1944, that we discovered who Berling really was, when he sent a telegram to Stalin with, among others, the words, "I beg you on my knees, get rid of this band of Trotskyists". He meant, naturally, not Trotskyists, but Berman, Minc and Zambrowski. He thought Stalin would heed his opinion, for Stalin wasn't exactly a philo-Semite either, but he overreached in his calculations: Stalin knew that if he listened to Berling, he would be in conflict with the whole governing group, including Bierut and Gomulka, so he told us: you have to get rid of him, and we did.

Berling was sent to the Frunze Military Academy in Moscow. He felt wronged. He sat down in the Polish embassy and declared a hunger strike, and he sat there and kept up his strike for several days. When I found out about it I wrote him a letter saying: end your hunger strike, it isn't necessary. I assure you that if you come back to Warsaw appropriate work will be found for you.

Berling ended his hunger strike. I expect he did so as a result of my letter, although perhaps there was someone else as well who influenced his decision – that's something I have no way of knowing. At any rate he returned to Poland and entered our military academy; later we made him deputy minister of State Farms. His further fate is known: he described it in his memoirs. I haven't read them, but I'm told they reek of anti-Semitism and loathing for the group which, in his view, removed him from the army. They don't interest me: that's a matter that's past and done with, painful and full of complexities.

Yet Sokorski writes that the conflict concerned General Berling's position: "Jakub Berman more than once expressed his surprise at my uncritical belief in the good faith of officers of the old Polish army."

That's a lie; I never uttered those words. The way Sokorski has learnt to fib, no one can keep up with him. I knew him when he was a young boy and I was always amazed at the way he could adapt to every argument. I respected Berling as a good military professional and I didn't know him well. But I did try to clear up this thing about Minc, because Minc was my friend. I discussed it with Wanda Wasilewska but she, like Berling, remained under the influence of General Zhukov of the NKVD; she considered him an authority, and for some time she inclined to his suggestions, although Zhukov was an extremely unpleasant character who also did us a lot of harm. Later Wanda came round to Lampe, with whom her relations had been strained for some time, and quite unnecessarily adopted an almost overly hostile attitude towards Berling. As often happens, she went to the other extreme. She wouldn't visit the army, she wouldn't see Berling and she wouldn't see any of his people, including Sokorski. It was all a bit typical of a woman. I tried to smooth things down a little, but it was difficult.

The real conflict came with postulates number one and two which outlined the future shape of Poland. Number one, drawn up by the minister Jakub Prawin, an old KPP man, but suggested by Sokorski, who in turn was inspired, I think, by General Shcherbakov, proposed a system of "organized democracy", and came in for a lot of opposition and discussion from First Division and ZPP activists. Recidivist legionary leanings from the time of Pilsudski were discerned in it, for the influence of the army over the future of the country was decisive in it and didn't even mention the PPR or the other parties. Thus the army, and not the party, was to be the decisive factor in Poland; the army was to rule over the future of the country, and this we couldn't accept. Not for that, surely, was the PPR created in Poland, nor, later, the Central Bureau of Communists in Moscow – to find that they were of marginal influence. A discussion arose, and out of it sprang postulate number two, drawn up by Hilary Minc and Roman Zambrowski. In their proposals it was the party and ideology that were accorded the decisive role in shaping the future of Poland. Zambrowski, however, also went a bit too far, in that his postulate proposed a parliamentary, liberal democratic system: this was a result of his illusions, not of any assessment of reality. Still, I wouldn't want to exaggerate the conflict over that. It was a normal discussion which undoubtedly contained deeper undercurrents, since it was instigated by our Soviet friends and really centred around one issue in the domain of tactics: an agreement on the type of system of rule that would bring better effects and prove the more durable in Poland – one based on obedient officers or on ideologically committed party men.

Lampe didn't like either proposal, and had considerable reservations about each of them. We tried to stifle this discussion, because no good would come of it, but Berling and Sokorski still harboured ambitions of leadership, and tried to push through their postulate number one at every opportunity.

The next conflict was between the communists from Moscow and the Home National Council.

There was no conflict.

So what was there?

After the capture of Fornalska and Finder we again lost contact with Poland and had no idea of what was happening there. We were genuinely concerned by the disturbing signals that had reached us before. The Comintern decided to send a group of its representatives to take stock of the situation on the spot and transmit information about what they found. From the first drop of eleven people two remained, while of the second group, which had contained almost seventeen people, twelve were immediately killed. We were at a loss to know what had happened, especially after the capture of Finder and Fornalska; we suspected some kind of provocation. But no trace of anything that might have confirmed our suspicions was found. We therefore came to the conclusion that it was an unfortunate accident.

Thus we knew little of what was happening in Poland, and the rapidly changing international situation demanded that we take some steps. The idea was born of establishing a representative body in the form of the Polish National Committee. The ZPP was concerned with refugees, welfare and education, while we wanted to broaden our base of influence and, in the face of the rapid progression of the war, to prepare the ground for a Polish government.

But there already was a government, in London, recognized by the nation.

But not by the Soviet Union, and Stalin would never have agreed to such a government. The Polish government had to be free from hostility to the Soviets.

And how did this hostility manifest itself? In opposing the appropriation of half our country? In opposing the murder and deportation to Siberia of our citizens?

You're talking nonsense. Who was it who threatened the young Soviet state after World War I? Mr Pilsudski! Lenin offered Poland very advantageous borders which extended far to the west, but they didn't satisfy Pilsudski, naturally, because he wanted to create a federation and bring the Ukraine and the Baltic states under his power. He marched on Kiev – why? *Cui bono!*

And why did Lenin march on Warsaw?

Because at that point it was no longer a question of Poland. Poland was considered a pathway to Germany, and in Germany, in the heart of Europe, a revolutionary situation was being sustained; hopes for a victorious revolution in Germany began to grow. Unfortunately they were not fulfilled. The defeat at Warsaw crushed all hope of a European revolution. After the Second World War, therefore, Stalin had to have a guarantee that the country bordering him – for Poland cannot be erased from the map of Europe – would be friendly towards the Soviet Union.

And he wanted to ensure this friendship by murdering our officers?

He also did what he liked with his own; the number of Soviet victims was also considerable.

What were you by the end of 1943?

I was secretary of the home section of the ZPP and secretary of the organizational commission of the newly formed PKN.

So the posts you held were not prominent or representative, but they were nonetheless the most important ones, because they were operational. Why did they choose you?

In my opinion Stalin was guided in his choice by two criteria. The first was the attitude towards the Soviet Union and to communist ideology, and Stalin was rather convinced of my attachment to both. The second was his assessment of the person as a whole: whether he would be able to achieve something, to have some power of suggestive influence over others, or whether he would be an empty thing filling a place. Stalin had probably formed his impression of me when I was still in Kushnarenkov. The political lectures I gave there must have made their way to Moscow in one form or another, and there reached Stalin.

Throughout all that time I remained in contact with Manuilski, who was then in charge of foreign affairs at the VCP(b) Central Committee. So when we came up with the idea of creating a Polish National Committee, I went with Manuilski to see Dimitrov, who was recovering from pneumonia and living on the outskirts of Moscow. That was my first opportunity to have a longer conversation with him. He asked about the people in the new PPR leadership, wanted to know who they were. Actually, I didn't really know, but since he mentioned Gomulka's name several times I told him that from what I'd heard he was a man who fully deserved to be trusted. I also told him about our new project of organizing a committee that would incorporate the idea of the Polish state and would be the beginning of Polish representation.

We didn't know at the time that the Home National Council was being planned in Poland, and we had to use the people we had available in Moscow to form the Polish National Committee. We set aside ten places for them, two for Polish Americans, two for London Poles, one for Poles from the Near East and five for Poles from Poland. I proposed to change the last to at least five, but my proposal was rejected. The majority thought that everything would go smoothly and evenly, and then only arithmetic, not logic, is important: ten here, five there. I was supposed to put up candidates from Poland after consulting with them. Wasilewska very much wanted Oskar Lange, whom she knew from their days in Cracow. As you know, Lange was in the United States at the time, and was quite friendly with Roosevelt, which must have raised a number of doubts in the minds of the Soviets. Stalin once spoke of him in rather harsh tones and Wasilewska immediately reacted; Stalin didn't often encounter that kind of reaction – perhaps never. But when he saw that his opinion of Lange had been mistaken he admitted that Wanda had been right and even said to her: I was wrong. That was something it wasn't easy to achieve with Stalin.

Did you succeed?

No. He would take up various suggestions but he never called it that. The first time I saw him was on 24 December 1943, at a reception for Poles at the Kremlin on the eve of the Polish National Committee meeting.

Presumably it was given in the same rooms in which Sikorski had been fêted a year before?

This time the guests consisted of several dozen people and us – a dozen or so communist activists. Lampe, unfortunately, wasn't included, as he had died about two weeks earlier.

You were completely under Stalin's spell, were you not?

For me Stalin was victory incarnate. He bore upon his shoulders the whole burden of the war with Hitler and he was the hope for the changes in Poland of which we expected so much. For me he was a man whose name was on the lips of millions as they went into battle and died.

In Siberia as well.

Of course there were some internal conflicts. The inability to reconcile those things with the war victories was a heavy burden. But when you were with Stalin that became secondary: the main thing for us was that Stalin was the victor. In the extremely difficult situation in which the Soviet Union found itself he had the strength and the ability to concentrate a powerful fist, which he used to crush Hitler. Stalin was the director of that victory; history will appreciate that.

How did he behave?

As a superb strategist, he undoubtedly used his tactical ability to control his behaviour. He sometimes had brilliantly perceptive flashes of insight, moments of elation, moments of anger and moments of thoughtfulness, or even deliberation, when he was in no hurry to respond. He wasn't particularly prone to revealing his thoughts, nor was he always inclined to sincerity. He generally spoke slowly, with a bad accent, but we didn't find this jarring, because after all there are many nationalities living in the Soviet Union and not all of them speak entirely correctly. He was short of stature and his face was pockmarked.

Did he have the Kremlin yellow complexion?

No, I wouldn't say so; on the contrary, he did his best to give the appearance of health.

Did he practice any sports?

I shouldn't think so, although his dachas, of which he had several, and which we often used to visit near the end of the war, contained various sporting equipment. We played bowls there, which I always made a terrible mess of, had cheerful conversations and told jokes.

Political ones?

Those as well. Minc would remember them if he were alive; he had a good memory and was good at telling them. Stalin didn't take part in our amusements and only made his appearance at supper or later, at the film, which was screened especially for us. He liked American films, ultra-political ones; he would become excited then and share his comments with us. But it was above all at supper that he had a good time. He ate and drank a lot. Later his doctors must have ordered him to cut down on his drinking, because there was something the matter with his liver, so he diluted his wine and vodka with water, half and half. Whenever we came to Moscow for a longer visit after the war our stay always ended with supper, followed by a film. It became a custom that we never left without having had a meal together. Naturally, the whole ritual of deciding who would take part from our side and who from theirs was observed.

What were the criteria?

I don't know; at any rate Bierut and I were always there. A few times some PPS people were also invited, even on their own, I think; that was when there was the proposal to create a unified front and unite them with the PPR, and Stalin was very anxious to win them over to the idea; his parties were one of the methods he used towards such ends.

What were the others?

He could be a charming man, and when he was counting on someone's cooperation he was full of warmth, even concern, towards him. On our way back from holiday in Crimea, for instance, he would always enquire in great detail whether we'd liked it, whether our families had enjoyed it, whether we'd had a good rest; he also made such enquiries of Gomulka. Little things like that – the human touch, which always brought you closer and endeared him to you.

Supper began at ten o'clock, did it not?

It always started late in the evening and lasted until dawn. The food and drink were exquisite; I particularly remember a delicious roast of bear. Bierut always sat next to Stalin, and I sat beside Bierut. Stalin would propose toasts: the first one to "Comrade Bierut", then to "Comrade Berman", and although the toast to Bierut did contain some warmth, both were brief and basically formal. Then he would put on a record, generally Georgian music, which he adored. Once, in 1948, I think, I danced with Molotov [laughter].

Surely you mean with Mrs Molotov?

No, she wasn't there; she was in a labour camp. I danced with Molotov – I think it was a waltz, or at any rate something very simple, because I don't know the faintest thing about dancing, so I just moved my feet in rhythm.

As the woman?

Yes, Molotov led; I wouldn't have known how. Actually, he wasn't a bad dancer. I tried to keep in step with him, but what I did resembled clowning more than dancing.

What about Stalin – whom did he dance with?

Oh, no, Stalin didn't dance. Stalin wound the gramophone, considering it his duty as a citizen. He never left it. He would just put on records and watch.

He watched you?

Yes. He watched us dance.

So you enjoyed yourselves.

Yes, it was pleasant, but with an inner tension.

You didn't have fun, really?

Stalin really had fun. For us these dancing sessions were a good opportunity to whisper to each other things that couldn't be said out loud. That was when Molotov warned me about being infiltrated by various hostile organizations.

Was it a threat?

No, it was called a friendly warning. He took advantage of the situation – or perhaps he'd even arranged it himself, since he was the one who asked me to dance – to mention, in passing, a few things which he thought it would be useful for me to know. I took note of them and didn't say anything in response.

Were there any women present?

None. You never saw any women around Stalin. Those matters were arranged with extreme discretion and never filtered out beyond his closest circle. Stalin was always very careful that there shouldn't be any gossip about him; it's always very dangerous when tongues wag about a man like that. Stalin understood the danger of gossip and he wanted to give the impression that every inch of him was pure and uncorrupted.

Were you waited on by soldiers?

When I was there we were served by waitresses in ordinary dress. Once one of them, quite a tall girl, was serving tea, and she stopped next to us for a moment as she was setting out the dishes. Suddenly Stalin burst out: "What's she listening to?" It gave me a shock, because for the first time I saw a different side to Stalin: here was a man who could react with such violent distrust towards a waitress – someone who had been checked a thousand times over before being admitted to direct contact with him, someone totally reliable in every way. I thought then that his state must be bordering on the pathological.

I also remember another occasion that was very typical of him. It took place near the end of the forties. I was in Moscow with Bierut, and during an interval between talks I told Stalin that we wanted to publish an album devoted to KPP activists, and include in it the names of Kostrzewa and Warski. Stalin approved this project, and then suddenly began to talk about Kostrzewa in glowing terms: such a wise woman, such a good communist, so dedicated to the party. Bierut and I listened to this in astonishment; we couldn't reconcile what Stalin was now saying with her death ten years before.

A good time to ask, then.

You don't ask stupid questions, Miss Toranska [smile].

I understand. Well, then, what was served on 24 December 1943, Christmas Eve? A roast of bear or carp?

I don't remember. Besides, that reception has been written about in detail by many of its participants.

The following day was the first of several devoted to a session of the Polish National Committee. The session was presided over by Wanda Wasilewska, and the deputy was Andrzej Witos, whom she had just extracted from labour camp – a bit by accident, in fact, since she'd been convinced that it was his brother, Wincenty Witos, who was in a Soviet camp.

The session was drawn out; there was much to discuss. The main problem was that we weren't sure what attitude we ought to adopt towards the new PPR leadership, about which we didn't know very much.

Because after the loss of two trusted communists, Nowotko and Finder, Gomulka had become first secretary?

Yes. He was the most distinguished activist at the time – he was secretary of the PPR in Warsaw – and Janek Krasicki had not yet brought Bierut in from Byelorussian Minsk. At a later date attempts were made to vilify Gomulka with a variety of insinuations concerning the deaths of Fornalska and Finder. Such suspicions could only be the product of a diseased imagination.

Another issue which came up in the course of the PKN session was that of ministry posts. I was proposed as a candidate for the directorship of the propaganda ministry, but I requested the withdrawal of my candidacy and instead put forward for consideration a prewar professor who undoubtedly enjoyed a certain renown in Poland, especially in academic circles.

You didn't plan on being a minister yourself?

No.

What plans did you have?

I didn't have any particular plans. But I was aware of the fact that as a Jew I either shouldn't or wouldn't be able to fill any of the highest posts. Besides, I didn't mind not being in the front ranks: not because I'm particularly humble by nature, but because it's not at all the case that you have to project yourself into a position of prominence in order to wield real power. The important thing to me was to exert my influence, leave my stamp on that complicated government formation which was being created, but without projecting myself. Naturally, this required a certain agility.

An éminence grise *perhaps?*

No, because that expression suggests someone secret, confidential, concealed from the greater mass of people, whereas I intended to make public appearances and official speeches, but only as one member of the collective, not as the most important one.

On 28 December I was rung up by Manuilski. I excused myself from the Committee session and went with him to see Molotov. Molotov asked me the same questions that Dimitrov had asked: about the PPR activists and the situation in Poland. I told him everything I knew. At the end of the visit I said to Molotov: I'd like to take the opportunity of being here to make the following suggestion. We're approaching Poland, and the army has, as you know, been subject to ideological differences; it has also displayed tendencies to bypass the party and govern the country in somewhat legionary fashion. In fact, they don't mention the party at all, although they must know about its activities, which are quite prominent in our papers and over the radio. The reason for this is that we lack a central institution that would coordinate all political activity and would be able to direct both the ZPP and the army. Once in Poland it would strictly coordinate its work with the PPR.

Molotov heard me out and said: write it down.

Immediately after this conversation, therefore, I got together with Minc and Wierblowski in a private flat and we jointly drew up a memorandum. The gist of it was that the situation was ripe for our activities to be coordinated and that we, Polish communists, considering ourselves a component part of the PPR, request the creation of a centre of command analogous to the German one. I signed this memorandum and sent it to Molotov. To our surprise, a decision was made within a week. The secretariat of the VCP(b) Central Committee resolved that a Central Bureau of Polish Communists (the name was thought up by them) was to be created in Moscow. This memorandum of ours, which became the founding declaration of the CBKP, is on file in the party archives, although my name has been deleted from it, since it is considered an anonymous document, which is something it never was.

The CBKP was created in the first days of January 1944, and almost at the same time we found out that the Home National Council had been created in Poland. We were taken aback.

Had no posts been assigned to you in the KRN?

No, presumably because of the lack of efficient communication between us.

After the creation of the KRN the Polish National Committee became unnecessary, so it dissolved itself, while the CBKP began its activities. First we were assigned one office, then another, and by a resolution of the VCP(b) secretariat we began our work.

Not many people knew about you. Werfel didn't, for instance.

We weren't a party or an organization of any kind, after all, merely an office – as the very name indicated – established to coordinate political work within the Soviet Union. There had to be someone to supervise the army, which was ablaze with ambition to govern the new Poland, and the Union of Polish Patriots. We also bore the burden of mediating between the Central Committee of the VCP(b) and the PPR, and as the situation developed we also became an advisory body to the PPR. But our attitude towards the PPR had been a loyal one from the outset: we were one of its component parts and we were there to help Poland in its struggle with the occupying forces.

That's very cleverly conceived.

Miss Toranska, Sokorski also suggests something along these lines, claiming that the CBKP was very cleverly conceived to take over the country and subordinate the PPR to itself, but that's a load of rubbish.

Is it? And yet you began your work by checking the loyalty of ancient KPP members?

If that's what Werfel says, then he's wrong. I wouldn't advise you to rely on his opinion, although I consider him a very useful man: he had a very flexible mind which easily adapted itself to new circumstances. What we did do was to have conversations with certain comrades who we thought would be useful in rebuilding the country and whom we wanted to use in the new Poland. Surely that's not a sin, but rather the ability to anticipate.

What was your position in the bureau?

I was a member of the leadership.

Quite. Three of you founded it – Minc, Wierblowski and yourself – but its leadership was also made up of Wasilewska, Swierczewski, Radkiewicz and Aleksander Zawadzki as the head.

Rubbish, Zawadzki wasn't in Moscow then and only very rarely came to see us. Those are myths created later. As for the make-up of the bureau, that, like its name, was decided not by us but by the VCP(b).

Why did they put in Zawadzki?

I don't know.

Then please decipher for me the following fragment of his life. In the years 1939–41 he worked in Pinsk: in the Soviet militia, in the town communal administration, as director of the culture and leisure park, and with Red Aid. When he fell ill he was sent to Sochi for treatment. From there he went to Gomel and Moscow. From Moscow, at the end of November 1941, he and his wife were sent to Stalingrad, and from there to the Aksai estate on the Volga, where he worked as a planner, something he knew nothing about. In July 1942 the German army was approaching Stalingrad, and Zawadzki was sent to the work battalion to build fortifications. After a few months he found himself in hospital and straight from there, not yet entirely cured, he was sent to work in a coal mine near Novosibirsk as a loader and miner. In mid-September 1943, after some complicated manoeuvres and interventions, he came to Siedlce, and by 7 November he was already inaugurating a ceremony to commemorate the October Revolution. In January 1944 he became second in command of the Political and Educational Affairs Corps in Sokorski's place; a few weeks later he became a general and put the communists in the army through a loyalty check. You have to admit it's quite an American-style career.

Well, yes. In 1941 Zawadzki refused to be parachuted into Poland because he was afraid, and hence his later difficulties.

He was obliged to comply?

Not formally, no, but the opinion was that he hadn't come through.

So: Zawadzki wasn't in Moscow, and nor was Swierczewski; Wasilewska was in charge of the Union of Polish Patriots, which was subordinated to the CBKP; Lampe was dead. Which leaves you, next to Radkiewicz, as the most important person in Moscow, the director of future decisions.

All the work of the CBKP was basically carried out by the four of us: Radkiewicz was the secretary, Wierblowski became an instructor on propaganda affairs, Minc became an instructor on economic affairs and I was assigned to contacts with Poland – a section of great importance, delegated to me because it was considered that as I had already deciphered coded messages from Poland in Kushnarenkov, I was familiar with what was happening there. Of course, I wasn't all that familiar with it, only to the extent of what I was able to glean from the coded messages (and not all of them at that, since I don't suppose they showed me all of them), but I suppose it's true that I was better informed than others.

In January 1944 I received a letter from Gomulka. It was addressed to Dimitrov, that is, to the Central Commission of Party Control of the VCP(b): "Wieslaw" did not yet know of the existence of the CBKP in Moscow and had sent the letter to the VCP(b) in the usual way. It was an intelligent and very well-written account of their situation in Poland. He wrote that the party's pro-Soviet stand, and in particular its consent to hand over Vilnius and Lvov, was barring their way to exerting a broader influence over society; and he included a clever comment to the effect that even if such a position were supported by the brotherhood of St Antony, it still wouldn't do much good, because the Poles would stubbornly continue to treat us as Soviet agents. That was actually something we were aware of without needing him to tell us, and he made no suggestions about how to overcome that attitude, so we had to work it out for ourselves. We assumed that if there was any point to the war at all, it was the opportunity to broaden the scope of socialist influence in the world, and particularly in Europe. That opportunity had to be taken advantage of. We had no illusions about being able to gain control over the so-called "big four" prewar parties which made up the London Representation, but we did want the PPR to extend its activities over a broad range of party supporters and sympathizers, as well as over the non party masses. We relied on the approach of the Red Army to give rise to a variety of hopes, especially among those who were still hesitating: populists or democrats who had become more radical in the course of the war and gone over to the left to become, in effect, our sympathizers. But, as we tried to suggest to Gomulka, they could be won over to our ideas if we refrained from slogans which were too radical and from making claims which would scare off the moderate elements or reinforce negative opinion about us.

I tried to explain to him that coming out with a radical programme would complicate not only our situation but also that of the Soviet Union in its relations with the anti-Nazi coalition. Thus the PPR had to keep in mind the intricate structure of the international situation and should refrain from launching campaigns which might put us or the Soviet Union in conflict with the Allies or contribute to frightening them away from talks with us. For these reasons we said that any programme of social change put forward by the PPR should be presented with the utmost moderation. Thus there could be no talk of nationalization without compensation or of agrarian reform without compensation.

In coming out with their stringent demands, the PPR activists in Poland were doubtless responding to pressure from the lower party ranks, which thought in terms of KPP slogans. We tried to temper these surges of radicalism and finally, I think, we managed to get our position across and convince them. In any case, the moderate formulations we drew up were to be found in the July Manifesto of the PKWN, which, as you remember, was very restrained.

But you were the ones who wrote it.

Yes, but the PPR delegation approved it. The Manifesto was initially drawn up by a PKN commission, under the chief editorship of Minc, and in later stages he was aided by, among others, Drobner and Spychalski. The final draft was written by Minc, together with Wierblowski and myself, the night before it was sent to press. It was printed in Moscow and subsequently sent over to Chelm and Lublin to be reprinted. The PPR would not have had the physical means to publish such a document.

Gomulka either didn't understand our politics, or understood it wrongly. One day, in the spring of 1941, he sent us a coded message asking whether the PPR should anticipate uniting with the Central People's Committee created by the RPPS along with syndicalists and democrats, and then take on the role of the opposition in the "representative" Council of National Unity. I was astonished at his failure to grasp the result of the war and the new configuration of forces that was already taking clear shape. But I did my best to enter into his way of thinking and that of others who were active under the occupation. I tried to tell myself that we, in Moscow, were operating with different categories: knowing the international aspect of things, we also knew where various interests crossed and how far compromises of one sort or another could be taken. They, on the other hand, were under enormous pressure from a public opinion that had been moulded by the mentality of the inter-war years and considered the London government as an extension of the state. Nevertheless, I realized that, all such excuses notwithstanding, Gomulka's suggestion attested to his complete ignorance of what was going on. We sent a negative reply to his message, stressing that it was totally misguided and incorrect. For us to unite ourselves with any party would mean consigning ourselves to eternal opposition, would it not? Whereas we had decided to aim for broadening the KRN's base at the expense of other parties and thereby greatly to extend our influence. In order to implement such a programme, however, we needed time, and time was what we didn't have.

I was the one who edited the reply to Gomulka, but it was signed by Zawadzki in his capacity as the official head of the CBKP. In the next coded message he sent, "Wieslaw" tried to exonerate himself by saying he had been under the influence of Churchill's speech when writing his previous letter and had supposed that the Soviet Union was going for some kind of compromise; for this reason he had wanted to assume a position of compromise in advance, as it were, in the belief that he would thereby make the Soviet Union's situation that much easier. What does this show? It shows that "Wieslaw", being in Poland, was very far removed from the winding course of world politics: he didn't understand it and he was lost in it. In contrast, he was overly influenced by pressure from certain circles operating with concepts from World War I. We were slightly worried by this state of affairs, since there were no effective means of communication between us and we weren't sure exactly how the PPR would steer events. They wrote us letters and we answered them, limiting ourselves to advice and asking for explanations when something was unclear; but time was pressing, and decisive events were approaching. The exchange of letters between me (since it was mostly I who wrote them) and "Wieslaw" intensified, and yet the correspondence did not enable us to understand their problems, nor them our intentions. We insisted that a delegation from the KRN come to see us. It came in May 1944.

The delegation put up at Wasilewska's dacha outside Moscow. I went out there, and on that occasion renewed my prewar acquaintance with Spychalski. We slept in one room, so we were at liberty to talk till morning. I asked him questions about what was happening in Poland and he, with great sincerity, described it to me; thanks to this I was able to get a better understanding of the PPR's situation in Poland.

How many members did the party have, according to him?

Spychalski wasn't particularly proud of its numbers. I don't remember the figure he gave me, but it wasn't in the tens of thousands, which we'd suspected anyway. But the party did have its cells throughout the country, and thanks to this Spychalski, when telling me about Poland, was able to refer to specific facts or events, particularly in the military sphere, with which he was especially concerned.

Did he talk about the factional struggle within the PPR?

I don't think so; I don't remember him doing so.

Because that was when Bierut sent a letter to Dimitrov in which he reported that Gomulka's attitude was unstable, sectarian and opportunist, and required intervention on the part of comrades from the USSR.

I didn't know anything about that letter, nor, probably, did the other members of the CBKP. Still, I'm not excluding the possibility that there was such a letter. There was indeed a very fierce factional struggle being waged within the Central Committee of the PPR at that time. The faction led by Gomulka thought that, despite various reservations and hesitations, they should join the London Council of National Unity. This position was supported by, among other things, an article which appeared in the *Trybuna Wolnosci* [*Tribune of Freedom*] on 1 July 1944, entitled "Our View". I didn't discuss any of this with Spychalski. At one point he expressed the opinion that by building a broader front we should be able to get through to various groups by way of penetration – you understand what that means, I take it? I didn't agree with him, and expressed my dissent in guarded terms. I had not only moral but also political reasons for not liking the method of penetration. I was, of course, in favour of winning over our enemies, or individual activists, but by means of persuasion, not by –

Recruitment?

Exactly; not by devious and roundabout means. Spychalski later wrote in his memoirs that he didn't know why I had a grudge of some sort against him, didn't understand what it was I reproached him for, but he failed to explain the nature of the disagreement which arose between us and which should not be overlooked.

The delegation was received by Stalin and succeeded above all in arranging for the transport of arms to Poland, which we had been trying to get for some months. Back in February we'd already sent a resolution to the Soviet authorities requesting that more arms be sent to Poland. We explained that with the approach of the Red Army there was growing unrest, the activities of various groups were increasing, and parts of these groups could be enlisted to fight under the leadership of the PPR. The Soviet authorities, however, had been distrustful of our resolution and kept delaying the decision – here again we discerned the hand of General Zhukov.

We also extended the membership of the CBKP by including Minc and Spychalski. So there were now seven of us instead of five. We didn't do this ourselves, of course, since we were not empowered to make such a decision alone, but we presented Minc as a brilliant economist who had played an important role in editing the text of the PKWN's Manifesto, especially the part dealing with agriculture, because when a discussion arose, the Soviet comrades didn't have a very good idea of the agrarian structure in Poland and Minc had to spend a long time explaining it to Stalin, Manuilski and others.

So the text of the July Manifesto was agreed upon with Stalin himself?

Of course: Stalin was very interested in how the situation in Poland was developing. Besides, it was not so much a question of his approving its content as of us explaining our position, since it didn't accord with the Soviet comrades' experience. They operated on the basis of what they remembered from their youth, and considered their own agrarian reform programme as the best model to emulate. So they urged us to distribute land to the middle stratum of peasants as well, which was impossible in Poland because there wasn't enough land. But they stuck to their version, remembering that there had been a lot of kulak land in Russia and that large tracts of it had been available. Minc was brilliant in arguing with them. He calculated the number of hectares within the prewar Polish boundaries (without including the western territories, since he couldn't yet treat them as a *fait accompli*) and the number of people who needed land; the proportions clearly showed that there wouldn't be enough land left over for the middle stratum of peasants. But still they stubbornly stuck to their viewpoint, basing themselves on doctrinal or doctrinaire assumptions. We spent a long time trying to puzzle out a solution to this jigsaw, playing for time. Then they insisted that if we failed to carry out an agrarian reform in time, we would find we had made a grave mistake, and the interests of the state would be harmed; you will pay dearly for it, they said, if you leave it too late.

They were right, of course, and their advice was sound, given out of concern for us. Finally we found a solution. We included a clause in the resolution to the effect that the middle stratum of peasants would also benefit from the agrarian reform, but only those with large families, which had the additional advantage of dividing them.

But you claimed Poland would be independent.

What does that have to do with independence! Independence is one thing, agreeing on the text of the Manifesto or the principles of agrarian reform is another. Besides, the Soviets were only doing this, and giving us advice, out of concern for us; they wanted our revolution in Poland to take the form they were familiar with, the best one in their view, because it was victorious. They couldn't, after all, shed their own mentality and jump into someone else's. I'm deeply convinced of that and I wish you would also try to enter into their way of thinking. I know it's not easy, because we've all been brought up on certain notions of international law, but although it's true that those notions have been to a great extent devalued, it's still not a matter of indifference to us whether the violation of that law is handled with kid gloves or not. Besides, they didn't intend to violate it. They wanted to help us, to advise us, not to interfere in our internal affairs. Poland was supposed to be independent, and that was something wanted not only by us, but by Stalin as well. Even in May 1943, when he was answering questions from journalists on the *New York Times* about whether he wanted a strong, independent Poland, he replied that he did, without qualification.

Did he? Because three and a half years before that he hadn't, and on 31 October 1939, at a meeting of the Supreme Soviet, Molotov was thundering (not on his own initiative, as you know better than I): "Nothing remains of that grotesque [or "bastard"] creation of the Versailles Treaty . . . there can be no question of a return to the old Poland."

Just a moment, just a moment. It's true that in 1942 and at the beginning of 1943 the notion of a seventeenth republic was still being propagated; Zofia Dzerzhinska was one of its advocates. Naturally, I didn't agree with her. And, while not wanting to be suspected of nationalism, I could still support my position by international considerations. It was only in 1943, when the idea began to ripen, that I voiced my opinion: I sent a letter to Dzerzhinska in which I summarized all the arguments against it.

Just at that time a series of articles appeared in the Comintern journal about the need to acknowledge the national identity of particular countries in the future bloc, to build a national front and to preserve national traditions. So I wrote to Dzerzhinska that I didn't see much point or advantage in creating a seventeenth Soviet republic, particularly since it would go against the slogans propagated by the Comintern, and that I maintained my insistence on Poland's being a sovereign, independent state. Dzerzhinska naturally did not reply to my letter, but she probably passed it on to the appropriate people. But that didn't matter: I hadn't committed a mortal sin and there were always other people I could appeal to whose authority was higher than my own and who had argued for the dissolution of the Comintern in 1943 on the grounds that the individual parties needed greater liberties and should not be hampered by directives from the communist international. In some sense Stalin also supported this argument.

Stalin's one overriding aim in all this was, of course, to ensure that Poland would be bound to the Soviet Union by firm ties of loyalty and friendship; however, he didn't insist on its necessarily becoming a part of the Soviet Union. He knew enough to see that this would be both pointless and unrealistic. The interests of the alliance against Hitler required that every nation be guaranteed its right to an independent existence. Thus the issue of Poland concerned not only the Soviet Union, but the world.

After Stalingrad the wave of victories turned in the Soviet Union's favour; it was becoming indisputable that its role in negotiations would be dominant and that peace in Europe would be a peace in large degree dictated by the Soviet Union. We also realized that thanks to this Poland would be given an historic chance to effect fundamental changes in its shape and structure.

What were the conditions on which you obtained her?

I don't understand.

Then let me be specific: why, when Mikolajczyk came to see Bierut in Moscow on 7 August 1944, requesting aid for Warsaw when it was being destroyed, did Bierut give no reply?

How was he supposed to reply? There was a choice of goals: either to collect together scattered forces and make superhuman efforts to save Warsaw, or to frustrate Churchill's plans to invade the Balkans and break off half of Europe for himself. It was a complicated web of circumstances. Gomulka was behaving like a blind man. We were a little more experienced and we knew how to negotiate, but our insistent requests for help for Warsaw made no difference.

But you see, the trouble is that you never even tried.

How do you deduce that?

Because the tragedy of the Uprising was doubly advantageous for the Soviet Union, and hence for you as well: you used the Germans to weaken the Home Army, a potential source of opposition to the communist party, and you also gained an argument of extremely strong propaganda value against the Polish government, which had provoked the Uprising and thereby directly contributed to the destruction of the city and the deaths of 100,000 people.

In no way were we involved in provoking the Uprising; we hadn't even been warned about it. However, we were obviously aware of the consequences of an alliance with a power as great as the Soviet Union, and we realized that its superiority over us would be great; as to that we had no doubts. But we knew that at that moment, in 1944 and 1945, we had to win the war, and that Stalin's aid in establishing our frontiers would be predominant. So we wanted to take advantage of his dynamism entirely for the good of the country.

You'd already handed over Vilnius and Lvov by then?

Well, yes: there was no chance of any eastern borders other than the ones Stalin was offering.

There was a chance to keep Lvov. On 13 February 1945, two days after the end of the Yalta Conference, where the question of Lvov had not been decided, James F. Byrnes, director of war mobilization in the United States, said: "The question of who will obtain Lvov has not yet been definitively decided."

Those were just short-lived illusions that he and others were harbouring. The only chance we had was the Puszcza Bialowiejska, and we took advantage of it.

Because bison, as Osobka tried to convince Stalin, are neither Poles nor Byelorussians.

[laughter] That's right, that's a true story. You could sometimes win Stalin over by humour.

And by what else?

Stalin was a really good politician, you know, and there were certain matters we wanted to persuade him about. So we used a variety of arguments.

Not guile?

That's indispensable when you need a convincing argument, isn't it? You appeal to the ones which might have an impact at a given moment and you bypass others which you think would have no effect. Conversations, after all, aren't just monologues on one side or the other; they involve a confrontation of thoughts, finding a way of putting the problem that will bring the two sides together in an understanding and lead to the joint formulation of an idea.

And if that's impossible?

Then you either accept it or you don't.

Did you accept the borders Stalin offered you?

There was some discussion about the Bialystok province, which had been taken over after 1939. But Stalin didn't insist on it, because the question of nationalities was clear there. The issue of Lomza led to some differences, but they were minor; it was only a question of details in the boundary line.

Because you'd already given them the Rzeszow area as well, hadn't you, with its railway network and several oil refineries?

We gave them away because Russia wanted oil and we had to agree. Besides, we received some compensation in the form of other territory.

But without oil?

Without oil, true, but you see, that oil was a bit . . . of a sham.

But what right did you have to dispose of Polish territory?

Miss Toranska, your reasoning is based on pure fiction. One could make various plans after World War I, as Mr Pilsudski did, although not with great success, but after World War II such myths became absurd. It was a question of reality, not law; and what was real were the agreements made by the Big Four in Teheran and Yalta.

Of course. Only the trouble, you see, is that you handed over those territories before *the conference in Teheran and* before *the conference at Yalta. You gave them away in 1939, and after that not only did you fail throughout to support the Polish government in its desperate attempts to wrest away, precisely for reasons of nationality, so much as a single bit more, but indeed you – to put it euphemistically – hindered it in those efforts.*

Rubbish. Our acquiescence or lack of it was of little importance, especially where the eastern territories were concerned, because their loss was determined by the course of the war. Hence it would have been anachronistic to discuss their status in 1944 or 1945. It was time to fight the great battle for the Oder–Neisse Line, and Stalin put up a fierce fight against anyone who attempted to undermine it.

In his own interests.

Naturally, we knew that like any politician he would be guided by the interests of his own country. But our interests converged, because we also wanted to obtain the western territories, in other words to achieve aims which directly involved Polish interests and to consolidate our gains. There was, for instance, a disagreement over Szczecin with the German communists, who wanted it badly; but it was the Soviet Union's stand that was decisive.

As well as Truman's line.

I don't know; we were the ones who got Szczecin. Stalin was extremely adept at getting the better of the people he was negotiating with.

Weren't you afraid you would be the next in line for that?

I must confess it didn't enter my mind. The main thing was to obtain the things we most wanted from the West: the most advantageous border for Poland, which meant a new shape to the state.

What you obtained, in effect, was a Poland – which won the war, did it not? – that was 22 per cent smaller than it had been before the war, while Germany, which lost the war, was 18 per cent smaller.

Those are pretty arbitrary calculations, naive, even. The land we obtained was richer. The territories that we gave up in the east were much poorer than the western ones, and it would have cost us a lot of effort to build the number of factories we obtained in this way. I'm not even sure a dozen years of sweat and toil would have sufficed for us to build them.

How many of them were transported to the Soviet Union?

Some estimates must have been made, but I'm not familiar with them. I also doubt whether they brought any real gain. For instance, cattle were herded from Germany and the Recovered Territories, but most of them died on the way, and our resourceful peasants found various ways of bribing the guards, so there's finally no way of telling how many they managed to herd in. Such, I'm afraid, are the rules of war.

Nevertheless we protested against the transportation of factories, and tried to prevent it; we considered this our main task. The Soviets treated the Recovered Territories as their personal spoils of war and considered the wealth contained there to be not ours but German, and thus their claim to it inconstestable. They created their own

Spoils of War Divisions, whose main task was to aid in the rebuilding of their country by pinching as much as possible. They were particularly successful in this during the first few months, when we were not yet entirely in control of the situation and the liberated territories were governed by Soviet military commanders. That was presumably when they managed to bring out quite a lot, but even then there were many things we managed to wrest away from them. I personally made trips to see Molotov about factories in Police, near Szczecin; they were sufficiently important to fight for, and we succeeded: their dismantling was stopped. I have the feeling Molotov helped us in that, and Minc frequently intervened in Moscow as well. Our arguments that we had to pull the country out of the ruins in which it lay were for the most part sympathetically received by Stalin and Molotov.

But they gave no order to cease the transportation entirely?

While wartime activities were still going on it would have been inconceivable, and afterwards it became an open question, remaining to be answered. But even then you had to understand that the war had greatly ravaged the whole western part of the Soviet Union, and the Soviet government, faced with general poverty and enormous losses, wanted to strengthen its industrial potential at least a little. That was the reasoning of the experts who made the decision to amass as much as possible. In practice, however, it turned out they weren't gaining all that much, because the factories were dismantled quickly, sloppily and unprofessionally, and transported in inappropriate conditions, so that they ended up broken or damaged. That, actually, was the argument we used when we intervened with the Soviet authorities.

Still, there was some kind of legal basis for the transportation, was there not?

There were general instructions, because they thought that everything they'd conquered belonged to them; in addition, the distribution of forces permitted them to think and act in that way.

You could have appealed to international opinion. After all, the British or American armies didn't go around looting all the countries they liberated.

My dear woman! Don't you understand there was a war on? The Red Army had its sights set on getting through to Berlin and taking over half of Germany, so obviously there were two forces in control of the liberated territories: us on the one hand, and Soviet military representatives on the other. There was one way out of that complicated tangle of problems and interests, and we were aiming for it: namely to remove the Soviet military commanders from Polish territories as quickly as possible, prevent them from taking control, and take the government of the country entirely into our own hands as soon as we could. Taking it over entirely naturally demanded time. The representative of the Soviet government in Poland was Bulganin, so it was through him, and sometimes directly through Molotov, for my relations with him were closer than they were with Stalin, that we worked. Stalin understood our problems and indeed I have to admit that he was very much on our side. His attitude is borne out, for instance, by the following facts. When our people entered Chelm and Lublin (unfortunately I contracted pneumonia at the time and had to put off my arrival in Poland for ten days, but Minc and Radkiewicz were already there in their capacity as members of the CBKP) they began to establish contact with the local organizations and to negotiate with the military command. The Soviet commanders, and more specifically Zhukov from the NKVD, suddenly issued an order to the Polish population to hand over all their radio transmitters to the authorities. Our people were outraged at this, for it was a violation of our jurisdiction and showed disregard for our own authorities. So the next time Minc met with Stalin he told him that such an order had been made and that General Zhukov had issued it. When Stalin heard this he said one word: *ubrat* [get rid of him], and Zhukov was dismissed. They sent him to the security service in Novosibirsk. That was our settling of accounts with this gentleman, who had done so much to get on our nerves, and a real victory for us. Still, it was lucky for us that Stalin got angry and Zhukov's further antics were no longer to his liking.

That's one example of the kind of game that was being played out then, in a situation which was far from simple. On the one hand we understood that there had to be some discipline, that there had to be military commanders and Soviet bases; on the other hand there was the civilian government represented by us, empowered gradually to take control of the territory and aiming as quickly as possible to straighten out the administrative matters involved in doing so. Stalin understood this tangle of problems facing us and wanted, consistent with what he had promised, to hand over power to us.

Who had power over the Polish population?

We did. According to the agreement with the Soviet Union, decrees could be issued to the Polish population by them as well as by us, but only after we had approved their content.

On what basis, then, were Polish citizens deported to Soviet camps?

The Red Army did deport people, that's true, but in its own defence and only during the war and in the first months of unrest after it, until peace came. Then it ceased.

But it still managed to deport 40,000 people [according to London sources], including my father.

But he came back, didn't he?

Yes, after three years. Mikolajczyk claims in his book that already in July 1944 a KRN delegation in Moscow had signed a secret agreement consenting to the arrest of Poles who were suspected of anti-Soviet opinions – which meant practically everyone – and to their deportation to Russia.

I know nothing about it and I doubt that such an agreement existed, for there is no trace of it in my memory. And in any case, I don't think we would have signed a document of that kind. We were extremely active in our efforts to get these people out and bring them back to Poland, and our representatives in Moscow frequently intervened in the matter. I remember we succeeded in bringing about the release of some people who had been arrested in Vilnius. I personally went to see Bulganin on their behalf, but he, naturally, kept saying that he wasn't familiar with the case and would have to make enquiries.

And what did General Serov say?

I didn't talk to Serov, in fact I'd never seen him.

Hadn't you? And yet Korbonski wrote: "I heard an account of a conversation between the number one communist Jakub Berman and the NKVD General Malinov (i.e., Serov). When Berman tried to convince him that it would be in the interest of calm in Poland to send Home Army soldiers back from Russia, even to camps in Poland, he was silenced with the threat: 'I am surprised, Comrade Berman, at your concern for people who certainly won't contribute to building democracy in Poland but who, on the contrary, will hinder it. Besides, they are being kept in camps in good conditions, and if you wish . . . you can go and see for yourself.' After this obvious hint Berman retreated, silenced, and never brought up the subject again."

Korbonski's making it all up. I didn't know Serov, and that account sounds rather like a travesty of my later conversation with the Soviet ambassador to Poland, Lebedev, which I repeated to the minister of education, a populist and a follower of Mikolajczyk, when he came to see me. We discussed matters of agriculture, and I mentioned that I'd just been to see Lebedev and tried to persuade him that given our political interests we wanted all the Poles in Poland. They would, of course, have to spend some time in prison here, and only afterwards would we begin releasing them gradually. But I said nothing about camps and no one suggested that I go anywhere. It's all rubbish.

No one threatened you?

No. Let's not exaggerate.

And you weren't afraid?

No.

You mean you agreed to the imprisonment of Polish citizens in the Soviet Union?

Miss Toranska, our agreement or lack of it made absolutely no difference. Lebedev didn't take up my suggestion and, that being the case, there was nothing else I could do. I could only deplore the fact that such things were taking place and that we were helpless in the face of them. They all thought, Stalin foremost among them, that we had to be protected, rescued, helped, because in our stupidity we were demanding or requesting the return of those Home Army soldiers, who wanted to kill us off. That was Stalin's view, and no efforts to change it would have had any effect.

How did he justify the continued imprisonment of communists?

We intervened in every case where we knew that there were no grounds for holding someone. But we didn't manage to reach all of them, because Russia is a huge country and people were often kept in tiny little backwaters. Why our efforts on their behalf took so long, in some cases until 1956, is a mystery to me. That's not the only thing that turned out to be impossible to arrange then, or to be a lost cause from the outset.

On 27 March 1945, the following people were lured into a trap in the suburbs of Warsaw, an area which was not near to the front: Jan Jankowski, deputy premier of the Polish government; the commander in chief of the Home Army; and the president of the Council of National Unity. The Soviet General Ivanov, that is,

Serov again, had earlier sent them, through couriers, assurances on his word of honour that it was only for talks. His word of honour doesn't seem to have been worth much, as all three of them vanished. On the following day a further thirteen heads of the main political parties, who had been active in the underground throughout the occupation, disappeared. Three of them were representatives of the British government [sic] *to the Commission of Three, which was supposed to consult about the future Government of National Unity. [Translator's note: the author presumably intends to refer to Poles put forward by the British to participate in these talks.] For a month and a half, the Soviet authorities denied, as they usually do in such cases, any knowledge of what had happened to them. It was on 4 May, in San Francisco, that Molotov admitted that they were in Russia, awaiting trial on the charge of "sabotage in the rear of the Red Army".*

Their arrest took us by surprise and even shocked us in some sense, because it had been made without consultation with us and ran counter to all our political plans regarding the "big four" pro-London parties; we had been aiming to divide their members and had great hopes for getting the populists to break away from them. It was Gomulka's dream to win the populists over to our politics, and he was willing even to sell out the KRN in order to achieve this aim. We had already established contact with them, and talks had begun. The arrest of the sixteen upset all our plans, as it was a blow that struck to the heart of these talks. It provoked, as it had to have done, negative reactions throughout the country, and it put a stop to all attempts to reach some kind of agreement with the other parties, divide public opinion, or even win over particular individuals to a stance that was more pro-Soviet or loyal to us. For these reasons we decided to protest. Four of us (Minc, Bierut, Gomulka and myself) wrote a coded message to Moscow which I translated, since my Russian was best. I wrote that the arrest of the sixteen was hindering our efforts to broaden our range of supporters and could therefore do us great damage. Of course, I wrote very cautiously, mincing my words.

Why on earth was that?

Well, I had no information as to the nature of the charges against them.

Were charges of any kind grounds for putting Polish citizens on trial before a Soviet court for possible offences they may have committed in Poland?

In theory you're right, but you're thinking in terms of peacetime, when law and order has been restored and the division of power established. But we, despite all our shock, had to acknowledge that the war was still on, and a war's a war: people get killed, and when they're suspected of espionage they get shot within twenty-four hours, no discussions, on both sides.

No. The British and American armies also took part in the war, but they didn't go around arresting or shooting heroes of the opposition movement in countries they had liberated.

We hadn't given our approval and they did it without consulting us. Presumably they had their plans and their decisions and didn't take much account of our wishes. They didn't reply to our coded message, either.

But you see, the problem is that when Mikolajczyk asked Bierut to intervene in July 1945 in Moscow, when the trial was under way, Bierut said to him: it would make Stalin angry, and besides, we don't need these people in Poland now.

I don't trust Mikolajczyk's account because he was interested in presenting us in the worst possible light. I don't know if Bierut said that, but even if he did use those words, he said them in a certain tone and with a certain inflexion to his voice. Even the way you put the stress on words can change the meaning of a sentence. I wasn't in Moscow then, because I wasn't part of the group that was negotiating the make-up of the Government of National Unity which was being created there, but I was surprised, and in some sense even pained, that these negotiations were going on parallel to the trial.

On 21 April 1945, when you signed the treaty of friendship, mutual aid and postwar cooperation with the Soviet Union, which was supposed to provide a "guarantee of the independence of the new democratic Poland", as well as "assure its strength and wellbeing", you could have included a clause requiring the release of all Poles from Soviet prisons and camps, could you not?

It wasn't a question of us or of the Soviet Union in that treaty. It was drawn up as a compromise with the coalition against Hitler. But what exactly are you getting at?

At the fact that you brought yet another disaster upon this nation.

That's not true. We brought it liberation.

Did you?

Yes, we did. We didn't come to this country as its occupiers and we never even imagined ourselves in that role. After all the disasters that had befallen this country, we brought it its ultimate liberation, because we finally got rid of those Germans, and that counts for something. I know these things aren't simple. We wanted to get this country moving, to breathe life into it; all our hopes were tied up with the new model of Poland, which was without historical precedent and was the only chance it had had throughout its thousand years of history; we wanted to use that chance 100 per cent. And we succeeded. In any case we were bound to succeed, because we were right; not in some irrational, dreamed-up way we'd plucked out of the air, but historically – history was on our side.

More specifically, the Red Army and the NKVD.

Naturally, you can claim now that the Red Army sympathized with the communists – yes, it did. And you can also accuse us of having been in the minority, and yes, we were. And so what? Nothing! That doesn't mean anything! Because what does the development of mankind teach us? It teaches us first of all that it was always the minority, the avant-garde, that rescued the majority, often against the will of that majority. It was spat at and misunderstood, or it lost and perished. Let's admit it honestly: who organized the uprisings in Poland? A handful of people. That's simply the way history is made. You only have to look at how other countries in Europe or Asia were liberated. In China the communist party didn't have any support either, I'm sure.

Secondly: the question of being in the majority is never entirely clear, especially in Poland, where people have a completely different mentality. Here the nobility was stronger and more numerous than it was in neighbouring countries and for hundreds of years it played a dominant role. It was only in the nineteenth century that it began, and not without some pain in the process, to absorb new elements and extend the concept of the nation to other social classes. That was when the nation began to take the shape we know now.

Thirdly: we weren't as few as all that. Even before 1920 the communists had their red groups in Poland, and in the elections, if you analyse them carefully, we sometimes got a million, even a million and a half, people voting for the communist party ballot – a party that was hidden, illegal and persecuted.

More precisely, you received 132,000 votes in 1922, 900,000 in 1928, and 850,000 in 1930, and you had from two to seventeen deputies to the Sejm.

I'm not claiming that the whole of the proletariat supported the communist party before the war, because the proletariat was divided. Part of it was Christian Democratic and part of it was PPS, but part of it was also communist. After the war a large enough section of the population supported the changes we were proposing; we knew their numbers would grow with each month, the peasants because of agrarian reform and the workers because of nationalization. Some PPS members also went through a complicated process of uncertainty and hesitation. If you put them all together, it would turn out that our numbers weren't at all small.

Did you bring in Soviet advisers from the start?

We didn't bring anyone in; they came by themselves.

But you agreed to have them there.

But, my dear lady, we couldn't refuse to have them. We could after Stalin's death, and then, as you know, we did limit their role. But it wasn't possible earlier. Stalin thought they were helping, not hindering us.

Did you talk to him about it?

We couldn't; Stalin would never have agreed to any kind of discussion of the subject, he thought it was too touchy. And besides, they were supposed to be helping us, rescuing us.

How many of them were there?

It's not a question of numbers; the point is that they were there. It could have been just one person in the department, and that would have been enough for him to exert a considerable influence on decisions.

What about blocking their access to information? Couldn't you have done that?

There's no point in that, it doesn't work. These people are quite cunning and experienced; they're security men, after all, they're trained to smell deceit of any kind. So there's no point in plotting strategies which can easily be seen through; it's far better to discuss everything with them openly and honestly and if necessary to oppose particular decisions.

With what effect?

Varying. But it's not true to say that they reigned supreme over us. I saw little of them myself. Sometimes they'd come along to meet me or to introduce themselves; mostly it was a department head who came. I'd speak with him briefly and I could sense, from the way he spoke or asked questions, a certain aggressive doggedness peculiar to people in this type of work. It didn't surprise me. But these conversations were more in the nature of a polite formality.

Because, as Mikolajczyk writes, all your discussions of strategy took place at Gomulka's flat every Thursday, is that right?

Nonsense, that's utter rubbish; it just proves that he had no idea of what really went on. These people were mainly in the security apparatus, and even if they did make some suggestions, they were never directly involved. Besides, they didn't throw their weight around here nearly as much as they did elsewhere. Radkiewicz would be best able to talk about their activities, as he dealt with them every day. If he wanted to, of course.

For the moment he doesn't

And he probably won't.

Why?

I've got a certain theory about him, but I won't discuss it.

You mean he was one of theirs?

No, ours, just very obedient. He was an ancient partisan and a member of the Central Bureau of Communists; when we created the Polish Committee of National Liberation in Moscow he joined it as minister of public security. I didn't join the PKWN, as you know. I became undersecretary of state for foreign affairs and worked closely with Osobka-Morawski, so I had no influence on the selection of personnel in the Ministry of Public Security.

Really?

It's a myth invented later that Berman was the lord and master who handed out positions and ruled over everything, kept a telephone with a line to Beria on his desk and took instructions from him or consulted him on all matters. That's completely ridiculous. I don't deny that certain matters were passed on to me, and in many cases I made a positive or a negative decision, maintaining what I considered to be the utmost caution, but I had no contact with Beria, I didn't telephone anywhere, and even when I went to Moscow to see Stalin, which I did two or three times a year, it was only very rarely that I saw him.

Why?

Because Stalin included the people he wanted in talks and dinners with us, and apparently he didn't want Beria. Molotov was there as a rule, as head of foreign affairs, and often Mikoyan, with whom we discussed the economy, and from time to time other members of the Politburo would come as well, if we were discussing something about Poland which was within the scope of their profession or interests. But no gathering ever included all the members of the Soviet Politburo at the same time.

Then who formed your security services?

Until 1947 the Ministry of Public Security was controlled by Gomulka, who, it must be said, took a great interest in it from the outset, indeed you might say he took great care of it. So it was to him that all the reports were brought. He could, and sometimes did, pass particular matters on to me for further consideration or checking, but even then he always took an interest throughout in the way those cases were handled.

Who gave Romkowski his post as deputy minister in the Ministry of Public Security?

He'd been there from the beginning, like Mietkowski, Swietlik, and Luna Brystigier. The posts in most departments, in fact, were filled in the first few years, the only exception, I think, being the investigative department.

I met Romkowski in Moscow, but I'd heard about him before. He was a communist who was devoted to the party; he'd been in a Polish prison before the war and spent a long time being educated in the Comintern "Lenin group", along with Gomulka – they'd even shared a room.

Which didn't prevent him from arresting Gomulka later.

No, indeed it didn't, but, as I discovered recently, he voiced his opposition to it, as I did. Of course it wasn't heeded. During the war he was a member of the VCP(b) and fought with the Soviet partisans.

One of yours?

In my opinion, yes. Indeed, we assigned him to security in the hope that he would be able to handle the Soviet advisers. He was a decent person, but unfortunately he succumbed to bureaucratization very quickly. The security apparatus is extremely demoralizing for people: the licence and freedom to act practically without any kind of control spoils and rots them.

Whose man was Mietkowski, the second deputy minister in the Ministry of Public Security?

I don't keep that kind of register on people, Miss Toranska, and I had no access to files of that sort. Of Mietkowski I knew only that he was a decent person who disliked making decisions of any kind. He was quite fortunate in his function: he dealt with the financial and economic affairs of the ministry, that is, with repairs, or with the number of posts, but not with the question of who would fill them. He had no direct part in any operational work, unless it was as a member of the ministerial body. He had a nice biography: he'd fought in Spain and been a member of the VCP(b). We enlisted him to work with us when he was still in Moscow, assigning him to the Central Bureau of Communists when we were beginning to build it up. Whether he'd already been recruited by then or whether it happened a bit later I don't know, nor do I think one should assign too much weight to facts of that kind. The Russians undoubtedly worked through certain people they'd recruited beforehand, but the process of recruitment didn't come to a stop with the war; it went on, and it continues to go on. Besides, it was not only the people who occupied the highest positions who were recruited; people of lower rank were recruited as well. What the scope of such methods was I don't know.

What about Luna Brystigier?

I met Luna in Moscow; she worked at the ZPP headquarters. Later she came to Lublin. In Lublin they were looking for suitable people to strengthen the security services and, as she herself later told me, she was forced into working in security by Gomulka and Bierut. Apparently she wasn't terribly keen on it, because she was afraid of the responsibility and didn't consider herself very well qualified for that type of work, but Bierut and Gomulka appealed to her duty to the party and ordered her to go, so she went. She became director of the social department and was in charge of dealing with the clergy and cultural circles. Within a short time it turned out that Bierut and Gomulka had been right in their choice, for Luna became a really outstanding employee of security and clearly shone above other directors or heads of department, who were not noticeable for their talent and often resorted to clumsy methods. She was also an extremely intelligent woman, and quite pleasant to look at; she had a degree in history from Lvov and was bright and perceptive. The matters entrusted to her required very delicate handling, considerable knowledge and high qualifications. She was supposed to investigate and report on the mood in artistic circles and assess which of the people belonging to them were honest and which were not. A myth was created about how she succeeded above all in demoralizing literary circles. Presumably she maintained a wide network of contacts with various people; it was part of her job. She could do whatever she wanted or saw fit. Whether, as has been claimed, she also recruited agents, I don't know. Those are secrets which you don't reveal even to good friends, but they make up a normal part of the work in security. It is, after all, an institution created to defend the system, and it should be its duty to indicate particular dangers or particular moods which might threaten the state. But I never heard of her using any kind of repression against artists, writers, musicians or intellectuals. She was one of those directors who came for advice in difficult matters. She came to me with exceptional matters, concerning the clergy and various social groups, if she was in doubt. The minor ones she decided on her own, or else with the departmental body, which met from time to time and made decisions. I know she was sometimes able to impose her opinion and get her way; I also know the in many cases she tried to maintain some degree of independence by resisting particular suggestions made by the Soviet advisers, which was not easy, as there was one for every department. So I'm sure that, whether she wanted to or not, she made the majority of her decisions in accordance with the wishes of the leadership, or else they were made by other channels behind her back, while she was left to bear the brunt of subsequent reproaches.

Who recruited Rozanski, director of the investigative department of the Ministry of Public Security?

It's hard for me to say, since I didn't know him well. Before the war he'd been a lawyer – a defence lawyer, I think – but I never came across him in party work. I only met him in Lublin, and by that time he was already working in security. I only saw him two or three times after that. I supposed he must have been recruited earlier, and not by us.

And what about Fejgin, head of the Ministry of Public Security's department in charge of combating enemies within the party?

Him as well, I imagine. I knew him when we were students. He was a decent chap and I liked him. Very intelligent, quite active in the KZMP. He'd spent some time in prison in Poland. I expect that the unfortunate events which were later to tell upon his position must have taken place earlier, when he was in Lvov after the outbreak of the war. Maybe he got himself entangled in something then and couldn't find a suitable way out. If that was what happened, he had to pay quite dearly for it later.

What about his deputy, Swiatlo?

A miserable creature. A number of people were recruited there.

And Konrad Swietlik?

I didn't know him. Remember, I had no direct contact with any investigative officers.

Who hired them?

Radkiewicz. There's only one thing I can tell you, and that is that we were aware of this state of affairs and made efforts to counteract it. Even back in the Central Bureau of Communists, before our departure to Poland, we were looking for people who wouldn't be weighed down by this dual obligation. We'd had some bad experiences with General Zhukov, who sent people to work in Poland during the war in his capacity as an NKVD officer, and we didn't want a repeat of that kind of situation. Did we succeed? In some cases yes, in most of them no. Those were very intricate matters, involving complex relations. Especially since the Politburo was not single-minded.

What about Mazur?

Mazur gave me the impression of a broken man. I don't know the details of his life, but I do know that he suffered terrible beatings and acute repression in the Soviet Union, while his behaviour after his return to Poland gave one considerably to think: he complied with all suggestions that came from the East. I don't know whether he did so out of conviction or because of instructions he received. I don't know and I don't even want to think about it, because it's none of my damned business. There were many such people.

How many in the Politburo?

I don't recall.

What about Jozwiak?

He was a POW member [Translator's note: Polish Military Organization: a conspiratorial and clandestine military body formed in 1914 under the leadership of Pilsudski] who later became a totally committed communist. But there were a few things in his life that I found puzzling. He crossed the German–Russian border under the occupation: how? He was a friend of Bierut's, and yet he wasn't made a member of the Politburo in Lublin from the beginning, only much later: why? Even Gomulka wondered about it at one point.

We've already discussed Zawadzki, so what about Zenon Nowak?

I met him after the outbreak of the war, in Lomza, and didn't see him after that until 1946. During the occupation the Germans deported him to a labour camp in Czechoslovakia, where he was liberated by the Red Army and settled down, together with his wife, in Kiev. When I was in Kiev in 1946 I paid a visit to Wanda Wasilewska, and she said: you know, Zenon Nowak works here.

I was quite amazed. At a time when every one was desperately eager to go to Poland and work for the party, here was our old activist in some subordinate little post. I sent for him. Our meeting was a dramatic one; Nowak launched into a very vague discourse from which I was able to gather that he had been recruited in Czechoslovakia. I went back to Warsaw and wrote to Moscow asking for him to be sent back to Poland. He came, and we made him secretary for Poznan.

I also knew many people who'd been recruited there, in prison, and who after their return to Poland played a variety of dirty tricks which often forced us to dismiss them from their posts, even though we suspected, and sometimes even knew, that they were in a position which forced them to act as they did.

What about Jerzy Borejsza, Rozanski's brother?

No, although I regret to admit that he, too, had been recruited.

In Lvov, after 1939, according to Aleksander Wat.

Indeed worse than that – before the war. It's a great pity; I thought he was a decent man. Rosalia Lampe as well. Lampe was editor-in-chief of the journal *Wolna Polska* [*Free Poland*] in Moscow and Borejsza was his deputy, so naturally it was Borejsza, not Lampe, who was in charge of the journal. He was friendly with Lampe, he used to visit him at home. When Lampe suddenly died of a heart attack Borejsza came round even before the body had been removed. Rosalia greeted him as a friend, but he began sniffing around the flat, so she kicked up a fuss. Without taking any notice of her, he continued to ferret around for Lampe's notes and didn't leave until he had found them. He returned them, I think, after some time, presumably after having made a copy. After the war he became president of the publishing cooperative "Czytelnik" ["The Reader"], where he mainly collected non-party writers, and later editor-in-chief of the journal *Odrodzenie* [*Rebirth*], which was similar in tone. In 1951 he was criticized at some plenum or other for defending petit-bourgeois ways in his "Czytelnik-style" press. He came under heavy attack from Minc and Zambrowski. I tried to come to his defence, since I considered these accusations to be unfounded and contrary to the facts, but I was unsuccessful, and Borejsza was ousted from his post.

Then who?

Wolski-Piwowarczyk, one of the most tragic figures, broken in camp and probably recruited there – in what circumstances it's hard to say. Suffice it to say that, after his premature release from camp, he came to Moscow with certain specific tasks to fulfil, the recruitment of people being foremost among them. Quite a lot of people knew about this. He was also said to be connected with the affair of Erlich and Alter, leaders of the Bund in prewar Poland who were murdered in the Soviet Union in 1942. After the war he became a government representative for repatriation affairs and minister of public administration. He used to come to me with declarations of love which were probably not entirely honest, but I'm not certain that he was plotting anything against me at the time. It obviously depended on the instructions he received. In the spring of 1950 his case came up for discussion at the plenum, and on that occasion he launched a furious attack on Zambrowski. He made no mention of me, which was probably deliberate. A resolution was passed to expel him from the party and from all his government posts. At that point I could no longer control myself and said to him: please leave. It was very tactless and in fact quite unnecessary, because he would have had to leave the meeting in any case, so urging him to do so was simply impolite. I later regretted having lost my temper like that.

According to Staszewski, he was an informer for Ambassador Lebedev, and was discovered when Stalin said to Bierut: you know, there's a man of yours, a certain Wolski, who informs on you, and Lebedev sends me the reports. According to Bienkowski, on the other hand, it was not a question merely of denunciations – they were part of the normal course of things – but of more serious intrigues. What were they?

Wolski was aiming, naturally as a result of instructions he'd received, to effect certain changes in the Politburo, and concentrated his main fire on Zambrowski by spreading all sorts of rumours about him in order to undermine his position. The point was not, of course, to get at Zambrowski, but rather at me, and this is how his actions were assessed not only by me but by the Politburo as well. We treated it as an intrigue aimed at breaking up the leadership. I never saw any of Wolski's denunciations, but I did see Stalin's letter to Bierut, which was sent after Wolski's expulsion from the party. Stalin wrote: you did the right thing with such-and-such, who was interfering in your internal affairs. A very significant letter. Stalin had apparently come to the conclusion that in the circumstances which had arisen he had to take some kind of decisive action which would restore our confidence in the Soviet Union. So he decided to treat us as a sovereign body that was empowered to expel Wolski while at the same time giving us to understand that he would not defend him.

History, my dear lady, is much more complicated than it might appear from textbooks, and people and their actions should not be defined by roughly drawn and overly simplified schemas. Difficult experiences don't always harden you; sometimes they can also break you.

In 1945–6 the distribution of forces was as follows: on your side you had 300,000 Red Army soldiers and security forces 230,000 strong, 200,000 soldiers and 120,000 ORMO [Voluntary Reserve of the Civic Militia] forces, most of them recruited by coercion, as well as 350,000 members of the PPR; against you there was a nation of 24,000,000 people worn out by the occupation but not yet reduced to submission, Mikolajczyk's PSL, which had 800,000 members, the PPS, with over 200,000 members, and the Catholic Church, which had the support of at least 90 per cent of the population. What was your plan?

What plan?

To take them all over or destroy them – a brilliant one, incidentally.

[Laughter] The plan was neither particularly brilliant nor consistently carried out. That, of course, is how I assess it as I look back on it. On the basis of facts, not speculation, the period which I helped to shape can roughly be divided as follows: the years 1944–8, 1949–53, and 1954–6. In the first of these stages things were not yet stabilized; we were fighting a civil war, we weren't recognized and we had no authority. It is largely thanks to Gomulka that we were able to control that difficult situation, for he was at that time going through a surge in activity. He was the first to begin implementing the Soviet system of government in Poland – although not a literal copy, it was in large degree modelled on the Soviet Union – and, despite his profound attachment to tradition, he was able to overcome his inhibitions and lead Poland down a new road, totally different from the one it had followed for a whole millennium. Giving Poland this new form became the dominant idea of his life. All his dynamism, his energy, his firmness and his intelligence were invested in it. His intelligence was limited, I admit, and narrow, but it was intelligence nonetheless. It's a pity it was so often torn by internal doubt and struggles between his various complexes, which were often disproportionate to the situation and resulted mainly from his awareness that there were many things he was incapable of. For things were difficult, and their difficulty was reflected in the transcript of the PPR plenum which took place in May 1945, a few months after the liberation of Warsaw. In addition to fighting our enemies, we also had to wage a struggle against factions within the party.

A struggle on two fronts, as usual.

That's how it was. Those transcripts now read like a crime novel.

Did the Katowice province propose the incorporation of Poland into the Soviet Union?

I don't remember anything like that. What I do remember is Minc's speech – it was beautiful. He spoke with great honesty about all the problems and difficulties, about the state of flux Poland was in, about how we were trying to turn the tide and managing, in spite of all adversities, to maintain the people's government and to seize one outpost after another as soon as the opportunity presented itself. After all, when we were taking power everyone was expecting another war and waiting for . . . Anders to ride up on a white horse and change everything. The Polish intelligentsia boycotted us in large degree.

So those elements of internal emigration that we can see today are nothing new in Poland; they existed then as well, even on a greater scale. For instance, you could work in a hospital if you wanted to cure people, but you couldn't take up an administrative position in the Ministry of Health, oh no! That was out; it wasn't done, it wasn't well looked upon, it was unpatriotic and not befitting a real Pole. But a boycott like that can never last very long nor take in all sections of society; and thus we were able to create large divisions among certain parts of the population. For the main task, one which we'd set ourselves from the beginning, was to divide public opinion and cause new elites to emerge. We also wanted to use the old, prewar elites to the full by including them in the building of socialism. For this reason we took on, among others, Boleslaw Krupinski, a great mining expert, and Eugeniusz Kwiatkowski, who'd been a deputy premier before the war and had constructed the city of Gdynia. It was largely thanks to Minc that we were able to get these people; he knew how to convince them and win them over.

You expelled Kwiatkowski in 1947.

That was the Cold War, unfortunately. But Krupinski remained. At the same time we tried to create a new elite from among workers and peasants, which would be able in future to take over from the old one. Hence our great efforts to develop education, eradicate illiteracy and spread culture as much and as far as we could. Hence, also, our attempts to privilege young people from working or peasant backgrounds who wanted to take up education, especially higher education. This was far from easy, because at the beginning the universities were hostile to us, especially in Cracow, and we had to wage a difficult and dramatic struggle with them.

In order to disseminate culture, which had been widespread before the war?

Of course, it wasn't just a question of education or illiteracy – those are just details – but rather of changing the country, of building a completely new Poland of a shape and structure previously quite unknown in its history. That was what the struggle was about. Poland, after all, had been there for a thousand years; during that thousand years it had amassed a number of ideas, complexes, opinions, convictions and beliefs. And suddenly new people come – from here or from Moscow, it doesn't matter – and turn the country upside down in order to form it from an entirely different mould. They extend it in the west, they cut it back in the east, instead of Jagiellonian they make it the country of the Piasts, they change the criteria that had been there before, they question and criticize established opinions. I don't know now whether it was always the right thing to do; it really wasn't a question of who was right but of a revolutionary movement, which by its very nature breaks old habits and old norms, old forms, structures and myths, some of them very deeply entrenched in people's mentalities, and builds new ones. Do you imagine all that can be changed simply and easily? No, of course not; of course it all required enormous efforts to break through, as the Russians say. It was a struggle, a struggle which continues to this day, and people still don't understand the meaning of it. But I assure you that if we hadn't rebuilt the country and at the same time built up industry, we wouldn't exist now. We were able to handle the repatriation of millions of people; within a short time we were able to populate the Recovered Territories in their entirety. The struggle for those territories was one of our main tasks during the first five years; it was a battle waged and won, and even the peasants from the other side of the River Bug, who were probably the most hostile to us, saw a better life opening up before them when they entered the Recovered Territories. True, it wasn't all that easy for them at first; but they managed to settle down and get on with their lives somehow, and finally they saw, they had to see, the greater prospects that lay before them. Could those be compared to the shacks and huts they'd left behind? Of course one could wonder afterwards whether as a country we had a lot of independence or a little, who was a good Pole and who was not – there were various considerations. Doubtless not all our calculations and predictions proved right, but in the general balance we didn't do badly. The balance of our achievements was deformed by the doubts that arose in the years 1980–1, which witnessed a great step backwards – all that we'd achieved in previous years was diminished. But time will do its work, just as it did during the first postwar years. Time and the right tactics to change the public mood. We were able in much more difficult circumstances to achieve significant changes of opinion among engineers, economists and architects. The architects we were able to win over mostly through the rebuilding of Warsaw, which became a matter of honour for them. We also succeeded in influencing the writers, and used every conceivable means to do so. We started a journal called *Kuznica* [*The Forge*], which managed to attract a considerable percentage of the militant intelligentsia, as well as the journal *Odrodzenie* [*Rebirth*], with a much broader and more liberal platform, and here, too, many intelligent people gathered.

You suppressed it in 1950, did you not, when you founded the journal Nowa Kultura *[*New Culture*]?*

We didn't suppress it; we amalgamated them into one journal, with a line that was better adapted to the times. It was especially important to us to enlist the cultural circles on our side. I often met with them in the Council of State and even kept up personal contacts with many great writers and film makers in the hope that this, too, was a way of gaining their support. I tried to create an atmosphere in which they would be eager to work, to be active. And I succeeded. Not with all of them, of course, but with many, particularly the younger ones, who wanted their day-to-day work to have some real effect. After that the opinions which until then had been prevalent in the Catholic camp changed, or were even shattered. Some people began to work in the PAX organization, actively contributing to the creation of the new system, while the rest, those who didn't belong to PAX, joined in the discussions we had launched and began to form a favourable opinion of the changes that were being effected in Poland.

Did you create PAX in order to break up the Catholic Church?

No, the formation of PAX is connected with an entirely different story. At one point, when he was in prison after his arrest by the NKVD, Boleslaw Piasecki had a conversation with General Serov. I don't know how it came about, but afterwards Serov declared him to be a brilliant young man [In Russian: *genialny malchik*]. Piasecki must have succeeded in convincing him that he would be able to form some kind of counterweight to the Catholic Church in Poland, either based on sufficiently strong popular support or in the form of a centre of opposition within the Church, and I think that was probably when he told Serov about his proposal to form PAX. I don't think anyone suggested it to him, since he was talented, intelligent and clever enough to think it up for himself. The idea must have appealed to Serov as a new speck of light in an area that was very hard to bring under control, and Piasecki himself must have made such an impression on him that Serov helped to obtain his release.

So it wasn't Stalin?

No, Stalin wasn't concerned with such details, he didn't have time. Piasecki had Serov to thank for his release. As Beria's deputy, Serov was a figure of sufficient stature to be able to make such decisions himself.

What other tasks did Serov allot him?

He didn't have to; a release from prison is always obligation enough. In any case, I don't know the details, and I don't even want to go into the matter, because these things are of a too confidential nature. Piasecki was released and immediately afterwards, in 1945, he formed PAX. I don't know what kinds of threads later continued to bind him to Moscow; I can only say that the Soviet embassy supervised PAX throughout, in one way or another. PAX did not intend, however, to break up the Church, as such an enterprise would be doomed to failure, but rather to split and divide opinion in the Catholic camp.

And this process of change and division was also helped along by the simultaneous application of blind and ruthless terror by which you wanted to frighten people into complying, was it not?

Rubbish.

Well, then, here are a few facts from September 1945: A security services commander in Bochnia murdered the mayor of Bogucice, the head of the local dairy, Wladyslaw Kukiel, and a PSL activist; he also tortured the mayor of Lapanow and shot to death a member of the PSL's local executive committee who, before being shot, had his nails torn out, his tongue cut out and his eyes burnt out with a poker. The chief officer of a village near Siedlce was killed in the presence of the villagers, who had their houses burnt down by the security services. The security commander in Rzeszow and the PPR secretary in Przemysl together dragged a member of the PSL executive committee out of his house; he was later found in a forest with thirty bullets in him.

Well, you know, I didn't deal with that kind of material and I didn't analyse it. I admit that we gave way to euphoria at first and underestimated the pro-London underground. The underground, too, was at first dazzled by the speed with which we were establishing the new government, but later it launched a struggle against us. Not all of it, of course – there were cases of Home Army people coming over to our side and volunteering for our army – but in some areas the struggle was still being waged. It was longest in the Bialystok, Lublin and Rzeszow provinces. Then there was the tragic incident where an attempt was made to influence our army; there were cases of desertion in one regiment and we had to go through a lot of difficulties because of that.

All the Polish soldiers were deported to Siberia.

That's exaggerated, but I don't have the exact figures.

In November 1945, in the vicinity of Tarnobrzeg, over 500 men were arrested because they had called a meeting to honour the memory of Wincenty Witos, who had just died; in the region of Ostrow Wielkopolski 150 people were placed in a camp which had previously held Germans; in Kepno 300 people were dragged from their houses and many of them never came back.

I'm not familiar with these facts and I don't know why people describe them; it only harms the cause and serves as justification for the underground. Let's be honest about this. First of all, Poland was in a state of revolution, and a revolution's a revolution – there will always be victims, because those are its laws, and there's nothing I can do about it. Didn't the French Revolution make an armed entry into Europe? Weren't people killed then? You'll be telling me in a minute that in France the revolution was supported by a sufficiently large part of the population, while in Poland it wasn't. That's a lie. We had our adherents too. Second, when we were taking power the situation was unstable and we were fighting a civil war. They shot at us and we, out of necessity, shot at them; the shooting was fierce and people were often ruthlessly liquidated. Hundreds of party people, security people, and soldiers from the Internal Security Corps were killed; everyone who was suspect was stopped on the road. Even my wife was stopped once, on her way to an inspection.

But they let her go?

So what! Some were let go and some weren't. And why did they shoot at us? It wasn't out of a love of shooting, after all, but in order to overthrow us and take power themselves. It was either us or them. We had to counter force with force.

*According to Krystyna Kersten [*The Political History of Poland, 1944–1956*], "The scope of repression in all its forms was very wide; moreover, it was only partially a function of the force of the opposition encountered by the government. The people who met with repression were not only those who were brandishing weapons, but also people engaged in political activity which did not go beyond the liberties guaranteed by the Yalta agreement, and the peasant population as well." And here are the figures: 50, and before elections to the Sejm even 100, death sentences per month, announced in the* Glos Ludu *[*People's Voice*] alongside potato and onion prices, as well as 100,000 (by the calculations of the Ministry of Public Security) or 150,000 (according to the later Ministry of Internal Affairs) people held in security prisons and dungeons.*

That's nonsense, what she's written. I'm not familiar with these figures, but you have to understand the principle. I'm not claiming there was a civil war in Poland, but there were certain elements of a civil war. And in a civil war either one side is right or the other is; never both. I'm not even denying the force of the ideals for which those young boys fought in the forests; I'm only saying that, unfortunately, they were fighting for the wrong cause, a lost cause from the outset, because it was based on ridiculous assumptions.

There were 20,000 of them, and of that only a few thousand in the forests, so who were you shooting at?

I don't know how many there were. We shot at them because what else were we supposed to do? Allow ourselves to be shot? Or put up our hands and give ourselves up? Surely you can see that that's precisely what would have led to a real catastrophe. The Soviet army would have come in and crushed everything. EVERYTHING. I don't understand your logic.

Poland, you claimed, was to be independent.

It was, but we were stuck at a certain stage of history which had to be overcome, and we overcame it, we saw no other way. We gradually calmed the atmosphere in the country, and the wave of tension began to fall, or rather to move to another level.

What was the point of the referendum supposed to be?

We saw it as a prelude to future elections, enabling us to get a view of a cross section of prevailing moods.

Whose idea was it? Osobka claims it was his.

That's not true; strictly speaking it was mine.

So Mikolajczyk was right. He'd suspected from the start that the PPS was acting as a screen, and that you planned the referendum in order to avoid elections to the Sejm, to which you were bound by your promises to the Western governments.

No. The point was on the one hand to make a survey of public opinion and on the other to try, on the basis of this survey, to split public opinion thoroughly and separate the grain from the chaff. Obviously, we knew we wouldn't attain full unanimity; what we wanted was to take up the struggle against our enemies and get people to make a decision and come out in favour of one side or the other: Mikolajczyk's or ours. That was why the questions were so important, and why we pored for so long over their formulation.

Were you the one who thought them up?

No, I don't consider myself their author. A larger group of people was convened, and after lengthy discussions they formulated those three questions. They were good questions, because they put Mikolajczyk in a difficult position. He was forced to take a negative stand on one of them, since otherwise there would have been no point in his taking part in the whole affair, but he wasn't quite sure which one. After all, he could hardly question the Oder–Neisse border or the plan for agrarian reform, which left the first question: do you want a senate? And so, although no one even dreamt of a senate, that became the criterion by which the population was divided. We launched a massive campaign, we managed to get our message across to a broad section of the masses, and we achieved our goal. The result showed a divided public opinion.

What was the result?

I can only say I had hoped, naturally, for a better one. Obviously, if I hadn't expected a better one I wouldn't have come out with such a proposal. But still, I thought that even the result we did manage to achieve was worth something from an overall point of view. For apart from the results themselves you have to take into account the enormous amount of work we put into the campaign. Naturally, in many places we had to make a number of various so-called corrections. In some places they were greater and in others smaller, but I couldn't undertake an analysis of their scope. Nevertheless, you can speak in terms of correcting the results, but not in terms of rigging them.

The results you announced in Cracow were genuine. Why?

Probably because the intensity of the opposition there was greater than it was elsewhere.

Apparently you were going to punish the residents for it by displacing them.

That's nonsense, idiotic nonsense; I never came across any suggestion of that kind.

That was what the president of Cracow threatened.

A piece of nonsense. It never even entered our heads, and in any case it wouldn't have been feasible. We didn't achieve full unanimity in the referendum, but nor was its result an all-out defeat for us. Our predictions turned out to be incontestable: no one even dreamt of a senate and no one intended to return the Recovered Territories.

Didn't they? Because Mr Starewicz said that the people living in the Recovered Territories voted against the Oder–Neisse border and to this day he is, unfortunately, unable to understand why.

Those were aberrations; that kind of thing always happens. And anyway, why should we be surprised at some peasants when today, thousands of clever, educated members of the intelligentsia harbour stupid and senseless views? They're the ones we ought to be surprised at, not those peasants, uprooted from their villages somewhere on the other side of the Bug, who, even though they were given better farms and excellent housing, still longed, quite simply longed, to return to the place they were used to. Those were their first years on alien soil, and they hadn't yet adapted to the new conditions of life there; the process of adaptation isn't nearly as simple as one might wish.

Was the process of proletarianizing the peasants an easy one? No, it wasn't easy anywhere, not in Western Europe, either. How, then, could the process of assimilating the peasants on the Recovered Territories be an easy one? It couldn't. But I don't think Starewicz is right in his views. It may be that individual communities or groups came out against the Oder–Neisse border, but I don't think that everyone, *en masse*, was taking a stand against it. I don't believe that. Many soldiers settled on the Recovered Territories; I'm sure they didn't vote that way.

So how did they vote? PSL statistics show, on a necessarily fragmentary scale, that in 2,004 out of the 11,070 voting districts, 83.54 per cent of the vote was against you.

I can't say. Probably it was like that in some districts, while in others we had a majority.

Why didn't you at least reveal this fact?

My dear lady, you can't, not if you want to stay on. If we'd had an alternative – if we win, we stay, if we lose, we hand over power – then of course you can tell the whole truth. But here we were compelled by the situation: in an election, we can't go by the criterion of a majority, because there isn't anyone we can hand over power to. There wasn't then and there isn't now.

I don't understand.

Well, whom would you have had us hand over power to? To Mikolajczyk, perhaps? Or to those even more to the right of him? Or to the devil knows who else? You'll be telling me in a moment it would have been democratic if we had. So what? Who needs that kind of democracy? And we can no more have free elections now than we could ten or twenty years ago, even less so, because we'd lose. There's no doubt of that. So what's the point of such an election? Unless, of course, we wanted to behave like such ultra-democrats, such perfect gentlemen, that we took off our top hats and bowed and said: fine, we're going to get some rest, go ahead and take power.

Well?

Well what [shouting]? Well what? Why do you say "well"?

Because that's just what you should do, exactly that.

I don't want to be rude.

Well, then, I will: you're hated here.

Miss Toranska, politics isn't something you do for pleasure, and it's not something you do in order to be loved and understood. I know things are bad now, but there are some prospects that we'll make them better. We will make them better, I'm deeply convinced of it. We'll find a way out of the situation, despite all its zigzags and contortions. Maybe not in my lifetime, but we will. It's not at all true that Poland is doomed to destruction, to total destruction.

But you're considered to be the cause of all the evil that has befallen this nation, don't you see that?

That's the result of mental backwardness, yes, backwardness [shouting]! You can't live by nineteenth-century concepts. Two great powers arose, and spheres of influence were defined and agreed. We found ourselves in the Soviet sphere of influence, which was lucky for us, because it helped in implementing a number of changes, although I agree that it also introduced many restrictions – no one's denying their existence. They had to meet with resistance on the part of a population raised on and accustomed to an entirely different set of ideas. But don't people undergo a process of evolution? Don't they change when reality contradicts their ideas?

You really don't see?

It's certainly true that people here are weighed down by complexes which the Czechs, the Romanians and even the Hungarians don't have, because they didn't experience either the geographical or the social perturbations that we went through: but clinging to absurdities, imagining that we live on the moon instead of on the Oder and the Vistula, is completely ridiculous. It's on a different planet that you can reflect, or meditate, or write poetry, not here. Here we have a different world, different threats, different dangers and different prospects. Was it plausible at any moment to imagine that Poland would be again the country it had been between the wars? In this configuration? With this distribution of forces? Surely that's inconceivable. You have to be deaf and blind not to see that we, the Polish communists, rescued Poland from the worst.

Sikorski, Anders, and finally Mikolajczyk – didn't they want to?

Whether they wanted to or not, that doesn't make any difference; it's not intentions that count, it's an understanding of politics. That understanding was something the gentlemen from London lacked, Mikolajczyk in particular. He refused to see that if the road of communication to Europe leads through Poland, the Soviet Union has to be certain that road won't be cut off.

He would have guaranteed roads of communication.

You don't know what you're saying. I knew them and I know what they represented. Mikolajczyk would have fallen over himself, and he wouldn't have given the Soviet Union any guarantees of safe roads.

How do you know?

I know, because I got to know him very well. He wanted to deceive. Yes, that's right, deceive [shouting]! He wanted to pretend that Poland was Finland, but Poland couldn't have been Finland, because Finland lies in a different part of Europe. It doesn't pose a threat to the Soviet Union and it isn't a strategic road, and that's why it could be permitted methods of government of one sort or another; but that was something we couldn't permit ourselves. And that's quite apart from the question of ideology, of the social aspirations to lift up those lower masses of millions of people – aspirations which we had, but Mr Mikolajczyk didn't, because in fact he was basically fighting for the kulaks.

For Poland, Mr Berman.

What kind of Poland [shouting]? For a kulak Poland, a Poland of landed squires! I wouldn't want to offend him, of course, but that was his ideology. Did it accord with the interests of the poor? Did it accord with the interests of the proletariat?

Mikolajczyk was fighting for a Poland that would be . . . Polish!

So were we, so were we. From the very beginning we were in favour of preserving traditions and separate national identities. Granted, we were selective, but every turning point brings with it a revaluation of traditions. Nineteenth-century Poland saw many different trends, but we didn't lump them all together as part of the national heritage;

we distinguished between the progressive and the reactionary ones. Basically we appealed to democratic traditions, but perhaps we narrowed them too much; perhaps there were others we didn't acknowledge and which we should have included. But mistakes of this kind are normal for a revolution still in progress. Much greater mistakes were committed in the East, and those, too, were acknowledged as such and abandoned. There are also some things we've abandoned and are abandoning now. That's something all politicians do if they think realistically; it's only Mikolajczyk and the gentlemen from London who wouldn't admit their mistakes. I've said repeatedly that I'd give Mikolajczyk an F in geography, because all he had to do was look at a map and see where Poland was and what its fate depended on in a given set of circumstances or a given distribution of power. Mikolajczyk couldn't grasp that the Soviet Union had to ensure that Poland was secure, in other words that it wouldn't rear up; and in a sense this meant that it had to be completely subordinated – yes, that's right, subordinated.

Did you guarantee them this ?

Yes, because there was a twofold dependence between us – between the Polist communists and the Soviet Union. It was not only political, concerning the state, but also ideological; in addition we represented a certain programme and were guaranteeing its implementation.

And . . . couldn't you cheat?

Cheat whom?

The Soviet Union, precisely in guaranteeing them those roads of communication.

But why should we have cheated them?

So as not to cheat us.

We didn't want to cheat anyone.

Very well, then: in the July Manifesto of 22 July 1944, you wrote: "The PKWN formally proclaims the restitution of all democratic liberties, the equality of all citizens without regard to race, creed or nationality, the freedom of political and professional association, of work and of conscience."

You're not taking into account the atmosphere in which this document was drawn up. In the Manifesto we also announced the nationalization of the means of production, and said that we would proceed at once to seize only property that had belonged to the

Germans, which we did, while as regards Polish capitalists or landowners who had been active in the opposition movement we proposed payment of life pensions or compensation. We also didn't rule out the possibility of awarding compensation to foreign property owners connected with the anti-Hitler coalition. That was what we had to promise in view of the Allies and the interests of the coalition. We later modified the principles of nationalization.

Well, then: as a result of your negotiations with Mikolajczyk a year later in Moscow concerning the creation of a Provisional Government of National Unity in place of the KRN (that was when Gomulka was proclaiming: power, once won, is something we shall never give up. You can shout that the nation's blood is being spilt, that Poland is governed by the NKVD. . . . You have a choice: either we reach an accord and join forces to rebuild Poland together, or we go our separate ways), you agreed that such a government would include the four prewar coalition parties and that the populists would obtain one-third of the positions in it; you promised to hold elections to the Sejm on the principle of a universal, equal, proportional, direct and secret ballot, which you failed to do; you announced an amnesty for Home Army soldiers, only to arrest them once they had come forward; and you promised that the Red Army, along with all other civil, party and security organs belonging to foreign powers, would be evacuated, which also turned out to be untrue.

What exactly is it that you're trying to prove by all this?

That you lie; that you're continually lying.

Just a minute, just a minute. We said various things about various matters, but at different times. In 1945 our perspective and prospects were different from what they became by the second half of 1947, not to speak of 1949. But the aim always remained the same: to create a different Poland, homogeneous as to nationality, without illiteracy, highly industrialized, with a high standard of living and a developed culture, permitting millions of people to take a huge social leap forward. That's how we imagined it; that was our vision of it.

And in order to realize it, the security services burnt down over 300 farms in the Pulawy district; they held a man from Stargard in a cold cellar with his feet immersed in water which froze; they hung people upside down, squirted water up their noses and squeezed iron bands so tightly around their heads that they fainted; in Bochnia they stuck splinters under the fingernails of prisoners, and in Cracow and Lodz they beat the soles of their feet. All these killings, burnings and tortures, on a scale unknown in Poland for centuries, were elements of the election campaign for the referendum and for the first and last Sejm in which the PSL took part – elections you intended to win even before they had taken place, as Stalin wanted.

I admit the greatest number of abuses was committed during that first period. There were many arrests, some of them justified, some not, and the sentences passed were not always just. But you must understand that danger creates fear, and the danger was great: the struggle with the armed bands was continuing and there was a fighting opposition that was supported by the PSL, which greatly complicated the situation and also put Mikolajczyk in an uncomfortable position, as it involved temptations which he couldn't resist. However, we found a fair solution before the elections, and we proposed it to Mikolajczyk. We offered to create a common bloc that would give the opposition or the semi-opposition as many seats as possible, hoping thereby to prevent electoral surprises that would force us to take wrong or unsuitable action. Unfortunately this did not work, and Mr Mikolajczyk was the reason it didn't work. I personally negotiated with Szwalbe, who acted as mediator between the PPR and the PSL, and through him transmitted our conditions to them. At first we offered them 25 per cent of the seats in the Sejm, and later one-third. That was as much as we were able to offer, given that, along with our allies, the SL, the SD and the PPS, we wanted to retain a majority. Mr Mikolajczyk, however, took an extremely aggressive stand, demanding at least 75 per cent of the seats for the PSL, which was not only unrealistic but quite simply a fantastic flight of fancy. Obviously, we couldn't give up our ability to decide the fate of the country, because then all our plans for the future would begin to crumble, wouldn't they?

And so you had to correct the results again?

Let's put the matter honestly: could it have been avoided? Could we have avoided correcting the results if it turned out that they led the way to disaster?

It would have been more honest not to cheat and not to hold elections.

A simple answer, but that wasn't feasible, because our international commitments would have been violated, and our recognition as a government depended on them. It was a pity Mikolajczyk didn't have the sense to content himself with leading a loyal opposition; maybe then things would have been different.

How?

Maybe Mikolajczyk would have resigned, or fled, in two years instead of a few months, by which time we would have gained more experience in working with opposition elements, which would certainly be useful to the party now. Because there's no doubt, of course, that he would have fled or resigned. Cold War currents were approaching, and they essentially determined the way the PSL ended.

What did you intend to do with Mikolajczyk if he didn't escape?

He wouldn't have kept his post, that's for sure. But I didn't think he'd escape.

After the PSL was liquidated it was time to deal with the PPS and, on the principle of fighting a battle on two fronts, with Gomulka.

No, the first clash with Gomulka wasn't the result of his speech about the role of the PPS; it took place almost a year earlier. In the autumn of 1947 the Soviet Union proposed the creation of an Information Bureau of Communist and Workers' Parties; it wasn't supposed to be a re-creation of the Comintern, but rather an attempt to coordinate the activities of particular parties on a principle of unanimity and not, as before, on a majority basis. First Gomulka went to see Stalin, and then I went. I was going on holiday to a health spa in the Caucasus and stopped in Moscow on my way; Stalin found out I was there and had me summoned to the Kremlin. Four members of the Politburo met as a body: along with Stalin, there was Voroshilov, Zhdanov, Molotov and Furtseva. They sat me next to Zhdanov, and I noted with some surprise that he used the familiar form of address when speaking to Stalin, which was extraordinary, as Stalin wasn't on first-name terms with anyone, except possibly with Molotov, and even then only when they were alone.

Tea was served. I knew by then that this was not to be just a social event, although Stalin was being unusually solicitous and polite. He put the matter modestly. I learnt that some sort of confidential meeting of European communist parties was to be called and that it might result in a communiqué. At this meeting the Information Bureau was to be created. Voroshilov suggested that the meeting take place at the Kremlin, presumably wanting a repeat of something in the nature of Yalta, but the others proposed Poland. I had no objection to this, and everyone took up the suggestion.

Stalin hadn't fully briefed either me or Gomulka beforehand about what this Information Bureau would be. He had simply stressed that in the current international situation, with America trying to put pressure on everyone, we had to concentrate forces on our side as well. Such an argument naturally had an effect: America had become extremely aggressive and was on the attack; we had to concentrate our forces to repulse that attack, and the Bureau was an opportunity to consolidate the communist parties and defend the entire socialist camp against enemy aggression. So Stalin's idea was a good one, especially in that it did not stipulate any restrictions; on the contrary, Stalin stressed that each party would retain its independence within the Bureau and would make its own decisions about its internal affairs. In that context, therefore, I saw nothing to worry about in the Bureau's creation.

After this conversation I wrote a letter to Gomulka, in which I gave him a detailed account of the meeting, and I went off on holiday. I knew Gomulka sensed that the idea of the Bureau might conceal other, further-reaching aims than those presented to us; indeed, we sensed this too, but you have to base yourself on facts, not premonitions, and the facts looked innocent enough.

The meeting took place in Szklarska Poreba. The Polish party was represented by Bierut and Minc: I was there as an adviser. The substance of this meeting differed considerably from the version Stalin had presented to Gomulka and me. Gomulka began to get agitated: Stalin had deceived him, he said; we would vote against the creation of the Information Bureau. I was horrified. I knew what the consequences would be if Poland voted against: the negotiations would have to be broken off or postponed. I tried to get this across to Gomulka: surely you must see, I said, that it would mean a total breach, a crack in the entire balance of power; can't you see what it would mean if Poland were to break away and disturb the unity of the camp? It would mean that it was betraying the Soviet Union and putting it in jeopardy . . . and I don't need to spell out for you what disasters would befall us then.

What?

Our whole leadership would be got rid of and blasted to hell, naturally, and the people who would come after us would be terrible, so terrible it's better not to think of it. But my attempts to get this across to Gomulka had no effect whatsoever. He behaved like a child that doesn't know what kind of world it's living in and won't face up to reality. He had some kind of complex and he succumbed to it, he couldn't resist it. I got into a car and went to Warsaw. The Politburo met and I reported the situation. We realized that we were bound by certain canons, certain allegiances, and that although we might be able to tone down some of their negative aspects, which in fact we did try to do, we knew we had to maintain solidarity and stick with the group as a whole. So we stood up to Gomulka and passed a motion committing him to a solidarity vote in favour of the Information Bureau and binding him to accept the resolution in whatever form the Soviet Union proposed it. However, we did leave him room to formulate certain reservations that we had regarding various aspects of the issue. He had to submit to our decision.

The other delegations, of course, were in favour from the start, I take it?

Of course. Especially Djilas, who's so militant now. At the time he was terribly eager to oblige, and hammered away at the French and Italian parties because they'd dismantled their party militia and hadn't fought for power after the fall of Germany. A disagreement had arisen earlier about whether or not the militia should be dismantled; in the end it was dismantled, on Moscow's initiative and with its approval, but Djilas failed to mention this at the meeting, and instead took on the main role in reprimanding these parties for their decision. He probably did it to frighten them a bit.

In the interval between talks, before the resolution to form the Bureau had been passed, I got into an argument with Zhdanov. I told him we should return to the principles of the Comintern's Seventh Congress in 1935 – a pivotal Congress at which a people's front had been proclaimed – and refrain from condemning social democracy entirely, since it was the link that would allow us to establish ourselves firmly in Western Europe, and we would need Western Europe in order to set it against America.

This was a continuation of my ideas back in 1943, when I had drawn up a memorandum concerning relations in postwar Europe and presented it to Togliatti. I'd written that our strategic goal after the war would be to establish close economic and cultural ties with Western Europe in order to safeguard it against American penetration, for I anticipated that as a result of the war America would consolidate its strength, become a great power and launch a battle for Western Europe in an attempt to subordinate it to itself – a prediction which in fact began to be borne out immediately, as shown, among other things, by the Marshall Plan, which, although it cost the USA a great deal, nevertheless had enormous advantages for them. Togliatti didn't reply to my memorandum, but he doubtless informed the Russians of what it contained.

This was the line of thought I continued in my conversation with Zhdanov in Szklarska Poreba. Zhdanov was rather harsh in his response, saying: don't you start throwing your weight about; in Moscow we know better how to apply Marxism–Leninism. That, of course, was not a declaration I could argue with, and there the conversation ended.

After the meeting it was suggested that the Bureau's headquarters should be in Warsaw. We summoned up our courage and tried to get out of this, justifying our refusal rather indirectly on economic grounds. We said we were just in the course of negotiating with America, applying for loans and trying to claim back the gold of the Polish government in London, and that it would be neither convenient nor tactically wise for us to complicate these talks. We simply didn't want a clear involvement in something the West wouldn't like, especially in view of the fact that we weren't sure in what direction the Bureau would develop.

But wouldn't having the Bureau's headquarters in Warsaw give you some possible influence over its decisions?

You shouldn't count on it; the Soviet delegation will always get its own way. We didn't have our heads in the clouds, you know; we knew they'd always be coming and bothering us. Maybe they didn't lord it over us as blatantly as they did elsewhere, because we were more familiar with all their little tricks, but still we preferred not to shoulder all the blame for the results of this undertaking without knowing exactly what course the Bureau would follow or what resolutions it would pass. We also didn't want all the attention focused on Warsaw if anything went wrong, nor did we want to take all the responsibility for the consequences of the whole affair. Besides, agreeing to it would have forced us to dissemble, or to play a double game, whereas we never at any point wanted to deceive the Russians or be disloyal towards them. We did, of course, want to push through certain aims which we found suitable and which were in our interest, but never at the price of playing dishonest games or tricks with them. So we were in favour of participating in the work of the Information Bureau, but as a reliable member of the collective, not as the leading party. We anticipated, rightly, that its activities would be limited only to propaganda measures against American aggression (which in the end were not very effective), to discussing the situation and passing resolutions. It was, quite simply, a stillborn child.

Not quite. In June 1948 the Bureau condemned Yugoslavia and the right-wing nationalist deviation in the Polish party, and it bound all the parties in the bloc to collectivize the countryside. These condemnations acquired a dramatic flavour through the fact that T. Kostov, who did the condemning for Bulgaria, was got rid of a year later; A. Pauker, who did the condemning for Romania, suffered the same fate two years later; and R. Slansky, condemning for Czechoslovakia, followed their example four years later.

One of the sources of conflict with Yugoslavia, apart from various minor matters which always crop up in this kind of set-up, was the desire to put Central and Eastern Europe in order. Various forms of federation were suggested, where each section would be a strong element of the bloc. We were supposed to form a federation with Czechoslovakia, which in principle was fine with us, but we didn't want to force them into it, and they – understandably, given the disparity in size -- were not so enthusiastic and basically didn't want a federation. Yugoslavia and Bulgaria, or possibly Albania, were to form another pair, while Hungary, according to this plan, was to remain alone. All these ideas remained at the negotiating stage, since there was also some disagreement within the Soviet Union, and there were discussions and arguments. Stalin was in favour of the federation of Poland and Czechoslovakia, but he was against uniting Bulgaria with Yugoslavia. Presumably he had reasons and calculations of his own. Dimitrov, whose stand had been pro-Yugoslavia from the beginning, found himself in hot water.

And died?

Yes, a year later.

Like Kostov?

Kostov, who had favoured the union, was shot; I don't know whether it was because of that. There were many pretexts available. But Dimitrov died normally. The myths that are created in order to embarrass the Soviets shouldn't be taken at their face value. They've committed enough sins; there's no need to magnify them by adding ridiculous ones.

That was the background to the conflict with Yugoslavia. Quite frankly, I was reluctant to go through with the condemnation. I thought that perhaps we could reach some kind of compromise and avoid a needless scandal.

And? Did you condemn Yugoslavia?

What else were we supposed to do? Stage a repeat of Gomulka's attempt to make trouble at Szklarska Poreba?

After a year the Bureau had exhausted its possibilities for effective action and achieved little else apart from flinging insults about. From what I heard, the Soviet Union also realized that it was an institution without a function. Meetings became increasingly rare and speeches less fiery, and in order to breathe some life into the Bureau Stalin proposed Togliatti as its head, which would have given new meaning to its activity. Togliatti, however, deftly declined, excusing himself on the grounds that such a function would involve a trip to Bucharest, and the Italian party did not wish him to leave since his presence in Italy was indispensable. Thus he repeated a move similar to the one we had made when the Bureau's headquarters were being discussed, but in different conditions, and therefore also with greater effect. As soon as he refused it became clear that the Bureau's activity would gradually wane; and after Stalin's death the international situation was differently structured – the Korean business came to an end, the Vienna compromise began to operate – and the Bureau in effect ceased to exist.

Gomulka couldn't see things from our point of view. He wouldn't grasp that the Bureau's creation was a necessary evil, that certain situations had to be waited out, and that in the meantime we should look after the affairs of our own country – although keeping in mind the interests of the whole socialist bloc, since they were common interests. He was still troubled by the suspicion that the Bureau would limit the autonomy of the Polish party. After the meeting at Szklarska Poreba he suggested that we go to see Stalin and obtain his signature on the transcript of the meeting that guaranteed our western border. He didn't realize that this would only offend Stalin. Indeed his idea wasn't the result of a hostile attitude to the Soviet Union – he's always been loyal towards them, I've no doubt as to that – it's just that there were certain things that Gomulka failed, unfortunately, to understand. He couldn't grasp that we were part of a particular group which had an interest in what was happening in Poland, had influence over our internal situation and had to be sure that we were a loyal member of it. He couldn't grasp this because he lacked sufficient political acumen and also often displayed insufficient experience in dealing with people, facts and circumstances. Because of this he was unable to defend Polish reasons of state without at the same time sparking off a sharp conflict with the Soviet Union. The fact that he had not, unlike us, lived for a longer period of time in the Soviet Union worked against him. He'd gone through his party training there, true, and he'd spent a little time in Lvov, where he had had a tertiary role as the director of a small factory, but he had never had the opportunity to familiarize himself more closely with the structure of Soviet government and its complicated mechanisms, and this was a very considerable impediment for him in his dealings with them.

You mean it was alien to him?

He simply didn't have a feel for it.

Followers of Gomulka in turn accuse you, Bierut and Minc of being unfamiliar with Poland.

That's rubbish, I don't even want to argue with it. In June 1948 Gomulka decided to make a speech at the plenum without getting its content approved beforehand by the Politburo. I warned him against it, but Gomulka's always been stubborn. I therefore told him to make it clear in his speech that he was expressing only his own, personal view, otherwise I would be forced to take him up on it in public and to stress that we were not in agreement with it. He acknowledged my point and loyally announced this at the plenum.

"We" meaning you, Bierut and Minc?

Yes. Gomulka's stand was yet another sign of his deviation from the party line, and evidence that the conflict was intensifying. I took the floor. In the transcript of my speech I deleted the parts concerning Gomulka's suggestion about going to Stalin to obtain his signature on the document concerning our western border, as I thought it was too compromising.

What did Gomulka say about the PPS that was so terrible?

That we should appreciate the traditions of independence to which it was bound.

Well, shouldn't you?

That depends on how you treat the subject and what role it assumes in the party's programme as a whole. The PPS undoubtedly played a part in the struggle for Poland's independence, but the general trend of the PPS during the World War I period was a legionary one: the PPS, like Pilsudski and his legions, sought Poland's independence in the victory of one of the rival camps. The communists, on the other hand, took the view that our interests hinged on an alliance with the workers' movement in Russia, and that the revolution which would break out there would bring with it hopes for liberating Poland and for the creation of an independent Polish state. Thus the conflict between us and Gomulka didn't revolve around minor matters, but around a hierarchy of principles: should Poland's independence be linked with the PPS view of things, which was in some sense a legionary one, or with the victory of the revolution?

Mr Berman, does it make any difference now, after sixty years, or then, after forty?

It was a real problem in view of the approaching amalgamation of the two parties, for which we had to work out a common ideological platform. After all, we wanted to unite the parties in order to strengthen the workers' potential, not weaken it. And what made uniting them all the more urgent was that the PPS was to a large extent pervaded by opposition elements. I clearly remembered the talks with the PPS at the time the PSL was still active: even then the PPS wanted to be the pointer on the scales that held the balance between us and the PSL, trying to obtain as many trumps as possible and to play a major role as mediator. All this, combined with the PPS's past, provided no guarantees that it would be a party with which we could settle down to smooth cooperation. In addition, after the dissolution of the PSL, the PPS was flooded by masses of people looking for shelter. Thus in order to take the situation in hand and establish unity in both the political and the ideological sense, it was essential to unite the two parties.

Is that what they decided in Moscow?

No, in Warsaw.

You mean all the fraternal parties had the same idea in the same year?

Yes, because it was a sort of general trend to think that the unity of the working class depended to a large extent on an accord with the socialists. This was a result of the trend established back in 1935 at the Seventh Comintern Congress, when the communists' attitude towards social democracy was changed and cooperation became the word of the day.

So it was a dogma.

Not only that; it was above all dictated by the logic of events which involved all the socialist countries and by the sequence of events on the international scene. If they had been different, if we had not been isolated as a bloc, then we would probably have been able to tolerate the coexistence of several parties for a longer time. But the international situation was pressing us to close ranks and consolidate our internal position more quickly, especially since we were also aware of the difficulties created in Poland by the activity of a semi-opposition party, which in a sense is what the PPS was. All those who didn't support us were beginning to back the PPS and were flooding its ranks, even contrary to the intentions of its leadership.

But why did you talk of uniting when it was a question of subordinating?

It was a question of uniting, both in a qualitative and a quantitative sense.

Or perhaps there were some, including Gomulka, who wanted to unite, while you, Minc and Bierut wanted to subordinate?

No. We wanted to unite on a political platform that was, of course, well defined, retaining those elements of the PPS tradition which were most valuable, while Gomulka wanted to unite in a way that would strengthen his position in the PUWP.

Perhaps you could explain what this consisted in.

Our intention was to establish not only unity of action, but also unity in the political and ideological sense, in other words an organic unity which would to some degree take account of the quantitative and qualitative potential represented by the PPS, along with certain ideological elements which would play a role in the future united party. In the meantime, however, a change of circumstance took place which somewhat altered our original ideas.

The plenum began in June 1948 and was adjourned; it was adjourned again in July, and we set the date for the third, decisive, session in late August/early September. It coincided with a change in international relations: we were entering the Cold War phase and our relations with Western countries were shrinking. We did our best to bring this struggle up to a more cultured level, but we weren't always fully successful.

On 25 August the Congress of Intellectuals for Peace opened in Wroclaw. The idea came from Jerzy Borejsza, who saw it as something of great importance. On 6 August, three weeks before the opening, he wrote to me: "If they don't make us call everything off the day before the Congress, and if the USSR sends a delegation of sufficient stature, then this Congress could become a major event; and if we play it right in the internal market, it could serve as an excellent *intermezzo* between one symphony *furioso* and the next symphony *furioso* which we shall shortly begin to play out."

What happened was different. The Soviet delegation to the Congress was received by Zhdanov, first secretary of the Leningrad party organization and Stalin's favourite boy, as it set out for Wroclaw: the only Politburo member to be on first-name terms with him. Zhdanov probably gave the delegation some last-minute instructions. We were soon to discover what they were. The Wroclaw Congress was attended by about 500 delegates from 45 countries, and this in itself already augured that it might become an important and valuable event. Unfortunately, the Soviet delegation decided to break it up. It arrived bristling with tension and fiery speeches, and was clearly putting pressure on us to support their hurrah-style attack on the Western countries. Fadeyev made a ferocious speech, even brutal in parts, which outraged many of the Western intellectuals. And quite rightly, too, for the content of some parts of his talk was indeed simply stupefying. We decided not to print in the Polish press utterances which were aggressive, malicious or just plain insulting. They appeared in the *Literaturnaya Gazetya*, but not here. Actually, that was not the only display of courage on our part. Fadeyev's speech caused some Western intellectuals to leave the conference hall immediately, and many others were planning to do so. That was when we lost Huxley, among others, who lodged a declaration of protest, left for London, and was lost forever to the communist movement after that. There was a danger that others might leave Wroclaw as well and that the Congress would fall apart.

I was in Warsaw, and in the evening I got a phone call from Borejsza, who was in complete despair and asking for help. I had a talk with Bierut and set off by car to Wroclaw. From there, after assessing the situation, I rang Molotov, applying the principle, well known – to speak parabolically – in the Catholic world, of appealing "from an ill-informed pope to a well-informed pope". The conversation lasted about fifteen minutes and it wasn't an easy one. I tried to dissuade Molotov from the idea that there was anything to be achieved by breaking up the Congress and tried to convince him that it would be harmful to our cause. I got the impression that in Moscow, among the Soviet comrades, there were differences of opinion on the subject as well, probably between Molotov and Zhdanov. At any rate, after my conversation with Molotov new directives were issued in Moscow and Ilya Ehrenburg made a beautiful speech which entirely changed the atmosphere of the Congress. After that it ran its course to the end on a note that was quite different from what had been planned, undisturbed even by the sudden death of Zhdanov, which took place on the second or third day of the proceedings. He suffered some kind of attack.

Despite the tense atmosphere in which it took place, the Congress of Intellectuals in effect turned out to be a success for the forces of peace and progress of all continents, and a demonstration of their unity and solidarity. Our insistence on ending it on a peaceful note, and our intervention in Moscow, could not, of course, significantly influence a change in the intensifying political trend; it was, however, an attempt to hold back the approach of the Cold War. We knew by then that it was inevitable, but we tried to lend it a more European character. It was also an attempt to defend not only our own Polish initiative, but also our own road to socialism and our cultural ties with Western Europe, since my whole idea of the battle for the Wroclaw Congress had one aim in view: not to break with Western Europe, not to break away from European culture, and not to allow ourselves at any price to become walled up in only one part of the world. And we succeeded. Unfortunately not for long.

And a few months later, in May 1949, at a party conference devoted to cultural affairs, you said: "We must inspire disgust for art which is laden with formalist cynicism and lack of ideals, for decadent capitalist art, for American cosmopolitanism; we must be passionate and ruthless in combating fascist trends; we must above all combat reactionary Catholic trends."

The Cold War to a greater or lesser degree left its imprint on the whole of our cultural policy, there's no doubt of that.

Did Gomulka not understand the necessity of that, either?

No, he didn't understand our tactics at all. In August/September 1948 the third part of the plenum began and I noted with regret that he didn't realize we had come to a new juncture in world politics, didn't see that we were at a turning point between two epochs and that the time had come to state firmly where we were and with whom we were going, and he still wouldn't go along with decisions which we deemed to be the only right ones.

What decisions?

About a speedier industrialization of the country and about starting preparations for changes in the countryside – decisions, in other words, which would speed up the process of socialist transformation, although we didn't call them that then. The logic of the new historical phase dictated this. We had to take up a struggle. It was, as I said in my speech, not a struggle against Gomulka but a struggle for Gomulka. I asked him not to run away to Sulejowek, because there was no point in it. For me Sulejowek was a symbol of flight, of withdrawing and turning away, not of return. At that point our paths and Gomulka's diverged and never again met, which I regret.

At the August/September plenum I appealed to Gomulka so fervently that I thought I'd finally got something across to him. His speech was much milder than the one he had made in June; he backed down on a number of issues and presented a self-criticism. Perhaps he was beginning to realize that we were concerned not with destroying him, but with the merits of the issue, and that we weren't necessarily wrong in our view of them.

Did he support collectivization?

No, but then we didn't want collectivization, either.

How could you not have wanted it if it's inscribed in the doctrine?

We didn't. And Stalin also told us we didn't have to collectivize our countryside. I remember a conversation I had with him in 1946. He told me then: we were in a situation where we had to collectivize, but you don't. Literally.

Really? Because two years later –

Two years later circumstances were different.

They were better. Food rationing had just been abolished.

But it was very unlikely that this state of affairs could be maintained. We were just entering the Cold War phase and we had to set our sights on quicker industrialization and greater socialization. But even then Minc clearly said we would have no collectivization, while in 1948, at a meeting of party activists, he gave a speech in which he declared that our collectivization could not be a repeat of Soviet collectivization, since they did it without machinery, but we couldn't do it until we had machinery, which meant that we would only decide to go through with it when we had the appropriate equipment and financial possibilities, in other words not for a while.

Really? Because a month or two later –

Later there was a meeting of the Information Bureau in Bucharest, at which I proposed an amendment to the resolution to the effect that the word "collectivization" be replaced by the word "cooperativization". But I exposed myself to Stalin's anger: he was irritated and insisted upon collectivization. So I had to back down from my proposal for the sake of maintaining the unity of the leadership. Gomulka was angry, even though he knew of my proposal and the background of the decision, and held it against me that we had finally voted in favour of collectivization. Spychalski, who had also attended the meeting, later told me that he tried to explain to Gomulka when he got back that I had put forward a proposal to amend the resolution, but that it had turned out to be unrealistic. But Gomulka remained obstinate, maintaining that no, the Polish delegation shouldn't have voted in favour of that resolution. He later claimed he had been defending private farms, which was true, but only in part, because we also defended private farms.

Did you? In what way?

We didn't want to implement collectivization of the Soviet kind, with repression, by coercion, hastily and brutally. I won't go into the details now of why it took the course that it did in the Soviet Union, because we know why. Collectivization, like every reform, has its costs, and someone has to pay for it. You can obtain the means for it from industry, but in the Soviet Union this was impossible, since that part of the national revenue which could be used for production expenses or for the countryside was spent on armaments, and this pushed technical progress and the already low workers' standard of living down even lower; it was impossible to extract any more from it. So the collectivization they implemented there was carried out at the expense of the countryside.

How many corpses?

I don't have the figures, but I know it didn't go at all smoothly, indeed it was quite dramatic. We didn't want that, and the Information

Bureau's resolution gave us the possibility of carrying out collectivization on the scale and in the way that we deemed fit. We adopted three types of cooperatives to be implemented: the first was complete, the second partial and the third transitional. We thought it rational to have a multiplicity of forms of cooperatives, so as to give the peasant an opportunity to choose. He could opt for the first type of cooperative, or he could choose the second or third, where fewer demands were made, as the scope of personal property was greater there, and where he was given the time to decide for himself whether or not he liked collective management, whether or not he wanted to renounce his right to property.

Didn't you know?

We knew they wouldn't want to for the time being, that's true, and that collectivization was frightening to them, and that it's no easy matter to deprive a peasant of his land –

– which you'd only recently given him with great fanfares, right?

But you see, peasants in Hungary, Czechoslovakia and East Germany did manage to reconcile themselves to it somehow. The right to property hasn't been around for ever; the feeling of ownership isn't something you can't live without, it's not something you can't overcome.

Why should one overcome it?

In order to live better. We wanted the peasant to discover for himself that working in a production cooperative provides him with decent living conditions, frees him from servitude and lightens his load of the most harrowing work. The peasant's way of life comes to resemble that of a worker: he begins to exist in different social structures, has an eight-hour day, holidays, rest. I'm looking at the countryside now, talking to peasants; not rich ones, because they'll always manage, but average ones, petty farmers, the ones eking it out on the verge of poverty. This one farmer, for instance, has twelve bits of land scattered about over a huge area: it's a lot of sweat to manage all that. This kind of scattering about is the bane of our agriculture. So we thought in terms of cooperatives that would combine scattered farms.

As the first stage?

It was a solution for one or two generations, because of course we knew that overcoming the urge for property was a difficult process; not even the most rational arguments will convince a peasant to forsake it; he has to overcome it himself. After that we intended, like Hungary, to start building up plots of land attached to farms; that way the peasant could have the feeling that he owned a bit of land, and the state would draw considerable advantage from it. In Hungary half the dairy produce and almost all the fruit come from such plots, because the peasant wants to get as much as possible out of them. Here, too, the returns would be considerable, and would be quite a sizeable supplement to the day's wages that the peasant earns in the kolkhoz.

And what do we get from the kolkhoz?

It's true we lost money on the cooperatives, but then progress has its costs, doesn't it? Do you think proving the advantages of the socialized sector over the private one shouldn't cost anything? It's got to cost something! And it's worth it to subsidize a cooperative and put extra money into it from time to time if it's going to bring any profit in future. Even now you can see, in the dozen or so that are left, that people live better there than they normally do in the countryside.

You mean that starving at least seven million peasants in the Soviet Union during collectivization took place out of concern for human life?

Let's be honest about this: the peasant can also put a knife to our throats if we don't have any back-up instruments in the countryside. We mustn't be totally dependent on their private farms. Why is it that we're now having such a terrible time grappling with these problems? Why are they so terribly difficult to deal with? Because we haven't got any more wheat for bread. And the amount of persuading we have to do to get these peasants to give us their wheat!

They provide wheat in the West.

That's because the level of production has always been very high there.

And why isn't it high in the Soviet Union?

Miss Toranska, collectivization is a very good thing if you go about it in a decent, reasonable way and if it's combined with a large industrial potential and with the means to invest. So one should, without questioning the idea itself, go on to consider how to implement it more cheaply and more reasonably, and maybe try some kind of parallel route which would provide the central authorities with strategic solutions to the difficulties of production. Gomulka also understood this after 1956, and, being unable to go back to cooperatives even to the slightest extent, opted for the system of state farms. He wanted to approach the countryside by another route, for he discovered for himself that the existence of a margin, whether in the form of state farms or in the form of cooperatives, provides some leeway for a government, since it guarantees the provision of bread to cities regardless of the peasants' attitude towards us. Of course, he didn't succeed with the state farms, either.

Did Polish peasants prove more obdurate than Czech or Hungarian ones?

No, we were the ones who proved more flexible.

So why?

Without human enthusiasm, without the support of the young, without eagerness in the effort, it couldn't succeed.

You had the young.

Yes, but on no account did we want to force the issue, and we also recognized the true distribution of power and the resistance there was in the countryside.

You mean you yielded in the face of their strength?

I mean that we thought we ought to inch our way forward slowly and with extreme caution, and gradually, very gradually, persuade people, win them over, show them the advantages.

How many cooperatives did you establish?

Not many. Collectivization encompassed 10, maybe 12 or 13 per cent of the whole of agriculture and it didn't look as if there would be more. But later, in 1956, almost all the cooperatives dissolved themselves within the space of just a few days; even the ones that could have developed further. I don't want to argue with these reactions, because in some sense they were unavoidable, but I'm convinced they didn't take place without approval.

In 1949 the countryside and the Church were trying, desperately and confusedly, to defend themselves; but by then the best of the independence activists were already in prison, the PSL no longer existed, there were no private shops, self-managing organizations, associations, crafts, not a single noncommunist society and not a single independent newspaper. The party had extended its tentacles over all areas of social, cultural and intellectual life. It was everywhere: in nurseries, in factories, in hospitals, even in funeral parlours. Thus the time had come when it could, free from internal threats, proceed, through its Bierut–Berman–Minc leadership threesome, to build a socialist Poland, could it not?

No, I think that's a false presentation of the whole picture. After the November 1949 "vigilance" plenum, at which I did not speak but which incontestably left its mark, to a greater or lesser degree, on the whole of our politics, Gomulka, Spychalski and Kliszko were expelled from the Central Committee. A period of complex and difficult processes of development had come upon us, and was to last until 1953 – until the death of Stalin. But this period wasn't just one black stain, as people now try to portray it, not at all. I'm not claiming everything we did was right; I don't deny we didn't avoid mistakes, nor do I reject suppositions that we could have avoided them. But that is not where the crux of the matter lies, so one shouldn't portray that period as a disastrous one, where everything was done by coercion and against the grain. That's not true; it wasn't like that. Those were also years of great awakened hope for a better Poland, years of extraordinary surges of enthusiasm. The six-year plan aimed to transform Poland from an agricultural country into an industrialized one. Of course, one can wonder now whether we should have implemented the process of industrialization in such an intensive way; we were often forced to do so by the international situation, but perhaps this was a mistake, since it caused a drop in the standard of living. But the population accepted this plan; people were burning to get down to work, and they worked. They were tired only when they didn't have enough to eat. And they didn't get enough to eat because when we arrived, and Poland lay in ruins, we had only our bare hands to rebuild it with, and in building new factories we had to work to create accumulation at the expense of the worker. When it exceeds 25 per cent, which was the case then, it is always at the expense of basic consumption. Western Europe in the nineteenth and the beginning of the twentieth centuries created it by syphoning off incredible amounts of wealth from its colonies, but that kind of wealth didn't come to us out of the blue, and the accumulation had to be got from somewhere.

Why, then, did you reject the Marshall Plan?

There was some hesitation everywhere, in the Soviet Union as well. We tried to take a bit before 1947, and during the initial period, before its announcement, we did manage to get quite a few things. But after that considerations dictating its rejection became overriding. It must be realized, after all, that money brings dependence; and no aid can be accepted with impunity. And you can't cheat, either. Cheating on a global scale doesn't work, it can never be managed. We had to see this realistically, and the whole thing boiled down to solving the puzzle of whether to build at the expense of consumption, which could bring the risk of upheavals along with it, and indeed this happened in 1956, or not to build and resign ourselves to a situation with no prospects. We decided on dynamic development, and one solution remained: how to manoeuvre things so as not to lower the workers' standard of living excessively and at the same time to build as many factories as possible which would bring returns in the future.

Had you by then also abandoned the steady development proposed by the PPS and the Central Planning Bureau?

Yes, because the Cold War was approaching, forcing us to industrialize the country more quickly and thus also to increase the percentage of accumulation. Was it a mistake to exceed it? Perhaps. Sometimes it was done from necessity and sometimes as a result of incorrect calculations or false prognoses.

What percentage of the national revenue went on arms?

Quite a large one, around 15 per cent, maybe even more – I don't remember the figures. The point is that you can only stand back and avoid it up to a certain limit, but it's impossible to go beyond that limit. So the only thing to do was to manoeuvre our way. Minc displayed a lot of talent then – he was undoubtedly the most talented person in our leadership. But our friends were saying, not without justification, that if we were partners, then we shouldn't shirk it. Of course, they were right, and it was hard to argue with that. There are times, after all, when you can't cut down on arms spending, rather you have to increase it. It can't be helped – either you're a partner or you're not.

But surely you weren't, not even in principle.

Certainly, this sovereignty of ours became stronger, greater and more independent after Stalin's death – that's why I introduced the division into the years before his death and the years after – but even then, during his lifetime, we tried to ensure the greatest possible autonomy and independence for Poland. That was what the Polish road to socialism was about; that was how we understood it.

But you didn't ensure it!

That's not true. There were indeed attempts, after 1949, to check our independence to some extent, and our efforts to retain it in full were stifled by the extraordinary pressure of the Cold War atmosphere and by a genuine threat from America, but even then we tried not to allow Polish affairs to suffer. For what was happening was that America had decided to appropriate the whole of Europe for herself. She wanted to invest in Europe (hence the Marshall Plan) in order to make it dependent on her. Her aim was for us and the other countries of the Eastern bloc to break away from the Soviet Union. Such were her intentions, and neither the Soviet Union nor we – we all the less – could agree to this, because for us it would probably have ended in disaster from the point of view of the state, quite apart from the ideological point of view. For us to break away from the Soviet Union would have meant losing the Recovered Territories, and Poland would have become the Duchy of Warsaw. Yes, that's right, the Duchy of Warsaw. There's no other possibility that I can see.

And who was supposed to take these western territories away from us? America?

The Germans, naturally. Because America immediately placed her bets on Germany and made efforts to unite it, and if she had succeeded, a victorious Germany would have been created, and thus an aggressive and greedy Germany, ten times worse than it is now, just as Hitler's Germany turned out to be worse than Wilhelmian Germany. It would have posed a complicated problem for us, and maybe even a new threat, for a united Germany would have become a pro-American Germany, and thus hostile to the Soviet Union and to us. And the existence of a pro-American centre bordering on the Soviet Union would lead to an inevitable clash, because the whole of Europe would be in danger of being subordinated to America. In such a situation we would immediately be the first to foot the bill, since we would be the first to be exposed to the dangers of such a clash. We're in the middle, after all; we'd be crushed to bits, and then the Recovered Territories would be taken away from us. The whole Adenauer strategy was directed towards taking the Recovered Territories away from us at the appropriate moment, and that's what would have happened, I've no doubt at all about that. Because, look: it's been so many years since the war, and yet the issue of Vilnius and Lvov is still alive in Polish society, so how alive must the issue of our western territories be in Germany. Germans lived en masse on those territories; millions, millions of Germans were born and raised there. I'm convinced that if circumstances were favourable they would claim that land back, without, of course, giving anything in return.

Which would be only logical, after all, because they could hardly be expected to start waging a struggle with the Soviet Union over our Vilnius and Lvov, which in the meantime have undergone a complete transformation as regards nationality. And then what would be left of Poland? Well, what? The Duchy of Warsaw! Of course, one might even reconcile oneself to a Duchy of Warsaw, but would it be the fulfilment of those pretentions to be a great power which are so deeply rooted in the mentality of the Polish nation? Historical opportunity is something you either seize or you lose; we, the communists, seized it and made it a reality. We based ourselves on the status quo, and we were able to polonize the western territories, to manage, incorporate and homogenize them. The new shape of Poland became our trump card. I don't know when the Poles will get that into their heads. I don't mean the uneducated, backward ones, but those enlightened, rational, thinking members of the Polish intelligentsia. I'm waiting for the time when it finally gets through to them that Poland will always be a lost cause in any other constellation than the one we succeeded in winning as its only historical chance. I don't know when another one will come along – perhaps in a few decades; I can't predict, I'm not a prophet, and besides, playing at prophecies would be risky. We're in a state of development, of flux; everything will still go on changing, modifying, evolving. At this point there's only one thing I can say: we, the communists, rescued Poland from the worst fate; if it weren't for us, it would be a Duchy of Warsaw, a truncated scrap, a mean, pathetic little Central European state with very limited possibilities of development, or it wouldn't be there at all.

Just to get things clear: did the PSL want a truncated little scrap?

My dear lady, they lived by illusions – yes, that's right, by illusions, just like our extremists from Solidarity, who also didn't know what they were leading up to, because if they'd realized it, they would have turned back. We, the communists, had the Soviet Union's guarantee of our western borders, and what did they have? Daydreams, illusions that they would succeed in breaking away from the Soviet Union and establishing full emancipation. Every politician must think realistically and weigh up the odds, but they weren't able to do that. And you don't know what they would have got up to, but I know: we would have ended up with the western territories being taken away from us. Maybe not immediately – it's possible we would have been allowed to keep them for a few years in one form or another – but in the final effect we would most certainly have lost them.

And the PPS didn't understand this either?

No.

And nor did Gomulka?

No, he didn't, because otherwise he wouldn't have protested against the creation of the Information Bureau, and that would also have ended in disaster for us, since even then there was the risk of losing the Recovered Territories to the GDR.

The GDR didn't exist yet.

Well, then, in some other configuration – I don't want to play at hypothesizing right now.

But it's important, because your hypotheses are based on the assumption that Poland was created by the grace or generosity of Stalin, and not that its shape was determined by the Big Four. But Stalin really couldn't make it any smaller, even with your consent, just as America couldn't unite Germany without the consent not only of the Soviet Union, but also of France, England, Belgium, and Holland, without risking a war.

A Third World War was hanging by a thread, and if America had been sure that Poland wanted to break away from the socialist bloc and that the whole business would fall apart at that point, it would probably have made up its mind to take action.

What kind of action?

I don't know specifically, but after all it's not for nothing that Weinberger went to Yugoslavia just now with the offer of a loan. They want to strengthen centrifugal tendencies and play out one strategy with regard to us and a different one with regard to Hungary or Yugoslavia. But do we stand to gain anything if war breaks out? Don't you understand that a war would be disastrous for us? That we would be flattened?

Yes, I know, like a pancake. So in other words nobody understood anything, and you, Bierut and Minc – the Moscow group, as you were called – knew everything best.

Stalin also understood, and he shared our concern. In 1952 he tried to put forward the idea of a united, but neutralized Germany, in other words of a Germany that would be united on the condition that it would be friendly towards us and neutral regarding us. But nothing came of this, and in that situation there was one thing for us to do: at all costs to maintain the status quo in Europe as agreed upon in Potsdam.

At what price?

Of course we paid a high price, in coal for one thing.

I mean the moral cost.

Certainly, but what was there to do? Stalin would have regarded any opposition to his politics as a sign of disloyalty on our part, which would have led him to reject responsibility for the future shape of Poland. So we had a choice: either we put ourselves in a position where the Soviet Union does what it wants, with us in the middle, and whatever happens to Poland depends on the Soviet Union, or we try to find some sort of compromise which would give us the possibility of waiting it out until better days. A web of complexity. In the final analysis Poland never had any alternative, either then or now, other than to endure in the shape it's in and at all costs to maintain the shape it's in, because it's our only chance. And for the sake of that chance, for the sake of those borders, it was worth making many concessions and agreeing to many sacrifices. Because sacrifices are a transitory thing, painful only for single individuals, whereas the shape of Poland and its greatness are a basis for the development of future generations.

No. The basis is the nation, with its tradition and its culture, both reactionary and progressive, in your terminology, because they, and not its borders, shape the nation's spirit and identity. But you chose the third, and most frightful, option: the sovietization of the nation.

No, that's not true! Even if we did to a large extent model ourselves on the forms of the Soviet system or make use of Soviet experiences (which is after all understandable, since the Soviet Union was the only country that was trying to build socialism, so we could transfer various experiences to Poland, there's no sin in that), still we never copied them automatically; we always, I repeat, always, tried to secure, as far as we could, the greatest possible measure of autonomy for Poland, and resisted suggestions and even moral pressure to shape Poland to the Soviet mould and make even more use of their experiences. We always tried to defend Polish autonomy, both in its cultural aspects and in its economic development. We retained autonomy in matters in which we thought it had to be retained. One example is the Catholic Church, towards which we took the attitude that we would absolutely not hinder the carrying out of Church functions, which was entirely contrary to what was going on in Russia on a huge scale.

We'll get to the Church later.

But what does this acknowledgement of a pluralism of world-views show? Surely that, far from being helpless and powerless, we were able to influence the course of events and tried to direct it. When times were gloomy and difficult, when it may not have been possible to take a clearly opposing stand – indeed it wasn't possible later, either – we manoeuvred, toned down certain things, smoothed them over and steered a course around them. And it wasn't at all the case that we carried out all the directives of the Soviet advisers. After all, there were dozens of people they wanted us to arrest, and we resisted that. No, no, they weren't all-powerful here at all, and nor did we take our submissiveness as far as our neighbours in Czechoslovakia, Bulgaria or Hungary did. We formed disciplinary commissions to determine whether or not people were being beaten in prison; we successfully defended Tatar and the other Polish officers from a death sentence, to a great extent thanks to me; we didn't allow sentences to be passed at the trials of communists and we didn't bring Gomulka to trial.

Did the idea of Poland becoming a seventeenth republic reappear then?

No, that's not true.

Were Poland's national anthem and emblem to be changed?

No, that's not true.

They were changed in the neighbouring countries.

Perhaps my memory fails me, but I don't recall our ever considering that. Still, it's possible that someone put forward such an idea, and we, as the leadership, firmly rejected it.

Apparently it was Stalin who turned it down, when Bierut went to see him about it.

That's possible. There are enough people around who want to ingratiate themselves. But Stalin was too experienced to give his stamp of approval to such ideas. He showed this many times, for instance in 1952, when we went to see him about our new constitution. We showed him the introduction to it, a preamble which said among other things that Poland in the past had been oppressed by two occupying powers, Austrian and German. Evidently the people who had drawn up that particular bit were afraid that Stalin would be opposed to any mention of the Russians as an occupying power, so they left them out altogether. Stalin said the tsarist occupying power should be included, because it would have been ridiculous to leave it out and didn't have any anti-Soviet implications at all, so we put it in, and what Stalin said was certainly helpful to us.

You asked him about it?

Well, what's wrong with that? Surely you can ask anyone for advice, there's no harm in that, and it certainly doesn't attest to their supremacy or to our consent to be dictated to in any way. Besides, the change in the preamble to include all three invaders, without leaving out the Russians, was to our advantage from the political point of view.

Did the draft of the constitution that had been sent to Moscow for approval come back with eighty-two corrections?

Rubbish, there was nothing there to correct apart from the preamble.

Mr Chajn didn't make a mistake, he was on the commission.

So was I. There were two, a state one and a party one, and I was head of the party one. It's true I wasn't at all the commission's meetings, but I did see the final draft of the constitution, and I don't remember any points of contention of substantive significance. So if there were any corrections, and perhaps there were, they were minor, insignificant and purely formal, and I may not have been informed about them, since they didn't alter the nature of the constitution. Perhaps it was a question of whether or not to introduce certain analogies to the Soviet constitution, which is quite well drafted as far as democratic principles are concerned and very liberal, although unfortunately not always put into practice. So, if there were any corrections, they were no calamity. As for the major ones, in the preamble, we saw them as a gesture on Stalin's part.

And because of that the Poles had to lose every football match with the Soviet Union?

Well, would you have us refuse to play with them?

No, just allow a free result.

Well, yes, a free result is all very well, but it was at those matches that the old anti-Russian sentiments, and the new anti-Soviet ones, came to the fore, and they weren't the result of our propaganda, although I must say I wasn't particularly pleased with it, but of the changes we had effected.

And for that we have to thank the Soviet Union every day?

What else could we do? Not say anything at all? Pass it over? I'm not saying that there weren't various journalists or activists who went overboard in their enthusiasm. We know the kind; each of them wanted to show off in his reports: look how well I've done it. I tried to influence them, I organized press conferences from time to time, but not always with good results. Maybe I wasn't too clever in what I said, either. So it's no doubt true that there was a lot of exaggeration, oversimplification and even crudity in our propaganda; people routinely trotted out the appropriate phrases. But after all, you couldn't not write that it was thanks to the Soviet Union that we effected the changes we did; that it was thanks to the Soviet Union that we obtained the western territories!

Let's leave them and stick to the nation, for which you even thought up leading workers, also on the Soviet model.

The leading workers' movement was a genuine movement; the battle for productivity wasn't just an invented slogan, it was very eagerly taken up by our youth. Of course you can ridicule and caricature it now, and even then some people may not have liked the rows of leading workers marching in the front ranks at First of May demonstrations, but you must remember that those people worked with the conviction that they were achieving great things, as indeed they were. But later people tried to smear it all with filth. And why? Why smear with filth even those girls who were allegedly whoring there? And even if such things did go on, so what!

Then you have to write about them.

I'm not claiming we didn't fight against the negative things.

But in the newspapers you only described the positive ones, ad nauseam.

I wasn't against criticism, and indeed I myself criticized many things, but criticism has to be intelligent. Because do you think those negative things could have been avoided? Did the great movement to rebuild Europe in the nineteenth century take place without them? No! It took place in conditions that were much worse. We escaped child labour, which existed on a mass scale then. Children ten or twelve years old were yoked in to the industrialization of Europe.

Our industrialization took place in conditions that were ten times better and more humane than those in the West. And if this was accompanied by various bad or unpleasant side effects, these were nonetheless only secondary phenomena. Of course, one might ask now whether, when the leading workers' movement burnt itself out, as it had to have done after five years, other forms of action shouldn't have been found to replace it. One can argue about whether our inventiveness in the attempt to transform this movement into something different, something better and more intelligent, was sufficient; whether we should not earlier have abandoned that way of doing things. Probably we should. But that's not the point; the point is what was achieved within that framework, and that was a very great deal. Would the Nowa Huta steelworks have been built? Would the Old City of Warsaw have been rebuilt? Would Warsaw itself, which after all isn't one of our worse achievements, have arisen and grown into what it is now?

Certainly it would. And maybe it would have been prettier if you hadn't rejected Le Corbusier's offer to have a team of some of the world's most distinguished architects draft plans for its rebuilding as a gesture of "help and regard for its courage".

I don't remember the details, but it's possible that such a thing happened. Le Corbusier and others watched the rebuilding of Warsaw with great interest. But we couldn't take advantage of their advice, because in the Soviet Union at that time they had switched over to a grand style of architecture, with columns, and Le Corbusier in particular began to be seen there as too audacious an innovator who had to be rejected. We probably knew that by then.

Because he was imperialist?

No, no; because he was an innovator. Le Corbusier had already been dethroned in the Soviet Union and was burdened with accusations of being super-modern while the Soviet Union itself entered an era of a return to classical architecture, with columns and imposing structures.

And so in order to curry their favour you got us the Palace of Culture and Science, even though apparently you could have chosen a housing estate.

You shouldn't believe that. There was no choice. When Stalin came out with the suggestion of erecting some sort of symbol of Soviet aid or friendship here, Minc dreamt of a housing estate, but Stalin rejected the idea, even though we wanted to name it after him. And he had the final say, because after all he was the benefactor, and he wanted his gift to be something great, splendid, symbolic and unrepeatable. A housing estate couldn't fulfil those conditions, because with time people would forget whose gift it was and how it had been named. Stalin wanted a palace that would be visible from any point in the city, and he wanted it to house cinemas, theatres and cultural centres. I have to admit that the Soviet architects made great efforts to make it as attractive as possible. They made special trips to Zamosc and to the Lublin region in order to study mediaeval and Renaissance Polish architecture and later incorporate its elements into their work. They didn't do a very good job of it, but that was what their efforts had been aiming at, and they thought they were creating the most beautiful work in the world for us. And the palace cost the Russians a packet, because of course they paid for everything themselves.

With money from our coal?

True, we did send them coal for free, or practically for free, but we chose that alternative because we wanted to avoid joining coal cooperatives, which they had suggested. If we sent them coal, we could write down the amounts while waiting for better days, and it was thanks to that that Gomulka was later able to send them a bill for it; but if we'd agreed to form cooperatives with them, we would have lost our control over the whole of the Polish mining industry. Minc reasoned on the assumption that if one cooperative was formed, further ones would follow, and each one would pose a threat to our economic sovereignty. He was very skilful at rejecting them, although such cooperatives had already been formed in China and Romania and were forming in Czechoslovakia.

Did you like the Palace of Culture?

Bierut liked it. He more than any one of us was fascinated by the style of architecture in which Warsaw was being rebuilt. He was terribly involved emotionally, he made the most frequent comments on the matter; he would even suggest certain solutions to the architects.

Like churches with cut-off spires and a Moscow-style Palace of Culture?

There were such projects, yes, but our architects amended them and finally they weren't carried out, which also didn't happen all by itself, but required the appropriate suggestions, supervision and control on our part. Bierut's ideas weren't always of the best kind, but he was in love with them. Everyone loves his own ideas. Still, it must be said to his credit that the speed and vigour with which Warsaw was rebuilt was undoubtedly due to him.

What was he like?

Stalin had a lot of respect and esteem for him, and he was right to choose him as the leading figure in Poland.

Was he intelligent?

He was undoubtedly intelligent, it's just that he was –

Uneducated?

No, it wasn't that. Bierut was self-taught, the scope of his interests was very wide, he read a lot and was quite well-read in literature, he was enthusiastic about astronomy and architecture – but, you see, he had some complexes that he couldn't break out of: loyalty to the Soviet Union and an almost fanatical faith in dogma, which told on the decisions he made. Unlike Lampe, Bierut in his youth had been part of a group that was supposedly more flexible, and had some time for bourgeois democracy, among other things; but whereas Lampe had succeeded in ridding himself of many of the dogmas that weighed upon him, Bierut became more and more rigid in his opinions over the years and was unable to shake off many prejudices which by then had become outdated. But in spite of this, we were bound by ties of friendship and a mutual sympathy that were quite firm, and we worked together very well. Bierut would often give me his speeches to read and was only confident in making them after he had discussed them with me. I generally made minor comments and sometimes insertions, and he accepted them. He also valued my advice and rarely failed to follow it.

I was closer to Bierut than Minc was, because Minc in general didn't make close friendships with anyone and was a little distant. (That's him in the photograph on the wall. He was a good friend of mine.) Bierut respected him a great deal for his clear head and his economic knowledge, which often came to our rescue. There's no doubt Minc was a very wise man, although he also found it impossible to avoid the mistakes we all committed. During the first years of People's Poland he would boldly propose prewar non-party experts for leading positions, but he later abandoned this practice, succumbing, like all of us, to the chilling climate of suspicion and the Cold War.

You were the ones who built up that climate: you, Bierut and Minc.

To a very limited extent. Generally speaking, the international situation – the Cold War and the conflict in Korea – created a pathological wartime mentality: pathological suspicion and the feeling of being hemmed in. A similar mood took hold in the Soviet Union, and they went too far in stoking up that atmosphere, all of which naturally had an impact on our own situation as well. But you have to realize that these were the results of a specific international situation, which was one of confrontation. The West was mobilizing its resources and was firmly set on breaking us off from the Soviet Union, a situation repeated in 1980 and 1981. Reagan's plan, so relentlessly put into effect, was clear, and its goal indisputable: to break up the balance that resulted from the Second World War and wrest Poland out of the Soviet orbit. We had to defend ourselves. This climate of confrontation was undoubtedly the source of the acts of repression carried out by the security services; it was precisely as a result of this atmosphere that senseless, sometimes blind arrests of the guilty and the innocent took place, that accusations were made against them which sometimes bordered on caricature. It was as a result of this mood that anything that went wrong in a factory began to be labelled as sabotage, which of course was horrendous, but the inspiration for it flowed from the Soviet Union.

But it was taken up here.

I don't deny the adverse consequences of the pressure of the Stalinist apparatus on our apparatus; I don't deny that they caused great damage. But even then I felt this was something temporary, flowing not from the nature of the Soviet state but from the situation of the time, which was an accidental consequence of a tangled web of historical factors and of Stalin's attitude and role, and that it had to end and change some time.

You were head of that apparatus.

That's a myth; all I did was hold a watching brief in my capacity as a member of the Leadership of Three.

So who made the decisions?

Bierut supervised everything, and on every issue he had the final say. If there were any noticeable differences of opinion, they concerned only the more minor matters, not the key issues. Perhaps I shouldn't say this, because naturally I wouldn't want to put any blame on

Bierut, who displayed exceeding kindness towards me and to whom I owe much, but a certain style was established then which also became prevalent later, under Gomulka, whereby the "First Man" dominated the other members of the Politburo. All the parties fell in with this style in the name of unity and solidarity, which are a guarantee of strength, since it was thought that differences always reveal internal weaknesses. In our Troika Minc dealt with economic affairs, while I was assigned culture, education, institutions of higher education, the Polish Academy of Sciences, propaganda, foreign policy, ideology and supervising the security services. After Gomulka's departure Bierut asked me to oversee the Ministry of Public Security along with him and I agreed, which was probably a mistake, because I got all the blame afterwards. I took on the overall supervision of security while Bierut supervised Military Information, in other words intelligence and counter-intelligence matters, the defence of the state against penetration by foreign intelligence services, and the fight against espionage. This division of authority was respected by them as well as by us. Over a dozen departments were active in the ministry; each had its own adviser and would summon a body to resolve any matters that were doubtful. When differences were serious or the gravity of the matter considerable, they would refer the matter to me, to Bierut or to the Troika. In addition to the bodies which adjudicated at the departmental level, there was also a ministerial council, which included the minister, the deputy ministers and some heads of departments. They reported the results of the work of this council to me, Bierut or the Troika, depending on the matter in question. From time to time I received visits from Radkiewicz, who would come to make a report or to ask my advice on some matter or other. But more often than not he would go to Bierut. I had more contacts with deputy ministers, mainly with Romkowski.

None with Vosnesensky or Skulbaszewski, Soviet colonels and heads of Military Information?

They came to see me a few times on various matters, when they couldn't get to Bierut or when he was away from Warsaw, for although I did try, in accordance with the rules, not to deal with Military Information, I was sometimes forced to do so, especially during Bierut's absences. Minc saw people from the economics department – after all, I couldn't be an expert in every field. The matters that were sent to me for decision were minor, everyday affairs, and anything that was more important was decided at meetings of the Troika or by Bierut himself. I'm not saying this in order to evade responsibility for the mistakes committed by security. I probably didn't contribute to a happy outcome in all decisions, but I do think that I protected a lot of people from many bad things. I tried, when trials began to take place on a large scale, to get them cancelled or at least not to allow death sentences to be passed, and I applied these tactics to the extent that I was able to. It was difficult, because many of these cases concerned Military Information, not security, and also because the influence of the Soviet advisers on investigations and sentencing was definitely harmful. So there were unfortunately quite a few cases that were outside my jurisdiction or which just didn't reach me, and in spite of various attempts at persuasion on my part I was unable to obtain a positive resolution of them, since it turned out that my arm wasn't long enough. I set down as my aim two things, which to me were a matter of honour: no death sentences and no trials of communist leaders. And I succeeded in both. The first, unfortunately, was only a partial success, because there were quite a lot of death sentences, albeit not in the main trials of Home Army officers, but on the sidelines, where I had no control over them.

Let's take things one by one: immediately after the August/September plenum of 1948 you arrested Alfred Jaroszewicz, and a month later Wlodzimierz Lechowicz, the minister of provisions.

That's something that still isn't clear to me even today, and what lies behind it hasn't been completely disentangled.

So Bierut was right when [at the 1949 plenum] he thundered: "Their activities resulted in the murder of Comrade Nowotko by a provocateur, the arrest and murder of Comrades Finder and 'Jasia' Fornalska, and the arrest and assassination of Comrade Janek Krasicki . . ."?

No, there were absolutely no grounds for burdening them with responsibility for that; it remained in the realm of legend and supposition. Jaroszewicz and Lechowicz worked for the Second Unit of the General Staff of the Polish Army before the war, that is for "Two", the "defence" unit that was concerned with intelligence and counter-intelligence.

And they were agents of Soviet intelligence?

I've no evidence of that. During the war they joined the GL and the Home Army and worked with Spychalski; after the war, when

Spychalski became head of intelligence and counter-intelligence in the Polish People's Army, he hired them to work for him. After 1948, when we entered the *pyeredyshka* period, a breathing space, and the danger of enemy penetration was increasing, these facts could awaken a certain amount of suspicion. Which is understandable, because great danger always gives rise to fear. And especially since Jaroszewicz and Lechowicz, in an attempt to defend themselves against the charges, tried to dissolve them by making various and often provocative accusations against other people. Then the Soviet advisers would follow this up and try to slip us dozens of people to arrest as collaborators or people suspected of collaboration with the prewar defence unit. The circle of suspects widened.

To 104 people, from Home Army officers to communists.

That exacerbated the atmosphere of jeopardy even more. I used to get material containing charges based on the testimony of people from the defence unit, charges which concerned even some distinguished communist activists. I was presented with a list of names of people I knew personally, with extraordinary charges appended to them – Trotskyism, for instance. In the Soviet Union, Trotskyism was, as you know, a criminal offence, so that the necessity of bringing someone to trial for it was unquestionable here as well. Investigations had to be made. Whether they were made honestly or not it's hard for me to say. We tried to reject such charges in many cases, considering them to be absurd. I managed to nip a few investigations in the bud, naturally thanks to Bierut's support, but there wasn't much I could do, since I didn't have the right kind of evidence at my disposal. The suspicions were too tangled or muddled to be refuted, and then only the element of time could help. And that's what I tried to play on, by not allowing sentences, and thus determining the outcome.

Lechowicz and Jaroszewicz were sentenced after almost seven years of horrifying interrogation, in July 1955, two years after Stalin's death; and a year later, in 1956, they were released and totally rehabilitated, along with the rest of them.

An injury was certainly done to them, but it was a consequence of the general atmosphere. Lechowicz's case, in fact, was supposed to be directly connected with the case of Spychalski.

He was imprisoned in May 1950. But before that, in August 1949, you arrested Herman Field, who had come to Poland in search of his brother Noel, whom he believed missing but who in fact had already been arrested.

The affair of the Fields, American left-wing sympathizers, broke out when the investigation concerning Lechowicz and Jaroszewicz, along with all its ramifications, was in full swing here. A very intricate tangle of suspicion, which was given international overtones, took hold of the entire bloc. Mass arrests took place in every people's democracy. Everyone who knew or had been in contact with the Fields was arrested, and since the Fields had contacts among a large number of communists, the circle of arrests was wide. I was in Moscow then, with Bierut. During a break in the meeting, Stalin, when the three of us were standing together, suddenly asked me about Anna Duracz, a member of my secretariat and the daughter-in-law of Teodor Duracz, a famous prewar lawyer who defended communists. I immediately realized what he was getting at. Anna had been in the AL and had ended up in a Nazi camp as a participant of the Warsaw Uprising; later she went to Switzerland for a cure, along with many other Polish women communists. There she and the others were looked after by Noel Field. At the end of 1946 he came to Warsaw and tried, through his acquaintance with Anna Duracz, to see me. He told her that he wanted to ask me to help clarify his own situation; earlier on he had been in contact with the Comintern, but the contact had been broken off in 1937–8, and he now wanted to renew it. I did not consider it appropriate to meet with him, but I agreed that he should write me a letter explaining his case. Naturally, I showed this letter to Bierut, but the attempt to clarify his situation, or at least to enquire about it, remained unanswered. That was where my part in it ended. But once he had been arrested and accused of treason, espionage, Trotskyism, cosmopolitanism and the devil only knows what else, and connected with, even put in the dock alongside, Laszlo Rajk, his case took on a new dimension.

I told Stalin about Anna Duracz but he was not convinced by my explanation. That, as it turned out, was to be my last conversation with him and Anna was arrested shortly afterwards.

You – the Polish leadership – arrested her, is that right?

A directive came from Stalin, and there was nothing I could do, because it was a move directed against me personally, and indeed that was how everyone regarded it.

Why against you?

Stalin must have come to the conclusion that I had disappointed him.

You?

It's hard to explain, but that's the only way I can account for his change of attitude towards me. He must already have heard about what I'd said during the discussion with Zhdanov at Szklarska Poreba before the creation of the Information Bureau in the autumn of 1947, and about my suggestion in June 1948 to replace the word "collectivization" with the word "cooperatization", and perhaps about other things as well that I'm not aware of. He couldn't have been pleased about it and probably decided that I'd let him down, and according to his way of thinking, if a guy's let you down he can be suspected of everything, even of being an American spy. At that point all you need is just some small detail, like, for instance, the fact that my secretary had been in contact with Field – you put the appropriate interpretation on it and there you are, my case becomes crystal clear.

Did Stalin come up with that himself?

I don't know; maybe someone suggested it to him. Beria might have, but so could various other zealous types. You see, for Stalin everything had to be connected, and according to him I was just right for a cosmopolite.

A what?

A cosmopolite. In 1948 Stalin launched a programmatic struggle with cosmopolitanism. That was when their newspapers began to print people's real names in brackets –

What? How?

Well, quite simply, when you mentioned a Jewish activist who had a Russian pseudonym, you would give his real name in brackets, and that was a sign that the man had been marked down for removal and his post was going to be filled by someone else.

Anti-Semitism, then?

Yes, indeed, but Stalin called it cosmopolitanism.

Was he an anti-Semite?

Well, that's oversimplifying it, but he certainly wasn't free from it. He didn't show it outright, obviously, or make a blatant public display of it, but he had quite a lot of that internal ballast in him. In the Soviet Union in the 1930s frequent mention was made, especially against the background of Hitler's criminal politics, of Stalin's statement on 12 January 1931 to a correspondent of the Jewish

Telegraph Agency from the United States: "National and race chauvinism is a vestige of the customs of cannibals, proper to the period of cannibalism. Anti-Semitism, as the extreme form of race chauvinism, is the most dangerous vestige of cannibalism. Anti-Semitism is a convenient lightning-rod for exploiters, protecting capitalism from the blows of the working masses. Anti-Semitism is dangerous for people, it is a false trail which causes them to wander off the right path. For this reason communists, as consistent internationalists, cannot fail to be relentless and sworn enemies of anti-Semitism. The USSR most rigorously combats anti-Semitism as a phenomenon that is profoundly hostile and alien to the Soviet system. Under Soviet law, active anti-Semitism is punishable by the death penalty."

This is a precise quote from that statement. How can it be reconciled with facts which are in such blatant contradiction to it? Ostensibly it cannot, but you have to understand that Stalin, too, like many people, was a man of contradictions.

Cant and hypocrisy, Mr Berman.

No, no, such epithets are too crude. The task of the historian should be to analyse and discover the source of this callousness in some areas and extreme sensitivity in others, which show that Stalin was profoundly torn and full of internal contradictions, as I call them, bordering on the abnormal, even, but far from submitting to a simple interpretation.

It's only by that contradiction that I can explain to myself why Stalin, when talking to us, to me or to Minc, would sometimes stress words in a characteristic way or tendentiously deform them, while at other times he could be charming to us, when he wanted to be or when he wanted something; or why on the one hand he eliminated activists of Jewish origin while on the other he agreed to the creation, in the 1930s, of the autonomous Jewish district, Birobidjan, where the beginnings of a state were to be formed as a basis for a future Jewish Soviet Republic, which was what activists from the Jewish section of the VCP(b) were asking for. These activists were connected with the Yiddish, Jewish-national movement; they looked after Jewish art and education, the theatre in Moscow, which was a leading one, and the cultivation of Yiddish literature and publishing; they sold books in Yiddish for a worldwide readership and made quite an impact abroad with them; they tried to preserve the Jewish tradition in its secular structure. At the start Stalin supported their activities, for his concern for the Jewish community was calculated as a way of showing that here was a country, a socialist country, which cared for a national minority and even considered creating a separate republic to ensure its better development.

This trend continued until the Great Purge; the repression took in many Jewish communist activists. A lot of them were killed, and the vitality of the autonomous district of Birobidjan was stifled. The closing off and sealing up of that district ensued and it never regained its vitality. There was still some kind of journal in existence there – the organ of the district authorities – and Jewish schools and a few cultural centres in the region were kept going, but it was a rather consumptive life, with no expansion, no absorption of new elements – just vegetation. Then, at a certain point during the Second World War, an opportunity arose to revive Birobidjan and the Jewish community in general. The Jewish press, and Jews working in the Russian press, began to play a more important role and became more visible, and the Jewish Anti-Fascist Committee was created, which had great propaganda value. Stalin fully understood and appreciated this. At one point the Committee even sent a delegation, which included a group of writers, to America, where it played an important part in obtaining help for the starving population of the Soviet Union in the difficult conditions of the war which was being waged.

Is that why they were sent?

No, that would have been too crude. And Stalin wasn't so much interested in money – a few million dollars, or even ten million or more, wouldn't have represented a significant sum in the budget – as in gaining America's sympathy for Soviet problems. After the victorious end to the war the situation gradually began to change. In the second half of the 1940s Stalin's suspiciousness increased; he started looking for enemies everywhere and deluded himself into thinking that the Jewish minority would be an excellent framework of support for American aggression. He was extremely suspicious of the idea, proposed at the time by certain activists, of extending the Jewish settlement in Crimea, which had been abandoned by the Crimean Tatars. He decided that Crimea could become a base for a possible American raid, because Jews were the best people for the job due to their international family connections. In addition, before that, the evolution of the Soviet Union's attitude towards the creation of the state of Israel had been characteristic and significant.

As we know, the communist movement had always represented an anti-Zionist position, condemning the Zionist party because it attempted to win over the Jewish masses with the aid of Zionist illusions. We in the KPP also vigorously combated Zionism, indeed sometimes fights broke out with them, for instance in the universities, especially during the Arab uprising in Palestine. But after the great calamity of the war and the extermination of the Jews in Poland – for that was the main centre for the extermination of European Jews – there were renewed efforts, mainly on the part of Zionist organizations, to ensure the future of the Jews who had survived the pogroms, and it was proposed that a centre be created where Jews might lead a normal life as a state or a semi-state. Stalin was in favour of the idea, especially as Palestine was being occupied by the British and the cutting edge of that policy was directed against him. I won't go into his motives in any greater detail; in any case the Soviet Union was one of the countries which supported the creation of the state of Israel. The state was created, the British were ousted from Palestine, and the attitude of the Soviet Union towards Israel changed, particularly when the newly created state began to take on an anti-Arab character in the sense of territorial expansion. Some people in the Soviet Union began to fear that a problem of dual loyalties might arise among the Jewish minority as an inevitable result of this process. Especially since Mrs Golda Meir became Israel's ambassador to Moscow and enjoyed great sympathy and authority among Soviet Jews. The friendship with Israel began to cool off, and Stalin used the slogan of the struggle with cosmopolitanism as a tool for ousting Jews from various positions. Jews began to be persecuted; there were trials and arrests, and accusations were flung about. One of the victims was Molotov's wife, who was a specialist in the perfume industry and even had considerable achievements in the field to her name. But because she'd at some stage been interested in the Jewish settlement in Crimea, and may have expressed a favourable view of it somewhere, that was proof enough, you understand, to deal with her and send her to a camp.

But I don't understand – what about Molotov?

The repression had a happy ending for him: he remained in his post.

And he didn't help her?

He helped her in the sense that she was sent to a camp, because after all she might have been killed, mightn't she? They must have forced him to divorce her, because that's what he did, and after Stalin's death, when she returned to Moscow, they continued to live together until the end of her life.

They also dealt quite gently with Michoels, a distinguished actor, director of the Jewish theatre and a favourite with the public. He died in a faked car accident, and for the sake of appearances was even given a grand funeral. But Michoels was an exception: other people were dealt with much more simply, shot by a firing squad on the basis of sentences passed by military tribunals. The flower of Yiddish literature and Jewish culture was destroyed.

In fact 238 writers, 106 actors, 19 musicians and 87 painters and sculptors, all shot to death or murdered in the camps. Only Ilya Ehrenburg remained.

Ehrenburg had never belonged to that circle and hadn't participated in the discussions about a Jewish republic. He was, first and foremost, a Russian journalist, and became very popular in the Soviet Union through his articles during the war. Stalin had a weak spot for him. I don't know whether it was because Ehrenburg had emigrated for some time and then come back, or perhaps for no particular reason. Stalin sometimes liked to help or even just show sympathy towards a distinguished intellectual or talented writer. He might ring one up all of a sudden to say a few warm words, or summon him suddenly and do something for him – as in the case of Bulgakov, for instance, for whom he got a job after years of unemployment, or Pasternak, whom he rang up on the spur of the moment to give him encouragement when he was having trouble publishing his books. The books didn't in fact get published, but a legend arose around these gestures of Stalin's which circulated widely and won people over to him. Stalin knew how to do such things.

Stalin dealt brutally with the flower of Yiddish literature, taking no account of the consequences his actions would have abroad. Abroad, after all, people admired the Soviet Union for having this flourishing centre which published its own literature and had a wonderful theatre, and no one over there would have believed that a writer whose works they had all read was involved in espionage.

Did you?

No, of course I didn't. I knew it was all a load of rubbish. Utter rubbish.

And?

Oh, my dear lady, all this was happening in an aura of victory and this rescue of the Jews from extermination by the Nazis. Our protests wouldn't have meant anything.

Did you try?

No. We never discussed the subject of the struggle with cosmopolitanism with them and they in turn put no pressure on us to carry it into Poland, or if they did, it was done very discreetly.

So who was it who planned the establishment of camps for cosmopolites in Mazuria?

I heard about it, but only afterwards. They probably either put that out to circulate as a rumour, not a directive, or treated it as a confidential decision.

They were supposed to be built by the army.

The commissariat, in other words.

You mean Rokossowski?

I doubt it. The commissariat was in general under Polish, that is Rokossowski's, command, but that decision didn't necessarily have to go through him. I'm guessing, of course, since I've no facts.

And did you hear about the building of a prison for cosmopolites?

I don't believe it, I don't believe it; that's a lie made up later.

Could you not have known?

Of course I could. Remember my situation was difficult, because I was already under suspicion. My secretary knew Field, I was a Jew, and in addition I'd met with the group from the Jewish Anti-Fascist Committee near the end of the war, before it left for America. I'd never made a secret of it, but that didn't mean anything, because they were accused. I became the perfect candidate for a Slansky, and that was the direction in which all the preparations were headed; I don't know how it would have ended if Stalin hadn't died. But the Field affair was becoming the direct way of getting at me.

That was when Bierut displayed real toughness of character, firmness and loyalty towards me. He wouldn't succumb to pressure and to the end he continued to defend me against the accusations, although Stalin tried to break him.

How?

I'll give you just one example. At one point Stalin asked Bierut: who is dearer to you, Berman or Minc? Bierut realized that his answer would signify his assent to the next move, so he answered in the way children do when asked whom they love more, mummy or daddy – both equally. He was also subjected to more brutal forms of repression.

Like what?

I won't say.

Threats against his family?

No, Stalin wasn't such a cad as that; no need to exaggerate. He could afford to give a little offence, but when he knew someone was going to cooperate with him – and Bierut's cooperation was guaranteed – he had to conform to certain niceties, and his behaviour didn't go beyond the limits of the acceptable.

Was Bierut afraid?

There were moments, yes, but I don't want to discuss it.

You mean he yielded to pressure?

Not in everything, no, I wouldn't say that. Not in my case, even though everyone thought he was mad to defend me against accusations of cosmopolitanism and subsequent dismissal from my posts, maybe even a trial. I'm sure it was a difficult decision for him.

Was there no struggle with cosmopolitanism in Poland?

Yes, there was, because copying the model of the Soviet Union was obligatory in every sphere, and even though I was constantly discussing the subject with Bierut, who of course was also hostile to it, the struggle with cosmopolitanism did seep through into Poland, regardless of our position on the matter. The problem itself was so acute in the Soviet Union that we even noticed some elements of that struggle in Gomulka's speech at the 1948 Conference on Unity. Gomulka had earlier received an invitation from Stalin, and Stalin had spent many hours in discussion with him; I don't know its contents, but Gomulka presumably got such an earful about cosmopolitanism there that he retained certain references to cosmopolitanism as a danger in his speech. I tried to argue with him, naturally without calling things by their true name and not always with happy results, because in my speech I based myself on some information about the Home Army that they'd slipped me. In 1949 Gomulka departed, and the struggle with cosmopolitanism began to be noticeable in our propaganda. We curbed and restrained it, so that it never assumed the proportions it had with our neighbours, but we did note individual instances where its full flood was unleashed. In the party press there was hardly any at all, but it was noticeable in the PAX press, although there, too, it was very discreet and almost hidden – for instance, an activist of Jewish origin would be criticized for what he was rather than for what he did. The practice of giving people's true Jewish names in brackets was not, of course, employed, so it took on an oral rather than a printed existence. And it fell on fruitful soil, because Polish society as a whole is very anti-Semitic.

You can say that? You?

Because that, unfortunately, is the truth. My daughter was often called a dirty Yid at school.

And you don't see why?

No, because, like Bierut, I was against too large a concentration of Jews in certain institutions; it wasn't the right thing to do and it was a necessary evil that we'd been forced into when we took power, when the Polish intelligentsia was boycotting us. But I assure you that if I recommended anyone for a post or shifted someone from one post to another, it wasn't because I loved one more than the other. In my politics concerning personnel I was guided by what made more sense and would prove more effective. At the same time I tried to avoid injury and humiliation when people were dismissed from their posts.

What about when they were imprisoned? In 1948–9 you arrested members of the Home Army Council of Aid to Jews, the "Zegota".

Yes well, all organizations connected with the Home Army were included; the scope was wide.

Mr Berman! The security services, where all or nearly all the directors were Jewish, arrested Poles because they had saved Jews during the occupation, and you say that Poles are anti-Semites. That's not nice.

It was wrong that that happened. Certainly it was wrong. At that time I didn't yet have any facts about what this "Zegota" did; it was only later that my brother told me about it. It was a small group, but very dedicated, and it took emormous risks to look after Jews during the war. I myself met a woman who'd managed to bring several dozen Jewish children out of the ghetto. Wladyslaw Bartoszewski had been very active in the "Zegota", as had my brother Adolf, after he managed, with its help, to escape from the ghetto to the Aryan side. We later released them all.

Wladyslaw Bartoszewski was in prison almost seven years.

I don't know how long he was imprisoned, but I certainly don't deny he was persecuted; he did his time.

And what did your brother have to say about it?

Adolf told me about the "Zegota", but not until many years later, and then, in 1950, he emigrated to Israel. He was an activist in the Central Jewish Committee, whose freedom of action had already been considerably restricted; he sensed the mood, saw that the possibilities for active work were shrinking, and at a certain point was ready to leave Poland.

And you weren't?

No. I was, of course, interested in what was going on in Israel, especially since I was quite familiar with the people there, and my brother urged me very strongly to come, finding it marvellous. Israel certainly deserves interest and notice, but I decided not to make the trip. The circumstances weren't right. I weighed up all the pros and cons and decided it wouldn't make any sense to go. In my case tourism assumes a different significance; it's not just an ordinary trip. So I didn't think that, in my critical situation, I should get myself into even deeper waters by an escapade to Israel or any other capitalist country; people here would have taken an unfavourable view of it and I would have been exposed to various comments and interpretations. Even without that, enough things were being imagined about me. And after that I didn't really have much opportunity. Even after 1956, there wasn't as much freedom as you think.

You wouldn't have got a passport?

I didn't try, but I suspect I wouldn't have, unless I'd declared that I was leaving for good, especially after 1968; but obviously I didn't want to do that, and I would never do it.

Everyone from the "Zegota" was rehabilitated after 1956.

Certainly; it was a group of extraordinarily noble people.

Is that all?

Look, you must understand: that was 1949–50. I already had some idea of my situation and Stalin's attitude towards me. So I thought that if I got involved in certain things, if I acted against the wishes of the Soviet advisers, then reports about my activities would reach Stalin, who would say, what kind of behaviour is this? So I had a choice: either leave or manoeuvre. Twice I handed in my resignation to Bierut, not across the board but only concerning my supervision of security. I had enough of those ministries, damn them, and I'd have had enough work to keep me busy all day even without security, but Bierut was opposed to my leaving. And my relations with him were such that I couldn't be categorical about it and say, right, I'm leaving, I don't want any of this and I don't care what you think about it. I had to make concessions and stay. So I decided to manoeuvre. I limited my participation in many significant matters or, at least, I limited my involvement to passing them on to someone else, or I asked Bierut to take a decision and only took decisions on minor matters myself. I also often cut myself off from contacts with security, which were unpleasant for me, for a few months or even half a year. Bierut used to tell me then: listen, whom can I count on if you won't help me? He would appeal to me so fervently that I would come back again after the break. Whether my manoeuvring tactics were deft enough or not, history will judge. Perhaps it would have been more sensible to dig my heels in and resign from the supervision of security altogether – who knows. For me the results would definitely have been positive, but I don't know whether it wouldn't have had an adverse effect on many decisions which would have been taken without me.

Because, of course, the people who replaced you would have been worse, right?

Either they would have been worse or no one would have replaced me at all and all the blame would have fallen on Bierut.

Apparently Radkiewicz also tried to resign, but stayed on.

Indeed, such situations did arise. He would say he was ill or tired, but those were just excuses; it was the situation in general that he didn't much want to participate in. We also considered for a while whether or not to keep him on.

You wanted to replace him with Moczar?

No, never. Anyone but him. Moczar was arrogant and hated, and even then went around proclaiming his anti-Semitism.

In May 1950 you arrested Spychalski.

I defended him throughout, even more than I defended Gomulka later, because I did it with more conviction. But I did think that the charges against him weren't entirely without foundation. The first was his attitude to his brother, a Home Army officer, with whom he had maintained quite close contact during the occupation; the second was his hiring of Lechowicz and Jaroszewicz for Military

Information, two people who had worked in the Second Unit under the prewar regime. I suppose it must have been his lack of experience or understanding, but in 1950 these facts were given only one interpretation. So he was accused, not unreasonably, of lack of vigilance. Thus the charges were certainly real enough, although not so serious as to warrant his arrest. That was why I continued to defend him and wouldn't agree to his imprisonment. People would say to me, look, if he escapes – that was the argument they constantly used – it'll be your head on the block. I didn't want any heads to roll, but I found it hard to believe that Spychalski would escape. Bierut, however, was full of suspicion against him, just as he was against Gomulka. Finally Wanda Wasilewska arrived from Kiev and told me that a plot was already prepared for Spychalski's abduction or escape.

On whose instructions did she come?

I don't know the facts; I can only make suppositions. I would think she was ordered to come by General Serov, who was stationed in Kiev and whom she knew well from the time of the war when she used to visit Khrushchev at the party committee. Still, for some years I was bothered about how Serov could have known about my reluctance, and recently, when I was at Julia Minc's, I finally found the missing link in my hypothesis. Julia remembered a minor but significant fact. When Spychalski's case was in progress, Wolski-Piwowarczyk asked her one day: what does Jakub think he's doing? Sending Spychalski out to the Recovered Territories to make it all the easier for him to escape?

We did in fact delegate Spychalski to the city government in Wroclaw, but we didn't have any ulterior motives in taking this decision. He had to be sent somewhere, and as an architect in the ruined city of Wroclaw he could be particularly useful.

At that point I understood the whole mechanism. Wolski-Piwowarczyk's version had made its way to Kiev, where Wanda found out about it, and hence her alarmist arrival.

But why come to you?

Judging by what Julia said, Wolski must have implied to the appropriate people that I was clearing the way for Spychalski's escape, that it was I who was making it possible for him to do so, so I was the main suspect. They could have thought of about ten other people who might have been similarly involved in Spychalski's alleged escape, but that's not important; the important thing was that such suspicions did arise and were passed on.

Did Wasilewska present any evidence?

No. I think Romkowski spoke to me about evidence, but only generally, without specifying what it was.

So throughout all this time Wasilewska was still interested in what was going on in Poland?

Certainly. But in this case I think her intervention was the result of her personal attitude to me; we were friends.

Some people claim it was even more than that.

Perhaps, who knows. But that's not the point. After Wasilewska's intervention I gave in. You've got to understand: the authorities in charge of Spychalski's case were claiming that a plot had been hatched, and I had no evidence which might have refuted those charges. Everything was rigged, of course, because Spychalski wasn't intending to escape. I was pressed up against the wall and I couldn't avoid taking the decision. I had a choice: either to believe Spychalski when he said he wouldn't escape, and I had no grounds for doing so, or to believe that he would escape. If this second version had turned out to be true, I would be the one to answer for it.

You arrested Gomulka because he also wanted to escape, didn't you?

I did hear such a version, and I even opposed it. It made no sense, because the conflict with him wasn't on that level. I said that certainly, we did hold some things against Gomulka, but that they were of a political, not a criminal nature, and didn't concern his wanting to escape.

Why, then, did you arrest him?

I had no influence on that decision, especially since I was ill in hospital. But when I found out about it I protested against it most vigorously, although in vain. I didn't, of course, make my opposition to it known *urbi et orbi*, but I exchanged sharp words with Bierut – with him alone, of course. It's only recently that I discovered that Romkowski had also protested against it and had made his opposition known, quite independently from me and probably without even being aware of my position on the matter. I suppose he was guided by the fact that he'd known Gomulka back from their time at the "Lenin school" together, when they had shared a room.

Who, then? Radkiewicz?

I shouldn't think the matter went through Radkiewicz.

So it was Bierut?

It couldn't have happened without Bierut's approval, of course. Bierut had some sort of complex about Gomulka which had remained with him since the time of the occupation and which I found difficult to understand, although of course that's no excuse. No, Bierut certainly didn't believe that Gomulka was a traitor, but he couldn't fully trust him, and he hesitated in deciding what to do about him. I think the Soviet advisers took advantage of Bierut's psychological condition, and I wouldn't rule out the possibility that Stalin himself persuaded him to give the order to arrest Gomulka.

On what formal grounds?

Gomulka came under suspicion.

Of espionage, as usual?

No one caught Gomulka at it and we never believed in his treason, but his name had already been mentioned two years earlier at Rajk's trial in Budapest, and obviously not by coincidence. Granted, not yet within the context of suspicion of espionage, as it was later, at Slansky's trial in Prague, but in the form of implications, veiled for the time being, that there were connections between them. Representatives of our security services were being invited to Budapest at the time, because the Soviet advisers were determined at all costs to exploit Rajk's case to our advantage and pressed us to organize the same kind of trial here.

Apparently two weeks before the trial, while being interrogated in the presence of two of your security functionaries, Rajk withdrew his previous confessions of treason and espionage.

That's highly unlikely; I don't remember any such thing. I only know that among our people who attended the trial were Zambrowski, who worked in the army then, and Romkowski, and they returned filled with doubt and scruples. Romkowski said to me: the trial didn't hang together; it didn't look like an open and shut case; a number of points gave rise to doubt. That's all I remember.

Rajk was executed.

Yes, but he was rehabilitated after 1956.

We were under strong pressure to give Gomulka a similar trial. It was suggested that a few comrades should attend the next trial –

Slansky's, in Prague. With this purpose we sent out a party delegation of four or five people. Gomulka's name was mentioned at this trial also, and this time his connections with Slansky were pointed out with no holds barred. But no proof of his guilt was presented, because there was none. No one could come up with any testimony implicating Gomulka. Despite this, however, since he had been in contact with Slansky, Slansky's shadow was to hang over him.

Slansky and ten other comrades were executed.

Yes, and they too were later rehabilitated.

And why do you think they arranged all these show trials in Bulgaria, Hungary and Czechoslovakia? Quite simply in order to involve the whole bloc. But we didn't go as far as our neighbours and refused to allow Gomulka to be put on trial. We rejected all the charges against him. In this sense we were an exception, because we were the only ones who didn't allow leading figures to be wrested out of the party leadership.

And why did Stalin arrange these trials?

My dear lady, every deviation, every manoeuvre, gives rise to the question of who gains from it, and it was in that light that Gomulka was assessed. I don't in the least wish to justify the situation, but you do have to understand that the charges were trumped up because of the principle of combating the enemy to the end –

Until his destruction, as in the Soviet Union in 1938?

Let us ask ourselves, first of all, why Stalin did that then; surely he wasn't crazy? No, he wasn't crazy. He got that idea and followed that path because at some point he discovered or came to the conclusion that accusing his enemies, who were hindering him and spoiling his plans, on political grounds alone would not be convincing, and that in order to get rid of them and liquidate them he would have to destroy them morally as well. That's how I see it. You also have to remember that all this was happening when Hitler was rearing up more and more and the Soviet Union faced a very real danger from Germany, so that unity of action and the closing of ranks were also essential. A similar situation was repeated, on a smaller scale, at the end of the forties and the beginning of the fifties: you have to remember that whenever the international situation intensifies, the result as a rule is, first, a sharpening in debate, which hinders the consolidation of forces in the face of the enemy, and, later, an intensification of the internal situation. At that time, too, there was a real threat from America and the entire bloc had to unite in the face of that threat. Hence the removal, in many parties, of distinguished activists. Nor do I rule out the possibility that there might have been some other additional reasons which led to these senseless and most serious charges that were imputed [sic] to them. It was a gloomy and bitter time which had to be waited out and in which I adopted what were to my mind the only suitable tactics: to play for time, to prevent death sentences from being passed and fates from being sealed, to await the time when people could be released.

On the day after Gomulka's arrest the trial of General Tatar and eight other Home Army officers began. Coincidence?

No, coincidences like that don't happen. There were attempts, through very far-reaching insinuations, to connect the two cases. Perhaps not directly, but as part of the search for evidence of Gomulka's guilt, evidence which, as I've said, did not exist.

The trial began on 31 July 1951. Was this done so that on 1 August, on the seventh anniversary of the Warsaw Uprising, all the papers might run first-page stories about the Polish heroes: "a pack of bandits", "the filthy progeny of crime", "Pilsudski's dwarfs", and so on?

I must confess I didn't see the coincidence in those dates. I did of course know, however, that the direct aim of the trial was to strike a hard blow against the Home Army and its activists in London. I'd just had an operation and was not yet entirely recovered, but they sent me the documents of the case before the trial because it was a matter for the direct supervision of security. I think I went over them with Minc, and made a few corrections, but I couldn't perform miracles. The testimony was various and sundry and a sufficiently incriminating picture emerged from it all.

What picture?

That they'd formed a conspiracy with the aim of overthrowing by force the system of People's Poland.

Naturally. And had they?

The important thing was that the documents presented to me showed that they had. They contained testimony of the accused confessing their guilt, the testimony of witnesses, in short everything necessary for a conviction, and it all held together so logically that there was nothing to latch on to. The only thing I found doubtful concerned the gold of the prewar Polish government which General Tatar had withdrawn from deposit in England on his way back from emigration and brought back to Poland. I wasn't entirely certain whether his efforts to obtain it had been made with malicious intent, in order to buy his way in and catch us on his hook, as the investigation attempted to prove, or out of concern for his country. The first possibility could not, of course, be ruled out, but I wasn't convinced of it. So I latched on to this and in conclusion wrote an indictment in which I recommended that neither Tatar nor the other defendants should necessarily be sentenced to death. That was the only thing I could do. What I proposed was this: let's sentence them and then wait and see what time will bring; perhaps some years later we will finally get at the truth.

Luckily I succeeded in persuading Bierut of my point of view, because obviously I couldn't have brought it off on my own. The discussion with him wasn't easy. I explained that condemning people to death was pointless because instead of serving the cause it worked against it, and I was so strenuous and categorical in my insistence that Bierut finally conceded my point. It may also have been partly due to the fact that he felt constrained regarding me, as I'd just recovered from an illness and was a bit angry with him for arresting Gomulka. He summoned Romkowski and declared that there should be no death sentences. Romkowski was stupefied. Actually, they were all stupefied.

All, meaning who else?

Meaning the Soviet advisers, who'd worked and worked on this trial and had prepared themselves for huge sentences. I think they were expecting four or five death sentences. They were very much counting on me, but they miscalculated and were disillusioned, while the world was stunned. Here was the first trial, in other words a show trial, and not a single death sentence, although of course the ones that were passed were heavy –

Four life sentences.

I think that the judge, in pronouncing sentence, described Romkowski's visit to Bierut and all the credit went to him, and rightly. Unfortunately, however, Tatar's trial was an exception which didn't determine the rule. In the other Home Army trials, the minor ones on the side, where the pressure exerted by the Soviet advisers was extremely harmful, there was nothing I could do, and quite a lot of death sentences were passed.

By the minor ones on the side you mean closed ones held in prison cells, like the ones in Lefortovo or the Lubyanka?

In prison, yes, but not in cells. There was a special room for them, so that the formal requirements were supposedly fulfilled. This was explained by saying that it was for the protection of the prisoners, in order to avoid the risk of taking them elsewhere, because they might be rescued on the way to court. You know, the usual kind of talk they always give you there.

Was that how Colonel "Nil", Emil Fieldorf, died?

I don't recall the case.

Curious. I've been asking nearly everyone about it and none of you gentlemen seems to know the name, although the man was a national hero. He was head of the Home Army's Directorate of Subversion, "Kedyw"; he planned the assassination of Kutschera and the prisoners' rescue operation; and he was the commander of the "Nie" ["No"] organization. First the NKVD arrested him under a false name and sent him to Siberia, and then the Polish security services arrested him when he got back.

If he belonged to the Home Army leadership his case certainly can't have been dealt with on a low level. Still, it must have passed me by.

Was his death sentence also passed by an independent (as you claim) court?

With you it's all so simple. Independent or not, a court bases itself on the documents presented to it by the investigative authorities. If those authorities were able to influence Bierut, who after all was incontestably an honest and intelligent man, and yet believed in Gomulka's or Spychalski's guilt, then surely they could persuade the court as well. Every prisoner feels constrained in court, and you have to be exceptionally tough to resist its pressure.

Fieldorf, Moczarski, Kuropieska, Lechowicz, and many other people all did – up to the end!

I don't know, really; all this is just speculation. It's certainly true that our courts were not among the best and the problem, in my view, lay not in that trials took place in the prison grounds, but in that judges were, unfortunately, prepared for what to expect from the outset and therefore not always impartial.

Those were the only kind you appointed.

We didn't appoint them; the Soviet advisers did. Judges came from the security apparatus, as in the Soviet Union, because the advisers introduced their own judicatory methods over here, so our judiciary was appointed according to the Soviet model.

Did they also determine sentences?

Sentences were in accordance with the provisions of the criminal code and dependent on the nature and extent of the offence. We intervened only in the most serious and vital cases; for the rest the penal procedure was normal.

Mr Berman!

I agree, those weren't normal courts and the judges were not among the most discriminating, but you must understand that these judges also wanted conscientiously to fulfil their duties to the party, which the necessity of state imposed upon them. You know how it is, surely. Sometimes the interest of the individual has to be subordinated to the interest of the state, and when the state is threatened suspicions are magnified in order to render them more plausible. I don't deny that a number of sentences were incorrect, and perhaps if they had been passed by different judges we would have avoided many mistakes. But then, it wasn't all that easy to find judges who would be able at the same time to retain both their loyalty to us and their loyalty to the accused, which is essential in order to pass a just sentence.

When I hear any of you gentlemen say the words "just", "equal" or "socialist", I feel my flesh creep.

[Smile] It was unfortunate that the idea was repudiated, but this took place not as a result of its falsification but owing to the failure of certain developmental trends which became manifest more sharply than one could have predicted, and also owing to the fact that certain forces hostile to socialism took up the offensive. [Sic.]

Yes, well, perhaps we'd better stick to the facts.

I don't want to whitewash them, because I know they are disgraceful. But that, unfortunately, was how that mechanism worked, and there was nothing I could do about it. My own situation, after all, was particularly difficult, since the Soviet advisers knew roughly what Stalin's attitude towards me was; even if they weren't told about it directly, they were certainly in some way predisposed towards me, be it only, for example, in the sense that they knew they didn't have to take my opinion into account.

On 11 November 1952, you arrested General Waclaw Komar.

We entered a phase when Spanish Civil War veterans began to come under suspicion of treason. An atmosphere of distrust built up around Komar's department; Komar, who had been chief of staff of the Second Unit of the Polish army, had put that unit together mainly out of comrades who were close to him; he employed mostly Spanish war veterans for intelligence work. Almost all these people were eliminated.

You mean imprisoned?

Yes, that's right; Wacek was arrested, and so were Leder and Flato. Throughout that time I tried to keep a finger on their case, in the sense that I tried to annul decisions which were leading up to their trial. What I could not do, however, since I didn't have sufficient facts at my disposal, was to obtain their release.

Their innocence wasn't sufficient?

Their innocence would have been sufficient, but first it had to be proved – after all, they were facing specific charges. I won't go into whether they were real or illusory, but they were charges, and during the investigation they had to be cleared up. That's what we tried to do.

Did you know Komar or Leder?

Of course.

So what was there to clear up?

Miss Toranska, the true/false, guilty/innocent distinctions are unfortunately very fluid in a situation where the atmosphere is filled with suspicion and that suspicion is constantly being stoked up. I couldn't just assume from the outset that everyone accused of espionage was innocent, because then I would have had to assume that hostile intelligence services had ceased to concern themselves with Poland and folded up their networks here, which would have been ridiculous. So the question was whether we always netted the right ones and whether security was lucky in its catches. Probably there were real catches and there were mistakes. But every case had to be thoroughly investigated.

With the aid of torture?

Komar wasn't tortured. If he was, the torture was only psychological, not physical. In other words, threats were made that his family would suffer consequences: they used methods which are generally employed in such cases. I heard nothing about his being beaten, nor did he later complain of it.

You mean he lied? He, Leder and Flato, along with Generals Kuropieska, Tatar, Mossor, Kirchmayer, Skibinski and finally Moczarski, who described forty-nine kinds of torture used on him?

I read that, and I don't deny those facts. We appointed a commission to check whether or not people were being beaten, and when we came upon certain abuses we submitted a few people to disciplinary proceedings – we meaning Bierut and myself. And we did punish a few, or maybe a dozen or so officers, I don't remember exactly how many. We prosecuted them under disciplinary procedure. They were reprimanded and suspended from the carrying out of their official duties or dismissed from work for several months, even half a year. Still, I agree that this was more for show than a genuine punishment, so of course it could only be effective for a short time, and it didn't change the mechanism – which continued to churn. This happened because, first of all, the security apparatus began, as it did in the Soviet Union, to rise above the party and to acquire a supraparty meaning; it was able to manipulate all the sources of information and we were often helpless in the face of it. Second, control over the kind of closed clan which security became was especially difficult, because everyone covered up for everyone else and you had to have someone to base yourself on if you ever wanted to prove anything against anyone. So someone had to betray those inside secrets – professional secrets, let's say.

And thirdly, you preferred not to know, right?

It's not true that we didn't want to know. We simply didn't believe that that kind of bestiality was going on. I agree, we may have been blind. We didn't give any credence to gossip and treated it as hostile propaganda, because of course there were countless rumours and hostile insinuations about us. Surely you must see that one has to be aware of the climate one's living in, and the climate then was such that even many people from the security apparatus, especially its more ideological part, gave credence to certain myths, legends and dangers, and they acted the way they did not under the influence of pressure from advisers or their superiors, but in the conviction that repression was the right thing.

My God! Tearing out fingernails? Crushing kidneys? Keeping people in water? Out of conviction?

If I'd known I wouldn't have tolerated an officer like that for five minutes.

Well, then, you should have gone to the prison [shouting] to visit your friends!

It's true I didn't do that, first of all because I was constrained in my movements, and secondly because I didn't really believe the rumours.

And you're going to tell me you didn't know how people hated you?

My dear lady, do you think it's conceivable that someome should decide to bring about a catastrophe just because he wasn't liked?

What are you talking about?

Well, of course you could say, *Après moi le déluge*, but that's not how a communist thinks. A communist should see the world as it develops and try to change it. He should be responsible for his actions and save the nation from catastrophe.

So you, the communists, were sacrificing yourselves for your country?

Not sacrificing ourselves, but fulfilling and continuing to fulfil our duty towards it, for the simple reason that if we don't work and suffer then Poland will be crushed to bits [shouting]! I don't know when that truth will get through to those millions, but I've no doubt that one day it will, and then it'll begin to dawn on them how great a danger we rescued them from.

That's masochism.

Why masochism?

What, then! Part of the nation spits on you, the other part curses you, and about 90 per cent doesn't want you.

Well, let's say 90 per cent, I won't haggle about percentages. If we were wrong, or if reasons were dreamt up or plucked out of thin air, then of course someone could come along and say it was madness – I agree. But we are right, in the most rational way, and the prospects which I've already outlined for you several times were and are real ones, there's nothing I can do about it. And as to the fact that we were few, and still are, history teaches us that the minority always rescued the majority.

I'm at a loss for words . . . so perhaps . . . you could say something about your life. You lived on Klonowa Street.

I had the ground floor of the house, Bierut had the first floor and for a while Szwalbe had the second. I had four rooms and quite a nice ante-room. In 1945 I was treated to a dacha near Warsaw. My villa was situated next to Radkiewicz's and opposite Bierut's. Hilary Minc had one a bit further along.

I led a quiet life. I would get up at eight, sometimes at half past seven, eat breakfast with my wife and then we'd go to work – my wife to the Institute of Rheumatology and I to the Central Committee or the Office of the Council of Ministers. I was there at nine. We had a maid.

One that they sent you?

Of course. The Ministry of Security had a government protection department. It organized our holidays and our official trips, it sent us our maids and appointed our bodyguards – I got four or five in shifts round the clock. They all had their specific tasks.

From whom did they take orders?

They didn't report to me, as you can imagine [smile].

But you were their head.

That's got nothing to do with it. They collected information about me and about everyone else they looked after, from the minister onwards, and passed it on somewhere. Who visited me and what my office hours were. They couldn't hear any conversations because they sat out in the corridors or in the hall, and outside in the summer.

Not in the house?

No, they were outside, but within reach. In any case I only held conversations in closed offices.

Weren't they bugged?

I shouldn't think so. I would come home between three and four, have lunch with my wife and daughter, and then go back to the Central Committee. Sometimes I'd drop in at home for supper, but they often sent up sandwiches to the office. My office, two offices, actually, one at the Council of Ministers and the other at the Central Committee, were large, bigger than this room. They had two telephones – one was a normal local line and the other a special line where you could be connected with Moscow. We didn't have a direct line because it wasn't necessary; with the special phone you got your connection immediately. Stalin organized a system of working late into the night, and this applied not only to us but also to the entire territory of the Soviet Union and the bloc. He normally started work at about six o'clock in the evening and would contact everyone between six and midnight or one in the morning. So everyone who could be useful to him waited for his call, knowing that he might ring at any moment.

So you sat there waiting for the phone to ring?

We didn't just sit there doing nothing; we did various things during the time, and also made telephone calls to people in the certainty that all of them would be there at that hour, and of course we also knew that one of them might ring with a question or with some information.

On Sundays as well?

No, Sundays were reserved for social meetings with other members of the Politburo; I mainly met with the rest of our Troika, that is Bierut and Minc. We visited one another for supper or afternoon tea, or just for coffee. We had more scope in the summer because we could also go for walks in Konstancin, short ones, within the closed grounds of our villas. But even then we did an enormous amount of work. I must admit we were rather poor on social life.

Did you discuss your arrested colleagues among yourselves?

We were all aware of the grimness of the situation. In December 1952 two terrible trials took place: twenty-three death sentences for cosmopolitanism in Moscow and eleven in Prague, among them Slansky's and Clementis's. And on 14 January 1953, they announced the discovery of a Kremlin doctors' conspiracy, which augured another purge. The smell of terror was in the air.

Zygmunt Modzelewski came to see me to intervene on behalf of Komar's group, and in particular Leder, whom he'd known before the war and was friends with his family. Leder was in fact the son of a distinguished KPP activist. I said to him, listen, there's nothing I can do right now, because of the situation being what it is. But I guarantee you that I'll manage to get them out somehow within a year or a year and a half. And I did.

Not so fast, Mr Berman. On 5 March "the heart of the leader of freedom stopped beating"; the "liberator of the Polish nation" who "gave us life, gave us freedom, was the father of us all", "the Great Stalin," died –

– I didn't go to the funeral, for understandable reasons –

– and the most threatening and dangerous time for the Polish nation began. It began on a rather innocent note: first of all you renamed Katowice "Stalinogrod".

Out of stupidity. I abstained from voting.

There was a vote?

Yes, there was.

Did Bierut propose it?

I don't remember.

Who was in favour?

The motion was carried by a majority, so there's no point in counting. In such cases various incidental, minor and irrelevant reasons often play a part. But I can tell you, as consolation, that we managed, with considerable help on my part, to bury the idea of erecting a statue to Stalin in front of the Palace of Culture and Learning.

Later, nineteen out of the ninety-one Polish officers who had been sentenced to death in the preceding years were executed.

I'd rather not talk about that, as it was a sad affair and it might show Bierut in an unfavourable light; Bierut was a noble character and it is thanks to him that you're talking to me at all. So please cross that out.

I was in the Belvedere, walking down the corridor, when he accosted me and said, listen, take these files, read them and tell me what I'm to do next. I replied: I won't take the files because I know how they're put together. But I do have just one request and piece of advice for you: don't give them death sentences, because when a case isn't closed it's still possible that somehow it will finally be cleared up, and as long as the person's alive there's still a chance, even if he suffers for a few years, that he'll be released.

I went home, and even had some pangs of conscience that perhaps it would have been better if I had taken those files; but I really did believe there was little to be gained from looking at them. They contained testimonies and confessions and everything was neatly set out and polished. There would have been nothing for me to latch on to. The only thing I could do was to play on the moral argument that it was better to hand out heavy sentences than death penalties. But Bierut didn't follow my advice. It rarely happened that he completely disregarded my advice, but this time it did happen. Unfortunately he placed too much faith in those documents.

And then, finally, it was time for the Church. On 28 September 1953, after a series of attacks and trials of clergy, you arrested the Primate, Wyszynski.

I was against it, but I couldn't influence a change of decision. Besides, they planned not to arrest him but to intern him in a monastery, where the conditions would supposedly be better, but that didn't really make much difference at that point, since the whole thing was senseless. There are various moves, you know, that you make in political games and intrigues, and they're not always wise or fortunate. I definitely include the arrest of the Primate among the unwise ones, because Wyszynski was made into yet another martyr and the Church, instead of being weakened, was strengthened.

Who committed this "mistake"?

Bierut.

With no help from your "friends"?

No. The imprisonment of the Primate was our decision, taken by our government. Specifically by Bierut, for the Church was his domain and this was no minor matter but involved a Primate in a Catholic country. Still, you have to understand that in this case the decision didn't concern so much the Primate as a person but the Church as such.

You wanted to break it up?

There was no chance of that, so we didn't even try. But it's always the case that each side tries to gain as many trumps as possible. The Catholic Church went through phases of extending its influence to a greater or a lesser degree, imposing greater or lesser restrictions, and we had to adopt some kind of attitude towards that. In addition Bierut's decision was influenced by the general situation, or rather by the coming together of several unfavourable elements. On the one hand operations to discredit the Church had already been in preparation when Stalin was alive, and on the other, apparently already by 1953, it turned out that the line represented by the patriot-priests and by PAX would not stem the activity of the Church.

By "patriot-priests" you mean the ones who tried to break up the Church from within?

No. The patriot-priests weren't aiming to break up the Church, because such an undertaking would have been doomed to failure, but they tried, together with PAX, to create a Church opposition – a centre that could both act as an exchangeable element in negotiations with the Church and restrict the Church's vigour and aggressiveness, since the Church was undoubtedly considered to be, if not an openly political organization, at least one whose attitude to the system and to all the "godless" ideas connected with it was rather unfavourable and reluctant. However, for a long time, and especially until 1947, we wanted to win the Church over, and particularly to win over the faithful.

More specifically to subordinate it.

No, no. We took the view that a pluralism of world views should be retained, that citizens should be granted absolute freedom of religion, and that we would not hinder the Church in the carrying out of is religious functions – which, as you know, was quite contrary to the attitude adopted by our neighbours. We didn't want to wage a battle with the Church and we tried to avoid doing anything unpleasant or unwise. In the beginning I think we succeeded. State dignitaries took part in the Corpus Christi procession while Church dignitaries participated in cutting the tapes at the inaugurations of new schools or factories. With the passing of time, however, as the international situation became more acute, bringing with it a wave of Cold War attitudes, so also our relations with the Church changed and yielded to certain deformations, which distorted our initial plans. As late as 1950 we were still trying to reach an agreement: together with Wyszynski we signed an excellent document, later modified somewhat, and it played a positive role, albeit not for long, since it was, unfortunately, not always abided by.

Mostly on your part.

One side will always accuse the other while defending its own position and claiming that it is beyond reproach, even though this is impossible when an enormous mass of people, a live organism consisting of many individuals with various temperaments, views and attitudes, is concerned. We accused them, they accused us, and I don't by any means wish to claim that the blame for this lay with the Primate Wyszynski, who was a man of wide horizons, appreciated the importance of the agreement with us and seemed to me to be quite well-disposed towards Bierut, which would indicate that Bierut knew how to talk to him. But Wyszynski had no influence on the prattling of some priest or bishop or other.

What were the specific charges on which he was arrested?

This repression – and I agree it was stupid – was the result of the general situation, and has to be seen as part of a whole. Stalin's death was followed a few months later by the Berlin Uprising and by the turbulent course of the June events in the GDR, and certain elements here also began to believe that something was changing, that perhaps the map of Europe would change. An activization and consolidation of the opposition groups took place, particularly in the Church, and Bierut attempted to stifle this.

Who helped him?

Mazur and Luna Brystigier, the latter delegated by the Ministry of Public Security to collect information for him.

Was she the one who, also at this time, prepared the show trial of the Bishop of Kielce, who like many clergymen was sentenced for espionage?

I shouldn't think so, although she probably knew the details of his case, as it was within the scope of her work. But I suspect that she prepared certain documents which she then passed on to the criminal investigation department of security, where, as you know, Rozanski worked, and any doubtful-looking or even uncertain information which she passed on and which he and his people in turn subjected to deeper investigation – investigation which was, in addition, not always conducted by proper or honest methods – had the effect it did. In fact we dismissed him, as you know.

Not for some time, Mr Berman.

A year later, after the November meeting.

And after Swiatlo's escape and his broadcast at Radio Free Europe, right?

Before that we had not yet been in possession of direct and documented accusations against him which would justify dismissing him from his post.

Hadn't you? Because almost the whole of Poland –

– myths to the effect that someone is a sadist may be real or they may be illusory or dreamt up with malicious intent. If I'd known, not for a minute would I have –

– and Radkiewicz, as this honest man –

– undoubtedly –

– why didn't he take an interest in these accusations?

I've already spoken about the beatings: we subjected several people to disciplinary proceedings and a few people from the investigation department, of which Rozanski was head, were also dismissed at that time. I'm far from wanting to claim that what happened was a good thing, and we certainly shouldn't have waited until we had accumulated so much evidence against Rozanski, but taken more decisive action earlier. First we shifted him over to the State Publishing Institute, as director, and a few months later, when so many charges against him had accumulated that he had to be arrested, we instigated criminal proceedings against him. I was still in office then. And that was also when we began to look into all the investigations, especially the ones conducted by Military Information, because they had amassed a lot of various kinds of rubbish, more absurd than what security had collected. Thus began the period which I had promised Modzelewski would come, and it was I who brought about, through Bierut among others, the appointment of a special commission, with the participation of Ochab, to look into the cases conducted by Military Information.

You appointed the commission because General Komar testified that Bierut and Mazur were the leaders of the espionage network in which he worked.

I didn't hear about Bierut, at any rate that was something they didn't show us – maybe they concealed it. But it's true that in the meantime Komar, trying to defend himself, started to talk rubbish and he reached a stage where he was implicating everyone.

You as well?

I don't think so, at any rate I didn't hear of it. Perhaps they didn't want to hurt me. But Komar mentioned Mazur, Zawadzki, Modzelewski – anyone you could think of, actually!

Years later, when I met him at the cemetery – all sorts of people meet there – he came up to me and asked whether I didn't hold it against him that he'd spewed out all those names. I replied, listen, there's a wise men's saying that in order to accuse someone and blame him for something, you have to imagine yourself in a similar situation. I can't imagine your situation, so I can't hold a grudge against you for having been foolish. I can only assert that you were, because the things you did were undoubtedly foolish and indecently foolish at that, because you couldn't really have predicted what consequences they would bring for the people whose names you mentioned.

Accusing members of the Politburo of being involved in espionage was a desperate attempt on Wacek's part to reduce the entire investigation to the absurd. He was probably hoping that someone would finally think twice and look at his case differently. That sort of calculation is risky, however, and it could have brought fresh disasters with it.

We appointed the commission independently of his testimony, but rather because Stalin had died and we were beginning to undo all the cases.

Did you appoint it as a move against Rokossowski?

Certainly, since he was the direct head of Military Information.

He didn't object?

He can't have been overly pleased that someone was interfering in his department, but he made no protest. But times had already changed, and we began to send home many of the Soviet advisers. Some of the military, judges on our Supreme Court, came to me before their departure asking me not to write bad reports on them because they were afraid they'd get a thrashing when they got home. And some of them did get sent to prison. Skulbaszewski was sentenced to a few years and Voznesensky to as much as ten. Ochab's commission talked to the people who had been arrested and for many of them the prison regime was changed; this was even reflected in what they later wrote. Kuropieska, for instance, who must have been inside longer than anyone else, considered it a kindness of sorts when he was transferred from the Military Information prison to the security prison and, paradoxical as it may sound, he felt more secure in the security prison, because he was no longer exposed to the direct attacks which had so tormented him in the Military Information prison. The commission had direct access to the case files; the absurdities committed during the investigations, which reached their peak in Military Information, increasingly came to light; and cases began to be cleared up, disentangled and dismantled, while people were cleared and released.

Not so fast, Mr Berman. In the meantime you were also demoted.

No, no, I don't think so. I continued to take part in all the meetings of the Politburo and to carry out all my previous functions. I can speak of being dismissed earlier, when the threat of Stalin hung over me and in consequence I had to impose certain restrictions on my movements and didn't want to involve myself in everything.

In 1954 you ceased being secretary of the Central Committee.

Because I became deputy premier, in other words I was promoted.

Really?

It was a sort of kick upwards, I agree. Someone was anxious to have me out of the Central Committee secretariat. Not Bierut, naturally, although he did – I presume, since officially I know nothing about it – succumb to pressure from Khrushchev, who, although not an anti-Semite in the popular sense of the word, nevertheless had various complexes of that sort. He claimed there were too many Jews in the administration. His words were zealously taken up by others and put forward as arguments. Khrushchev thought it would be conducive to calming the atmosphere and defusing the situation if I were dismissed and all the blame for the preceding period fell on me. The matter was discussed at the Kremlin, where they considered what post I should be entrusted with, and I'm told that Molotov, looking for some kind of honourable way out, suggested at one point: maybe we should make him deputy premier, then he won't suffer any discrimination. Bierut agreed to this solution, but people in Warsaw, who were familiar with the backstage of politics, interpreted my departure from the Central Committee secretariat correctly and didn't consider my deputy premiership a promotion.

Were Starewicz, Kasman and Staszewski dismissed for the same reasons?

I couldn't say.

So Molotov supported you to the end?

I met with him quite frequently, especially at the beginning, when we worked together on dozens of things concerning Poland. And later also, when I had a political problem of some kind, I would turn mainly to him. This was also true in 1948, during the Peace Congress in Wroclaw. He was polite to me, but then they were all very polite – Kaganovich, and Mikoyan – all of them, in fact. Politeness is part of the ritual. But I think the only gesture of sympathy I ever met with was from Malenkov, when I came to Moscow after a few years' break in 1954, for the first time since Stalin's death, and Malenkov raised a hand in greeting and said, *Zdrastvuy, Yakov*. I didn't know him very well, only to the extent that he was a member of the Politburo and took part in meetings with us, so we could sit side by side and talk about this or that, but I never discussed anything of major importance with him.

Who was the first to be released? Gomulka?

I don't know if he was the first, but he was cleared of the charges against him after a few years and he came out at the end of 1954. It could have been earlier, but that's how it worked out. Other people also started to come out. A whole crowd of them came out. My Anna Duracz and all the people tacked on to the Field affair. We were helped by the fact that the Field affair had gone bankrupt in Hungary as well, and the Hungarians were beginning to withdraw from it. It was senseless: a lot of people were wronged, many suffered, and Gecow even died.

The rest of the Home Army people were still inside.

Releasing people was a process, after all, not a one-off act, so clearing up cases and releasing the arrested required time and took place gradually. The espionage cases were the worst. Two of them dragged on for an alarming length of time. I raged about the fact that in 1955, when almost all the communists had been released, Wacek Komar and Marian Spychalski were still inside. But Bierut slowed down their release. His mind was full of a whole complex of suspicions which I couldn't cut through. I blame this on his rigid, doctrinaire views, which also accounted for, among other things, his faith in all those documents that security slipped him. He believed in them; really believed in them.

Didn't you?

For me those suspicions were totally discredited by then, but not yet for him. It depends on your attitude to the investigative documents you read: one person interprets them in a certain way because he wants to clear the suspect while someone else gives more credence to the interrogators. Bierut continued to believe the accusations, and that's why I didn't raise the issue of Spychalski's or Komar's innocence or guilt in my conversations with him, but suggested instead that they should remain at liberty during the investigation and trial, since their cases would then take on a totally different character. I discussed Komar with him many times. Since this produced no results, in the spring of 1955 I raised the issue of his release at a meeting of the Politburo. But I remained isolated in my position. I even became ill then: I had a mini-stroke and had to stay in bed for several weeks. In the autumn of 1955 I again raised the matter of release, this time Spychalski's, and again in vain. My motion was struck down.

What was Minc in favour of?

I don't remember. In any case Bierut made the decision, and as always in matters of the highest state importance the voice of the First Man prevailed. They both remained inside until 1956.

Spychalski remained in prison until the Twentieth Congress and Bierut's death, as did the Home Army officers, who were only released by Ochab on the basis of the amnesty that was announced in April 1956.

Three of us went to the Twentieth Congress: Bierut, Jerzy Morawski and myself. Bierut wasn't feeling well: he was weakened after a bout of flu and the sessions were a difficult ordeal for him. Mikoyan's speech at the beginning of the Congress already contained a promise of renewal. Mikoyan naturally didn't make any revelations, but the way the accents in his speech were distributed indicated that we were entering a new phase. I succumbed to the exalted mood and, influenced by these joyful happenings, drank a *bruderschaft* with Morawski.

On the last day of the Congress Khrushchev made a speech in a closed meeting that was for delegates only. Foreign guests were not invited into the conference hall. I was due to return to Poland the following day. Bierut received a copy of this speech and he lent it to me on the final night. Naturally it made a great impression on me, but I think I took it more calmly than Bierut, since I'd already had many criticisms to make of Stalin's actions earlier. In fact Bierut should also have had some. After all, "Jasia" Fornalska's entire family had been terribly hacked up during the Great Purge and when Bierut was in Moscow he continued to ask about her brothers, long murdered, in the deluded hope that maybe one of them was still alive and he might succeed in getting him out. So Bierut, too, should have been immune to a shock of this kind. But when you only know of individual instances, the process is different from what it is when everything is laid before you. Bierut was staggered.

He finally discovered whom he had been serving?

No, it's not even that he'd been serving him. Bierut simply couldn't understand what had happened to make Stalin do such things. In that context it didn't matter that bringing these horrors to light might lead to Stalin's being condemned or erased from history – he can't be erased whatever happens, because he defeated Hitler, and that is how he will continue to be seen in the history of the world, despite all the foolish acts he committed –

– crimes, Mr Berman.

And crimes, that's undeniable. But he committed them convinced that they were serving the cause of the revolution, and thus guided by ideological principles.

So did Hitler, Mr Berman.

Don't be silly. Stalin had an idea, a great idea – to defend the revolution at all costs.

Hitler wanted to defend the purity of the race.

No [shouting], no, you can't compare those things!

The effect was the same.

Such are the paradoxes of history. Very painful and difficult, but such they are, you can't get away from them. And that's why Khrushchev's speech at the Twentieth Congress turned out to be such a shock, and Khrushchev himself, regardless of whether he was always right when speaking on particular matters, displayed great strength of character by the very fact that he came out with such an arsenal of charges against Stalin. Bierut fell ill, but I didn't think his illness would be fatal. I left for Warsaw with Morawski. Khrushchev's revelations reached here very quickly. They caused a lot of perplexity, deepened the ferment and complicated the situation even more. There were even a few suicides: not everyone's nerves can withstand such tension.

Echoes of all these events reached Bierut from various sources. He often phoned from Moscow, mostly to me, and was very upset at the disorder which had arisen in Warsaw. I sensed he was a little upset at me for not being able to control the situation. I tried to calm him as best I could, saying that the situation was indeed difficult but that he shouldn't worry, we would get it under control. All of a sudden I got a phone call from Wanda Gorska, from whom I gathered that Bierut had contracted pneumonia and was dying. I flew to Moscow immediately. I got there just before two o'clock in the afternoon and after being greeted at the airport went directly to see Bierut. Wanda, who had been sitting with him the whole time, left the room. I asked the doctor who had been assigned to look after Bierut permanently for permission to see him, but he said, no, we're afraid that talking to you will agitate him too much, and that would not be appropriate right now. His refusal was very unconvincing and probably the result of instructions he'd received. It was painful to me, because I'd come to say goodbye and they wouldn't let me in. I gave way to despair.

After Bierut's death Zawadzki and Mazur came. Zawadzki was supposed to give a speech at the House of the Soviets and I helped him to edit it, since my Russian was better than his. Then they displayed the coffin at the House of the Soviets and formed us into rows beside it. I was put in one of the farther rows, while Mazur was assigned a place in a nearer one; I took this to be a sign which explained why I hadn't been let in to see Bierut and I realized that this was the end.

Two months later I left, in order to make it easier for the new leadership, and four months later we had October, which had a twofold significance: it brought to an end, in an extremely turbulent way, the slow thawing process which we had begun, and at the same time it released various bad strains that were lodged in the mentality of the Polish nation.

What caused it, in your view?

There's a fashion now for analysing crises; each one is turned inside out. But I think it's a pretty fruitless discussion which has no point unless it concerns particular economic mistakes.

What were the ones you committed?

It's hard to say, because every situation should be assessed together with all its intricacies and complexities. It's easy to plan something in your office, at your desk, and come to the conclusion that your idea is the best one. But putting it into practice is less simple, because it's the result of a tangle of various factors, including international ones. Our six-year plan, initially more modest in its assumptions, had to be modified not because we wanted to modify it but because the Cold War forced us to do so, imposing an increase in armaments beyond the proportion of expenditure already allocated to them, which led to a decrease in the standard of living and must have provoked discontent in consequence. Gierek would also have wriggled out of the internal economic collapse if it hadn't been for the international situation, and more specifically the general world crisis. Poland's own crisis was, after all, the product of that. Until 1975 the machinery was still turning somehow and it would have continued to turn if things hadn't cracked in the West. But they did crack there, and Gierek couldn't count on any help or on loans of any kind.

You claimed that a capitalist crisis had no influence on a socialist planned economy.

It couldn't not have an influence.

You claimed it didn't.

It has no influence in a situation where we have no economic ties with them, but we did, the whole time; indeed we wanted to extend that collaboration, not restrict it. Our aim was to develop our trade relations with all countries, not only within the bloc but with

Western and Third World ones as well. We tried not to allow our trade with the Soviet Union to exceed 30 per cent, because when it did, going up to around 40 per cent, we felt this was a bad thing, as it led to economic dependence which in turn led to political dependence. Our scope for autonomy, after all, depends precisely on that proportion. Now we've found ourselves in a situation where we're dependent on help from only one quarter, which leads to an even greater increase in those tendencies which our leadership tried to oppose.

The second factor in the Polish crisis is the reappearance of problems which had not been resolved earlier and essential reforms not implemented in time, resulting in an unfavourable attitude to our methods of government – often indisputably faulty and undoubtedly deformed, especially during the period of the Cold War, during the years 1949–53 and especially in 1953. But you have to understand that the repression which took place then, after the death of Stalin, idiotic as I agree it was, resulted from the coming together of some unfavourable circumstances. The Berlin Uprising had just broken out, throwing the entire GDR into anxiety and engulfing it in strikes, and various elements in Poland became active and started to believe that the map of Europe would change. This mood in turn was stoked up by Western radio stations, particularly by Radio Free Europe. That was when I coined the word *znieczulica* [anaesthesia], not suspecting that it would catch on so widely later. I noticed certain symptoms of atrophy, bureaucratization, administratization and alienation, not only in the social but also in the political sense, products of the Cold War period and the result of a failure to understand the processes that were taking place all around. One evening I began talking about it with my wife, searching for a term that would adequately describe this state. And that was how, together, we got from "hyperthermia" – overheating – to "anaesthesia". I made a speech, in the hope that the problem would be resolved and that its resolution would open up new prospects for Polish society. And it might have been resolved (a change of climate had taken place; we had started to try to raise the standard of living. This was possible because tensions in international relations had relaxed, the war in Korea ended and the Vienna compromise began to take effect) if our leadership had not fallen apart and if the events in Poznan had not broken out, disturbing the thawing process and undoubtedly warping the path of development that we had traced.

Gomulka didn't manage it in 1970, either.

It was senseless to give the order to shoot, but he did it out of a feeling of horror and concern for Poland – that was how he saw it in his mind. Just before his fall he was convinced he'd achieved something great, and indeed he had: he signed the agreement with Brandt. It was his life's dream to secure for Poland a guarantee of the western Territories; he put all he had into realizing it, and the agreement with the FRG is certainly a historic achievement on his part. But he overestimated it. It went to his head, until he thought that everything was allowed him. Then came the events of 1970 and it turned out that people weren't at all enthralled with him. Gomulka broke down. And he still continued to wait for a phone call from you know where; he was counting on them to back him. But no one called, and Gomulka was embittered. And over there they just decided he was all used up, so they latched on to Gierek, who didn't turn out to be a very worthwhile asset. But that was the political stupidity of the instigators of those riots in Gdansk and Szczecin, their narrowness and their inability to see how they were harming Poland by what they did.

Really? And whose stupidity was it in Poznan?

It's hard for me to give an opinion about what forces were at work there. Certainly there were visible trends towards stoking up the situation and making it more acute, which leads one to suppose that possibly there were some groups who were interested in stoking up the fire.

From security?

I don't think so. They were actually the ones who had nothing to gain from it – just like the Soviet Union. On the contrary, the Poznan events were undermining solidarity within the party, and they had been counting on that solidarity. I wrote to Ochab then, as I'd already been dismissed and was no longer seeing him, saying that while he should not deny that counter-revolutionary forces were at work in Poznan, he should, in his assessment of these events, recognize the importance of our mistakes and the extent of working-class discontent, as they were the deciding factors there. I appealed to him to look for new solutions which would allow us to find a common language with the working class and the right way out of the situation, not only in Poznan. Now, of course, one can ask whether the renewal we embarked on (because renewal it was – *sui generis*, let's say, but the only kind we could afford) was bold enough. One can ask whether we were right to use brakes in implementing it, to do it slowly and gradually, to phase through the process of liberalization. But why did we do this? We did it because we were afraid, afraid of what broke out in 1956 and 1980 but could have broken out already in 1954. Poland is a Pandora's box. It's easy to release evil spirits from it, but harder to get them back in later.

What kind of evil spirits?

It's a whole syndrome: dreams of a great Poland, of Poland as a great power, a Christ of nations, and of the Poles as the chosen nation. These myths, scattered around throughout Polish society, are still alive, taking on different shapes and forms in various periods and clothing themselves in ever newer shades. It's obvious! Why do you think Gomulka gained such great popularity in 1956, greater than anyone in postwar Poland had ever had, and which was in fact what brought him to power? Where did it come from? It came precisely from what we were afraid of and what was holding us back. He awakened, quite involuntarily, unwittingly and without intending it, incredible hopes of a return to the old Poland: the old Poland would return and resist the Soviet Union, if not openly then halfway or a quarter of the way, but in such a way that some kind of clash would come about between Poland and the Soviet Union –

– emancipation, Mr Berman.

Really? And what about that whole operation at the Solidarity Congress in Gdansk, with the appeal to the nations of the Soviet bloc – what was that aiming at? Obviously, at the disintegration of the Soviet Union! Was it really possible to delude oneself that anyone would tolerate this? That anyone would be able to swallow it? But they bought it. And then they started shouting "this is the final struggle" together – they remembered the International [bangs his fist on the table]!

Please don't get agitated; that was Karol Modzelewski.

Well, so what if it was Zygmunt's son? Zygmunt's son can be foolish too. An intelligent lad, actually, but he went too far and got lost, and forgot everything.

And what about that destruction of Soviet monuments and cemeteries – what does that show? No one organized that, those graves were destroyed spontaneously, en masse.

Mostly by the security services, according to Ochab.

That's what Ochab thinks, but I think otherwise and maintain that it was an explosion of incredibly intense hatred. Or take someone like Michnik! Why is Michnik speaking out against Yalta? What would we have done without Yalta? What would we be? A Duchy of Warsaw. At best. That's actually where the lack of logic and the disastrous thinking of the extremists lie: they don't realize that everything they do is a threat to the shape of Poland, narrowing it down to a Duchy of Warsaw. Where's the sense in that? Was there any deeper political thought there? If there was, it was harmful and base, but mostly it was all just thoughtless, leading nowhere and only attesting to the narrowness of Solidarity's mentality. It began with a very noble and worthwhile surge of enthusiasm, flowing from healthy sources and healthy roots, but from correcting mistakes, from renewal, from creating new principles, where did it finally lead? To the same thing all over again. To firing up dreams, by then somewhat muted and calmed, of French sovereignty, absolute independence, semi-independence, quarter-independence, who the hell knows what else. It was probably different in different circles, and all of them, unaware of the consequences, went on the rampage together! Following the intelligentsia. Their position – the position adopted by a broad section of the Polish intelligentsia – is something that causes me enormous pain. After all, these are sensible, rationally thinking people, so what is their aim, what do they want?

Independence, Mr Berman.

That's stupidity [shouting], lunacy, utter lunacy! We're living in a different epoch, a different age! Maybe after World War I you could still go around dreaming up various plans, as Mr Pilsudski did, although they weren't very happily conceived, either, but after the second war that was absurd. The world *has* changed, can't you see that? There aren't any sovereign states any more, only semi-sovereign ones. The degree of dependence can be lesser or greater, but it's always there. Look at what France, that great power, is doing. It's manoeuvring. De Gaulle still had sufficient character and strength of will to force through a more independent political line, but not Mitterand – he's marching in file, because that's how the world is and that's how you have to see it. And no amount of manoeuvring will get round that – don't count on it. And thinking that we'll sit down in our little corner and smile a little at each in turn is stupidity; it shows ignorance of geography and of elementary political principles. Poland can only be either pro-Soviet or pro-American; there's no other possibility.

There isn't [shouting]! Poland can't be uprooted from the Soviet bloc. How? Uproot it and then where would you put it? On the moon? Poland lies on the road between the Soviet Union and Western Europe, and its position is clear: either/or. There are no half-shades, because Poland can't float in the air. So the objective reality is this: either America succeeds in building up enough ferment here to overthrow us, whereupon intervention will naturally ensue because the overriding interests of the Soviet Union require it, and there will be so much bloodshed that all the nation will be drained of blood, which is no solution for anyone; or the whole bloc will be destroyed and Poland will become the Duchy of Warsaw; or a Third World War will break out and part of Europe or the whole of it will be laid waste. There are no other prospects that I can see, and I don't understand why Polish society and the Polish intelligentsia doesn't see them. I try to enter into their mentality and understand why they're provoking trouble, aggravating problems that are past. And I always reach the same conclusion: various pains, ailments and restrictions are blocking their view, and because of that they are unable to distinguish between major and secondary issues. But they will see them, and grasp them, they have to see them, probably after I die, because things being as they are now, *rebus sic stantibus*, the system is doomed to remain; you can improve it, moderate and soften it, but exist it must, and instead of wondering how to overthrow it we should muster our strength and effort to save the Poland we have created, a Poland which, for all its faults and mistakes, is a power, and finally rid ourselves of those absurd myths and unrealistic hopes, because they're *contra naturam*.

Contra naturam, *Mr Berman, is what the current state of affairs is.*

Exactly! Gomulka also finally understood that his popularity was only the result of dreams and illusions. Maybe he didn't see it immediately; perhaps he didn't see it fully until 1957, or maybe even not until 1958, I don't know, but I think it partly got through to him during the rally in front of the Palace of Culture. It gave him a great shock, because he finally saw both sides of the situation. On the one hand he knew certain dams had been breached, and it was a good thing that they had, but on the other he also saw that they would break more and more visibly and might end up undermining the whole postwar structure which is the basis of our presence in the Western Territories and of our existence as a state. Why? Because some people were asking themselves who was a good Pole and who wasn't, and others proceeded to act. We want to bring back the National Democratic Party, they shouted; we want to reactivate the Labour Party, shouted others; we want this reform and that reform. Gomulka was lost in all this. He launched into self-criticism, some of it right and some not, because he lacked the feel and understanding to distinguish between them. And since, in addition, his outlook was narrow, he did some silly things. And since he also lacked organizational talent and had many faults and a number of failings, as well as being too conceited and placing too much faith in arithmetical calculations, he managed to alienate several wise people who were devoted to the party, he had a stupid fear of the old intelligentsia and he stepped up the pace at the cost of any reforms. But what was the reason for all this? Concern, fear and terror. Because he finally saw, with full clarity, that a mood of independence had swept the country like a wave and that he had to stop it because he wouldn't be able to control it and in the end it would sweep him away. Like an ocean.

How long do you intend to fight against it?

Sixty years, a hundred years if need be [bangs his fist on the table]. Until we defeat it!

You didn't manage it in 150 years.

But we will [shouting]! The nation must mould itself into its new shape. It must.

No.

But my dear lady. I understand that for a nation to be able to shift to a new set of values, a new shape, it has to experience a breakthrough of a kind it has never known throughout its thousand years of history. One can't erase 150 years of oppression and struggle with Russia from memory all at once, because they left a profound mark on the national consciousness. No other country has to bear the burden of such experiences. Neither the Czechs nor the Hungarians nor the Romanians can be compared to us in that regard. The Czechs did experience change of a sort, but qualitatively it was not as staggering as what we went through. The Hungarians lost Transylvania after the Second World War, a wound which probably aggravates them still, but they also gained a lot: stability and a certain degree of wealth. Nor was the history of Romania as dramatic as ours. We are doomed to shoulder the enormous load of the experience of a thousand years, and therefore the process of breaking away from tradition and coming to love our new shape is not an easy one, and it can't take place smoothly, slowly and flexibly: it has to cause jolts, which will appear and return in one form or another from time to time. Especially as all these Jagiellonian illusions, combined with dreams of a great eastward expansion, continue to live in the Polish consciousness, because they were cultivated for centuries in various circles; every generation has been brought up on them and continues to be brought up on them, in spite of great efforts on our part. So they can't be erased overnight, and things can't be set straight by even the most carefully edited history textbooks or the most skilfully written articles – not that they were very intelligent, and they certainly should have made more mention of things they passed over. But it's a dream, an illusion, to think that a consciousness that had shaped itself over centuries can be changed in the space of thirty or forty years with the aid of one lecture or another or a film or a book. Teachers may be disappointed to see that the effort they've invested has had no effect: but it has had none because it couldn't have an immediate effect. But without placing my faith in the magical power of words I am nonetheless convinced that the sum of our actions, skilfully and consistently carried out, will finally produce results and create a new Polish consciousness; because all the advantages flowing from our new path will be borne out, must be borne out, and if we're not destroyed by an atomic war and we don't disappear into nothingness, there will finally be a breakthrough in mentality which will give it an entirely new content and quality. And then we, the communists, will be able to apply all the democratic principles we would like to apply but can't apply now, because they would end in our defeat and elimination. It may happen in fifty years or it may happen in a hundred, I don't want to make prophecies, but I'm sure it will happen one day.

Thank you.

April 1982–April 1984

APPENDIXES

Appendix I
ABBREVIATIONS

AK – *Home Army*: An underground resistance organization formed in 1941 and commanded by the Polish government in exile in London. With over 300,000 members, it was the largest clandestine military organization in Europe. It was dissolved on 19 January 1945; the communist authorities, with the aim of totally destroying it, urged its members to reveal themselves, promising safety and liberty. Almost all the soldiers who did so were arrested and deported to the East; others, who buried their weapons and returned quietly to their homes, were hunted down by the NKVD and the Polish security services.

AL – *People's Army*: A communist underground military organization which attempted to rival and discredit the AK. It arose out of the People's Guard, which was formed by the PPR in 1942 and at that time consisted of about 3,000 soldiers. In 1944 the newly created Home National Council (KRN) rebaptized it the People's Army. Official communist sources give its membership at around 50,000.

CBKP – *Central Bureau of Polish Communists*: A communist organization created in Moscow in 1944, officially to represent the PPR in Poland but in fact to supervise and control it.

CPSU – *Communist Party of the Soviet Union.*

CPWB – *Communist Party of Western Byelorussia.*
CPWU – *Communist Party of Western Ukraine.*
These were Soviet-controlled annexes of the Polish communist party, their existence being due to Moscow's policy of "independence" for western Byelorussia and Ukraine. They were dissolved along with the KPP.

CRZZ – *Central Trade Union Council*: A trade union headquarters controlled by the communist party, it was the only trade union council in Poland until the creation of Solidarity in 1980. It was dissolved in 1981, together with "all trade unions" – a formula conceived to allow for the dissolution of Solidarity.

FJN – *Front of National Unity*: A communist umbrella organization created in 1957 to provide a semblance of unity, incorporating the PUWP and all other "parties" and organizations. It existed in name only, its only role being that of an all-encompassing organization from whose membership election ballots might be drawn up. It was dissolved after the creation of Solidarity and replaced by a replica with another name.

GL – *People's Guard*: See AL, *supra*.

KBW – *Internal Security Corps*: Special army units for internal use, such as the quelling of riots.

KOR – *Workers' Defence Committee*: A group founded in 1976 initially as a reaction to the repression of workers after the June 1976 workers' riots in Radom and Ursus. It provided workers and their families with legal and other assistance. In 1977 KOR changed its name to KSS "KOR" – the KOR Committee for Social Self-Defence – and took on the broader aim of collecting and publicizing material on abuses of human rights. The authorities considered it a threat and the group's members were harassed and frequently arrested by the police. KOR's activities paved the way for the creation of Solidarity. In 1981, after the first Solidarity conference, KSS "KOR" dissolved itself, finding that there was no more reason for its existence.

KPP – *Polish Communist Party*: Formed in 1918 from the union of the SDKPiL and the left wing of the PPS; part of the Communist International. Dissolved by Stalin in 1938 and thoroughly purged: most of its members were killed on Stalin's orders in 1938–9. During the war its members reconstituted themselves, with Stalin's approval, in the form of the Central Bureau of Polish Communists (CBKP), based in Moscow (see *supra*), and of the PPR, the party's official new name from 1941.

KRN – *Home National Council*: Founded by the PPR on 31 December 1943 and headed by Bierut, the KRN called itself the "true political representative of the Polish nation" and was to act as Poland's "legislative and executive body" until the constitution of the Sejm.

KZMP – *Union of Polish Youth*: Also known at various stages as the ZMP, the ZMS and the SZMP, this was a communist youth organization.

ONR – *National-Radical Camp*: An extreme right-wing party headed by Boleslaw Piasecki, in existence before and during the war.

PAX: An anti-Catholic, pseudo-religious communist organization created in 1945 with the aim of infiltrating the Church.

PKWN – *Polish Committee of National Liberation*: Created by the Soviets on 20 July 1944 and launched on 22 July 1944 in Lublin, with the "July

Manifesto", the PKWN was installed by Moscow as a temporary administration. It was replaced by the Provisional Government formed by the KRN on 31 December 1944.

PPR – *Polish Workers' Party*: Formed on 5 January 1942 by Marceli Nowotko, Pawel Finder and Boleslaw Molojec, who had been parachuted into Poland from the USSR for the purpose. (See KPP, *supra.*) In 1943, after the assassination of Nowotko and the arrest of Finder by the Gestapo, Gomulka took over as first secretary. In 1948 the PPR merged with the PPS to form the PUWP.

PPS – *Polish Socialist Party*: Founded in 1892; in 1906 it split into two factions: the PPS Lewica, or Left-Wing Faction, and the PPS Frakcja Rewolucyjna, or the Revolutionary Faction, headed by Pilsudski, who had also been the founder and editor of the PPS journal, *Robotnik* (*The Worker*). The Revolutionary Faction of the PPS saw as its main aim the recovery of national independence, while the PPS Left Wing, an internationalist party, merged with the SDKPiL (see *infra*) in 1918 to form the Polish Communist Workers' Party (KPRP), which in 1925 became the KPP. After the recovery of national independence the PPS was the most important workers' party in Poland. During the occupation it was part of the coalition government in exile in London; after the war the PPS was reactivated by some of its members who were allied with the communists in the PPR, and in 1948 it was merged with the PPR to form the PUWP. Activists of the old PPS were hunted down by the security services and imprisoned.

PRL – *Polish People's Republic*: Founded in 1945; formally constituted in 1952.

PSL – *Polish Peasants' Movement*: Founded in 1895. After the rigged elections of 1947 the leader of the PSL, Mikolajczyk, in danger of arrest, fled the country, and the PSL was dissolved.

PUWP – *Polish United Workers' Party*: Created in 1948 out of the union of the PPR and the PPS.

Red Aid – *International Organization for Aid to Revolutionary Fighters (MOPR)*. Founded in 1922 and active until 1947, at its peak it had sections in over 70 countries giving financial, legal and moral support to "victims of white terror" irrespective of party. More than half of its members lived in the USSR. Red Aid's source of funds was supposedly members' contributions, and it controlled an enormous publicity operation with (in the early 1930s) more than 90 newspapers and bulletins.

RPPS – *Workers' Polish Socialist Party*: Founded in 1943 from the left-wing section of the PPS; it continued to exist during the war and later merged with the PPS.

SD – *Democratic Movement*: Founded in April 1939 and remained underground during the war. After the war the name was taken over by the communists, and the SD, like the SL, became part of the communist system.

SDKPiL – *Social Democracy of the Kingdom of Poland and Lithuania*: Created in 1900 from the union of the SDKP (Social Democracy of the Kingdom of Poland), founded by Julian Marchlewski and Rosa Luxemburg, with the SDL (Social Democracy of Lithuania), founded by Feliks Dzerzhinsky; in 1918 the SDKPiL merged with the PPS Left Wing and formed the KPRP (see PPS, *supra*).

SL – *Peasants' Party*: A communist organization created after the dissolution of the PSL; again, the name was taken over by the communists.

VCP(b) – *All-Union (bolshevik) Communist Party*: The name of the CPSU from 1925 to 1952.

ZNAK: A group of Catholic writers and journalists gathered around the monthly ZNAK and the weekly *Tygodnik Powszechny*. In 1956 the officially authorized ZNAK group of deputies to the Sejm was formed.

ZPP – *Union of Polish Patriots*: Founded in Moscow in 1943 and headed by Wanda Wasilewska; it marked the beginnings of the future communist government in Poland. It was the ZPP leadership which, in 1944, launched the idea of a "temporary Polish government", and thus led to the creation on 20 July 1944, in Moscow, of the PKWN.

ZSL – *United Peasants' Party*: The result of a union between what remained of the PSL after Mikolajczyk's flight and the SL, a communist pseudo-peasants' party.

Appendix II

INDEX OF PROPER NAMES

ALBRECHT, Jerzy (1914–): Party activist. Before the war: member of the KZMP and the KPP; during the war member of the PPR, arrested and sent to a concentration camp by the Gestapo. After the war: member of the PPR Central Committee; 1948–68, member of the PUWP Central Committee; March 1956–November 1960, secretary of the Central Committee; prominent figure in the events of October 1956; 1956–60, deputy head of the Council of State; 1960–8, minister of finance. Fell out of favour in 1968. A signatory, in December 1977, of an open letter to the Second PUWP National Conference criticizing Gierek's policies.

ALSTER, Antoni (1903–68): Before the war: member of the KPP; 1930–1, student at the Comintern Advanced Party School. Spent the war in the USSR. A political officer in the Polish army formed in the Soviet Union, later appointed head of that army's political education section. In 1944 head of the military section of the PPR Central Committee in Lublin. 1948–64, member of the PUWP Central Committee; 1952–5, in charge of cadres as departmental director in the Central Committee; 1955–6, member of the Committee on Security; 1956–61, deputy minister of internal affairs. Retired in 1968 and died that same year.

ALTER, Wiktor (1890–1941): A leader of the prewar Bund. Arrested in the USSR, together with Henryk Erlich, in September 1939; condemned to death in August 1941. However, being Polish citizens, both he and Erlich were released in accordance with the Sikorski–Maisky pact, only to be arrested by the NKVD once again in December 1941 and executed on the charge of treason.

ANDERS, Wladyslaw (1892–1970): Polish general; took part in the September campaign in 1939. Wounded, arrested by the NKVD while in hospital in Lvov. Released in 1941 after the Sikorski–Maisky pact. Commander of the Polish army formed in the USSR, which was drawn from Polish citizens released from the camps. In 1943, having led this army out of the USSR and into Persia, he formed the Second Army Corps, which later played a prominent role in the capture of Bologna and Monte Cassino. In 1946, along with 65 other senior officers, he was stripped of his citizenship by the authorities of People's Poland. After the war he was a member of the Polish government in exile in London.

ANDRZEJEWSKI, Jerzy (1909–83): Writer, author of the book *Ashes and Diamonds*, which was made into a film by Wajda; associated with Catholic circles before the war. A member of the Home Army during the occupation, he became a communist after the war but left the party in 1957. One of the founders, in 1976, of the Workers' Defence Committee, KOR.

BARTOSZEWSKI, Wladyslaw (1922–): Writer and historian. During the occupation a member of the Home Army and head of Zegota, an organization of aid for Jews. (He was later awarded an Israeli medal.) Arrested and imprisoned by the communist authorities on trumped-up charges in 1946, released in 1954. Interned for several months after the imposition of martial law in Poland in December 1981 for his role in Solidarity.

BERIA, Lavrenti Pavlovich (1899–1953): Stalin's henchman. Head of the NKVD from 1938; responsible for the murder of millions of people. 1942–6, minister of internal affairs in the USSR. Liquidated by his political rivals after Stalin's death in 1953.

BERLING, Zygmunt (1896–1980): Polish general. Fought in Pilsudski's legions and in the Polish September campaign in 1939. Imprisoned in the USSR, released in 1941 after the Sikorski–Maisky pact. Chief of staff of a division of Anders' army, he remained in the USSR after this army's departure and in 1943 became commander of the First Kosciuszko Division. Later commander of the First Polish Army. In 1944 he became deputy director of the ministry of National Defence in the PKWN; 1948–53, commander of the General Staff Academy; 1953–6, deputy minister of State Farms and deputy minister of agriculture. In 1963, already retired, he was promoted to the rank of general.

BERMAN, Adolf: See BERMAN, Jakub.

BERMAN, Jakub: See biography at head of interview.

BIENKOWSKI, Wladyslaw (1906–): Journalist, party activist. Before the war: member of the KZMP; member of the central editorial office of the KPP. Joined the PPR in 1942. Member of the KRN. 1945–8, member of the PPR Central Committee, where he was a departmental director and a member of the Central Committee secretariat; a close associate of Gomulka's, dismissed from the Central Committee in 1948 at the time of the "struggle against right-wing deviationism". 1949–56, director of the National Library; November 1956–October 1959, minister of culture; dismissed from his post in 1960. Expelled from the PUWP in 1968 for his book, published by the émigré press in Paris, on the mechanisms of socialism. Continued to publish abroad on the subject of the communist system in Poland.

Bierut, Boleslaw (1892–1956): Communist activist. Before the war: NKVD agent, studied at the Advanced Comintern Party School and at the school for the KPP. Comintern agent in Bulgaria, Czechoslovakia and Austria; arrested in Poland in 1935; in prison at the time of the dissolution of the KPP. During the occupation he emerged as the president of the KRN, a post which he held from January 1944 to February 1947. February 1947–November 1952, president of the Polish Republic, a post he took up after the rigged elections of 1947. September–December 1948, general secretary of the PPR Central Committee, after Gomulka's dismissal from that post; December 1948–March 1954, PUWP Central Committee chairman; November 1952–March 1954, prime minister; March 1954–March 1956, first secretary of the PUWP Central Committee. Died in Moscow after the Twentieth CPSU Congress in 1956.

Borejsza, Jerzy (1905–52): Communist journalist. Brother of Jacek Rozanski (see *infra*), who headed the interrogation department at the Ministry of Public Security. Before the war: 1922–7, active in left-wing organizations in France and Spain; in 1929 he joined the KPP. He spent the war in the USSR. With the Red Army's entry into Lvov, the Soviets appointed him director of the *Ossolineum* publishing house and later editor-in-chief of *Free Poland*, the organ of the Union of Polish Patriots. In 1944 he was made head of the "Czytelnik" press and responsible for non-party publications. In 1948 he was general secretary of the International Congress of Intellectuals in Wroclaw. He retired in 1950.

Bromberg, Adam (1912–): Editor, director of the PWN academic publishing house from 1953 to 1968. Expelled from the party during the anti-Semitic campaign of 1968 and arrested shortly thereafter on the charge of leading an international criminal organization with the aim of subverting the State. His case was dropped after two years of investigation and he was given permission to emigrate. He now runs a Swedish publishing house.

Broniewska, Janina (1904–81): First wife of the poet Wladyslaw Broniewski (see *infra*) and a friend of Wanda Wasilewska. She spent the war in the USSR and was active in the Union of Polish Patriots. After the war: secretary of the Union of Polish Writers, a party organization where her role was to watch over the political loyalty of the members.

Broniewski, Wladyslaw (1897–1962): Revolutionary poet; a socialist gradually turned communist. During the war he was arrested, together with Aleksander Wat, by the NKVD in Lvov and imprisoned until the signing of the Sikorski–Maisky pact in 1941. He then joined Anders' army and went with it to Persia, Iraq and Palestine. After his return to Poland in 1945 he wrote propaganda poetry for the regime, although he did not become a party member.

BRYSTIGIER, Julia (1902–73): 1944–56, departmental director in the Ministry of Public Security, in charge of cultural affairs and in particular of infiltrating youth organizations and the Church. Before the war a member of the Hashomer Zionist scout oranization in Lvov. Joined the KPP in 1930. In 1939, after the Red Army's entry into Lvov, she became head of International Workers' Relief in Lvov and then in Samarkand, and was later active in the Union of Polish Patriots. In 1956 she began to write novels under her maiden name, Preiss.

BUDZYNSKA, Celina (1908–): Communist activist; emigrated to the USSR at the age of nineteen. Her husband, a hero of the October Revolution, was executed during the Great Purge of 1937. She herself was sent to a labour camp for eight years. Released in 1945, she returned to Poland, where she held executive posts in schools for party cadres. She left the party soon after the imposition of martial law in December 1981.

BUKHARIN, Nikolai Ivanovich (1888–1938): A communist theoretician. Played an important part in the October Revolution. In 1918 he was a member of the so-called left-wing deviation. A close associate of Stalin's for a short time in the 1920s, by 1929 he was the leader of the so-called right-wing deviation. He was expelled from his party posts when Stalin decided to impose forced collectivization. In 1934 he was editor-in-chief of *Izvestia*. He was also one of the editors of the Soviet constitution. In 1938 Stalin accused him of Trotskyism and conspiracy against the State. A confession of his "crimes" was forcibly extracted from him during a rigged trial (the last of the Moscow show trials). He was sentenced to death and executed.

BULGAKOV, Mikhail Afanasievich (1891–1940): Soviet writer of short stories, plays and novels. Author of *The Master and Margarita*, which he began in 1928 and continued until his death in 1940, and of *The White Guard*. Attacked by the party for the tone of his writings, which was often satirical, by 1930 he was completely barred from publication. He has only recently been rehabilitated in the Soviet Union, but even now only abridged editions of some of his works are published there.

BULGANIN, Nikolai Alexandrovich (1895–1975): A member of the communist party from 1917; Marshal of the Soviet Union. In August 1944 he was appointed representative of the Commissars of the People of the USSR to the PKWN. In February 1955 he succeeded Malenkov as president of the Council of Ministers. In 1958 he supported Molotov, Malenkov and Kaganovich against Khrushchev; in September of that year he was expelled from the Presidium of the Supreme Soviet.

CHAJN, Leon (1910–83): Lawyer and journalist. Spent the war in the USSR, was one of the organizers of the Union of Polish Patriots and a political officer in Berling's army. He was a communist plant in the Democratic Party (SD). After the war: 1944–69, member of the SD Central Committee; 1944–61, general secretary of the SD; 1961–5, deputy chairman of the SD Central Committee; 1944–9, minister of Justice; 1949–52, vice-president of the Chief Board of Supervision; 1953–7, deputy minister of Labour and Social Security; 1957–65, member of the Council of State.

CHOU EN-LAI (1896–1976): Chinese politician. Took part in the foundation of the Chinese Communist Party in 1920 and in the Long March of 1934–6. 1949–58, minister of foreign affairs of the People's Republic of China; 1949–76, prime minister of the People's Republic of China; a moderating influence during the Cultural Revolution of 1966.

CHOU T'EH (1886–1976): Chinese politician and army marshal; commanded the first Chinese Red Army during the Long March. 1937–45, commander of the Eighth Army and the Eighteenth Army Group against the Japanese; 1946–54, commander-in-chief of the People's Liberation Army; 1946–9, drove the forces of Chiang Kai-shek out of China.

CLEMENTIS, Vladimir (1902–58): Slovak lawyer and communist politician. In 1948 he was appointed minister of foreign affairs of the Czechoslovak Republic. In 1958 he was accused of treason and hanged. He was posthumously rehabilitated in 1963.

CYRANKIEWICZ, Jozef (1911–): Party activist. Member of the PPS; during the occupation a member of the resistance movement supported by the government in exile in London. Arrested but escaped in 1939; active in the WRN in Cracow; arrested again in 1941 and sent to Auschwitz until 1945. 1945–8, general secretary of the Central Committee Executive of the PPS after the genuine socialists had been removed – he supported the union of the PPS and the PPR, in other words the liquidation of the PPS; 1948–75, member of the PUWP Central Committee; 1948–71, member of the Politburo (supported Gomulka in October 1956); 1947–52, prime minister; 1952–4, deputy premier; 1954–70, prime minister (resigned after the 1970 workers' revolt in Gdansk and Szczecin); 1971–2, head of the Council of State; 1972 onwards, head of the National Peace Committee.

DIMITROV, Georgi (1882–1949): Bulgarian politician. Active in the revolutionary movement from 1903; imprisoned from 1905 to 1917. Went to Moscow in 1920 and from there, as a Comintern agent, to Germany. Arrested by the Nazis on the charge of setting fire to the Reichstag. Released in 1934, after a prominent trial. He returned to the USSR, where he became a Soviet citizen. Head of the Comintern until its dissolution in 1943. 1946–9, general secretary of the Bulgarian Communist Party.

DIMSCHITZ, Benyamin (1910–): Soviet politician and token Jew, for purposes of display, in the Soviet government. Joined the VCP(b) during the Great Purge of 1937. Received the Stalin prize in 1946 and 1950. Appointed a member of the CPSU Central Committee in 1961, deputy of the Supreme Soviet in 1962 and, also in 1962, deputy head of the Council of Ministers. He held a variety of ministerial posts.

DJILAS, Milovan (1911–): Yugoslav politician, author of *The New Class* and *Conversations with Stalin*. An associate of Tito's from 1936. Appointed to the Yugoslav CP Central Committee in 1937 and to the Politburo in 1941. In 1941 he organized the resistance movement in Montenegro. Dismissed from office in 1954 after a clash with Tito and finally imprisoned, he became Yugoslav's most famous dissident. He lives in Belgrade.

DROBNER, Boleslaw (1883–1968): Socialist activist. Imprisoned and sent to a camp by the NKVD at the beginning of the war; spent the rest of the war in the USSR, where he was active in the Union of Polish Patriots. In 1944 he became director of the Ministry of Labour, Health and Social Security in the PKWN; in 1947 he was a PPS delegate to the Sejm; 1952–65, PUWP delegate to the Sejm; October 1956–February 1957, secretary of the Provincial PUWP Committee in Cracow, his only party post.

DURACZ, Anita (1923–76): Secretary to Jakub Berman. Took part in the Warsaw Uprising as a soldier in the AL. Arrested in 1949 in connection with the Field affair; released five years later. Emigrated to Sweden in 1968; died in Israel in 1976.

DZERZHINSKÁ, Zofia (1882–1968): Wife of Feliks Dzerzhinsky. Durıng the war she was director of "Kosciuszko" radio and worked for the Central Bureau of Polish Communists in Moscow. She held a variety of offices in the VCP(b).

DZERZHINSKY, Feliks Edmuntovich (1887–1926): The first Chekist. A Pole, founder and head of the Cheka, known after 1922 as the OGPU (later successively the NKVD and the KGB). One of the organizers of the October Revolution. By 1917, when at the age of almost forty, he was freed from Moscow's tsarist gaol, he had spent eleven years in tsarist prisons or forced labour in Siberia. One of the founders of the SDKPiL. 1919–20 People's Commissar for Internal Affairs; 1921–4, People's Commissar for Communications; 1924–6, Chairman of the Supreme Council of National Economy.

DZERZHINSKY, Jan (1911–): Son of Feliks and Zofia Dzerzhinsky. A Comintern functionary.

EHRENBURG, Ilya Grigorievich (1891–1967): Russian writer and journalist. Twice emigrated to Paris: in 1908 (until 1917) and 1921 (until 1942).

During this latter period he served as correspondent for several Soviet journals. A Jew and a favourite of Stalin's, he was awarded the Lenin International Peace Prize in 1952, when hundreds of Jews were being sentenced to death in the USSR on the charge of "cosmopolitanism". Author of *The Thaw* (1956), in which he made a timid and half-hearted attempt to describe the Stalinist terror.

ERLICH, Henryk (1892–1941): Leader of the Bund in prewar Poland (see ALTER, *supra*).

FADEYEV, Alexandr Alexandrovich (1901–56): Soviet novelist, author of *The Defeat*, a novel about the Civil War, and *The Young Guard* (1945).

FEJGIN, Anatol: Interrogator and head of an investigation department in the Ministry of Public Security; colonel in the political police. From 1944 onwards held various offices in security; one of the organizers of the security department dealing with the investigation and elimination of anti-Soviet influences within the party. Also in charge of drawing up dossiers on all party members (with the exception of Bierut, whose dossier was kept in Moscow). In 1949 became head of the department and responsible mainly for weeding out "right-wing nationalist deviationists" within the party. Expelled from the party and removed from his post after Swiatlo's defection, he was arrested in 1955, tried *in camera* in 1957, and sentenced to twelve years' imprisonment for employing "unauthorized methods of investigation".

FIELD, Herman: An American, brother of Noel Field (see *infra*); arrested in Warsaw in 1949, while attempting to search for his brother. Held and interrogated for five years by the Polish authorities, who denied all knowledge of his brother. Left Poland after his release.

FIELD, Noel: American communist. In the 1930s he made contact with Soviet intelligence agencies. He spent the war in Switzerland as director of the Unitarian Service Committee, which helped refugees from Nazi-occupied Europe. In 1947 his connection with Soviet intelligence was discovered by the United States authorities and he decided to settle in Czechoslovakia. However, he was arrested at Prague airport, handed over to the Hungarian security services and imprisoned in Budapest, on the charge of working for Dulles in the OSS and participating in an international conspiracy against the socialist countries. His wife, brother and daughter were likewise arrested after crossing the Iron Curtain in search of him, as were several hundred other people throughout the Soviet bloc who had at any time been in contact with him. He was used as the "missing link" in the show trials which took place between 1949 and 1952, when many party members in high positions throughout the Soviet bloc were accused of espionage and conspiracy. Both he and his family were released after five years, following the defection to the West of Jozef Swiatlo (see *infra*), who informed the US authorities that they had been arrested.

FIELDORF, Emil (1895–1953): A general in the Home Army. Fought in Pilsudski's legions, took part in the 1939 September campaign, later helped organize a Polish army in France. Returned to Poland in 1940 as an emissary of General Sikorski to become the Home Army commander for North-west Poland and later head of the Home Army's intelligence section. Arrested and deported by the NKVD to Siberia after the occupation of Poland by the Red Army, he returned to Poland in 1948, only to be arrested once again, this time by Polish security. He was murdered in 1953, in circumstances which remain unclear.

FINDER, Pawel (1904–43): Communist activist. 1928–39, member of the KPP in Poland; in 1934 sentenced to ten years' imprisonment for subversive activity; 1939–41, in the USSR. Member of the First Initiative Group parachuted into Poland in December 1941 to organize the PPR. 1942–3, general secretary of the PPR Central Committee. He was liquidated by the Gestapo in October 1943.

FLATO, Stanislaw (1910–72): Military intelligence officer. Military doctor in the International Brigades in Spain; sent to a camp in France, then went to China in order to organize the medical services in Chiang Kai-shek's army. Spent the war in China and Burma. An officer in the Second (i.e., intelligence) Unit of the General Staff and deputy to General Komar after the war, he was sent to Canada as military attaché for People's Poland, and while there is said to have been involved in the recruitment of the Rosenbergs. Recalled to Poland in 1949, after Komar's arrest, he was arrested at the airport and imprisoned without trial until the spring of 1955. He died in 1972 in Berlin, where his family had emigrated after the anti-Semitic campaign of 1968.

FORNALSKA, Malgorzata (1902–43): Second wife of Boleslaw Bierut; part of the Second Initiative Group of the PPR which was parachuted into Poland in the spring of 1942. In Russia during the October Revolution, she enrolled in the Red Guard, then in the Red Army. After the Soviet Union's invasion of Poland in 1920, she helped to organize the Polish Provisional Revolutionary Committee, which was founded by Dzerzhinsky, Kon and Marchlewski. 1926–34, studied at the Comintern school and later worked for the Comintern in Moscow. Moved to Poland, where she was arrested, and returned to Moscow in 1939. Together with Pawel Finder (see *supra*), she was arrested by the Gestapo and shot in 1943.

FORNALSKI, Aleksander: Brother of Malgorzata Fornalska (see *supra*), killed in the USSR during the Great Purge.

FURTSEVA, Ekaterina Alexeievna (1910–74): Soviet political activist. Joined the VCP(b) in 1930; became first secretary of the city of Moscow in 1954. 1956–60, a CPSU Central Committee secretary; 1957–60, member of the Presidium; 1950–62 and 1966–74, deputy to the Supreme Soviet. Appointed minister of culture in 1960.

GECOW, Leon (1911–52): Communist activist. Took up Soviet citizenship in 1939 and moved to Lvov. Joined the Red Army in 1941 and Berling's army in 1944. After the war he held various posts in the PKWN Ministry of National Defence. Joined the party in 1947. In July 1949 he was arrested and accused of disseminating fascism, anarchism and Trotskyism; in 1952 he was sentenced to a prison term of unknown length (his wife was sentenced to six years). He died in prison two weeks later; possibly he committed suicide, but the circumstances of his death are obscure. He was posthumously rehabilitated in 1956.

GERÖ, Ernö (1898–): Hungarian politician. 1948–56, minister of security in Hungary; July–October 1956, first secretary of the party. Dismissed from his government posts later that same year; expelled from the party in 1962.

GIEREK, Edward (1913–): Member of the PUWP Central Committee from 1948 onwards; appointed secretary of the Upper Silesia Provincial Committee in 1951. 1970–1980, first secretary of the Central Committee, a post from which he resigned after the signature of the Gdansk accords in August 1980.

GOMULKA, Wladyslaw (1905–82): KPP member and union activist from 1926; thrice arrested and twice sentenced for communist activity. 1933–6, studied at the Lenin International School in Moscow; 1936–9, imprisoned in Poland, thus escaping the Great Purge; joined the PPR in 1942. Appointed general secretary of the PPR Central Committee in 1943; created the People's Guard (GL), the People's Army (AL) and the KRN. From August 1944 in the PKWN; deputy premier of the Provisional Government and of the Government of National Unity; Minister of the Recovered Territories until January 1949. Dismissed from his post as first secretary of the PPR Central Committee at the Second PPR Congress in 1948, when he was accused of "right-wing deviationism", but still elected to the Central Committee at the first PUWP Congress. Expelled from the Central Committee in 1949, arrested in 1951, released in 1954; accepted back into the PUWP in 1956. Appointed first secretary of the PUWP Central Committee at the Eighth Central Committee plenum in October 1956. In 1968 he took part in the anti-Semitic campaign and the campaign against the intellectuals, and was also involved in the invasion of Czechoslovakia. In December 1970, after he had quelled the workers' uprisings on the coast with the use of the army, he resigned from his post as first secretary of the Central Committee, and in 1971 he was expelled from the Central Committee. He died of cancer in Warsaw in 1982.

GOZDZIK, Lechoslaw: Worker-activist, secretary of the party cell in a Warsaw car factory; particularly prominent for his role during the "thaw" of October 1956. Officially accepted by the government at that time, he was to have been appointed deputy to the Sejm. After October, however, he was soon dropped, expelled from the party and subjected to harassment. He subsequently retired from the scene and moved to the coast to become a fisherman.

GRANAS, Romana: Director of the Central Committee Party School. Spent the war in the USSR and upon her return to Poland took up a succession of party posts. 1949–64, deputy member of the Central Committee. She left the party after the imposition of martial law in Poland in December 1981.

HOFFMAN, Pawel (1903–78): Dealt with propaganda and the press in a variety of party positions. In 1948 he became editor-in-chief of the communist weekly *Kuznica* (*The Forge*), which was later merged with the non-party journal *Odrodzenie* (*Rebirth*) to become *Nowa Kultura* (*New Culture*). He was dismissed from all his posts after 1968.

HOXHA, Enver (1901–85): General Secretary of the Albanian Communist Party from 1948; in 1941 he founded the Albanian Workers' Party. 1945–54, President of the Albanian Council of State. He broke with the USSR in 1961.

IBARRURI, Dolores (1895–): Militant member of the Spanish Communist Party; popularly known as *La Pasionaria*. In 1939 she went to Paris as a refugee, then moved to Moscow, where she held the posts of general secretary (1942–60) and later president of the Spanish Communist Party in exile.

JABLONSKI, Henryk (1909–): Historian. 1972–85, president of the Polish Council of State; before 1972 he had held a number of high posts, among them that of minister of higher education in 1968, when he was one of those responsible for the expulsion of university professors.

JAROSZEWICZ, Alfred: 1946–8, minister of supplies. Arrested in 1948, together with Lechowicz (see *infra*), on false charges of espionage and collaboration with the Gestapo; sentenced to fifteen years' imprisonment in June 1955, after a lengthy investigation which involved torture. Released in November 1956; rehabilitated in March 1957. His wartime allegiances remain a subject of controversy.

JASIENICA, Pawel (1909–70): Writer and journalist. Arrested during the war as a member of the Home Army, he was sentenced to death but later released. A vigorous opponent of the anti-Semitic campaign of 1968.

JEDRYCHOWSKI, Stefan (1910–): 1951–6, deputy premier; 1957–68, head of the Planning Commission at the Council of Ministers; 1968–71, minister of foreign affairs; 1971–4, minister of finance; 1975–8, ambassador to Hungary. Member of the PPR Central Committee (1944–8), the PUWP Central Committee (1948–75) and of the Politburo (1956–71). During the war he worked for the NKVD as censor of the Polish theatre in Vilnius, was a member of the ZPP in Moscow and a political officer in Berling's army. In 1944 he was head of the PKWN's propaganda department and PKWN representative in Moscow.

JOZWIAK, Franciszek (1895–1966): 1955–6, deputy premier. KPP member before the war; during the war chief of staff in the AL. 1945–8, member of the PPR Politburo; 1948–59, member o the PUWP Central Committee; 1948–56, member of the Politburo and head of the Central Commission of Party Control. His other posts include head of the militia (1945); president of the Chief Board of Supervision and member of the Council of State (1949–52) and minister of state control (1952–5). A member of the "Natolin" group, he was dropped and dismissed from all government posts in October 1956.

KAGANOVICH, Lazar Moiseievich (1893–): 1952–7, member of the Presidium of the Supreme Soviet. Member of the VCP(b) Politburo from 1930 and vice-president of the Council of People's Commissars from 1938. Responsible for establishing the communist party in Turkestan (1920–5).

KAMENEV (real name: ROSENFELD, Lev Borisovich) (1883–1936): In the 1920s a close ally of Stalin and Zinoviev; vice-president of the Council of People's Commissars. After 1926 he allied himself with Trotsky; he was expelled from the VCP(b) in 1932, and in 1936 tried for treason and executed.

KAPLAN, Regina (1908–): An activist for the Communist Party of Western Byelorussia; arrested in Poland and sentenced to fifteen years' imprisonment in 1933. Released after the outbreak of the war, she disappeared from the political scene.

KASMAN, Leon (1905–84): 1951–4 and 1957–67, editor-in-chief of the daily *Trybuna Ludu*. Member of the PUWP Central Committee (1948–68). KPP member before the war; he spent the war in the USSR, where he became a member of the VCP(b) and worked for the Comintern. Leader of one of the KPP groups sent to organize the PPR, he was parachuted into Poland in 1943; after the war he worked in propaganda. He was dismissed from his editorship at *Trybuna Ludu* after the anti-Semitic campaign of 1968.

KHRUSHCHEV, Nikita Sergeyevich (1894–1971): 1953–64, first secretary of the CPSU. A member of the VCP(b) [later CPSU] Central Committee from

1934 and of the Supreme Soviet from 1937; elected to the Politburo in 1939. Appointed by Stalin to the post of first secretary of the Communist Party of the Ukraine in 1938 and again in 1943, he was recalled in 1949 to become first secretary of the Moscow oblast. Member of the Presidium and of the Central Committee secretariat from 1952, he denounced Stalin at the Twentieth CPSU Congress in 1956 and crushed the Hungarian Uprising in October of that same year. He was removed from power by Brezhnev in 1964.

KIRCHMAYER, Jerzy (1895–1959): An officer in the Home Army. Arrested in 1951, together with General Tatar, on charges of treason and espionage, he was sentenced to life imprisonment. He was released and rehabilitated in 1956.

KIROV (real name: KOSTRIKOV, Sergei Mironovich) (1886–1934): 1925–34, secretary of the Leningrad Communist Party. He was murdered in December 1934, probably on Stalin's orders.

KLISZKO, Zenon (1908–): A close associate of Gomulka's from 1956 until 1970. In 1949, at the same time as Gomulka and Spychalski (see *infra*), he was accused of right-wing nationalist deviations and removed from his posts, which had included that of head of the cadres department at the PPR Central Committee (1945–8). He retired from office after the risings on the coast in 1970.

KLOSIEWICZ, Wiktor (1907–): 1950–6, president of the Central Council of Trade Unions. Associated with the "Natolin" group, he resigned from all his party positions, but continues, despite his retirement ten years ago, to hold a number of minor government posts.

KOLAKOWSKI, Leszek (1927–): Philosopher, currently at the universities of Oxford and Chicago. Accused of revisionism in 1956, he was expelled from the party in 1966 and dismissed from his chair of philosophy at Warsaw University after the student riots in 1968, which he was accused of having incited. He remains for many a symbol of the opposition movement in Poland.

KOMAR, Waclaw (1909–72): A general in the Polish army. 1936–8, fought in Spain; 1945–7, chief of the Second Unit of the General Staff; 1951–3, deputy minister of national defence. Arrested in 1953, released in 1956; in August 1956 he became commander of the Internal Security Corps; in October 1956 he was in charge of preparations for the defence of Warsaw from approaching Soviet tanks. Dismissed from his post in 1960, he became general director of the Ministry of Internal Affairs until 1967.

KORBONSKI, Stefan (1901–): Active member of the Polish Peasant Party. During the war a member of the Home Army, a representative of the government in London, and director of the clandestine radio station *Swit*. After the war, together with Mikolajczyk (see *infra*), he was a leader of the Peasant Party. He defected to the West in 1947.

KOSTOV, Traicho (1897–1949): Bulgarian party activist; deputy premier of the Bulgarian government after the war. Arrested in 1949 on charges of treason and espionage, he was sentenced to death and executed. He was posthumously rehabilitated in 1960.

KOSTRZEWA, Vera (1876–1939): One of the main organizers and ideologists of the KPP; emigrated to the USSR in 1924, where she became a member of the VCP(b) and worked for the Comintern. Dismissed from her party positions, reinstated between 1926 and 1929, she was arrested and sentenced in 1937, during the Great Purge. She died in a Soviet prison and was posthumously rehabilitated in 1956.

KOWALSKI, Aleksander (1908–51): Trained at the Party School in the USSR during the war, he was among those parachuted into Poland to organize the PPR. In 1948 he was accused of right-wing nationalist deviationism and dismissed from his party posts; attempts were made to implicate him in the Gomulka case. He died in a psychiatric hospital.

KRASICKI, Jan (1919–43): Trained at the Party School in the USSR during the war, he was parachuted into Poland in 1942. Arrested by the Gestapo in 1943, he died while attempting to escape.

KRUPINSKI, Boleslaw (1893–1972): An expert in the mining industry, he was in charge of mining operations in Silesia (1945–50). Dismissed from his posts in 1950, he became a lecturer at the Cracow Academy of Mining and Metallurgy.

KURON, Jacek (1934–): Historian and pedagogue, prominent during the student riots in March 1968; co-founder of the Workers' Defence Committee KOR (1976) and an adviser to Solidarity. Expelled from the party in 1953 and again in 1956. Arrested and sentenced to three years' imprisonment in 1965 on the charge of attempting to overthrow the regime. Arrested again in 1968 and frequently detained during the 1970s. He was arrested after the imposition of martial law in December 1981 and spent a further two and a half years in prison.

KUROPIESKA, Jozef (1904–): Officer in the Polish Army. 1945–6, worked on the General Staff; appointed military attaché to Great Britain in 1946. Recalled to Poland and arrested in connection with the case of General Tatar. Accused of treason and espionage and sentenced to death in 1952, he was released in 1956 after a second investigation and became chief commandant of the military district of Warsaw.

KUTSCHERA, Franz: German General, SS commandant of the district of Warsaw. He was executed by the Home Army in 1944.

KWIATKOWSKI, Eugeniusz (1888–1974): 1935–9, deputy premier. A chemical engineer, he oversaw the construction of the port of Gdynia and was one of the architects involved in the main industrial construction project, known as COP (Central Industrial Region), in Sandomierz. After the war he was briefly commissioned for a project to reconstruct the coastal region, but was dismissed in 1947.

LAMPE, Alfred (1900–43): KPP member from 1921; member of the KPP Central Committee and Politburo; KZMP secretary. Spent ten years in prison, charged with subversion. He spent the war in the USSR, where he was one of the founders of the Union of Polish Patriots. He died in Moscow.

LANGE, Oskar (1904–65): Economist. First ambassador of People's Poland to the USA. 1934–45, lecturer in the USA; 1949–65, professor of economics in Poland. A member of the socialist party, he was recruited early on by Wanda Wasilewska and became an influential supporter of the new regime in Poland. He supported the union of the PPS and the PPR.

LEBEDEV, Victor: Soviet ambassador to Poland from 1945.

LECHOWICZ, Wlodzimierz (1911–): Prominent member of the Democratic Party; journalist. 1947–8, Democratic Party deputy to the Sejm and minister of trade and supplies. Arrested in 1948; 1948–55, imprisoned, tortured, investigated; sentenced in 1955 to fifteen years' imprisonment; released in April 1956; rehabilitated in December 1956. 1957–73, member of the Democratic Party, and successively vice-president (1957–69) and member of the Presidium (1969–70) of the Democratic Party Central Committee; 1957–72, Democratic Party deputy to the Sejm. 1957–61, founder and editor-in-chief of the paper *Kurier Polski*. 1970–3, ambassador to Holland.

LEDER, Witold: The son of a communist murdered in the USSR during the Great Purge, he was arrested in 1949 in connection with the Field affair and imprisoned until 1955. After 1955 he worked for the party press.

LENSKI-LESZCZYNSKI, Julian (1889–1939): Communist activist in the USSR. Sent to France by the Comintern in 1924 to work with the French Communist Party. 1929–37, worked for the Comintern as general secretary of the KPP. Arrested by the NKVD during the Great Purge in 1937; executed in 1939. He was posthumously rehabilitated in 1955.

LIEOU-CHAO-K'I (1898–1969): 1943–9, general secretary of the Chinese Communist Party; 1949–59, vice-president of the People's Republic of China; in 1959 he succeeded Mao Tse-tung as president. He was expelled from the party in 1968, but posthumously rehabilitated in 1979.

LIPSKI, Jan Jozef (1926–): Journalist and writer. A prominent member of the intellectual opposition; founding member of the Workers' Defence Committee KOR in 1976. Interned in 1981, after the imposition of martial law, and one of five defendants in the recent KOR trial. Until his dismissal in 1982, he worked at the Literary Institute of the Polish Academy of Sciences. Subject to frequent acts of repression and harassment from the 1950s onwards.

MAISKY, Ivan (1884–1975): Soviet diplomat. 1932–43, Soviet ambassador to Great Britain. Took part in the Yalta and Potsdam conferences.

MALENKOV, Georgi Maximilianovich (1902–): Stalin's personal secretary from 1932; VCP(b) Central Committee member from 1939; 1941–5, member of the National Defence Committee; vice-president of the Council of People's Commissars from 1946. Succeeded Stalin as prime minister in 1953. Accused by Khrushchev of anti-party activities, he was expelled from the party, dismissed from his posts and sent, in 1957, to Kazakhstan as the director of a generating station.

MANUILSKI, Dmitri (1883–1959): Soviet communist activist. On the Comintern Executive Committee from 1924. 1928–43, secretary of the Comintern. Secretary of the Central Committee of the Ukrainian Bolshevik Communist Party from 1920 to 1922, he returned to the Ukraine after the dissolution of the Comintern in 1943 and remained there as deputy first secretary until 1953.

MATWIN, Wladyslaw (1916–): 1939–44 in the USSR; served in the Red Army, Berling's army, and was a member of the Union of Polish Patriots. 1945–6, secretary of the PKWN embassy in Moscow; 1946–8, first secretary of the PUWP Provincial Committee in Wroclaw; 1948–64, member of the PUWP Central Committee; 1955–63, secretary of the Central Committee; 1952–4, first secretary of the Warsaw PUWP Committee. 1954 and 1956–7, editor-in-chief of the paper *Trybuna Ludu*. A supporter of Gomulka in 1956. Later fell out of favour and became director of the Managing Cadres Training Headquarters.

MAZUR, Franciszek (1895–1975): Communist activist. 1915–30, in Russia, where he served in the tsarist army; VCP(b) member; in 1930 he was sent to Poland, subsequently arrested and sentenced to six years' imprisonment, thus escaping the Great Purge. He spent the war in the USSR. 1945–59, member of the PPR and PUWP Central Committees; 1948–51, deputy Politburo member; 1950–6, secretary of the Central Committee; 1951–6, member of the Politburo. A member of the "Natolin" Group in October 1956. Removed from his posts after 1956. 1957–65, ambassador to Prague.

MICHNIK, Adam (1946–): Historian, prominent in the opposition movement; took part in the student revolt of 1968; member of the Workers' Defence Committee KOR; Solidarity adviser. Interned in December 1981, after the imposition of martial law. Arrested in 1984 and convicted in a trial of union activists; released under an amnesty in August 1986.

MICHOELS, Solomon (1890–1948): Jewish actor and founder of the National Jewish Theatre in Moscow; a member of the Jewish Anti-Fascist Committee. He died in 1948 in obscure circumstances; the official cause of his death was a car accident.

MIETKOWSKI, Mieczyslaw (1903–): Brigadier general, connected with the NKVD; 1936–8, fought in the Spanish Civil War; spent the war in Moscow at the NKVD school. 1948–57, member of the PUWP Central Committee. Expelled from the party at the ninth plenum. 1945–54, deputy minister of public security.

MIKOLAJCZYK, Stanislaw (1901–66): Founder of the Polish Peasant Party; deputy premier, then premier of the Polish government in London during the war; deputy premier and minister of agriculture after the war. In 1945 he signed a pact with the communist government in Poland, resulting in the Provisional Government of National Unity. Faced with arrest after the rigged elections of 1947, he escaped to the West and the Peasant Party was dissolved.

MIKOYAN, Anastas Ivanovich (1895–): Soviet politician. 1926–38, People's Commissar for Commerce, Supplies, and the Food Industry, successively; 1946–55. Minister of Commerce. 1935–66, member of the Politburo; vice-president of the Council of Ministers from 1946; head of the Presidium of the Supreme Soviet from 1964.

MINC, Hilary (1905–74): Economist; 1944–56, member of the Politburo of the PPR and PUWP Central Committees; 1949–56, head of the Economic Planning Commission; 1944–9, head of the PKWN department of industry, minister of trade and industry. Creator of the three-year plan. Before the war: secretary of the KPP central editorial office (1929–39). 1939–44, in the ZPP leadership and the Bureau of Polish Communists in the USSR. Dismissed from all his posts in 1956, he confessed to being guilty of "errors and distortions". He had been the third most important government figure in People's Poland, after Bierut and Berman.

MINC, Julia: See biography at head of interview.

MOCZAR, Mieczyslaw (1913–86): The organizer of the 1968 anti-Semitic and anti-intelligentsia campaign. Immediately after the war he began working in security (chief of the security services in Lodz, 1945–1948). Deputy minister (1957–64) and minister (1964–8) of internal affairs. 1969–76, member of the Council of State; deputy member (1948–56) and member (1956–81) of the PUWP Central Committee; 1968–70, deputy member of the Politburo and Central Committee secretary; 1970–1 and 1980–1, member of the Politburo.

MOCZARSKI, Kazimierz (1907–75): Journalist; active member of the Democratic Party before the war; during the war head of intelligence and propaganda in the Home Army. Arrested in 1945; released and rehabilitated in 1956. Author of the book *My Conversations with the Hangman*, an account of his time in prison, where he had shared a cell with the SS general responsible for the liquidation of the Warsaw ghetto.

MODZELEWSKI, Karol (1937–): Historian and prominent opposition activist. Expelled from the PUWP in 1964; arrested in 1965, together with Kuron (see *supra*); sentenced in 1968, for the second time; released in 1971. press officer for Solidarity. Interned after the imposition of martial law in December 1981 and held without trial until his release in 1983.

MODZELEWSKI, Zygmunt (1900–54): Communist activist in France before the war; recalled to Moscow and arrested in 1937; released and rehabilitated in 1939. During the war in the ZPP and the Central Bureau of Polish Communists in Moscow. First ambassador of People's Poland to the USSR. He became minister of foreign affairs upon his return to Poland in 1945.

MOLOTOV (real name: SKRIABIN, Vyacheslav Mikhailovich) (1890–1986): Soviet politician. Member of the VCP(b) (later CPSU) Central Committee from 1921 and of the Politburo from 1926. 1930–4, head of the Comintern. 1939–49 and 1953–6, people's commissar for foreign affairs; 1941–6, first vice-president of the Council of State. Signatory of the Molotov–Ribbentrop pact (the Nazi–Soviet pact of 1939); took part in the Teheran, Yalta and Potsdam conferences. A Stalinist and opponent of Khrushchev, he was the leader of the anti-party group from 1956 to 1957. Removed from office and expelled from the party when Khrushchev took power in 1964; readmitted to the party in 1984.

MOLOJEC, Boleslaw (?–1943): A member of the First Initiative Group in the USSR during the war; parachuted into Poland in 1941 to organize the PPR. In 1942, for reasons which remain mysterious, he used his brother,

Zygmunt, to assassinate the first secretary of the PPR, Nowotko; it is unknown on whose orders he did this. Both he and his brother were executed on orders from the party in 1943.

MORAWSKI, Jerzy (1918–): Prominent in the party after 1956; accused of revisionism and removed in 1959.

NOWAK, Zenon (1905–80): KPP functionary (1924–38) and Central Committee member (from 1932); freed by the Russians from a labour camp, he joined the Soviet army in 1945. Upon his return to Poland in 1947, he became first PPR Provincial Committee secretary in Katowice and head of the cadres department at the PPR Central Committee. Member (1948–80) and secretary (1950–4) of the Central Committee; 1950–6, member of the Politburo. A leading member of the "Natolin" group. 1964–71, head of the Central Committee of Party Control; 1952–68, deputy premier; 1969–71, head of the Chief Board of Supervision; 1971–7, ambassador to Moscow.

NOWOTKO, Marceli (1893–1942): Member of the SDKPiL (from 1914) and of the KPP (from 1918); spent ten years in prison for subversive activity. 1939–41, in the USSR; parachuted into Poland in December 1941 to organize the PPR, of which he became first secretary. In 1942 he was murdered by Zygmunt Molojec and the latter's brother, Boleslaw (see *supra*).

NOWOTNY, Antoni (1904–75): Czechoslovak politician. First secretary of the Czechoslovak Communist Party (1953) and President of the Republic (1957). He was removed from power in 1968, during the Prague Spring.

OCHAB, Edward: See biography at head of interview.

OSOBKA-MORAWSKI, Edward (1909–): PPS member from 1930; head of the PKWN in Lublin in 1944. 1944–7, premier of the Provisional Government and the Government of National Unity; 1947–50, minister of public administration. In December 1956 he was crossed off the list of candidates to the Sejm.

PASTERNAK, Boris Leonidovich (1890–1960): Russian writer and poet; author of *Doctor Zhivago* (1957) and *My Sister, Life* (1922). Awarded the Nobel Prize in 1958, but forced by the authorities to refuse it.

PAUKER, Anna Rabinovich (1893–1960): Romanian politician; member of the Central Committee of the Romanian Communist Party. 1947–51, Romanian minister of foreign affairs.

PIASECKI, Boleslaw (1915–1979): Leader of the ONR [National-Radical Camp], an extreme right-wing nationalist group; fought in the September campaign. Arrested by the NKVD in 1945; released shortly thereafter to form the PAX association; editor of the daily *Slowo Powszechne* and the weekly *Kierunki*. Opposed Gomulka in 1956. Member of the Council of State from 1971 until his death.

PILSUDSKI, Jozef (1867–1935): Polish statesman, founder of the so-called "revolutionary faction" of the Polish Socialist Party. Organizer of the underground Polish Military Organization and the Polish legions. Head of state and commander-in-chief of the army during the Bolshevik war of 1919–21. On 15 August 1920, he played the leading role in a decisive battle in which the Soviet army was routed, and which enabled Poland to sign a peace treaty at Riga. He resigned from office soon afterwards. In 1926 he staged a coup d'état.

PONOMARENKO, Panteleimon (1902–): 1955–77, Soviet ambassador to Poland.

PRAWIN, Jakub (1901–57): In the USSR during the war; fought in the Red Army and later in Berling's army. After the war: military attaché in Berlin and director of the Polish National Bank.

PSZCZOLKOWSKI, Edmund (1904–): Deputy member (1948–53) and member (1953–68) of the PUWP Central Committee; 1950–52 and 1957–63, head of the Central Committee agricultural section; 1953–4, member of the Central Committee secretariat and deputy member of the Politburo; 1953–6, minister of agriculture. March–November 1956, head of the Committee on Public Security; 1963–7, ambassador to Moscow.

PUTRAMENT, Jerzy (1910–86): Writer. 1945–50, Polish ambassador to Paris. From his return to Poland in 1950 until his death he was an active member of the Union of Polish Writers, prominent for his advocacy of socialist realism in literature. He also edited several journals.

RADKIEWICZ, Stanislaw (1903–): KPP member before the war; trained in the USSR. 1941–3, in the Red Army; 1943–4, secretary of the Central Bureau of Polish Communists; member of the leadership of the union of Polish Patriots. July–December 1944, head of the public security department in the PKWN; 1945–54, minister of public security; 1954–6, minister of state farms; 1945–8, member of the PPR Politburo and Central Committee; from 1948 member of the PUWP Politburo and Central Committee. He left the Politburo in 1955; in 1957 he was expelled from the Central Committee and from the party. Reinstated to the party in 1960, from 1960 to 1968 he was the general director of the Bureau of State Reserves. He retired in 1968.

Rajk, Laszlo (1909–49): Hungarian communist. 1946–8, Hungarian minister of the interior. Sentenced to death and executed in 1949 after a prominent show trial in which he was accused of conspiracy against the State. He was posthumously rehabilitated in 1956.

Rakosi, Matyas (1892–1963): Hungarian politician; communist activist and Comintern agent. Secretary of the Hungarian Communist Party and vice-president of the Council of State from 1945; general secretary of the Hungarian Workers' Party from 1948. 1952–3, president of the Council of State; 1953–6, first secretary of the Hungarian Workers' Party. He was expelled from the party in 1962.

Rakowski, Mieczyslaw (1926–): 1957–82, editor-in-chief of the weekly *Polityka*: 1981–5, deputy premier. Until 1957 he held party posts dealing with propaganda.

Rapacki, Adam (1909–70): 1956–68, minister of foreign affairs. He was removed from office in 1968 for his opposition to the anti-Semitic campaign launched by Moczar and Gomulka.

Rokossowski, Konstanty (1896–1968): Career officer; Marshal of the Soviet Union. Evacuated to Russia in 1915, he took part in the Bolshevik revolution; sent to camp at the time of the Great Purge; released in 1941 and sent to the front with the rank of general. Sent to Poland by Stalin after the war. In 1949 he was made Marshal of Poland and minister of national defence; in November of that year he was coopted into the Central Committee, and in 1950 into the Politburo; in 1952 he was made deputy premier. Expelled from the Politburo in October 1956; recalled to the USSR in November 1956 and there nominated deputy minister of national defence for the USSR.

Romkowski, Roman (1907–68): Brigadier general. 1945–54, deputy minister of public security; 1948–55, member of the PUWP Central Committee. Expelled from the party in January 1955; in November 1957, sentenced to fifteen years' imprisonment for illegal detention of prisoners and the use of "unauthorized" methods of investigation.

Rozanski, Jacek (real name: Goldberg): Communist and NKVD agent before the war; spent the war in the USSR. 1945–54, head of the investigative department of the Ministry of Public Security; in December 1955, sentenced to five years' imprisonment; after a second investigation ordered by the Supreme Court, he was sentenced to fifteen years' imprisonment in 1957. He was released in 1960.

Rylski, Ignacy (real name: Lubiniecki, Jan) (1893–1937): Member of the KPP Central Committee Secretariat; he was murdered during the Great Purge.

SCHULENBERG, Count Werner von der: German ambassador to Moscow. He was executed for his part in the 1944 conspiracy against Hitler.

SEROV, Ivan Alexandrovich (1905–): NKVD general. 1930–41, posted in Kiev, where he organized the deportation of Polish citizens. After the war he organized the abduction and arrest of sixteen leaders of the Polish resistance. During the first postwar years he was the NKVD representative in Poland. In 1954 he was appointed head of the KGB, and in 1959 of the GRU (Soviet military intelligence).

SHCHERBAKOV, Alexandr Sergeievich (1901–43): Soviet politician and general; chief political administrator of the Red Army. He was appointed secretary of the VCP(b) in 1939.

SIKORSKI, Wladyslaw (1881–1943): Polish general; collaborated with Pilsudski in organizing the legions. Removed from his position in the army in 1926. After September 1939 he became head of the Polish government in exile. Signatory of the Sikorski–Maisky pact with the USSR, a treaty which allowed for the release of Polish citizens who had been deported to the USSR; however, the USSR broke off diplomatic relations after the discovery of the massacre of Polish officers at Katyn. After a number of attempts to reach an accord with the USSR, Sikorski died in a plane crash in 1943.

SKIBINSKI, Franciszek (1899–): Polish general arrested in connection with the Tatar case; he was released and rehabilitated in 1956.

SKULBASZEWSKI, Antoni (1919–): Deputy head of Polish military intelligence headquarters.

SLANKSY, Rudolf (1901–52): Czechoslovak communist: a member of the Czechoslovak Central Committee and Politburo from 1929; 1939–45, a member of the party leadership; 1945–51, general secretary of the Communist Party and head of the security police. Arrested in 1951, given a prominent show trial on the charge of espionage and treason, and executed; he was posthumously rehabilitated in 1968.

SOKORSKI, Wlodzimierz (1908–): 1926–31, member of the left wing of the PPS; 1931–5, in prison for communist activity. In the USSR during the war, he became deputy head of the Union of Polish Patriots in 1943. Political officer in the First Division. Returned to Poland in 1945. 1947–8, deputy minister of education; 1948–52, deputy minister of culture; 1952–6, minister of culture; 1956–72, head of the Radio and Television Committee; 1948–75, deputy member of the Central Committee. In 1980 he became president of the ZBOWiD organization.

SPYCHALSKI, Marian (1906–80): Polish general. During the war a member of the PPR and the KRN; organizer of the People's Guard. 1944–9, chief of staff in the Polish army (promoted to the rank of general), president of Warsaw (for a month), deputy chief political officer in the Polish army, first deputy minister of national defence; after his dismissal from the army he was minister of housing and an architect in Wroclaw. 1945–8, member of the PPR Politburo; 1948–9, member of the PUWP Politburo and Central Committee; expelled from the Central Committee at the third plenum, together with Gomulka; arrested in 1950; rehabilitated in 1956, reinstated in the Central Committee at the eighth plenum. 1959–70, member of the Politburo (removed after the 1970 workers' riots on the coast); 1956–68, minister of national defence. Nominated Marshal of Poland in 1963. 1968–70, head of the Council of State.

STAREWICZ, Artur (1917–): KZMP member; in the USSR during the war; 1944–8, PPR functionary and first secretary of the Wroclaw Provincial Committee. 1949–54, head of the Central Committee propaganda department; 1954–6, secretary of the Central Council of Trade Unions (removed after October 1956); 1957–63, director of the Central Committee's press bureau. He was a deputy member (1954–9), member (1959–71), and secretary (1963–71) of the Central Committee. A member of the "Pulawy" group. 1972–8, ambassador in London.

STASZEWSKI, Stefan: See biography at head of interview.

SWIATLO, Jozef (1905–): 1949–53, head of the security department dealing with "enemies within the party"; responsible for the arrests of Gomulka and Spychalski. Defected to the West in December 1953 and proceeded to broadcast a series of talks on Radio Free Europe. These broadcasts brought about a thorough purge in the security services: Rozanski was arrested; Radkiewicz, Romkowski, Fejgin, Mietkowski and many minor security officials were dismissed; some prisoners, among them Gomulka, were released; the ministry of public security was dissolved and replaced by two committees. Although the official line was that Swiatlo was an American agent and a *provocateur*, his talks led to the recognition that "violations of legality" had occurred. At the third plenum in 1955 the security organs were subjected to severe criticism; Romkowski and Fejgin were expelled from the party and arrested.

SWIERCZEWSKI, Karol (1897–1947): Polish general. In the Red Guard during the Russian revolution; later in the Soviet army. 1936–9, division commander in Spain; 1939–44, in the USSR, where he organized the Polish army; commander of the second army of the Polish Forces in 1944; 1945–7, member of the PPR Central Committee. He was killed fighting against the underground resistance.

SWIETLIK, Konrad: Brigadier general. 1948–59, member of the PUWP Central Committee; chief political officer in the Polish Army in 1946; 1950–4, deputy minister of public security.

TATAR, Stanislaw (1896–1980): Brigadier general; chief of the operational division of the Home Army high command during the occupation. Arrested in 1949 and sentenced to life imprisonment on the charge of conspiracy in the army – a fabricated case which involved many Polish officers. He was released and rehabilitated in 1956.

TOGLIATTI, Palmiro (1893–1964): Italian communist; co-founder of the Italian Communist Party in 1921. General secretary of the Italian Communist Party; 1944–55, vice-president of the Council of State; 1945–6, minister of justice.

ULBRICHT, Walter (1893–1973): One of the founders of the German Communist Party in 1919; communist activist in France and Czechoslovakia, then in the Soviet Union. Returned to the Soviet-occupied zone in Germany in 1945. 1950–71, first secretary of the United Socialist Party; 1960–73, president of the Council of State of the GDR.

VOROSHILOV, Kliment Yefremovich (1881–1969): Soviet general, member of the Bolshevik Party from 1903; took part in the 1905 revolution. 1925–34, people's commissar for the Navy; 1934–40, people's commissar for Defence. Appointed Marshal of the Soviet Union in 1935. 1946–53, vice-president of the Council of Ministers; 1953–60, head of the Presidium of the Supreme Soviet.

VOZNESENSKY, Dmitri: Soviet officer. 1950–4, head of Polish military counter-intelligence ("Military Information") headquarters; as such he was in charge of cases against Generals Komar and Kuropieska, and others accused of military espionage and conspiracy. Recalled to the USSR in 1954; he was tried in 1956 and sentenced to ten years' imprisonment.

WARSKI (real name: WARSZAWSKI, Adolf) (1868–?): A close associate of Rosa Luxemburg; a co-founder of the KPP and a representative of the Communist International. In 1929 he was accused of right-wing deviationism and expelled from the KPP. Arrested in 1937 during the Great Purge and subsequently disappeared; the circumstances and date of his death are unknown. He was posthumously rehabilitated in 1956.

WASILEWSKA, Wanda (1905–64): Polish communist activist in the USSR; she joined the VCP(b) at the outbreak of the war. President of the ZPP and close to Stalin, whom she was instrumental in persuading of the need to form a Polish army – Berling's army – alongside the Red Army. She was not appointed to any positions in Poland after the war, and settled in Kiev.

WAT, Aleksander (1900–67): Polish poet. Arrested in Lvov by the NKVD in 1940; released in 1941, after the Sikorski–Maisky pact. Returned to Poland in 1946 but never accepted communist rule in Poland and emigrated to the West in 1963. He died in France.

WERFEL, Roman: See biography at head of interview.

WIERBLOWSKI, Stefan (1897–1973): In the USSR during the war; a member of the Central Bureau of Polish Communists. After the war he worked mainly in propaganda.

WITOS, Andrzej (1878–1973): A member of the Peasant Party before the war, he was arrested by the NKVD in 1939; rescued by mistake by Wanda Wasilewska, who was searching for his brother Wincenty (see *infra*), he came to Moscow and joined the ZPP. For a brief period he was a member of the PKWN.

WITOS, Wincenty (1874–1945): Leader of the Peasant Party in 1913; prime minister three times between the wars. An opponent of Pilsudski; arrested in 1930 and sentenced to eighteen months' imprisonment. In 1945 he once again became leader of the Peasant Party, but died that same year.

WOLSKI-PIWOWARCZYK, Antoni Wladyslaw (?–1976): In charge of settling the Recovered Territories and of repatriating the Polish population of the eastern territories after the war. Later removed from his government posts, he was appointed director of the National Library in Cracow.

WYSZYNSKI, Stefan (1901–81): Polish cardinal; 1948–81, Primate of Poland. Arrested in 1953 and imprisoned until 1956: his arrest was the culmination of the government campaign against the Church in the 1950s. He had been a man of enormous authority; after his arrest he became a symbol.

ZABLUDOWSKI, Tadeusz (1907–84): In the USSR during the war as editor of the ZPP press. 1944–8, head censor in Poland; dismissed in 1948 on the grounds that he had once translated the works of Trotsky. Until 1968 he worked in publishing and the press; he was dismissed and expelled from the party during the anti-Semitic, anti-intellectual campaign of 1968.

ZAMBROWSKI, Roman (real name: NUSSBAUM, Rubin) (1909–77): Secretary of the KZMP Central Committee and of the Lodz KPP Committee before the war; spent the war in the USSR, where he was a member of the ZPP and a political officer in the Polish army. 1944–8, secretary of the PPR Central Committee; 1948–64, member of the PUWP Central Committee; 1948–63, member of the Politburo; 1948–54 and 1956–63, secretary of the PUWP Central Committee; 1947–55, member of the Council of State; 1955–6, minister of State Control; 1963–8, vice-president of the Chief Board of Supervision. A member of the "Pulawy" group in 1956; accused of revisionism and removed from his party posts in 1963; expelled from the party during the anti-Semitic campaign of 1968.

ZAWADZKI, Aleksander (1899–1964): KZMP and KPP member from 1922; in the USSR during the war, where he was one of the organizers of the ZPP; 1943–4, deputy chief political officer in the Polish army. Member of the PPR Central Committee; member of the Politburo from 1948; 1949–51, head of the Central Council of Trade Unions; 1951–2, deputy premier; head of the Council of State from 1952 until his death.

ZAWIEYSKI, Jerzy (1902–69): Actor and playwright; connected with Catholic circles. In October 1956 he became a member of an officially recognized group of Catholic deputies to the Sejm. He publicly condemned the anti-Semitic campaign of 1968 and died in obscure circumstances.

ZHDANOV, Andrei Alexandrovich (1896–48): Soviet politician; one of Stalin's henchmen. Member of the VCP(b) Politburo from 1939 and secretary of the Central Committee. He was influential in matters of foreign policy; he also combatted "bourgeois deviationism" in literature and the arts.

ZHUKOV, Georgi Sergeievich: An NKVD general, subordinate to General Serov (see *supra*); a dedicated Stalinist, he was the NKVD officer responsible for all matters concerning Poland during the war. Stalin later had him removed from office and posted to Siberia.

ZINOVIEV (real name: RADOMYSLSKI, Grigori Yevseievich) (1883–1936): A member of the top leadership together with Stalin and Kamenev, he played a part in the expulsion of Trotsky but was to ally with him later. Expelled from the party in 1934, he was accused of complicity in Kirov's murder, sentenced to death and executed in 1936.